Ceol Phádraig

Ceol Phádraig

Music at St Patrick's College
Drumcondra, 1875-2016

Edited by John Buckley and John O'Flynn

Carysfort Press

PETER LANG
Oxford • Bern • Berlin • Bruxelles • New York • Wien

Bibliographic information published by Die Deutsche Nationalbibliothek.
Die Deutsche Nationalbibliothek lists this publication in the Deutsche National-
bibliografie; detailed bibliographic data is available on the Internet at
http://dnb.d-nb.de.

A catalogue record for this book is available from the British Library.

Cover photo: Detail from altar mosaic of the original St Patrick's College Chapel.
Cover design: Brian Melville.

ISBN 978-1-78997-565-9 (print HB) • ISBN 978-1-78997-622-9 (print PB)
ISBN 978-1-78997-578-9 (ePDF)
ISBN 978-1-78997-579-6 (ePub) • ISBN 978-1-78997-580-2 (mobi)

© Peter Lang AG 2019

Published by Peter Lang Ltd, International Academic Publishers,
52 St Giles, Oxford, OX1 3LU, United Kingdom
oxford@peterlang.com, www.peterlang.com

John Buckley and John O'Flynn have asserted their right under the Copyright,
Designs and Patents Act, 1988, to be identified as Editors of this Work.
© the editors and contributors 2019

All rights reserved.
All parts of this publication are protected by copyright.
Any utilisation outside the strict limits of the copyright law, without
the permission of the publisher, is forbidden and liable to prosecution.
This applies in particular to reproductions, translations, microfilming,
and storage and processing in electronic retrieval systems.

This publication has been peer reviewed.

Contents

List of Contributors   ix
List of Figures   xiii
Abbreviations   xv
Acknowledgments   xvii

Introduction
   John Buckley and John O'Flynn   1

Chapter One: Fluctuating Fortunes:
St Patrick's College, 1875-2016
   Daithí Ó Corráin   7

Chapter Two: Music Performance at
St Patrick's College, Drumcondra
   John Buckley   25

Chapter Three: Music in Education and Humanities
   Patricia Flynn and John O'Flynn   59

Chapter Four: Composition and the College
   Rhona Clarke   85

Chapter Five: 'All are welcome':
Irish traditional music at St Patrick's College
   Teresa O'Donnell   105

Chapter Six: Vocal and Choral Music
   John O'Flynn   127

Chapter Seven: The Kodály Connection
   Yvonne Higgins   153

Chapter Eight: Engagement and Research
John O'Flynn   177

Chapter Nine: Music and Tourism:
Mapping Popular Music from St Patrick's College
Áine Mangaoang   205

Chapter Ten: The Fidelio Trio Residency
John O'Flynn   223

Chapter Eleven: Graduate Perspectives
Introduced by John Buckley   243

Afterword: St Patrick's College Music Department
and its place in Irish musical life
Niall Doyle   259

Appendix A: List of full-time music lecturers in
St Patrick's College, 1883-2016
Compiled by John Buckley   271

Appendix B: Programmes of lunchtime concerts
given by guest performers, November 2003 - March 2016
Compiled by John Buckley   273

Appendix C: Participation by choirs of St Patrick's College
at the Cork International Choral Festival, 1972-2015
Compiled by John O'Flynn   289

Appendix D: Music and music education
dissertations and theses, 2000-2016
Compiled by John O'Flynn   295

Appendix E: List of events during the Fidelio Trio
residency and festivals, 2012-2016
Compiled by John O'Flynn   303

Index   315

List of Contributors

JOHN BUCKLEY is a composer whose catalogue of original compositions extends to over 100 works. These have been performed and broadcast in more than fifty countries worldwide. He is a graduate of St Patrick's College Drumcondra and was a lecturer in the Music Department there between 2001 and 2016. He is a member of Aosdána.

RHONA CLARKE is an associate professor in the School of Theology, Philosophy, and Music at Dublin City University. She is a composer whose output includes choral, chamber, orchestral and electronic works. She has received commissions from RTÉ National Symphony Orchestra, the Cork International Choral Festival, Concorde, Music Network, Chamber Choir Ireland and the National Concert Hall, among others. Her works have been performed and broadcast throughout Ireland and worldwide.

NIALL DOYLE attended St Patrick's College from 1978-81. He taught in St Maelruan's NS in Tallaght before returning to college in TCD to study music while also working as a professional tuba player. From the early 1990s he has been a full-time manager, working as CEO of Music Network, as Director of Music in RTÉ, CEO of Opera Ireland and as a management consultant. He is currently Head of Music and Opera in the Arts Council.

PATRICIA FLYNN is Associate Professor of Music in DCU. She lectured in St Patrick's College Drumcondra from 1998 until its incorporation into Dublin City University in 2016. A graduate of UCD and the University of Huddersfield, her research engages with infrastructure for the arts in music and she works extensively with Music Generation, Local Authorities and the Contemporary Music Centre.

PAUL GILGUNN is a composer, educator, and musician who works across the peripheries of classical and popular music. He is currently focused on creating a body of new work encompassing avant-rock, improvised music, and post-minimalist composition. He holds a BA in English and Music (DCU), an MPhil in Literature (TCD), and a PhD in Music (Goldsmiths).

YVONNE HIGGINS is Assistant Professor of Music Education in the School of Arts Education and Movement in the DCU Institute of Education. Prior to taking on this role she has had extensive experience at primary level. She is a graduate of St Patrick's College and of the

Kodály Institute, Hungary, and has founded and directed school, community, and college choirs.

ÁINE MANGAOANG is Postdoctoral Research Fellow at the Department of Musicology, University of Oslo. Her research on popular music appears in *The Routledge Handbook for Popular Music Analysis,* and *Postcolonial Text* and *Torture* journals. Her forthcoming publications include the monograph *Dangerous Mediations: Pop Music in a Philippine Prison Video* (Bloomsbury), and the co-edited collection *Made in Ireland: Studies in Popular Music* (Routledge).

DENISE MORGAN graduated with a BA degree in 2013 from St Patrick's College, where she studied Irish and music. She completed a Postgraduate Diploma in Education in Trinity College Dublin in 2014 and is currently on the staff of St Mary's Secondary School, Baldoyle. She is a choral director and is also the Irish and Cultural Officer of Meath GAA.

CONALL Ó BREACHÁIN is a member of *We Cut Corners* - a multi-award nominated band trading in lyrically-deft, harmony-laden indie music. He has, along with his long-term musical collaborator, John Duignan, released four critically acclaimed albums, and performed across Ireland, the UK, Spain, Holland, Russia and in New York. The band has collaborated with the RTÉ Concert Orchestra, Conor O' Brien (Villagers), Paul Noonan (BellX1) and Lisa Hannigan.

DAITHÍ Ó CORRÁIN is a lecturer in the School of History & Geography, Dublin City University. A specialist on the history of Ireland in the twentieth century, his recent publications include chapters on Irish Catholicism in *The Cambridge Social History of Modern Ireland* (2017) and *The Cambridge History of Ireland* vol. 4 (2018). He is co-editor of the acclaimed *Irish Revolution, 1912-23* series published by Four Courts Press.

TERESA O'DONNELL is a harpist and musicologist. She is former Foras Feasa fellow and lecturer at St Patrick's College, DCU. She is co-author of *Sisters of the Revolutionaries: Margaret and Mary Brigid Pearse* (2017) and her research has been published in the *Journal of Music Research Online* and the *Journal of the Society for Musicology in Ireland*. Teresa is a renowned harpist and has performed nationally and internationally.

List of Contributors

JOHN O'FLYNN is Associate Professor of Music at Dublin City University and was formerly Head of Music at St Patrick's College. He is author of numerous publications on a range of subjects including music in Ireland, film music, popular music and music education; he is also active as a choral conductor and baritone recitalist.

MIRIAM O'SULLIVAN is a native of Killarney who graduated from St Patrick's College, Drumcondra in 1982. While teaching in primary schools for most of her career, she has been seconded twice, first to The Ark where she worked as Music Programmer, and subsequently to the Primary Curriculum Support Programme. She holds a performance diploma in flute from the London College of Music and is keenly interested in performing.

COLMAN PEARCE won many awards as a young pianist, and received an honours degree in music at UCD. While at college he began to conduct and in 1965 he was offered a contract as orchestral conductor by RTÉ. He was Co-Principal Conductor of the RTÉ Symphony Orchestra from 1978-1980, and Principal Conductor from 1981-1983, Principal Guest Conductor Bilbao SO 1984-87, and Music Director/Principal Conductor, Mississippi SO 1987-99. He was awarded a PhD in composition by St Patrick's College, Dublin City University in 2009.

GAVAN RING is an international opera singer and musicologist. He has performed leading roles at the The Royal Opera, Glyndebourne and Opéra Royal de Versailles with conductors such as Sir Mark Elder and Sir Simon Rattle. Gavan is a graduate of St Patrick's College, Dublin City University, the Royal Irish Academy of Music and the National Opera Studio in London.

List of Figures

1	St Patrick's College quadrangle Photograph by Paul Murphy	11
2.1	Kyung-Wha Chung and the RTÉSO St Patrick's College Auditorium, 1972 Image courtesy RTÉ Archives	37
2.2	Autographs by members of the Vienna Boys' Choir Belvedere House, St Patrick's College, 1969 Photograph by John O'Flynn	39
2.3	Éadaoin Ní Mhaicín and Niamh Molloy performing at a lunchtime concert, 2015 Photograph by Frances Marshall	48
2.4	Poster for We Cut Corners lunchtime concert, 2014 Sean Breithaupt & Yvette Monahan Photography	52
3.1	Seán Hayes, lecturer and Head of Music, 1949-1985 Photographer unknown	66
3.2	Seán Mac Liam and Teresa O'Donnell, 2012 Photograph by Patricia Flynn	75
3.3	Rhona Clarke, Patricia Flynn and Louise Curtis, 2012 Photographer unknown	79
4.1	John Buckley and Judith Weir (CBE), 2015 Photograph by Paul Murphy	99
4.2	Poster for Macalla/Echo, 2016 with Liam Ó Maonlaí Photograph by Phillip Lauterbach	101
5.1	Cover of *The Irish Minstrel*, No. 1, 1908	108
6.1	Annual return of vocal and instrumental teachers, St Patrick's College, 1915-1916 Photograph by John O'Flynn	132
6.2	Harmonium manufactured c. 1851 located in Room B118 ('Music Room'), St Patrick's College Photograph by John O'Flynn	134

6.3 Marion Doherty, Head of Music, 1985-2008
    Photographer unknown   144

6.4 Members of College Choir at the The Helix, 2011
    Photograph by Eoin Campbell   146

6.5 Members of College Choir at the Cork International
    Choral Festival, 2013
    Photograph by Hertz Oliveira da Silva   148

7.1 Colum Ó Cléirigh conducting at Galway Cathedral, 1974
    Photographer unknown   158

7.2 Front of programme for the Second International
    Zoltán Kodály Music Seminar, 1985
    Photographer unknown   164

7.3 Éva Andor and John O'Flynn, 2009
    Photograph by Paul Murphy   168

8.1 Poster for The Music Education Gathering, 2013
    Design by Mick McCabe   198

8.2 Keith Swanwick at St Patrick's College, 2013
    Photograph by Barbara Flynn   199

9.1 *The Dublin Music Map* (2016), cover
    Design by Simon Roche, illustrations by Maria Hildrick   216

9.2 *The Dublin Music Map* (2016), inset detail
    Design by Simon Roche   216

10.1 The Fidelio Trio at Belvedere House, 2015
     Photograph by Frances Marshall   232

10.2 Poster for the 4th Fidelio Trio
     Winter Chamber Music Festival, 2016
     Design by Alastair Keady, Hexhibit   233

11   Main entrance to St Patrick's College   257
     Photograph by Paul Murphy

Abbreviations

BA	Bachelor of Arts
BAJH	Bachelor of Arts Joint Honours
BEd	Bachelor of Education
BIMM	British and Irish Modern Music Institute
BMusEd	Bachelor of Music Education
BRelEd	Bachelor of Religious Education
CCÉ	Comhaltas Ceoltóirí Éireann
CHMHE	Council of Heads of Music in Higher Education
CMC	Contemporary Music Centre
CPD	Continuing Professional Development
DCU	Dublin City University
DAHG	Department of Arts, Heritage and the Gaeltacht
DES	Department of Education and Skills (previously, Department of Education and Science)
DIT	Dublin Institute of Technology
DOP	Dublin Orchestral Players
Dram Soc	Drama Society
DSO	Dublin Symphony Orchestra
ECTMA	European Chamber Music Teachers' Association
ECTS	European Credit Transfer System
EHEA	European Higher Education Area
ESAI	Educational Studies Association of Ireland
IFUT	Irish Federation of University Teachers
INTO	Irish National Teachers' Organisation
IKS	Irish Kodály Society
ISME	International Society for Music Education
KSI	Kodály Society of Ireland
MA	Master of Arts
MAI	Music Association of Ireland
MEND	Music Education National Debate
MLitt	Master of Letters
MPMiD	Mapping Popular Music in Dublin
NCCA	National Council for Curriculum and Assessment
NCH	National Concert Hall
NDRC	National Development and Reform Commission
NT	National Teacher
NUI	National University of Ireland
PCSP	Primary Curriculum Support Programme
PhD	Doctor of Philosophy
PRTLI	Programme for Research in Third Level Institutions
QUB	Queen's University Belfast

RÉSO	Raidió Éireann Symphony Orchestra
RIAM	Royal Irish Academy of Music
RTÉ	Raidió Teilifís Éireann
RTÉCO	Raidió Teilifís Éireann Concert Orchestra
RTÉLO	Raidió Teilifís Éireann Light Orchestra
RTÉSO	Raidió Teilifís Éireann Symphony Orchestra
SMEI	Society for Music Education in Ireland
SMI	Society for Musicology in Ireland
SPARC	St Patrick's College Repertory Company
SPCA	St Patrick's College Archive
TCD	Trinity College Dublin
TES	Teacher Education Section
Tradsoc	Traditional Music Society
UCC	University College Cork
UCD	University College Dublin
UL	University of Limerick
UNESCO	United Nations Educational, Scientific and Cultural Organization

Acknowledgments

The editors are greatly indebted to St Patrick's College Research Committee and the Irish National Teachers' Organisation for the subvention of book production costs. Thanks are also due to Dan Farrelly, Carysfort Press and Lucy Melville and colleagues at Peter Lang Publishing for their expert guidance, and to Áine Mulvey for her meticulous preparation of the index.

Our sincere thanks go to the many library staff, archivists and others who provided access to a range of handwritten, print, digitized and media materials, including: Orla Nic Aodha, Sophie Dowling and staff of the Cregan Library, DCU; Paul Murphy, Senior AV Technician, DCU Institute of Education; Teresa O'Farrell, President's Office, DCU; Tina Byrne, Senior Archivist and Records Manager, RTÉ Document Archives; Avice-Claire McGovern, Mary Broderick and Nóra Thornton, Special Collections and Manuscripts Department, National Library of Ireland; Sarah Burn, Potter Archive.

We deeply appreciate the committed work of music and humanities administrators at St Patrick's College over the past two decades who helped digitize many of the records accessed in preparation for this volume, notably, Emer Benson, Evelyn Cuddy, Carol Davis, Bronagh Farrell, Geraldine Healy, Barry O'Halpin and Annette Slattery.

The production of this volume has been greatly assisted by a range of colleagues and friends who provided additional materials or who furnished details on various aspects of musical life at the College, including: Albert Bradshaw, Patrick R. Burke, Gareth Cox, Paul Deegan, Marion Doherty, Lilla Gábor, Péter Erdei, Helen Fleming, Jean Hayes, Anne Marie Herron, Muireann Joy, Ailbhe Kenny, Peter McDermott, Darragh McGonigle, Seán Mac Liam, Nicole Martin, Cliona Murphy, Regina Murphy, Moya Ní Cheallaigh, Nicholas O'Carolan, John O'Carroll, Lorraine O'Connell, Peter O'Driscoll, Gráinne O'Flynn, Mary O'Flynn, Michael O'Leary, Breda O'Shea, Eoghan Ó Suilleabháin, Fiona Roche, Deirdre Seaver, Caitlín Uí Éigeartaigh, Fintan Vallely and Daniel Walsh.

Finally, our sincere and heartfelt thanks go to all the contributors to this volume for giving of their expertise and experience; they share our dedication to all those who created the musical heritage of St Patrick's College.

Introduction

John Buckley and John O'Flynn

Since its foundation in 1875, the activities of St Patrick's College Drumcondra and its graduates have been closely woven into the educational and cultural fabric of Irish society. For more than a hundred years the College's sole function was the preparation of students for teaching in the Irish primary school system. From the 1990s onwards a range of new programmes, including a BA in Humanities and an array of postgraduate degrees, was introduced in addition to the teaching courses. The College's graduates have taught hundreds of thousands, if not millions of pupils across the country and have made an invaluable contribution to the wellbeing of individuals, to the development of communities and to the advancement of the nation as a whole.

Music and music education have fulfilled a major role throughout the history of St Patrick's College. This book represents *a* history of music at the College until its incorporation into Dublin City University (DCU) in 2016, marking the end of St Patrick's as an independent entity. The book is not intended to be a comprehensive inventory of all the musical activities over that period, which would be beyond its scope or intention. Rather, it sets out to examine and interpret key developments, appraise the work of major contributors to the progress of music at the College and capture the activities of students and staff over the years. This is the first time that such a study has been undertaken, and it is hoped that it will evoke further memories and discussions among graduates of the College and others.

The development of music at St Patrick's College in many ways reflects the evolution of music in the country as a whole. The focus on choral music and on singing generally in the early years of the College, with a particular prominence given to the repertoire of native traditional songs, was in keeping with the aspirations of nationhood at that period. The book investigates developments in music instruction in the national education system as well as the activities of the Irish Cecilian movement and the Gaelic Revival. The close engagement of the College Choir with the nascent national broadcasting service 2RN (later RTÉ) in the 1920s further enhanced the relationship between St Patrick's and the state. In later decades the rejuvenation of Irish traditional music found vibrant resonances in the musical life of the College. In fact, many graduates were to become leading figures in the development of traditional music in the 1960s and later. Other musical genres including classical, jazz and various popular styles were fully integrated into the musical life of the College in more recent years.

Several chapters of the book endeavour to present a broad perspective spanning the entire historical period of the College. Chapter One, 'Fluctuating Fortunes' by Daithí Ó Corráin, explores the origins and development of the College over the years and provides a context into which the following chapters can be placed. Ó Corráin examines the role of music in evolving curricula and surveys the new programmes introduced to the College from the 1970s onwards. The second chapter, 'Music Performance at St Patrick's College' by John Buckley, surveys the role of the College in instigating and supporting the performance of music throughout its history. Musical performances organized both within the College and by external groups using the College facilities are discussed in detail. The range of music performed - including choral, orchestral, opera, instrumental, musicals and popular songs - is reviewed and analysed. The theme of performance extends into several other chapters in the volume. Chapter Five by Teresa O'Donnell focuses on the College's engagement with Irish traditional music. She reviews the various courses and approaches to the teaching of Irish traditional music in the College. The contribution of key figures – lecturers and graduates of the College – to the development of Irish traditional music nationally is assessed and the sense of historical continuity and development surveyed.

The singing of the college choir is mentioned in the *Freeman's Journal* as early as 1885, a tradition that was maintained throughout the College's history. In Chapter Six, 'Vocal and Choral Music' by John O'Flynn, the role of various choirs both within and beyond the College is discussed in detail. O'Flynn's chapter also explores the relationship between mandatory music syllabuses of the early to mid-twentieth century (termed 'vocal music') and extra-curricular choral activities in the realm of artistic practice. A closer look at the history of the various music courses offered at St Patrick's College over its one-hundred-and-forty-year history is presented in Chapter Three, 'Music in Education and Humanities' by Patricia Flynn and John O'Flynn. Three types of music course would evolve at the College over this time. The first of these, which developed from the earlier 'vocal music' syllabuses, became known as 'curriculum music' and embraced courses that prepared student teachers to teach music in primary schools. The second type of course was the study of music as a university degree subject, a development that came to fruition following the introduction of the College's BEd degree programme accredited by the National University of Ireland (NUI) in 1974. The academic status of music at the College was further enhanced through the BA programme established in 1994 following the institutional linkage with Dublin City University

(DCU). A third major category emerged at the end of the twentieth century, namely, that of music education as a field of academic inquiry. Flynn and O'Flynn also raise an important theme that resonates with many chapters in the book - that of the music department's dual investment in the areas of education and humanities.

Many contributions to the book focus on developments over the last half-century of the College's history. In addition to the accreditation of degree programmes and the gradual expansion of student numbers, significant changes over this period included the admission of the first female students from 1971, and a gradual process of secularization of the institution, marked by the departure of the Vincentian Order in 1999.

Chapter Four by Rhona Clarke charts the evolution of composition studies at the College, and begins with an overview of the harmony and counterpoint courses that were first included as components for academic music within the two-year college diploma (NT). First accredited by NUI in the 1960s, these were later expanded in the degree-level courses. Chapter Four continues with a consideration of group composition as a new area within curriculum music studies following the introduction of a revised primary school curriculum in 1999 by the National Council for Curriculum and Assessment, and goes on to chart the development of studies in free composition at BA, MA and PhD levels from the turn of the twenty-first century.

Following Chapters Five and Six that respectively address traditional music and choral music (discussed above), Chapter Seven by Yvonne Higgins, 'The Kodály Connection', charts and interprets the College's special association with in-service provision and curriculum development based on the approach of Hungarian music educator and composer Zoltán Kodály. Higgins demonstrates the impact music lecturers and graduates of the College made on the development of music education and choral music in Ireland from the early 1980s to the time of writing. Engagement and research are treated as distinct yet interrelated themes in Chapter Eight by John O'Flynn which examines developments and contributions by staff and students in the areas of in-service education, curriculum development, community music projects, postgraduate research, funded research projects and conference organization.

Chapter Nine by Áine Mangaoang details the music department's leadership of the applied research project 'Mapping Popular Music in Dublin' which was funded by the national tourist agency Fáilte Ireland. Mangaoang explores the project's reach to various networks, organizations and spaces across the Dublin area, and further considers the researchers' collaboration with other disciplines within the College including geography and visual arts. She describes how outcomes of this research not only included a published report and an innovative *Dublin Music Map*, but also intersected with new initiatives in local arts programming.

Chapter Ten, 'The Fidelio Trio Residency' by John O'Flynn documents a unique relationship that emerged between the world-renowned piano trio and the music department of St Patrick's College from 2012-2015. Co-funded by the Arts Council/An Chomhairle Ealaíon and the College, the Fidelio Trio residency made outstanding contributions to performance, composition, education, outreach, musicology and chamber music promotion at St Patrick's College and beyond. O'Flynn situates the chapter in a consideration of national arts-in-education initiatives and also with regard to the music department's unique balance of music and music education interests. The chapter also notes the continued association between the Trio and the College (and later DCU) through an annual winter chamber music festival which was established during the residency.

Finally, Chapter Eleven, introduced by John Buckley, focuses on the perspectives of college alumni. The chapter brings together reminiscences from graduates Miriam O'Sullivan, Gavan Ring, Colman Pearce, Conall Ó Breacháin, Paul Gilgunn and Denise Morgan in which they consider the impact that music studies and musical activities at the College made on their personal and professional lives. This resonates with an afterword in which Niall Doyle reflects on the book's various contributions in light of his own experience as a student at the College and subsequently as a leading figure in Irish musical life. Doyle provocatively concludes his commentary with a challenge to policy-makers and providers for primary level music education in Ireland.

The book includes five appendices. Appendix A provides a list of full-time music lecturers at the College from 1883-2016. Appendix B supplements the second chapter on performance with a list of lunchtime concert programmes by guest performers from 2003-2016. The extensive involvement of choirs from St Patrick's College at the Cork International Choral Festival between the years 1972-2015 is detailed in Appendix C. Appendix D provides a list of music and music education dissertations and theses from 2000-2016. Finally, Appendix E documents a comprehensive list of concerts, workshops and other events that took place during the Fidelio Trio Residency 2012-2015 and also includes programme details of chamber music festivals under the artistic leadership of the ensemble.

While the history of music at St Patrick's College can be said to have officially ended on the occasion of the institution's full incorporation into Dublin City University in October 2016, its legacy continues in several significant ways. The most far-reaching aspect of that legacy is that, along with the music department of Mater Dei Institute of

Education which was incorporated into DCU at the same time, the integration of St Patrick's College's music department signalled the presence of music as an academic discipline at the university for the first time. From 2016 music studies at undergraduate and postgraduate levels have been offered through DCU's Faculty of Humanities and Social Sciences while music education has been re-configured within the university's newly constituted faculty, the DCU Institute of Education. Aside from these significant institutional changes, staff and students based at what is now the St Patrick's Campus of DCU—as well as those at the university's All Hallows campus—continue to teach, study, perform, compose, research and otherwise engage with music. The endeavours of these present and future lecturers, scholars, teachers, students and musicians form part of a continuum of educational, societal and cultural impact that has been unbroken since the establishment of St Patrick's College in 1875.

Chapter One: Fluctuating Fortunes:
St Patrick's College, 1875-2016

Daithí Ó Corráin

From its establishment as a denominational teacher training college in 1875 until its incorporation into Dublin City University in 2016, the impact of St Patrick's College on the educational landscape of Ireland, as well as the wider social, cultural and political life of the country has been immense.[1] Generations of teachers have passed through its gates and in more recent decades they have been joined by graduates in the humanities. The story of the College and the history of Irish education are intertwined. The purpose of this chapter is threefold. It explains why the College was founded, the challenges that it faced and how the institution evolved over its 141-year history from a male training college to a co-educational one to a third-level institution that also offered programmes in the humanities. Second, a synopsis of the various developments in the primary school curriculum and their impact on teacher training will be provided. Lastly, and by no means least, the place of music in the College and the curriculum will be touched on.

A state-supported primary school system was inaugurated in Ireland in 1831 under the auspices of a state board of commissioners. The board, which replaced a multiplicity of ad hoc educational agencies, controlled the management of school buildings, curriculum, textbooks, teacher training and a system of inspection. The state's desire to create a non-denominational system was opposed by all the main churches because religious formation was regarded as a fundamental element of a child's education. The primary school system spread rapidly and became increasingly denominational in character. By 1900 almost sixty-five per cent of the 8,644 schools, which catered for 770,622 pupils, were denominationally homogeneous and eighty per cent had clerical managers.[2] During the nineteenth century there was a growing professionalization of occupations. As the number of schools increased, so did the need for trained primary school teachers, the vast majority of whom were untrained. Of the 7,907 Catholic teachers in 1883, three-

---

[1] Although the official name was St Patrick's College, the institution became popularly known as St Patrick's Teacher Training College. This designation fell into abeyance in the 1990s when programmes in the humanities were offered.
[2] T. Walsh, 'The National System of Education, 1831-2000', in B. Walsh (ed.), *Essays in the History of Irish Education*, (London: Palgrave Macmillan, 2016), pp. 10-11.

quarters had no training.³ After 1831 the National Board of Education established an interdenominational and co-educational training college at Marlborough Street with attached model schools.⁴ But this did not satisfy the Catholic hierarchy which sought denominational control over all aspects of education because 'if national schools were to become Catholic in character they should be staffed by teachers who had undergone a course of distinctly Catholic training'.⁵ From the 1860s until 1883 an arduous campaign was waged to obtain state support for denominational training colleges, as was the norm in England. To increase pressure on the government, the hierarchy banned Catholics from attending Marlborough Street and the model schools.

Cardinal Paul Cullen, the formidable Catholic archbishop of Dublin from 1852 until 1878, was determined to establish a Catholic training college for men. A national synod at Maynooth issued a pastoral on 31 August 1875 which announced the hierarchy's decision to open a new college in Drumcondra 'under the immediate care of the Vincentian Fathers'.⁶ The congregation provided two priests and a lay brother. Fr James Petit, the principal, and Fr Louis Bean, bursar, had previously taught at Castleknock College, a Vincentian secondary school in Dublin.⁷ The first Catholic training college in the country was established at No. 2 Drumcondra Road (later the Sacred Heart Home) and the first cohort of students was admitted on 31 October 1875. The accommodation for fifty students was soon increased to seventy. Initially, the duration of the course was one year. In January 1877 the adjoining building at No. 1 Drumcondra Road was leased. By the following year St Patrick's College provided a full-time course to almost 100 national schoolteachers, as well as a variety of short courses. St Patrick's was soon joined by other voluntary Catholic training colleges. In 1877 the Sisters of Mercy opened a training college for women on Baggot Street in Dublin which moved to Carysfort in 1903. By the beginning of the twentieth century three other Catholic colleges had been opened: De La Salle College, Waterford (1891) for men; and Mary Immaculate College, Limerick (1898) and St Mary's College, Belfast (1900) for women. Consequently, the number of trained teachers

---

³ T. J. McElligott, *Education in Ireland*, (Dublin, 1966), p. 7.
⁴ Between 1843 and 1867 a network of twenty-six model schools was established throughout the country.
⁵ C. King, 'The early years of the College, 1875-1921' in J. Kelly (ed.), *St Patrick's College Drumcondra: A History*, (Dublin: Four Courts Press, 2006), p. 93.
⁶ T. Ó Ceallaigh, *Coláiste Phádraig/St Patrick's College Centenary Booklet, 1875-1975*, (Dublin: St Patrick's College, 1975), p. 7.
⁷ Ibid., p. 8.

increased to forty-eight per cent (5,790) by the end of the nineteenth century.[8]

Without state support, the Catholic training colleges operated in straitened circumstances and the financial position of St Patrick's College was perilous in its early years. The Maynooth synod determined that a levy of £2 per annum should be contributed by each parish for the upkeep of the College in addition to hefty student fees of £20 per annum.[9] Many dioceses did not (or could not) contribute the expected amount. In April 1880 Edward McCabe, Cullen's successor as archbishop of Dublin, advanced a personal loan of £400 to keep the College afloat. The situation improved in early 1883. The end of the Land War, which had preoccupied the British government, and a demand by the Church of Ireland's Kildare Place training college led George Trevelyan, the Irish chief secretary, to indicate that the government was willing to provide grants to teacher training colleges 'under local management'. St Patrick's Drumcondra and Our Lady of Mercy, Baggot Street became recognized national teacher training institutions in 1883 and the Church of Ireland training college a year later.[10] The state grants were strictly grant-in-aid. The colleges remained fee-paying and were subsidized with grants of £50 per male student and £35 for female students. Capital or other expenditure was not covered and the grants could not exceed 75 per cent of the certified expenditure approved by the National Board each year. Problematically, the grants were paid on an instalment basis depending on student performance in annual examinations and as teachers for two years following graduation.[11] Unlike Marlborough Street, the duration of the teacher training course in the new denominational colleges was two years and intensive; provision was also made for a temporary one-year course for practising teachers. Examinations were conducted by the inspectors of the National Board.

Following recognition by the National Board in 1883, Cardinal McCabe arranged for the purchase for £3,000 of Belvedere House, half a mile from Nos. 1-2 Drumcondra Road.[12] The house, which stood on twenty-two acres, was originally built in the 1660s and remodelled in

---

[8] *Sixty-Sixth Report of the Commissioners of National Education in Ireland for the Year 1899-1900*, (Dublin: Stationery Office, 1900), Cd. 285, p. 30.
[9] King, 'The early years of the College', p. 97.
[10] S. M. Parkes, '"An Essential Service": The National Board and Teacher Education, 1831-1870', in B. Walsh (ed.), *Irish Education*, p. 74.
[11] King, 'The early years of the College', p. 101.
[12] McCabe was raised to the College of Cardinals on 27 March 1882.

the eighteenth century.¹³ From January 1874 the Christian Brothers used Belvedere House as a novitiate and the administrative headquarters of the congregation before relocating to a more spacious property in Marino. The Christian Brothers built a small primary school on the grounds of Belvedere House which was recognized by the National Board and served as the practice school of the training college. The 'new' St Patrick's College opened its doors in September 1883 just three weeks after the acquisition of the property. Fr Peter Byrne (1840-1920) became the new principal and was the driving force in the development and consolidation of the college. He recalled the challenges of the first session in 1883-4 and how 'some classes had to be held in the entrance hall ... and the stabling and other farmyard buildings, including a lofty barn'.¹⁴ The College was able to accommodate seventy-four students, although approved by the National Board for 100 Queen's scholars.¹⁵ More than one-third of the intake comprised practising teachers; the remainder had passed the Queen's scholarship examination and were admitted to the two-year course.¹⁶

The Belvedere House property was transformed during its first decade as St Patrick's College. The introduction of the Loans for Non-Vested Schools and Training Colleges (Ireland) Act in 1884 allowed the college management to borrow money from the Board of Public Works for new buildings and improvement works. Builders became a common sight around Belvedere House. A new study hall block was opened at the beginning of the 1885-6 session. Adjoining Belvedere House to the northeast, it comprised a study hall, a 76-bed dormitory, two lecture halls, a recreation hall and a refectory. Cardinal McCabe died in February 1885 and was succeeded by William J. Walsh. The new archbishop of Dublin paid his first formal visit to the College on 29 September 1885 to open the new building and used the occasion to highlight the inferior financial treatment of denominational training colleges. Marlborough Street training college was built and maintained at the taxpayers' expense, whereas the state paid only capitation grants to the colleges under local management. Walsh boldly declared that until the government treated all the training colleges equally he would refuse to act as manager of St Patrick's. His stance was supported by the Church of Ireland. In 1890 Arthur Balfour, then Irish chief secretary,

---

¹³ On Belvedere House, see J. Kelly, 'Belvedere House: origins, development and residents, 1540-1883', in J. Kelly (ed.), *St Patrick's College Drumcondra: A History*, (Dublin: Four Courts Press, 2006), pp. 9-40.
¹⁴ King, 'The early years of the College', p. 102.
¹⁵ Ó Ceallaigh, *Centenary Booklet*, p. 12.
¹⁶ Ibid., p. 16.

introduced a new funding scheme which included an undertaking that the state would repay capital expenditure. Walsh laid the foundation of another new building in October 1890 which formed an L-shape with the study hall block and became known as the science block on completion in September 1892.[17] The neighbourhood of Drumcondra grew rapidly in this period. The original primary school on the St Patrick's College grounds was replaced by new buildings in 1893 with accommodation for 625 children; the school was soon full.[18] Fr Byrne's last major building project was a new college chapel which was opened by Archbishop Walsh on 11 June 1899. The chapel faced the quadrangle and was approached, on either side, from the college buildings through a handsome cloister.[19]

Figure 1: St Patrick's College quadrangle, with the chapel on the left. Photograph by Paul Murphy

During the nineteenth century music did not occupy a central place on the school curriculum. When the National Board was established it looked to the methods of instruction deployed in the English school system. John Hullah (1812-84), an English music teacher and

---

[17] Ibid., p. 18.
[18] E. J. Cullen, *The Origin and Development of the Irish Vincentian Foundations, 1883-1933*, (Dublin: The Three Candles, 1934), p. 118.
[19] *Freeman's Journal*, 12 June 1899.

composer, adapted the method of instruction in vocal music devised by G.L.B. Wilhem in France in the 1840s. In this way, a French method of interval training designed for use in a monitorial system (where advanced students taught less advanced ones) was imported via an English adaptation into Ireland.[20] Under the Wilhem-Hullah method, music education became equated with a mechanical skills-based practice with an emphasis on vocal music. Moreover, the Hullah manual was ill-suited to Irish schools and contained not a single Irish air. That singing became the mainstay of the curriculum was understandable given the specialist skills, equipment and financial outlay required for the teaching of instrumental music. The 1831 curriculum was revised in 1872. The report of the Powis Commission (1870) into primary education introduced payment by results and from 1872 teachers' salaries were linked to the annual examination results of their pupils. This led to didactic and mechanistic teaching and the prioritization of the mandatory subjects of reading, writing, spelling and arithmetic. In 1872 vocal music was one of twenty-one additional subjects added to the curriculum. Uptake was poor and the teaching of singing was largely confined to girls' schools.[21] At the end of the century only seventeen per cent of Irish schools provided instruction in vocal music and the reports of the commissioners of education lamented teacher apathy. In 1899 of 8,700 schools in operation, only 1,470 had music as a subject of examination at the annual inspection. Furthermore, only one-quarter of the 12,000 teachers were registered as competent to teach music.[22]

Following a national and international review of education provision, the Revised Programme of Instruction was introduced in primary schools in September 1900. Under the new curriculum greater emphasis was placed on the practice of teaching. The traditional compulsory subjects were supplemented with a number of new manual and practical subjects such as drawing, physical drill, manual instruction (woodwork) and singing. In addition, the new curriculum also included as optional subjects instrumental music, French, Latin, mathematics and Irish. The commissioners considered the study of music 'a refining and intellectual pursuit ... calculated to have a

---

[20] M. Stakelum, 'A song to sweeten Ireland's wrong: music education and the Celtic Revival', in B. Taylor FitzSimon & J. Murphy (eds.), *The Irish Revival Reappraised*, (Dublin: Four Courts Press, 2004), p. 82.

[21] *Sixty-First Report of the Commissioners of National Education in Ireland for the Year 1894*, (Dublin: Stationery Office, 1895), C. 7796, p. 30.

[22] P. Goodman, 'General report on music instruction, 1900', *Appendix to the Seventy-Sixth Report of the Commissioners of National Education for the Year 1900*, (Dublin: Stationery Office, 1902), Cd. 954, p. 82.

cheering influence on school life generally'.²³ In 1883 Peter Goodman, an accomplished organist and conductor, was appointed the first music master in St Patrick's College. A decade later he became examiner in music with the National Board. Goodman promoted the study of music in the training colleges with zeal and devotion. For him:

> no other subject so brightens and enlivens the routine of school life, as sweet, pleasant music. It quickens all the faculties of the children ... When well taught, children display a love of music for its own sake which they show for no other school subject ... The child in whom the gift of song has not been developed may surely be said to want a sense.²⁴

When the revised programme was launched Goodman was appointed inspector of music instruction. He faced the formidable challenge of ensuring that vocal music was introduced in over 7,000 schools, where it had been unknown, and that 9,000 teachers acquired some knowledge of the subject. With the help of five assistants, he sought to guide both teachers and children. During the school day instruction was given in schools to the children and in the evenings teachers attended a two-hour class every day for five weeks in preparation for an examination at the end of the course. Teachers who failed the examination and demonstrated manifest want of any musical aptitude were excused from teaching the subject.²⁵ These efforts bore fruit and by 1904 vocal music was taught in 6,683 primary schools, instrumental music in 306.²⁶ Goodman died prematurely in June 1909 and the chief inspectors of the National Board paid generous tribute to his 'wholehearted devotion' to the cause of music and his 'untiring efforts to promote it'.²⁷

The teacher training colleges had adopted the tonic solfa system (the use of Hullah began to decline from the 1860s) and they also afforded

---

[23] Ibid.
[24] P. Goodman, 'General musical report for year 1897', *Sixty-Fourth Report of the Commissioners of National Education in Ireland for Year 1897-8*, (Dublin: Stationery Office, 1898), C. 9038, p. 271.
[25] P. Goodman, 'General report on music instruction, 1900', *Appendix to the Sixty-Seventh Report of the Commissioners of National Education for the Year 1900*, (Dublin: Stationery Office, 1902), Cd. 954, pp. 83-4.
[26] *Seventy-First Report of the Commissioners of National Education in Ireland for the Year 1904*, (Dublin: Stationery Office, 1905), Cd. 2567, p. 53.
[27] *Appendix to the Seventy-Fifth Report of the Commissioners of National Education in Ireland for the Year 1908-9*, (Dublin: Stationery Office, 1910), Cd. 5062, p. 8.

facilities for learning instrumental music, chiefly the harmonium which was found helpful for singing instruction in the classroom. The introduction of a new programme in the colleges in 1897, in preparation for the revised curriculum, also proved beneficial. For the first time vocal music could be included in the classification marks of Queen's scholars if chosen as the obligatory optional subject (from a menu of twenty subjects). The number of student teachers in Ireland selecting music increased from 259 in 1897 to 1,184 in 1900.[28] A decade later, in St Patrick's College 162 King's scholars were examined in music and thirty in instrumental music (harmonium).[29] Of the male training colleges, only St Patrick's and De La Salle offered the harmonium which proved more popular in the female training colleges. For example, 105 female student teachers were examined in the instrument in 1913-14 compared to only forty-seven of their male peers (twenty-six in St Patrick's and twenty-one in De La Salle).[30] This lack of interest may explain why Louis O'Brien, assistant professor of harmonium in St Patrick's since 1912 and a well-known choir director, was given a month's notice in September 1921 that his services were no longer required.[31] This period also witnessed the steady growth in the Irish language both outside and inside St Patrick's College. Father Byrne favoured the gradual extension of a course in the Irish language and in 1896 Eoin MacNeill, a founder of the Gaelic League and later the Irish Volunteers, was appointed professor of Irish. In 1906 he was succeeded by Tórna (Tadhg Ó Donnchadha), a noted Irish writer, poet, translator and collector of songs. Douglas Hyde and a Gaelic League delegation visited the college in 1914 and the following year Irish was given an

---

[28] P. Goodman, 'General report on music instruction, 1900', *Appendix to the Sixty-Sixth Report of the Commissioners of National Education for the Year 1900*, (Dublin: Stationery Office, 1902), Cd. 954, p. 87.

[29] T.F. Marchant, 'General report on musical instruction for 1910', *Appendix to the Seventy-Sixth Report of the Commissioners of National Education in Ireland for the School Year 1909-10*, (Dublin: Stationery Office, 1911), Cd. 5491, pp. 212-13.

[30] T.F. Marchant, 'General report on musical instruction for the school year ended 30 June 1914', *Appendix to the Eightieth Report of the Commissioners of National Education for the School Year 1913-14*, (Dublin: Stationery Office, 1915), Cd. 7966, pp. 173-4.

[31] D. Ferriter, '"For God's sake send me a few packets of fags": the College, 1922-45' in Kelly (ed.), *St Patrick's College*, p. 135. For a brief biography of O'Brien see K. Daly, 'O'Brien, Louis' in H. White & B. Boydell (eds.), *The Encyclopaedia of Music in Ireland*, Volume II (Dublin: UCD Press, 2013), p. 742.

equal place on the timetable with compulsory subjects.[32] About half of the student body took Irish.

Fr Byrne retired as principal in 1911. His was an outstanding legacy in terms of the development of the College and the broader educational environment unsurpassed by any of his successors, not even Fr Donal Cregan (who is discussed below). The chief inspectors of the National Board, professionally disinclined to fulsome praise, paid Byrne a generous tribute:

> ... to his sound judgement and fostering care the great success of the institution was largely due. He piloted it skillfully through the difficulties that attended its early days, and he may lawfully pride himself on the flourishing condition in which he has left it.[33]

Byrne was succeeded by Fr James Flynn. His term as principal (1911-17) was short but noteworthy for efforts to organize a three-year course and a pathway towards a university degree for student teachers. Though unsuccessful, these efforts presaged developments half a century later; an attempt to create a specialist three-year degree for teachers was also mooted in the 1940s. Flynn died in 1917 and was succeeded by Fr John Russell (1917-20) who was followed by Fr James Bennett (1920-22). The College did not survive the War of Independence period unscathed. In October 1920 John Carolan, professor of the science and art of teaching (teaching practice), died of wounds inflicting during a shootout in his home, 'Fernside' at 6 Church Avenue, Drumcondra between the Crown forces and the celebrated Tipperary IRA men Dan Breen and Seán Treacy.[34]

In the aftermath of the Irish Civil War, Catholicism and the reification of the Irish language provided a sense of shared identity and cohesion clearly distinct from Protestant England.[35] Perhaps fittingly, Fionán Lynch, a graduate of the college, was the minister for education in the provisional government from January until August 1922 and oversaw the establishment of the Department of Education which

---

[32] Ó Ceallaigh, *Centenary Booklet*, pp. 21-2.

[33] *Appendix to the Seventy-Eight Report of the Commissioners of National Education in Ireland, School Year 1911-12* (Dublin: Stationery Office, 1913), Cd. 7061, p. 9.

[34] The shootout took place on 12 October 1920 and Carolan died in the Mater Hospital, Dublin on 27 October. His remains were interred in Glasnevin Cemetery two days later.

[35] P. Corish, *The Irish Catholic Experience: A Historical Survey*, (Dublin: Gill and Macmillan, 1985), p. 244.

replaced the National Board.³⁶ In the opening decades of independent Ireland there was little serious re-appraisal of education policy beyond a dogmatic desire to restore the Irish language. As the education system had played a considerable role in anglicizing the country, it was assumed simplistically that it could also be used to reverse that process and spearhead a programme of Gaelicization. The first National Programme Conference in 1922 and the Second National Programme Conference in 1926 laid down a curriculum policy that remained largely intact until 1971 (there were minor revisions in 1934 and 1948). Irish became a compulsory subject to be taught for one hour per day in addition to further integration with other subjects. A requirement, subsequently much criticized, to use Irish as the medium of instruction in the infant classes remained in place until 1960. Timetable demands adversely affected the music programme which had, as might be expected, a greater emphasis on Irish music and tradition. Singing was largely confined to the teaching of songs in Irish and annual inspectors' reports expressed disappointment at the low level of proficiency of pupils in general music on leaving primary school. Standards of voice training, ear training and sight-reading remained poor.³⁷

From 1922 until 1937 Fr Edmund J. Cullen, a nephew of Cardinal Cullen but very much his opposite in temperament, became principal.³⁸ He was unenthusiastic about the government's prioritization of the Irish language above all other subjects. New regulations were introduced in 1923, whereby Irish became a compulsory subject for admission to the training colleges. That year all students took Irish in their final examinations in St Patrick's College and arrangements were made to teach as many subjects as possible through Irish as the 1920s progressed. Some members of staff had no Irish. Notably, Cullen continued to teach Christian doctrine through English which remained the language of record in the College and that used by the students. Teacher competence in the Irish language proved a notable difficulty. The Department of Education addressed this by providing in-service training and through the establishment of seven preparatory colleges between 1926 and 1929. They provided post primary education to

---

³⁶ Before the Irish Free State came into formal existence on 6 December 1922 there was a provisional government minister for education – Lynch with responsibility for primary education and a Dáil minister for education, Michael Hayes with responsibility for intermediate education. Both functions were assumed by Eoin MacNeill as minister for education from 30 August 1922.
³⁷ T. Walsh, *Primary Education in Ireland, 1897-1990: Curriculum and Context*, (Bern: Peter Lang, 2012), p. 178.
³⁸ Cullen had previously been president of St Patrick's College, Armagh, a Vincentian secondary school.

pupils, particularly those from the *Gaeltachtaí*, desiring to become teachers and twenty-five per cent of places in the teacher training colleges were reserved for those students, without further competition once the minimum Leaving Certificate criteria were satisfied. By contrast, students outside the preparatory colleges were selected on the basis of Leaving Certificate results and additional oral and practical tests at Easter.[39] The emphasis on Irish in St Patrick's College was matched by the centrality of religion in the experience of students with morning and evening prayer, daily Mass, frequent confession and communion. Until the late 1950s the college operated 'in the manner of a lay seminary. A disproportionate amount of time and attention was devoted during the 1930s, 1940s and 1950s to ensuring that the student-teachers fitted the model of a Catholic teacher'.[40] Pádraig Faulkner, future government minister and *Ceann Comhairle*, entered the college in 1936. He recollected that 'life in St Pats was very confined in those days'. A happier memory was a performance by the student choir, conducted by Gus Redmond, professor of music at the college, on Raidió Éireann.[41]

Teacher employment prospects declined during the 1930s and 1940s. Many students did not complete their course in St Patrick's as opportunities in the civil service and semi-state sector proved more enticing. In 1940 only thirty-nine new teachers were qualified by the College, as there was a surplus of trained teachers at this time. To meet this situation the Department of Education abolished provisions for pupil-teachers, reduced the number of junior assistant mistresses and imposed a marriage bar on married women teachers; it also reduced the number of approved students in St Patrick's to 150. The situation deteriorated during the 1940s. In 1943 there was no first year intake in Drumcondra and the following year the College was closed down and its staff dismissed. Fortunately, the closure was short-lived. St Patrick's reopened in September 1945 with only thirty-three students and five full-time teaching staff in addition to the principal, dean and bursar.[42] The future of the College was precarious. It was saved by three fortuitous factors. The first was demographics. Despite high emigration, the primary school population expanded during the 1950s. In 1951 the number of approved students in St Patrick's was increased to 185. Second, there was a reorientation of state educational policy and from

---

[39] S. O'Connor, *A Troubled Sky: Reflections on the Irish Educational Scene, 1957-68,* (Dublin: Educational Research Centre, 1986), p. 29.
[40] J. Kelly, 'Introduction', in Kelly (ed.), *St Patrick's College*, p. 4.
[41] P. Faulkner, *As I Saw It: Reviewing Over 30 years of Fianna Fáil and Irish Politics*, (Dublin: Wolfhound Press, 2005), pp. 11-12.
[42] Ó Ceallaigh, *Centenary Booklet*, p. 26.

the late 1950s it was belatedly recognized that investment in education was a vital component of Ireland's economic development. Lastly, the reforming vision and wise stewardship of Fr Donal Cregan, principal from 1957 until May 1976, capitalized on the aforementioned developments.

Concerns about the standard of student attainment in the preparatory colleges led to their discontinuation in 1961 (with the exception of the Protestant Coláiste Móibhí). A scholarship was introduced for students from the *Gaeltachtaí*. The consequent change in the admission system – now based on the Leaving Certificate and an interview – was welcomed by the authorities in St Patrick's and led to a more diverse intake of students. From 1959 onward the state underwrote the cost of the College's ambitious and transformative building programme to provide facilities for 450 students. Plans were designed by Andrew Devane of Robinson, Keefe & Devane and work commenced in 1962 on 305 study bedrooms arranged in five blocks (previously there was accommodation for 216), a new chapel, auditorium, communal area, gymnasium, administrative offices, music room, dining hall and kitchens. In addition, the existing buildings were renovated and adapted. The old chapel became a library and the remainder of the ground floor around the quadrangle was adapted for teaching purposes and included a language laboratory; a staff common room was also added. The first floor of the original study hall block and the science block were converted into lecture halls and classrooms. A modern science laboratory, tutorial rooms and offices for teaching staff were created on the top floor.[43] A symphony concert by the Raidió Teilifís Éireann Symphony Orchestra was held in March 1966 to open the new auditorium. Included in the programme was a new work by Dr A. J. Potter, commissioned for the occasion, based on the Breastplate of St Patrick and sung in Irish by the college choir.[44] The Department of Education also financed the establishment of the Educational Research Centre which began its work in temporary accommodation in January 1966 and acquired its own building two years later. The first issue of *The Irish Journal of Education* published by the centre appeared in 1967. The government demonstrated a greater commitment to educational research and evidence-based policy formulation. The transformed campus was ready by the beginning of the 1966-7 session and was formally opened on 4 May 1967. The redevelopment cost £1.5 million.[45] The government's investment was 'an act of enlightened self-

---

[43] Ibid., p. 34.
[44] *Irish Press*, 16 March 1966.
[45] *Irish Independent*, 1 May 1967.

interest ... which enabled the expansion of the College to provide a significantly augmented supply of trained primary teachers.'[46]

During the 1960s there were increasing concerns about the narrowness of the primary school curriculum and the inordinate amount of time devoted to the teaching of Irish. A new curriculum – the first thorough revision for almost half a century – was published in 1971. Its child-centred and active learning philosophy marked a radical change, as did the broader programme of instruction which was arranged under seven subject areas: religion, language, mathematics, social and environmental studies; art and craft activities; music and physical education.[47] Teachers' handbooks provided detailed elaboration of the syllabus and pedagogical approaches in each subject area.[48] The impact of increased exposure to music through radio and television was embraced and the curriculum sought to extend children's awareness of music through singing, music making and listening and moving to music.[49] The implementation of the new curriculum was disappointing. Even though music was a core subject, a survey by the Irish National Teachers' Organisation (INTO) in 1976 reported that fifty per cent of teachers were dissatisfied with their performance in teaching the subject.[50] A report by the Arts Council in 1985 found dispiritingly that a majority of Irish primary school children left school 'musically illiterate, with little vocal or aural training and with a repertoire of songs that is usually learned by rote'.[51] The perception that the music syllabus was too complex for non-specialist teachers endured. As Frank Heneghan observed, most newly trained teachers were ill-equipped to undertake the imaginative teaching of music 'simply because their own acquired skills are necessarily so rudimentary'.[52] In 1999 a new curriculum was introduced and in terms of music attempted a greater balance between process and product. Greater emphasis was

---

[46] J. Walsh, 'An era of expansion, 1945-75', in Kelly (ed.), *St Patrick's College*, p. 171.
[47] Walsh, *Primary Education in Ireland*, p. 261.
[48] The chapter on music appeared in *Curaclam na Bunscoile: Lámhleabhar an Oide, Cuid 2/Primary School Curriculum: Teacher's Handbook, Part 2* (Dublin, 1971), pp. 209-86.
[49] Walsh, *Primary education in Ireland*, p. 274.
[50] M. Stakelum, 'Primary music education: the misrepresentation of the ideals of curricula in research', *Irish Educational Studies*, 27:3 (2008), p. 286.
[51] D. Herron, *Deaf Ears?: A Report on the Provision of Music Education in Irish Schools*, (Dublin: The Arts Council, 1985), p. vi.
[52] F. Heneghan, 'Music in Irish Education', in G. Gillen & H. White (eds.), *Irish Musical Studies 3: Music and Irish Cultural History*, (Dublin: Irish Academic Press, 1995), p. 174; see also Walsh, *Primary Education in Ireland*, pp. 290-3.

placed on the development of musical concepts with three interrelated curricular strands: composing, listening and responding, and performing.[53]

The transformation of St Patrick's was not confined to the physical infrastructure of the College alone. The size and diversity of the student body increased significantly: it numbered 600 by 1971 and 950 by the mid-1970s. This was the product of four overlapping developments. First, non-resident male students from Dublin were admitted from 1968. Second, in a sharp break with tradition, the college embraced a co-educational model of teacher training so that by 1974-5 half of the student body was female.[54] By the 1990s the vast majority of student teachers were women and that trend has intensified. Third, from the early 1970s the College admitted a sizeable number of mature students to the two-year undergraduate teacher-training programme. Lastly, in 1971 a one-year fulltime graduate diploma in primary education was devised to cater for university graduates. A new extension – E Block – opened in 1982 which provided new lecture theatres, offices and a new library. It should also be mentioned that the first training course – a postgraduate diploma – in special education in Ireland began in St Patrick's in October 1961. Donal Cregan's programmatic reforms reached an apogee when the long-sought goal of obtaining degree status for primary school teachers was realized. A demand for a three-year university based course had occasioned a number of student protests in the early 1970s with regular pickets at the Department of Education on Marlborough Street. Famously, the car of Pádraig Faulkner, then minister for education, was surrounded by students in December 1971 when he visited his alma mater to present certificates to students who had completed their course.[55] In April 1975 St Patrick's was granted the status of a recognized college of the National University of Ireland along with Mary Immaculate, Limerick and Our Lady of Mercy, Carysfort; St Patrick's was linked to University College Dublin.[56]

In 1974 a new three-year Bachelor of Education (BEd) degree was initiated. It recognized the importance of intellectual development in addition to the principles and practices of education. Student teachers were required to study academic subjects to degree level: two academic subjects were taken in first year and one in second and final year. This

---

[53] Stakelum, 'Primary music education', p. 288; National Council for Curriculum and Assessment, *Primary School Curriculum: Arts Education: Music*, (Dublin: The Stationery Office, 1999).
[54] Ó Ceallaigh, *Centenary Booklet*, p. 31.
[55] *Irish Independent*, 18 December 1971; Faulkner, *As I Saw It*, pp. 67-8.
[56] On Cregan, see T. Kellaghan, 'Cregan, Donal Francis', *Dictionary of Irish Biography*, *Irish Catholic Directory 1977*, p. 353.

prompted the reorganization of the college into academic departments in the mid-1970s by which time the number of staff had increased to sixty-nine.[57] Under the purview of the Teaching Council, the BEd degree was reconceptualized in 2012 and its duration extended to four years. The revised programme has placed greater emphasis than hitherto on foundation studies, professional studies and teaching practice at the expense of traditional academic subjects in the humanities.

If the 1960s and 1970s were decades of rapid expansion, the bleak 1980s witnessed deep retrenchment as Ireland's economy struggled and its national debt ballooned. The Department of Education restricted student intake and the one-year graduate course was discontinued in 1981. The closure in 1988 of St Patrick's sister institution in Carysfort illustrated starkly that the future could not be taken for granted. Overstaffed and facing potential redundancies, St Patrick's had to evolve to survive. A two-year part-time in-service BEd was introduced in 1985 to allow diploma graduates attain a degree. In 1991 the graduate diploma in primary education was reintroduced. Efforts to provide a BA programme within the NUI in 1990 were vetoed by the Department of Education which instead directed that an institutional relationship be forged with Dublin City University (created in 1989 when university status was conferred on the National Institutes of Higher Education in Limerick and in Glasnevin). After protracted negotiations a linkage agreement was signed in August 1993. St Patrick's became a constituent college of the university and university structures such as a governing body and academic council were implemented. BA students were admitted in the same year and the annual intake increased steadily thereafter. The College provided degree courses in Music, History, Geography, Irish, English, Mathematics, French, Bioscience, Human Development and Religious Studies. The linkage agreement also facilitated the introduction of postgraduate programmes in both Education and Humanities. It was updated in 2008.

The Vincentian Order, which had administered the College on behalf of the archbishop of Dublin since its foundation, withdrew in September 1999. Succeeding Dr Simon Clyne, Dr Pauric Travers, former head of the History Department, became the first lay president. He oversaw significant growth in student numbers which by the second decade of the twenty-first century reached 2,600 on twenty different programmes in education and humanities from undergraduate to doctoral level. The largest programme remained the BEd as the demand for teachers soared. Increasing numbers occasioned a long campaign for government investment in the development of the campus. When a

---

[57] C. Sugrue, 'Three decades of college life, 1973-99', in J. Kelly (ed.), *St Patrick's College*, pp 240-1.

€15 million building project belatedly arrived it did so after the collapse of the Irish banking sector and the implosion of the country's finances. Once more the College faced an uncertain future. In the 1870s when St Patrick's was first established Cardinal Cullen envisaged the integration of the College into the Catholic University. That did not transpire but 141 years later under government directive, St Patrick's, the Mater Dei Institute of Education, and the Church of Ireland College of Education were incorporated into Dublin City University on 30 September 2016.

Bibliography

Appendix to the Seventy-Fifth Report of the Commissioners of National Education in Ireland, Year 1908-9, (Dublin: Stationery Office, 1910), Cd. 5062.

Appendix to the Seventy-Eight Report of the Commissioners of National Education in Ireland, School Year 1911-12, (Dublin: Stationery Office, 1913), Cd. 7061.

Corish, Patrick, *The Irish Catholic Experience: A Historical Survey*, (Dublin: Gill and Macmillan, 1985).

Cullen, E. J., *The Origin and Development of the Irish Vincentian Foundations, 1883-1933*, (Dublin: The Three Candles, 1934).

Curaclam na Bunscoile: Lámhleabhar an Oide, Cuid 2/Primary school Curriculum: Teacher's Handbook, Part 2, (Dublin: Stationery Office, 1971).

Daly, Kieran, 'O'Brien, Louis', in H. White & B. Boydell (eds.), *The Encyclopaedia of Music in Ireland*, Volume II, (Dublin: UCD Press, 2013), p. 742.

Faulkner, Pádraig, *As I Saw It: Reviewing Over 30 years of Fianna Fáil and Irish Politics*, (Dublin: Wolfhound Press, 2005).

Ferriter, Diarmaid, '"For God's sake send me a few packets of fags": the College, 1922-45', in J. Kelly (ed.), *St Patrick's College Drumcondra: A History*, (Dublin: Four Courts Press, 2006), pp. 133-157.

Goodman, Peter, 'General musical report for year 1897', in *Sixty-Fourth Report of the Commissioners of National Education in Ireland for Year 1897-8*, (Dublin: Stationery Office, 1898), C. 9038, 270-276.

Goodman, Peter, 'General report on music instruction, 1900', in *Appendix to the Sixty-Sixth Report of the Commissioners of National Education for the year 1900*, (Dublin: Stationery Office, 1902), Cd. 954, 81-88.

Heneghan, Frank, 'Music in Irish Education', in G. Gillen & H. White (eds.), *Irish Musical Studies 3: Music and Irish Cultural History*, (Dublin: Irish Academic Press, 1995), pp. 153-198.

Herron, Donald, *Deaf Ears?: A Report on the Provision of Music Education in Irish Schools*, (Dublin: Arts Council of Ireland, 1985).

Kellaghan, Thomas, 'Cregan, Donal Francis', in J. McGuire & J. Quinn (eds.), *Dictionary of Irish Biography*, Volume II, (Dublin and Cambridge: Royal Irish Academy and Cambridge University Press, 2009), pp. 987-988.

Kelly, James, 'Belvedere House: origins, development and residents, 1540-1883', in J. Kelly (ed.), *St Patrick's College Drumcondra*, (Dublin: Four Courts Press, 2006), pp. 9-40.

King, Carla, 'The early years of the College, 1875-1921', in J. Kelly (ed.), *St Patrick's College Drumcondra*, (Dublin: Four Courts Press, 2006), pp. 91-129.

Marchant, T. F., 'General report on musical instruction for 1910', in *Appendix to the Seventy-Sixth Report of the Commissioners of National Education in Ireland for the School Year 1909-10*, (Dublin: Stationery Office, 1911), Cd. 5491, 212-213.

Marchant, T. F., 'General report on musical instruction for the school year ended 30 June 1914', in *Appendix to the Eightieth Report of the Commissioners of National Education for the School Year 1913-14*, (Dublin: Stationery Office, 1915), Cd. 7966, 169-174.

McElligott, T. J., *Education in Ireland*, (Dublin: Institute of Public Administration, 1966).

National Council for Curriculum and Assessment, *Primary School Curriculum, Arts Education: Music*, (Dublin: Stationery Office, 1999).

Ó Ceallaigh, Tadhg, *Coláiste Phádraig/St Patrick's College: Centenary Booklet, 1875-1975*, (Dublin: St Patrick's College, 1975).

O'Connor, Seán, *A Troubled Sky: Reflections on the Irish Educational Scene, 1957-68*, (Dublin: Educational Research Centre, St Patrick's College, 1986).

Parkes, Susan M., '"An Essential Service": The National Board and Teacher Education, 1831-1870', in B. Walsh (ed.), *Essays in the History of Irish Education*, (London: Palgrave Macmillan, 2016), pp. 45-82.

Seventy-First Report of the Commissioners of National Education in Ireland for the Year 1904, (Dublin: Stationery Office, 1905), Cd. 2567.

Sixty-First Report of the Commissioners of National Education in Ireland for the Year 1894, (Dublin: Stationery Office, 1895), C. 7796.

Sixty-Sixth Report of the Commissioners of National Education in Ireland for the Year 1899-1900, (Dublin: Stationery Office, 1900), Cd. 285.

Stakelum, Mary, 'Primary music education: the misrepresentation of the ideals of curricula in research', *Irish Educational Studies*, 27.3 (2008), 281-293.

Stakelum, Mary, 'A song to sweeten Ireland's wrong: music education and the Celtic Revival', in B. Taylor FitzSimon & J. H. Murphy (eds.), *The Irish Revival Reappraised,* (Dublin: Four Courts Press, 2004), pp. 71-82.

Sugrue, Ciaran, 'Three decades of college life, 1973-99', in J. Kelly (ed.), *St Patrick's College Drumcondra: A History,* (Dublin: Four Courts Press, 2006), pp. 225-265.

Walsh, John, 'An era of expansion, 1945-75', in J. Kelly (ed.), *St Patrick's College Drumcondra,* (Dublin: Four Courts Press, 2006), pp. 158-183.

Walsh, Thomas, *Primary Education in Ireland, 1897-1990: Curriculum and Context,* (Bern: Peter Lang, 2012).

Walsh, Thomas, 'The National System of Education, 1831-2000' in B. Walsh (ed.), *Essays in the History of Irish Education,* (London: Palgrave Macmillan, 2016), pp. 7-43.

Newspapers and periodicals
Freeman's Journal
Irish Catholic Directory
Irish Independent
Irish Press

Chapter Two: Music Performance at St Patrick's College, Drumcondra

John Buckley

Early Years

The performance of music has consistently played a highly significant role in the life of St Patrick's College, Drumcondra, since its foundation in 1875.[1] In the intervening years the sound of music has been woven into the fabric of daily life in the College, in academic, cultural, and social contexts. Music has been heard on formal and informal occasions in classrooms, lecture halls, practice rooms, church, canteens, student common rooms, and of course, in the college auditorium.

The first available formal reference to a musical performance in the College appears in the *Freeman's Journal* of 30 September 1885 and describes the visit to the College on the previous day by the Rev Dr Walsh, Archbishop of Dublin. The principal purpose of Dr Walsh's visit was to inspect the new buildings, which had just been completed: 'When the Archbishop entered the hall, the hymn "Ecce Sacerdos Magnus" was sung by the choir, under the direction of the Rev John E. Flynn, Mr Goodman presiding at the organ'.[2] The report continues with a description of the hall as magnificent and gives the dimensions as eighty-four feet long and forty feet wide. This study hall would remain in general use for a range of formal events including a series of symphony concerts in the 1960s and would be superseded only by the opening of the new auditorium in 1966. The original hall was located on the second floor of what became known as Block D after the renovations and developments of the 1960s.

Beginning in 1883, and up to its incorporation into Dublin City University in 2016, it is possible to trace an unbroken lineage of music lecturers in the College (see Appendix A). Peter Goodman, the first formal lecturer in music at the College, placed particular emphasis on the achievement of music literacy through the tonic solfa approach and all college students were given detailed tuition in the subject. Subsequent to his work as a lecturer in music at the College, Goodman played a major role in the development of music in the Irish primary school system, becoming the first organizing inspector of music

---

[1] St Patrick's College was known as St Patrick's Training College Drumcondra until the introduction of the BA programmes in the 1990s. It will be referred to as St Patrick's College throughout this chapter.
[2] *Freeman's Journal*, 30 September 1885.

instruction, a role he undertook with indefatigable zeal and energy.[3] A later visit to the College by Archbishop Walsh on 11 June 1899 was celebrated by another choral performance. The occasion of this visit was the opening of the new chapel, which still remains the single most striking and beautiful building in the college complex.[4] During the High Mass, the choir under the direction of Joseph Seymour performed a wide-ranging, highly imaginative, and innovative programme. The music included Gregorian chant, motets by Franz Xaver Witt, sections from Gounod's mass for male voice choir and organ or harmonium (*Messe des Orphéonistes* 1870), and 'Tantum Ergo' and 'Laudate' by Seymour himself.[5]

In its account of the ceremony, the *Evening Herald* of the following day draws particular attention to: 'the singing of Dom Lorenzo Perosi's "Credo" and "Benedictus" as they are the first works of the young Italian priest, whose oratorios have recently attracted such attention in London'.[6] An indication of the advanced and adventurous nature of choral music in the College at that time can be inferred from this programme and in particular the inclusion of such recently composed music by Perosi (1872-1956). Perosi was a leading composer of church music, including oratorios and settings of the Mass, though he also wrote much secular music including concertos for clarinet, and for piano amongst other works. The oratorios referred to in the *Evening Herald* report are *The Transfiguration, The Raising of Lazarus,* and *The Resurrection of Christ*, all of which had been performed in London the previous month. His compositions are highly accomplished, with a concentration on melodic line, integrated textures, colourful orchestrations, and an awareness of Wagnerian harmonic language. It is nothing less than extraordinary that his music was performed in St Patrick's College as early as 1899.[7]

---

[3] M. McAuliffe Ryng, 'Peter Goodman: Ireland's First Music Inspector', *Oideas*, 51 (Spring 2005), 109-124.

[4] The interior is decorated with mosaics and marble columns and the building has a spectacular circular stained glass rose window on its east-facing side. An entirely new chapel, equally remarkable for its stained glass windows and elegant architectural proportions, was built as part of the campus developments in the 1960s.

[5] Joseph Seymour was a music lecturer in St Patrick's College between 1892 and 1910. P. Collins, & D. Larkin, 'Seymour, Joseph', in H. White & B. Boydell (eds.), *The Encyclopaedia of Music in Ireland*, (Dublin: UCD Press, 2013). pp. 927-928. Franz Xaver Witt (1834-1888) was a German church musician and priest.

[6] *Evening Herald*, 12 June 1899.

[7] M. Dubiaga, 'Musician to Five Popes: Dom Lorenzo Perosi', *Seattle Catholic*, 30 November 2005.

The choral tradition was maintained in the College throughout the early part of the twentieth century. According to Francis MacManus, who was a student of the college between 1928 and 1930: 'Once a year the students went to a musical comedy in the Gaiety ... During the intervals, the students' choir rose as one, and under the direction of one of their fellows, sang for the whole theatre'.[8] Ciarán Laighléis, a student between 1929 and 1931 adds a further colourful anecdote: 'Mr Redmond always had a four-part choir trained and ready to sing at college concerts and we always sang in Croke Park when our team was playing'.[9] It is apparent that singing was not confined to formal academic contexts, but formed part of the everyday life of students of the college at that time.

In the first half of the twentieth century, performances by the choir featured regularly in the annual presentations given by the students in the college. Referred to as *Cuirm Cheoil agus Drámuíocht na Macléinn*, these events combined drama and music. It is interesting to observe that the plays were presented in translation in Irish and a great deal of the music also consisted of choral arrangements of traditional Irish melodies.[10] This important continuity and development of choral music in the College is discussed in detail in Chapter Six.

'A feast of song' - broadening the audience on Raidió Éireann

During this time the college choir was to enlarge its audience beyond college-based performances, by becoming actively engaged with a new medium that brought it national attention, the radio. Ireland's first national radio service 2RN was established by the Department of Posts and Telegraphs and began broadcasting on 1 January 1926.[11] In its early years, 2RN was on air for approximately four hours each day and its broadcast content consisted predominantly of music, often of an extremely high calibre. The music was provided by a station 'orchestra', initially consisting of just three members, relays of BBC concerts, musicians live in the studio, and the playing of gramophone records.[12] Scripted talks on a wide range of topics were also a regular part of the broadcast schedule.

---

[8] F. MacManus, 'Fourteen Thousand National Teachers', *The Bell*, 1.2 (1940), p. 37. Francis MacManus (1906-1965) was a teacher, novelist and broadcaster.
[9] Ciarán Laighléis, 'Memories of the Past', 1994, SPCA, C/30/1.
[10] Music concert and dramatic presentation of the students.
[11] 2RN became Raidió Éireann in 1933.
[12] 2RN initially broadcasted from a studio in 36 Little Denmark St, Dublin moving to the General Post Office (GPO) in 1928. R. Pine, *Music and Broadcasting in Ireland*, (Dublin: Four Courts Press, 2005), pp. 39-50.

The choir of St Patrick's College was regularly invited to broadcast on the new station from as early as 1927, a clear indication both of the choir's musical ability and the high regard in which it was held nationally. Its programmes were presented in slots ranging from twenty to forty minutes in duration and consisted of standard repertoire for male voice choir, along with arrangements of Irish traditional songs. These arrangements were frequently undertaken by college music staff including Redmond or drew on earlier versions by Goodman. The first broadcast by the choir under its conductor Seán (John) Redmond was given on Tuesday 28 June 1927.[13] The programme consisted of 'The Soldiers' Chorus' from Gounod's *Faust*, 'The Comrade's Song of Hope' by Adam, and 'Cradle Song' by Brahms. Traditional Irish music was represented by 'Slán le Máigh' arranged by Goodman and 'Eamonn an Chnuic' arranged by Maguire.[14]

Further broadcasts by the choir, with similar type programming, were given in 1929 (26 May) and 1930 (22 May). The broadcast given on 24 May 1933 is of particular interest in that it also included the choir of St Patrick's Practising Schools under its conductor R. McNally.[15] The programme included Handel's 'Hallelujah Chorus', 'Hark the Solemn Music' by Donizetti and 'Peter Piper' by English composer Frank Bridge along with a series of arrangements of Irish traditional melodies by Goodman, Redmond, Annie Patterson, and others.[16] We can gain some insight into how this and other broadcasts by the college choir were received through the following report which appeared in the *Donegal Democrat*:

> Those people who are fortunate enough to own a loud speaker enjoyed a treat when the Choir of St Patrick's Training College, Dublin broadcasted on the 24th May. Irish songs predominated, and the programme was one that would impress itself on your memory. The students' rendering of 'O'Donnell Abu', 'Killarney's Lakes and Dells', and 'Oh, Breathe not his Name' was unsurpassable; The 'Hallelujah Chorus' and 'Hark the solemn music' were masterpieces ... The public are grateful to Mr Seamas Clandillon, manager of the Dublin Broadcasting

---

[13] *Sunday Independent*, 26 June 1927.
[14] Maguire's forename is not included in the broadcast schedule.
[15] St Patrick's Practising Schools were primary schools opened in 1895 within the grounds of the College, where students could practice teaching skills.
[16] Annie Patterson (1868-1934) was a composer and academic. B. Lalor, (ed.), *The Encyclopaedia of Ireland*, (Dublin: Gill & Macmillan Ltd., 2003), pp. 861-862.

Station, for making it possible for listeners to enjoy such a feast of song, and are hoping that this first-class choir shall be kind enough to broadcast in the near future'.[17]

More broadcasts were indeed to follow in 1937 (26 May), 1938 (30 April, 6 May), 1940 (30 April), and after a break, during part of which the College would close, 1950 (3 June), and 1951 (20 June).[18] The absence of any further broadcast recitals after this date by the choir of St Patrick's College was undoubtedly related to the establishment of the Raidió Éireann Singers in 1953.[19] Under its first conductor, Hans Waldemar Rosen, this outstanding full-time professional chamber choir quickly gained national and international recognition. In terms of vocal ability, musical scope, range, and professionalism, the establishment of the Raidió Éireann Singers was one of the most noteworthy musical developments ever undertaken by RÉ, and the ten-voice choir quickly dominated all broadcasts of choral music on Raidió Éireann.

This singularly important development in the performance and composition of choral music in Ireland had the unintended effect of diminishing the role of the choir of St Patrick's College and other external choirs in the RÉ broadcasting schedule. St Patrick's College Choir continued to be heard on Raidió Éireann from time to time however, though in a somewhat diminished role. Broadcasts of Mass, with choral singing from the college chapel were programmed throughout the following decades; High Mass for the Feast of the Ascension on Thursday 7 May 1964 was a typical example.[20]

Tibor Paul and Donal Cregan: A symbiotic relationship

Significant developments and expansion in St Patrick's College were well under way during this period. Student numbers rose in response to the need for teachers in the increasing primary school sector and by 1955 the college had an intake of over 200 students. The pace of transformation was greatly enhanced under the presidency of Fr Donal Cregan from 1957 to 1975.[21] Born in Newcastlewest, County Limerick,

---

[17] *Donegal Democrat*, 3 June 1933.
[18] D. Ó Corráin: 'Fluctuating fortunes: St Patrick's College, 1875-2016', in Chapter One of this publication.
[19] P. O'Kelly, *The National Symphony Orchestra of Ireland 1948 – 1998*, (Dublin: Raidió Teilefís Éireann, 1998), n. p.
[20] Broadcasts beyond this date are referred to in J. O'Flynn, 'Vocal and Choral Music' in Chapter Six of this publication.
[21] T. Kellaghan, 'Cregan, Donal Francis', in J. McGuire & J. Quinn (eds.), *Dictionary of Irish Biography II*, (Dublin and Cambridge: Royal Irish Academy and Cambridge University Press, 2009).

Cregan (1911-1995) was a highly imaginative and inspirational figure in the history of the College and arguably the single most important and influential figure in its history.[22] His tenure as president was marked by the introduction of new courses and programmes including the BEd, special education courses, the first intake of female students, and linkage with the National University of Ireland.

While Cregan was a somewhat remote figure from the perspective of the individual student, he nonetheless placed a major emphasis on personal development as the goal of education. He had a great interest in and knowledge of the arts in general, and had a particular love of classical music. His collection of box sets of Verdi operas and other works on 78 rpm records still adorned the music department in St Patrick's College up to its incorporation into DCU in 2016. From the perspective of the history of music performance in the College, Cregan's strong personal and professional rapport with the principal conductor of the Raidió Éireann Symphony Orchestra (RÉSO), Tibor Paul, led to an outstanding series of symphony concerts in the College during the 1960s.[23]

Hungarian born, Tibor Paul (1909-1973) was a graduate of the Liszt Academy of Music in Budapest, where Zoltán Kodály had been one of his teachers. Paul was appointed as both principal conductor of the RÉSO and director of music in Raidió Éireann in 1961.[24] He was an inspirational and flamboyant figure and clearly an outstanding conductor; contemporaneous reports describe his conducting as 'stylish', 'elegant' and 'dynamic'.[25] His musical background in central Europe, and in particular, his studies with Kodály, one of the leading composers and musical educationalists of the first half of the twentieth century, led Paul to a deep appreciation of the importance and

---

[22] J. Walsh, 'An era of expansion, 1945-1975', in J. Kelly (ed.), *St Patrick's College Drumcondra: A History*, (Dublin: Four Courts Press, 2006), p. 163.
[23] The Raidió Éireann Symphony Orchestra (RÉSO) was established in 1948. It became known as the Raidió Teilifís Éireann Symphony Orchestra (RTÉSO) in 1964, the National Symphony Orchestra (NSO) in 1990, and subsequently the National Symphony Orchestra of Ireland (NSOI). The orchestra is currently (2019) called the RTÉ National Symphony Orchestra (RTÉNSO).
[24] M. Bosworth, 'Paul, Tibor (1909–1973)', in *Australian Dictionary of Biography, Vol. 15*, (Melbourne: National Centre of Biography, 2000).
[25] G. Cox, 'Paul, Tibor', in H. White & B. Boydell (eds.), *The Encyclopaedia of Music in Ireland*, (Dublin: UCD Press, 2013), p. 826; C. Kelly, 'Déjà vu', *Comhnasc*, 18 (October 2015), pp. 10-11; C. Howell, *Forgotten Artists 24. Tibor Paul (1909-1973)*, http://www.musicweb-international.co/classrev/2017/Nov/Forgotten_artists_Paul.pdf

centrality of music in education and society generally. He aimed to make 'his' orchestra (RÉSO) a central feature of Irish culture and education and his relationship with Cregan was truly mutually advantageous in this regard.

The series of symphony concerts by the RÉSO in St Patrick's College began on 26 October 1961. According to the *Irish Press* of the following day, 'The orchestra (leader Geraldine O'Grady) has seldom been heard to better effect than in the wonderfully resonant Lecture Hall of the College'.[26] The programme consisted of Mozart's overture to *Il Seraglio* and his *Violin Concerto No. 5* in A, with soloist David Lillis.[27] After the interval, the orchestra performed Beethoven's *Symphony No. 8* in F. This first concert clearly had a decisive impact on the student body. Mary Mac Goris, in the *Irish Independent* on 28 March 1962 wrote: 'The professors say that since the first concert, last autumn, students have being going in great numbers to the Phoenix Hall, concerts, and operas'.[28]

The concerts in St Patrick's College were held biannually in the following years. The programmes were exciting, highly imaginative and wide-ranging, combining standard works of the Classical and Romantic periods with more contemporary compositions. The first half of the concert on 20 December 1962, for example, consisted of Haydn: *Symphony No. 103* (*Drumroll*) and Mozart: *Piano Concerto No. 20*, K.466, in which the soloist was the twenty-two year old Veronica McSwiney.[29] The second half of the programme was dedicated to Respighi's spectacular *The Fountains of Rome*, composed in 1916, and the vibrant and colourful *Dances of Galanta* by Paul's former teacher Kodály, composed in 1933 and inspired by Hungarian folk material.

While the concerts were principally intended for college students and staff, external audiences were also welcomed. The programmes were recorded and subsequently broadcast on Raidió Éireann, often in segments combined with material from other concerts; Haydn's *Symphony No. 103* from the above concert, for example, was broadcast on 1 February 1963 along with works recorded in the Gaiety Theatre. The concerts in St Patrick's College also received significant coverage in

---

[26] *Irish Press*, 27 October 1961.
[27] All concert details throughout this chapter are taken from the relevant programme notes, available in the Charles Acton Collection in the National Library of Ireland or from the RTÉ documents archive.
[28] The Phoenix Hall was the concert venue of the RÉSO between 1948 and 1962.
[29] Born in 1940, Veronica McSwiney had already performed six different concertos with the RÉSO by the age of nineteen. She went on to become one of the leading Irish concert pianists of her generation.

the national press. *The Irish Press* of 21 December 1962 sets the context of the previous evening's concert:

> An opportunity of hearing the Raidió Éireann Symphony Orchestra (leader Geraldine O'Grady) in the small but very resonant surroundings of St Patrick's Training College, was arranged last night by the President, Rev. D. F. Cregan, C.M. for students and friends of the college.

Referring to the soloist, the unnamed reviewer continues:

> It was also an opportunity to hear that young, talented, and attractive pianist, Veronica McSwiney, who gave a most polished account of Mozart's stormy D minor Piano Concerto .... She managed to colour the music, especially in the romantic B flat second movement, and it may be said that she kept her audience in thrall, communicating an interpretation as deeply thought as it was felt.

In reference to the same concert, the *Evening Herald* of 21 Dec 1962 draws attention to Paul's music education crusade, and in particular to the significance of an audience of future teachers from across the country:

> It was a social occasion disguising a mission. Tibor Paul is much devoted to the task of spreading the cause of music in Ireland and in last night's audience of trainee teachers he had the country in microcosm. There were few counties unrepresented .... The College President, Rev. D. Cregan, C. M., thanked the musicians and extended the hospitality of the College for which all were most grateful.

The concert on 17 Dec 1963 is particularly noteworthy in that the college choir had the opportunity to perform with the orchestra under Paul's direction. The first half of the programme consisted of Mozart's delightful *Divertimento No. 17* in D, K.334 and his exuberant motet of 1773, *Exultate Jubilate*, K.165 in which the soloist was Veronica Dunne.[30] In the second half of the programme the orchestra played Schubert *Symphony No. 8* in B minor (unfinished) and Sibelius *Finlandia* with the choral final section performed by the college choir. The concert concluded with familiar Christmas carols 'Angels We Have

---

[30] Born in 1927, Veronica Dunne is one of Ireland's best known opera singers and singing teachers.

Heard on High', 'See Amid the Winter's Snow' and 'Oíche Shéimh' also sung by the choir, and accompanied by the orchestra. The chorus master for the occasion was Seán Hayes, now in his fourteenth year as music lecturer in the College. Cyril Kelly was a first year student and member of the college choir for the concert with the RÉSO. In a special edition of the long-running radio show *Sunday Miscellany* broadcast from the National Concert Hall at Christmas 2013, Kelly gives a vivid and colourful description of the mesmeric impression that Tibor Paul made on the college students some fifty years earlier: [31]

> Tibor Paul, the conductor of the NSO (sic), was tall, of aristocratic bearing and autocratic demeanour. A native of Hungary, his explosive temperament and his swift, sabre like movements, suggested a lineage back to the legendary Hussars of his homeland. Prominently parked in the college car park, his flamboyant Studebaker ... and, boys-o-boys, was it spellbinding.[32]

On the night of the concert itself, the excitement was palpable as the audience began to arrive, lecturers in academic gowns filed into the hall and the orchestra began to tune up:

> Finally, Tibor Paul, a jet-black swerve of tails and dazzling breastplate, sprang onto the podium, inclining imperiously in our direction. Immediately, baton aloft like a lightening-rod, he smote the silence ... and the music rumbled ... And suddenly, our choir is singing ... the 'Hymn of Freedom'. Two hundred voices rising in rhapsody ... but most of all we are exultant because of our director, Mr. Hayes, who, there, before our very eyes, is almost levitating with relief and pride in our shared accomplishment.[33]

The triumphant hymn in the final section of *Finlandia* is generally known as 'Hymn to Freedom': 'Finland, behold, thy daylight now is dawning'. It is easy to understand the sense of awe and inspiration felt by the young students in the presence of such majestic music, with a full symphony orchestra conducted by the dazzling and flamboyant Tibor Paul.

---

[31] *Sunday Miscellany* is a regular Sunday morning programme on RTÉ Radio combining short articles and complementary music. Cyril Kelly is a frequent contributor to the programme.
[32] C. Kelly, 'Déjà vu', pp. 10-11.
[33] Ibid. Kelly gives the date of this concert as 10 December 1963.

The high level of cooperation and engagement between the College and the RÉSO evident from the above commentaries was to continue. Paul's letter to Cregan, dated 4 February 1964, for example, thanks the president for lunch and gives the full programme for the forthcoming concert on 10 March, which they had jointly agreed:

Rossini *Overture to the Barber of Seville*
Tchaikovsky *Nutcracker Suite*
Strauss *Horn Concerto No. 1 in E Flat major* (Soloist Victor Malirsh) [34]
Interval
Beethoven *Symphony No. 2 in D* [35]

The inclusion of a horn concerto was a bold stroke of programming in this otherwise standard but excellently devised programme. Apart from the four examples of the genre by Mozart, horn concertos do not hold a central part in the repertoire of symphony orchestras. The first horn concerto of Richard Strauss, completed in 1883, is a wonderful display of both the heroic and lyrical characteristics typical of horn music and would have greatly appealed to the audience.

New facilities for music performance in the College
During the 1960s Cregan oversaw wide-ranging infrastructural developments to the campus in St Patrick's College.[36] Beginning in 1962, an extensive building programme was undertaken. This included the renovation and modernization of existing buildings and the provision of many new facilities. These developments included entirely new student accommodation, dining facilities, the new chapel, a gymnasium, an auditorium, a music room, and a set of practice rooms. Three of these buildings in particular became central in further facilitating and enhancing music performance in the College: the music room, the auditorium, and the chapel. All three, and in particular the auditorium, provided a range of opportunities for music performance not previously available. Recitals, lunchtime concerts, carol services, musical productions, operas, song contests, choral performances and further symphony concerts took place in the following decades.

---

[34] Slovenian born Victor Malirsh (1928 - 2016) was horn player with the RTÉ National Symphony Orchestra and teacher at the Royal Irish Academy of Music.
[35] Letter from Paul to Cregan, SPCA, A/9/III.
[36] T. Ó Ceallaigh, *Coláiste Phádraig/St Patrick's College: Centenary Booklet, 1875-1975*, (Dublin: St Patrick's College, 1975).

The new auditorium in St Patrick's College provided a high quality performance space, superior in many respects to the St Francis Xavier Hall, the RTÉ Symphony Orchestra's home venue at that time.[37] The moveable apron at the front of the stage area and the system of audio cabling in the new auditorium in St Patrick's College greatly facilitated orchestral lay out and recording. The auditorium was officially opened on 15 March 1966 with a gala concert given by the RTÉ Symphony Orchestra, once again conducted by Tibor Paul. The opening work, Brahms, *Academic Festival Overture* could hardly have been more apt for the occasion but the most notable aspect of the concert however, was the first performance of a newly-commissioned work *Lúireach Phádraig* by the Irish composer A. J. Potter (1918-1980). Potter, widely regarded as one of the most significant Irish composers of the twentieth century, was highly prolific and fulfilled numerous commissions for a wide variety of situations and musical forces.[38]

Lúireach Phádraig displays Potter's great awareness of the musical forces for which he was writing – three-part student choir (tenors 1 and 2, and bass), and professional symphony orchestra. The vocal lines are relatively straight-forward and frequently in unison, though there are passages where the texture is in three parts, the latter always carefully doubled by the orchestra. The orchestration is colourful and imaginative and adds greatly to the expressive character of the score. The college choir was prepared once again by Seán Hayes, and the performance, which was recorded and subsequently broadcast, communicates a sense of assurance and vigour, in keeping with the celebratory nature of the occasion.

It is somewhat ironic that this high point of engagement between the RTÉSO and St Patrick's College was to be the final time that Tibor Paul would conduct there. He departed from RTÉ and Ireland in somewhat controversial and acrimonious circumstances.[39] While he was undoubtedly a gifted and charismatic conductor, he was also described by contemporaries as ill-mannered, dictatorial, and egotistic. This dual characterization was perhaps best captured by Gerard Victory, Paul's Deputy Head of Music in Raidió Éireann: 'He (Paul) was a catastrophically brilliant and tempestuous figure'.[40] Paul's parting from RTÉ in 1967 was due to contractual disagreements.

---

[37] With a capacity of 700, the St Francis Xavier Hall in Upper Sherrard St, Dublin was the home of the RTÉSO between 1962 and 1981.

[38] *Lúireach Phádraig* known in English as *St Patrick's Breastplate*, is a prayer attributed to St Patrick.

[39] See O'Kelly, *The National Symphony Orchestra of Ireland 1948 - 1998*; Pine, *Music and Broadcasting in Ireland*, p. 449.

[40] Pine, *Music and Broadcasting in Ireland*, p. 454.

Tibor Paul's departure meant that it would be several years before the RTÉSO performed again in St Patrick's College. The concert given on 9 March 1971 was directed by the orchestra's new principal conductor Albert Rosen, who had been appointed in 1969.[41] Two standard works from the orchestral repertoire, Mozart's overture to *The Marriage of Figaro* and Beethoven's *Symphony No. 3 'Eroica'* were featured in the concert alongside something of a rarity, *Concerto in A for Cello* by the Italian composer Giuseppe Caminiti. The concerto was performed by the composer's son Vincenzo Caminiti, who had come to Ireland in 1959 to join the RÉSO. Vincenzo was subsequently appointed leader of the cello section of the RÉSO in 1967, a position he held for ten years before returning to his native Palermo.[42] Giuseppe Caminiti's cello concerto was composed in 1935, but its musical approach is deeply imbued with the stylistic idioms of the late nineteenth century. The work combines vigorous dramatic flair with a profound sense of lyricism and highly idiomatic writing for the solo instrument.[43]

Albert Rosen conducted another concert with the RTÉSO in the auditorium of St Patrick's College on 1 January 1972. The soloist on this occasion was Kyung-Wha Chung, one of the leading international violinists of her generation, who performed both the Beethoven and Tchaikovsky violin concertos. At the time of the concert, Korean-born Chung was only twenty-three, but had already begun her stellar career and had previously recorded the Tchaikovsky and Sibelius violin concertos with the London Symphony Orchestra, conducted by André Previn for the Decca label.[44]

Chung was to return to St Patrick's College in January 1974 to perform the Berg *Violin Concerto* as part of the Dublin Festival of Twentieth-Century Music.[45] Founded by the Music Association of Ireland, The Dublin Festival of Twentieth-Century Music (1969-1986) presented biennial festivals, featuring the music of leading international composers alongside that of their Irish contemporaries and also including recognized masterpieces of the twentieth century. The

---

[41] Viennese born Albert Rosen (1924-1997) was appointed principal conductor of the RTÉSO in 1969 and retained his connection with the orchestra as principal guest conductor and conductor laureate until 1997.

[42] See Pine, *Music and Broadcasting in Ireland*, p. 172.

[43] A deeply felt performance of the first and second movements given by the RTÉSO and Vincenzo Caminiti can be found on a YouTube recording at https://www.youtube.com/watch?v=YijfAt1boJI.

[44] Kyung Wha-Chung, London Symphony Orchestra, André Previn, *Violin Concertos*, (Decca, SXL 6493, 1970).

[45] P. O'Kelly (ed.), *The Fifth Dublin Festival of Twentieth Century Music* (Dublin: The Music Association of Ireland, 1974). p. 10.

Examination Hall of Trinity College provided the main venue for the wide range of chamber music concerts, while the St Francis Xavier Hall was utilized for orchestral concerts.

Figure 2.1: Kyung-Wha Chung and the RTÉSO in rehearsal, St Patrick's College Auditorium 1972. Image courtesy RTÉ Archives

The 1974 festival is of particular interest to St Patrick's College, as two major concerts were held there on 5 January and 7 January. Apart from the Berg *Violin Concerto*, the concert on 5 January included a work by Italian composer Franco Donatoni (*Puppenspiel No. 1*) and Polish composer Witold Lutosławski (*Symphony No. 2*), with Irish compositions represented by Eric Sweeney's *Canzona*. The concert was conducted by Colman Pearce, also well known as both pianist and composer.[46]

The concert on 7 January 1974 featured the Pulcinella Ensemble with soloist William Pearson (baritone) and was conducted by Seóirse Bodley. The programme comprised the finest articulation of *avant-garde* European music at that time and received an excellent

---

[46] Colman Pearce was appointed principal conductor of the RTÉSO (1981-1983) and went on to establish a very close relationship with St Patrick's College when he undertook studies there towards a doctorate in composition. He was awarded a PhD in composition from St Patrick's College DCU in 2009. His reflections on his studies in the College are included in Chapter Eleven – 'Graduate Perspectives'.

performance from the ensemble. Most notable is that all five works in the programme were heard for the first time in Ireland, and those by Irish composers - Frank Corcoran (*Chamber Sonata*) and Bodley himself (*September Preludes* for flute and piano) - were world premieres. Franco Donatoni (1927-2000) was again represented, this time by his *Etwas Ruhiger im Ausdruck* and his fellow Italian, Niccoló Castiglioni (1932-1996), by *Tropi*, a work of great originality and delicate beauty. The main work, occupying the entire second half of the programme was the startlingly dramatic *Eight Songs for a Mad King* by the English composer Peter Maxwell Davies.

Apart from its engagement with RTÉ, St Patrick's College collaborated with a wide array of other musical organizations leading to a rich and varied concert life. Its partnership with the Irish-Austrian Society, for example, enabled a series of high-profile concerts with the Vienna Boys Choir in 1969 and 1970. The choir's origin dates back to the court of Maximilian I in 1498 and it is now regarded as one of the leading boys choirs in the world. The concerts in St Patrick's College on 22 March 1969 (repeated 23 March) and October 16 1970 (repeated 17 October) were given as part of the choir's Irish tours in those years.

The concerts were presented in three parts, the first consisting of a series of short classical pieces. The central part of the programmes were devoted to light comic operetta, *Signor Bruschino* by Rossini in the 1969 concerts and *Tales of Old Vienna* with music by Johann Strauss and text and musical arrangement by Richard Rossmayer in the 1970 concerts.[47] The final segment of each concert consisted of arrangements of folksongs from Austria and surrounding countries. The choir had a large and devoted following in Ireland at the time and the college auditorium was packed for all concerts, the *Irish Independent* of 17 October 1970 reporting:

> The Vienna Boys Choir gave the first concert of the 1970 season in St Patrick's Training College Drumcondra, Dublin, last night. A few days after booking opened, you could not have bought a ticket for love or money. And 800 contented patrons were present last night.

---

[47] Programme notes for the 1969 and 1970 concerts.

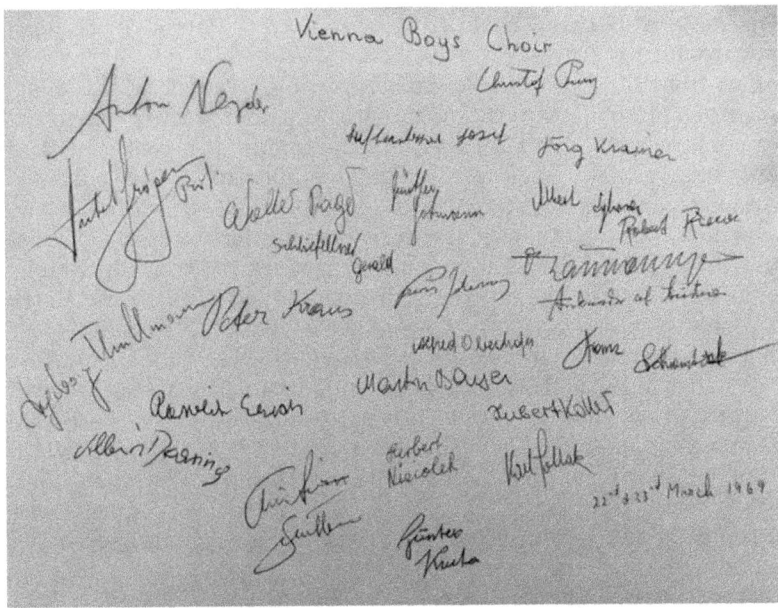

Figure 2.2: Autographs by members of the Vienna Boys' Choir, 22-23 March 1969 in the Visitors' Book, Belvedere House, St Patrick's College. Photograph by John O'Flynn

The College's association with the Irish-Austrian Society was to lead to further concerts in the auditorium. On 9 March 1970, the young Viennese pianist Rudolf Buchbinder gave a recital of Mozart, Beethoven, Chopin, and Debussy, 'a spell-binding recital of lovely music' according to Mary McGoris, music critic of the *Irish Independent*.[48] Though only twenty-four at the time of the recital, Buchbinder had already established an outstanding international reputation. At the time of writing (2019), he is frequently spoken of in legendary terms and is widely regarded as one of the world's leading concert pianists.

A further Irish-Austrian Society concert, took place on 18 November, 1978 when the Vienna Haydn Trio performed music by Haydn, Smetana, and Schubert. Formed in 1964, the Vienna Haydn Trio has become one of the world's leading piano trios, with numerous international performances and recordings amongst its body of work.

---

[48] *Irish Independent*, 11 March 1970.

Operas, musicals, and concerts in St Patrick's College auditorium

Apart from the close collaboration between St Patrick's College and such organizations as RTÉ and the Irish-Austrian Society, numerous external music bodies have used the auditorium as a venue for their presentations. The auditorium, and in particular its spacious, well equipped and versatile stage proved ideal for opera and musical shows as well as concerts. Amongst the many organizations to use its facilities was the Wicklow Opera Group,[49] which presented Mozart's *Il Seraglio* on 8 March 1980 as its first ever production[50] and Nicolai's *The Merry Wives of Windsor* on 22 November of the same year. The company also staged Smetana's charming opera *Dvě Vdovy* [The Two Widows] in November 1981, with Aideen Lane and Anne Cant as the widows. Further productions included *School for Fathers* by Wolf-Ferrari in March 1983 and a double bill *Susanna's Secret* by Wolf-Ferrari and *Il Tabarro* [The Cloak] by Puccini on 31 March 1984. The productions, which also travelled to a number of provincial centres, were accompanied by piano in place of an orchestra, making transport easier and significantly reducing expenses.

Productions of musical shows were also undertaken in the college auditorium by the O'Connell Musical Society.[51] The company's production of *Hello, Dolly!* opened there on 30 April 1984 and that of rock musical *Adam and Eve* on 3 December 1984. Composed by Alan Dee and first performed in 1976, the revival of the latter show in St Patrick's College starred Colm Wilkinson, playing the role of the Devil, as he had in the original production.[52] Writing in the *Evening Herald* on 4 December 1984, Thomas Myler draws attention to the fine score, the excellent voices of the cast, and the high quality production, in particular the choreography and the 'imaginative lighting by Denis Twomey'. Twomey subsequently became a lecturer and assistant registrar in St Patrick's College. Further productions in the college by the O'Connell Musical Society included *Sweet Charity* (opened 10 April 1986), which had premiered on Broadway in 1966 and *Oklahoma!* (opened 27 March 1987). The Society's staging of *Little Shop of Horrors*

---

[49] Wicklow Opera Group was founded in 1979, with the aim of producing little-known operas sung in English and using Irish singers.
[50] *Sunday Independent*, 2 March 1980.
[51] Founded in 1943, The O'Connell Musical Society is a non-profit theatre group based in North Dublin City.
[52] Colm Wilkinson is an Irish singer and actor, best known for his role of Jean Valjean in *Les Misérables* (in the West End and Broadway).

was a remarkable achievement as it was the first amateur performance of the work in the world.[53]

Amongst the many choral performances in the auditorium of St Patrick's College was that of Bach's *Christmas Oratorio* (7 January 1973) given by the Malahide Singers and Orchestra conducted by Brian Grimson. The impressive list of vocal soloists consisted of soprano Anne Cant, contralto Anne Woodworth, tenor Frank Dunne as the Evangelist, and bass Pádraig O'Rourke. Many leading instrumentalists played the obbligato parts and the leader of the orchestra was Thérèse Timoney.[54] A number of performances were also given by the Culwick Choral Society, which presented the Irish premiere of *African Sanctus* on 17 May 1978 with a repeat performance the following day.[55] The performances, which featured soprano soloist Eileen Donlon were introduced to the audience by the work's composer David Fanshawe.[56] Composed in 1972, *African Sanctus* is a setting of the Latin Mass juxtaposed with live recordings of traditional African music. The intriguing scoring of the work for soprano solo, choir (SATB) piano, tape of African music, and a large range of percussion with optional amplified guitars and keyboards expertly combines European and African musical styles. The work in thirteen movements is immensely colourful and exciting while also including sections of a more reflective character. Another premiere, *Hy Brasil*, a chamber opera or cantata by Irish composer Jerome de Bromhead was commissioned by the Culwick Choral Society and first performed in St Patrick's College on 30 April 1981, with an outstanding list of performers: Irene Sandford (soprano solo), Deirdre Cooling-Nolan (alto solo), Frank Dunne (tenor solo), John Milne (bass solo), John Dexter (organ), Culwick Choral Society, and orchestra conducted by Eric Sweeney.[57]

Amongst the many other choral events in the college auditorium were a concert of winning choirs from the 21st Cork International Choral

---

[53] *Little Shop of Horrors* is a rock musical with music by Alan Menken and lyrics and a book by Howard Ashman. It was first staged in New York in July 1982.

[54] An obbligato is an elaborate instrumental part accompanying a solo or principal melody in music. Thérèse Timoney is one of the leading Irish violinists of her generation and former leader of the RTÉCO.

[55] The Culwick Choral Society was established in 1898 by James Culwick. This large mixed voice choir specializes in oratorio and other sacred compositions. M. Stakelum, 'Culwick Choral Society', in H. White & B. Boydell (eds.), *The Encyclopaedia of Music in Ireland*, pp. 270-271.

[56] David Fanshawe (1942 - 2010) was an English composer and ethnomusicologist. *African Sanctus* remains his best known work.

[57] B. Harrison, *Catalogue of Contemporary Irish Music*, p. 51.

Festival (21 May 1974) and St Stephen's Singers (30 January 1979) in association with the College Musical Society. At a later date (April 1989) the regional finals of the *Irish Press* Choral competition also took place in the college.

Symphony concerts still maintained a presence in St Patrick's College auditorium throughout the 1970s and later. The Hertfordshire County Youth Orchestra gave a concert in the auditorium in August 1971 as part of its Irish tour. The seventy-four strong group of musicians aged from fourteen to twenty clearly excelled in their ambitious programme of music by Glinka, Beethoven, Walton, Wagner, and Borodin. 'A smooth interpretation of Wagner's *Siegfried Idyll* was succeeded by an exhilarating account of Borodin's *Polovtsian Dances* to bring a remarkable concert to a close' according to J.J.F. in the *Evening Herald* of 2 August 1971.

Though the RTÉ Symphony Orchestra does not appear to have performed in the college after 1974, the Dublin Symphony Orchestra (DSO) used the auditorium as a regular venue for their concerts and performed programmes of music drawn mostly from the nineteenth century.[58] The concert on 18 November 1977 was part of the orchestra's tenth anniversary celebrations and also marked the 150th anniversary of the death of Beethoven. Appropriately enough the entire concert consisted of Beethoven's compositions: *Egmont Overture*, *Piano Concerto No. 3* in which the soloist was John Gibson, and *Symphony No. 5*. The orchestra was conducted by Colin Block. Further concerts by the DSO were given on 30 April 1978, with soloist Alan Smale performing the *Violin Concerto* by Mendelssohn. One of the leading violinists of his generation, Smale became leader of the RTÉ Concert Orchestra in 1983 and subsequently, leader of the RTÉ National Symphony Orchestra between 1993 and 2013. Other soloists in the DSO concerts in St Patrick's College included Aisling Drury Byrne, who performed the tuneful and popular *Cello Concerto* by Dvořák, (26 January 1979) and pianist Lynda Byrne, who performed Beethoven's *Piano Concerto No. 4* (4 May 1980).[59] Symphony concerts were also given in St Patrick's College auditorium by another of Dublin's non-

---

[58] Established in 1967, the Dublin Symphony Orchestra (DSO) is one of the leading non-professional orchestras in Dublin. It gives regular concerts of standard orchestral repertoire along with compositions by contemporary Irish composers. J. McCay, 'Dublin Symphony Orchestra', in H. White & B. Boydell (eds.), *The Encyclopaedia of Music in Ireland*, (Dublin: UCD Press, 2013), p. 331.

[59] Cellist Aisling Drury Byrne studied with Paul Tortelier at the Paris Conservatoire and was leader of the cello section of the RTÉSO (later RTÉNSO) between 1978 and 2001). Lynda Byrne was a staff pianist with RTÉ.

professional orchestras, The Dublin Orchestral Players (DOP).[60] The orchestra's imaginative programme for its concert on 27 January 1973 comprised Verdi's overture to *Nabucco*, Smetana's symphonic poem *Blaník* and *Symphony in D Minor* by Franck. Caitríona Yeats was soloist in Handel's *Concerto in B flat for Harp*.[61] The DOP concert on 23 November 1991 featured cellist Moya O'Grady as soloist.[62]

A further array of events, at least part of which involved musical performances included a dance drama presented by the pupils of Hopefield Secondary School, Newtownabbey, Co. Antrim, and 'Breffni Parade', which was presented by the Cavan Association. Hopefield Secondary School undertook their tour 'in the interests of good cultural and social relationships between North and South' and their presentation, which included full symphony orchestra took place on 24 May 1968.[63] The 'Breffni Parade' expressed the following ambition: 'apart from organising (charity) fundraising events, they also wish to give entertainers from Cavan the opportunity of performing in Dublin'.[64] The Association presented concerts of Irish music and dance along with novelty and variety items on a number of occasions in the 1980s in the college auditorium. More significantly, the national finals of Slógadh, the youth festival with an emphasis on Irish music, traditional and other genres, and culture, were held in St Patrick's College on four occasions, attracting thousands of competitors and large audiences to the college. The national impact of Slógadh is discussed in more detail by Teresa O'Donnell in Chapter Five.

The relationship between St Patrick's College and the Kodály Summer Schools discussed elsewhere in this publication led to a fruitful collaboration between the College and the Hungarian embassy and various Hungarian music organizations. The exchange of choral concerts that emerged from this cooperation is discussed in Chapter Six by John O'Flynn. One of the most significant purely instrumental concerts was that given in the college auditorium by piano virtuoso György Oravecz to mark the 200th anniversary of the birth of Liszt. This recital was hosted by the Hungarian Embassy on 5 December 2011,

---

[60] The Dublin Orchestral Players is an amateur orchestra founded in 1940. The composer Brian Boydell was the orchestra's conductor between 1942 and 1966.
[61] Irish harpist Caitriona Yeats has held positions with many of the world's leading orchestras including the Norddeutscher Rundfunk Symphony Orchestra, the Boston Symphony Orchestra, the Cincinnati Symphony Orchestra, and the Danish National Symphony Orchestra.
[62] Moya O'Grady was a cellist with the RTÉCO.
[63] *Evening Herald*, 18 May 1968.
[64] *Meath Chronicle*, 12 April 1980.

an event reminiscent of the concerts organized in collaboration with the Irish-Austrian Society in the 1970s.

Musicals, choral music and song contests – 1970s onwards
Apart from its role as an outstanding venue for external musical organizations, the new auditorium in St Patrick's College also provided many opportunities for musical performance organized within the College itself. In the late 1970s the student union was active in organizing a variety of musical events including concerts by Christy Moore, Luka Bloom, and the Chieftains. Moore also recorded his anti-nuclear song 'Nuke Power' in the college in 1979 and this version is available on his album compilation *The Box Set 1964 - 2004*.

Under the direction of college music lecturer Colum Ó Cléirigh, a series of musicals were produced by Cantóirí Choláiste Phádraig, (St Patrick's College Singers) amongst them, *The Pirates of Penzance* and *The Merry Widow*. For the 1975 production of *The Pirates of Penzance*, Ó Cléirigh assembled a large cast and stage crew, totalling well over one hundred students. In addition to this, an orchestra mainly consisting of players from the RTÉSO and the Raidió Teilifís Éireann Light Orchestra (RTÉLO) was engaged.[65]

The production ran over three nights, Wednesday 26 February, Thursday 27 February, and Saturday 1 March, 1975. Previewing the production in the *Evening Press* of 13 February, journalist Terry O' Sullivan was clearly greatly impressed by the rehearsal he attended:

> The most exciting show since "Jesus Christ Superstar" – that's my preview of "The Pirates of Penzance," now in rehearsal by a cast of 100 in St Patrick's Training College, Drumcondra. The average age of the soloists, the pirates and the police is about eighteen ... among the cast there are some superb voices emerging.

Video recordings of one of the performances, kindly supplied to the author by Paul Murphy, fully endorse O'Sullivan's impression of the production, which was of a professional standard, with outstanding individual performances and a highly accomplished and polished chorus.[66] Modesty forbids my commenting on the standard of the orchestra; the programme confirms that the author was the second flautist. Cantóirí Choláiste Phádraig were to undertake further productions in the following years. Once again, a large cast and an

---

[65] The Raidió Teilifís Éireann Light Orchestra (RTÉLO), has been known as the Raidió Teilifís Éireann Concert Orchestra (RTÉCO) since 1978.
[66] Paul Murphy, senior AV technician, DCU Institute of Education.

especially assembled orchestra gave a number of performances of *The Mikado* from 6-9 March 1979, with an extra schools' matinee on 10 March. In retrospect, it is evident that this production drew together a group of college students which was destined to make a noteworthy contribution to the musical and cultural landscape in Ireland and further afield in the following years. Amongst the cast were Victor Merriman (Ko-Ko), Kathleen Tynan alternating with Deirdre Seaver (Yum-Yum), Deirdre Crowley (Pitti-Sing), and John O'Flynn (Pish-Tush).[67]

Other productions by Cantóirí Choláiste Phádraig under the direction of Ó Cléirigh included Franz Lehar's *The Merry Widow* 11 March 1977 and a revival of *The Pirates of Penzance* (1981). In March 1980 St Patrick's College also witnessed a three-day music festival co-ordinated by Ó Cléirigh. The festival culminated in a performance of Part 1 of Haydn's *Creation*, which took place in the college chapel. Apart from his direction of college musicals, Ó Cléirigh continued to contribute to the performance of choral music in the College through the participation of the college choir in the Cork International Choral Festival. Further documentation and commentary on this aspect of Ó Cléirigh's and Cantóiri Choláiste Phádraig's engagement with musical performance are discussed in more detail by John O'Flynn in Chapter Six.

Further enhancements of the choral tradition in St Patrick's College were undertaken by Seán Mac Liam, who joined the staff of the music department in 1977. As well as being an active composer and pianist, Mac Liam had a firm foundation in choral singing, having been a founding member of UCC Madrigal Group, and also a member of Madrigal '75, a vocal ensemble founded in Cork city by students of the university there. Mac Liam's interest and expertise in the vocal music of

---

[67] Merriman is currently Professor of Performing Arts at Edge Hill University in the UK and has made a notable contribution in the areas of teaching, criticism, and public engagement. He is author of *Because We Are Poor: Irish Theatre in the 1990s*, (Dublin: Carysfort Press, 2011) and was a member of An Chomhairle Ealaíon/Arts Council of Ireland (1993-1998). Kathleen Tynan enjoys a career both in concert and opera, and has sung at festivals in Ireland and internationally and is currently the Head of Vocal Studies and Opera at the Royal Irish Academy of Music. Mezzo-soprano Deirdre Crowley has performed in opera in Covent Garden and at Glynebourne amongst many other venues. Deirdre Seaver is a professional harpist, who has represented Ireland on many diplomatic and cultural occasions, both at home and abroad while John O'Flynn is a musicologist, performer, lecturer, and conductor. Between 2008 and 2016 he was Head of the Music Department of St Patrick's College and is co-editor of this publication.

the Tudor period would be further developed in his thesis 'The Sources of Continental Music in Britain c.1450 - c.1650', which was awarded an MLitt by Trinity College Dublin in 1989. On his appointment to the music department, he established a madrigal group comprised of music students and staff. The repertoire consisted predominantly of English and Italian madrigals and the group gave regular performances throughout the academic year. Participation in the annual Christmas carol service in the college chapel also constituted a regular element of the choir's performance calendar.

An increase in the group's membership changed its status in effect from that of madrigal ensemble to chamber choir. While the choir still performed the madrigal repertoire, it could now also undertake larger-scale compositions. Amongst the impressive range of works performed were masterpieces of the Baroque period including Vivaldi's *Gloria*, Pergolesi's *Magnificat* and Carissimi's oratorio *Jephte*. The performances were not, however, confined to music of the Baroque era; the *Requiem* by Gabriel Fauré composed in 1887 featured amongst compositions from a later period. The works were performed in the college chapel, with Niamh Williams as the piano accompanist, and were well attended by college students and staff.

The establishment of a series of lunchtime concerts in the college was a separate but related initiative undertaken by Mac Liam. These weekly concerts provided music students with an invaluable opportunity of performing in public. All students specializing in music were, in fact, required to perform at least one piece in one of these concerts. While the music performed was generally in the standard Classical and Romantic genres, there was always at least one concert in each semester devoted to Irish traditional music. Another noteworthy feature was the invitation extended to primary school choirs to perform in the concert series, St Paul's School, Greenhills being one of those presented. St Patrick's College Madrigal Group and Chamber Choir, under Mac Liam's direction, also performed in the lunchtime concerts. The venue for these concerts was the Music Room, designated as B118. This room and the connected group of offices and practice rooms were part of the college redevelopment programme undertaken in the 1960s. B118 is primarily a lecture room but can easily be adapted as a performance space with excellent acoustic properties and a capacity of approximately eighty.

The very substantial contribution to the great choral tradition of the College played by Marion Doherty is discussed in detail by John O'Flynn in Chapter six. Doherty who was Head of the Music Department between 1985 and 2008, was also responsible for the instigation of an annual student song contest. Students could compete within a range of categories including best arrangement, children's section, Irish section, and best original song. The panel of adjudicators was sometimes chaired by well-known radio or television personalities for example, Aonghus McNally in 1986. The annual song contest generated great interest and excitement amongst the student population of the college as expressed by Moya Ní Cheallaigh:

> In 1988 I took part in the college song contest, winning the arranger's prize for 'The Morning Sun' by Geraldine Galligan ... It was an amazing time in the Music Department ... it seemed like the whole college became musicians during that time. There was such excitement in the air ... [68]

The standard of winning songs was often exceptionally high as illustrated in the 1996 competition by the beautiful melancholy ballad 'By All Appearances' composed and performed by Karen Ryan. Ryan's backing group included piano, cello, violin, guitar, and another vocalist. The prize was one hundred pounds and equally importantly offered the winner time in a professional recording studio.[69]

Marion Doherty was also musical director for a concert performance of Gilbert and Sullivan's *Trial by Jury* in April 2008. The production was directed by Pat Burke of the English Department and featured music students Gavan Ring and Brian Gilligan, both of whom have established impressive professional careers as singers at the time of writing.

Lunchtime Concerts from 2003 onwards

Music lecturer Patricia Flynn took charge of organizing a series of lunchtime concerts in the early 2000s. In 2003 the administration of the series was undertaken by the present author, at the suggestion of Seán Mac Liam, who was acting Head of Music at that time and who had himself organized a successful series of such concerts from 1978 to 1985. Between 2003 and the incorporation of St Patrick's College into Dublin City University in 2016 twelve to fifteen concerts were presented each academic year, the total number being in excess of one hundred and sixty. The concerts featured either student performances or were presented by invited professional musicians. Student concerts were initially programmed around class year groups, encompassing a wide range of musical genres and styles. This diversity, which might normally be viewed as an impediment to integrated programme

---

[68] Email communication from Moya Ní Cheallaigh, 6 November 2018. Ní Cheallaigh was a BEd student in St Patrick's College from 1986-1989.
[69] Video recordings of these song contests have been kindly made available by Paul Murphy, senior AV technician, DCU Institute of Education.

planning, actually proved to be a great asset in that it embraced the varied musical interests of the students and affirmed their individual musical identities. Students were invited and encouraged to perform but without obligation. The concerts took place on Wednesdays usually in B118 (The Music Room) and had a duration of approximately forty-five minutes. They were generally over-subscribed by students offering to perform and were frequently attended to capacity with extra audience members listening in from adjoining corridors on occasions. Audiences were comprised of students from across all college courses, college administrative and teaching staff, pupils from nearby schools and members of the general public.

Figure 2.3: Harpist Éadaoin Ní Mhaicín and concertina player Niamh Molloy performing at the lunchtime concert on 29 April 2015. Photograph by Frances Marshall

The concert presented on 3 Nov 2004 by second year music students was indicative of the range and diversity of the programming and included music by Schubert, Debussy, and Gershwin along with popular style songs by Andrew Lloyd Webber and Eva Cassidy. A selection of Irish traditional jigs and reels was included as a central element and a total of fourteen students performed. As an illustration of both continuity and development, the programme given by first year BA and BEd music students on 27 February 2013 consisted of popular music ranging from Simon and Garfunkel's iconic 'Bridge Over Troubled Waters' (1970) to the Bombay Bicycle Club 2011 hit 'Shuffle' and 'Use

Somebody' (2008) by Kings of Leon. The latter song was presented in a striking performance close to the beautifully reflective melancholy of Pixie Lott's ballad–like version of 2009, an indication of an increasing selectivity and subtlety in student understanding of the importance of interpretation. The final item in the student concert featured a vibrant set of traditional Irish jigs and reels performed on a wide range of traditional instruments including flute, tin whistle, button accordion, and concertina accompanied by guitar. A noteworthy feature is that more than twenty students performed in this concert.

Student concerts sometimes adopted a thematic approach and these were presented by performers across all years of the college programmes at that time. Amongst the themes were 'The Three Sopranos' - Michelle Brennan, Louise Brennan, Lorraine McLaughlin (23 November 2005), and 'The Three Baritones' - Brian Gilligan, Gavan Ring, Cian Kearns (22 November 2006); both trios performed opera, sean nós, and popular style music. Other themes were 'Chamber Music' (6 May 2009; 2 Dec 2009), 'Opera, Pop, and Songs from the Shows' (29 April 2009), 'Best of Broadway' (6 April 2016) and 'Irish Traditional Music and Dance' (21 November 2007). With the exception of two occasions, individual students or student groups generally performed in just one, or at most two, items in each of these concerts. The exceptions were soprano Geraldine Meade (18 February 2004) and baritone Gavan Ring (23 January 2008) who each performed a full concert. Both students had already gained performance experience at local and national levels. Meade, accompanied by pianist Fergal Warren presented a wide-ranging programme of Baroque, Classical, and twentieth-century songs. Her performance was highly assured and her interpretations captured every nuance of the varied programme.

Though only twenty years of age at the time, Ring was already a well-established singer, having performed solo roles in oratorio and other genres in leading national venues including the National Concert Hall and the Helix in DCU along with international events. His programme for the lunchtime concert in St Patrick's College in 2008 attested to both the range and ambition of his musical interests; it included operatic arias and songs in English, French and German. Ring's sympathetic accompanist, as on many other occasions until her retirement in 2008, was head of the music department Marion Doherty. Her supportive engagement in those years was greatly appreciated by performers, organizers and audiences alike.

Many visiting Erasmus students became actively involved with the music department and frequently performed in the lunchtime concerts series.⁷⁰ This engagement was greatly to the mutual advantage of college music students and visitors. In keeping with the ethos of the Erasmus programme, it broadened the perspectives of music students in St Patrick's College and simultaneously embraced the musical interests and experiences of the visiting students. There was a particularly strong musical connection with students from the Charles University in Prague; amongst those who performed in the lunchtime concerts were Helena Velická (cello), who joined college students Clare King (violin) and Niamh Ní Shúilleabháin (violin) and professional pianist Fergal Warren in the *Trio Sonata No. 3* by Gregor Joseph Werner (1695-1766) on 26 November 2003. Violinist Dasha Knerova gave an outstanding performance of Bartók's *Romanian Folk Dances* on 14 February 2007 accompanied once again by Marion Doherty while violinist Anna Fliegerová performed *A Few Notes for Jim* for solo violin by John Buckley on 5 December 2007. During her semester as an Erasmus student in 2007 Fliegerová's contribution to the musical life of the College also included performances of Brahms *Violin Sonata No 1*, and Beethoven *Romance in G*. All her performances were marked by a combination of technical assurance and refinement, and a highly developed sense of music insight and interpretation. Fliegerová is now a leading professional violinist in the Czech Republic. Other Czech Erasmus students included pianist and singer Barboro Kozlova, pianists Anna Pragrová and Markéta Krucká, both of whom accompanied students in the lunchtime concerts and singer and pianist Květa Šmídová. Amongst the many Erasmus students from other countries, who have left abiding memories of their vibrant musical contributions to the college were Spanish saxophonist Oscar Marín, Hungarian singer Klara Szabó, Bulgarian guitarist Yavor Neved, and Greek singer Vicky Chalaftri.

All student performers were mentored by music department staff prior to performing in the lunchtime concerts, a process that became even more structured from 2009 onwards with the formation of formal music groups. These groups were organized on the basis of the students' own musical interests and would typically constitute two to six performers and display a wide range of genre and styles, including popular, rock, classical, folk and Irish traditional. Students were encouraged to select their own material and many developed a highly imaginative and refined approach to the art of arrangement. A favourite method was the overlapping of several songs sharing the same harmonic basis. In formal music terminology, this might be referred to

---

⁷⁰ Named after the Dutch philosopher, the Erasmus programme is an initiative run by the European Union. It provides opportunities for third level students to study in a different European country as part of their degree programme.

as a 'quodlibet', but the more colloquial term 'mashup' commonly used by the students, better captures the vibrant and exuberant musical results achieved. Two larger music groups, the college choir directed by John O'Flynn and from 2015 the DCU Orchestra, initially directed by Marie-Louise Bowe and subsequently by Rhona Clarke, regularly performed in the lunchtime series. As O'Flynn outlines in Chapter Six of this publication, the repertoire of the choir in these concerts included standard choral works along with popular arrangements and more contemporary pieces suitable for youth choirs. The orchestral programmes chosen by Clarke also drew on popular arrangements and fully accommodated both the specific instrumental array available and the range of performance expertise of the students.

The lunchtime series also featured a wide range of professional guest musicians. These performances were an essential component of the lunchtime concerts offering both variety and enrichment in programming and inspiring an ambition towards the achievement of high musical standards in the students. The concerts presented a wide range of genres including solo instrumental and chamber music, opera and song cycles, jazz improvisations and ragtime, Irish traditional music and rock. The programming was frequently highly inventive, timed with precision to avoid conflicts with lecture hours, and designed to appeal to and often challenge a diverse audience. Classical piano recitals regularly featured; amongst the performers were Fergal Warren, Anthony Byrne, Fionnuala Moynihan, Barbara Murray, Aileen Cahill, Svetlana Rudenko, and Martin O'Leary. Programmes were sometimes planned around the music of a single composer (Chopin: 21 April 2010 – Anthony Byrne) or focused on a theme (Irish composers: 17 February 2016 – Martin O'Leary). Piano concerts given by Colm 'Stride' O'Brien (7 December 2005; 16 April 2008) and Conor Linehan (21 November 2012; 21 October 2015) displayed different facets of the piano repertoire being devoted to ragtime and jazz improvisations respectively. O'Brien's natural sense of stage presence was greatly aided by his attire: colourful shirt and braces, armbands and of course a derby fedora with ribbon, all of which further enhanced his outstanding interpretations of stride and ragtime music.

Amongst the other guest musicians were harpists Geraldine O'Doherty and Aisling Ennis, guitarists John Feeley, Pavlos Kannelakis and Benjamin Dwyer and violinists Cora Venus Lunny, and Anna Fliegerová. Guest musicians, who had been students of the College included soprano Muireann Mulrooney, accompanied by pianist Dearbhla Collins (4 February 2015) and the rock-pop duo 'We Cut Corners' – John Duignan and Conall Ó Breacháin (19 February 2014).' Ó Breacháin's reflection on his time as a student in St Patrick's College can be found in Chapter Eleven, Graduate Perspectives.

Figure 2.4: Poster for We Cut Corners lunchtime concert on 19 February 2014. Sean Breithaupt & Yvette Monahan Photography

Other singers included Aylish Kerrigan, Imelda Drumm, Elizabeth Hilliard and Virginia Kerr. Kerr's programme included the world premiere of *Six Yeats Songs* by Colman Pearce, who was working towards completing a PhD at that time. Amongst the many other musicians were flautists William Dowdall, Julie Maisel, and Róisin Ní Bhrían, horn player Cormac Ó hAodáin, cellists Martin Johnson, Jenny Dowdall, Clíodhna Ní Aodáin, and Aoife Nic Athlaoich, and oboist Sanja Romic. The lunchtime concert series was also delighted to welcome international choirs as part of their Irish tours. The Willicher Emmaus Kantorei from Germany (21 October 2009) and Apáczai Csere János Choir from Hungary (12 March 2012) presented programmes combining sacred music and folksong arrangements while the Duluth Vocal Jazz Ensemble from the USA (13 October 2010) focused on jazz a cappella and popular contemporary songs.

Irish traditional music has always held a prominent position in the life of St Patrick's College as discussed by Teresa O'Donnell in Chapter Five and this focus is also reflected in the lunchtime concerts. While most concerts presented by students contained some Irish traditional music, there were also complete programmes performed by Thomas Johnston on uilleann pipes and whistles and Síle Denvir on Irish harp. Johnston was a research fellow and part-time lecturer in St Patrick's college between 2013 and 2016, while Denvir was a member of staff in the Irish Department. Denvir's Irish traditional group Líadan also gave an outstanding concert on 18 February 2015. Líadan has established a reputation across Europe, Japan and the Unites States. The group has been described by *Hot Press* Magazine as 'wildly talented' and as being 'The next major global force in Irish traditional music' by New York's *Irish Echo*.[71]

During the period of its residency in the College (2012-2015) the Fidelio Trio made a highly significant contribution to the lunchtime concerts. The Trio's engagement and commitment to musical life on the college campus and beyond is discussed in detail in Chapter Ten and a full listing of their concerts is given in appendix E. Their programmes for the lunchtime concerts combined standard works for piano trio along with contemporary compositions. An added advantage for the audiences was that many of the featured composers attended the concerts and frequently introduced their compositions. Amongst them were Judith Weir, Graham Fitkin, Joe Cutler, Linda Buckley, Stephen Gardner, Augustin Fernandez, Raymond Deane, Martin O'Leary, Jonathan Nangle, Benjamin Dwyer, Ann Cleare, Benedict Schlepper-Connolly, Piers Hellawell, and Dorothy Ker.

Two other noteworthy lunchtime concerts were given in this period by members of the music department, pianist Rhona Clarke (14 October 2015) and baritone John O'Flynn (9 March 2016). Clarke chose a

---

[71] Oldest Irish-American newspaper in the USA, established in 1928.

programme of music by Chopin including the *Ballade No. 3*, while O'Flynn, who was accompanied by Colman Pearce, performed a wide range of songs by Mozart, Berlioz, Fauré, Massenet, Tchaikovsky, Debussy and Joan Trimble. The complete listing of all lunchtime concerts given by guest musicians between November 2003 and March 2016 can be found in Appendix B. The music department was greatly assisted in organizing the lunchtime concerts by student committees. Publicity, setting up the room, stage management, distributing printed programmes, and other arrangements were all undertaken by the students. While the work of the lunchtime concerts committees served an immediate practical purpose, it also had a longer-term pedagogical intent. Many of the students involved were planning to become teachers or enter some aspect of the music profession and it was hoped that the experience of concert organization would prove to be invaluable in their future careers.

While a great number of musical events in St Patrick's College were directed by staff of the music department, student-led events also played a vibrant role in the musical life of the College. These included musical productions, open mic session and broadcasts of Irish traditional music. In recent years, a series of vibrant and professional level productions of musical shows were undertaken by the college musical and drama societies including *Annie Get Your Gun* in January 2000 and *The Wizard of Oz*, which received a number of performances in December 2007. The latter was a Dramasoc (College drama society) production with Chris O'Sullivan as music director and choreographer. Further productions included *The Wiz* in association with the Students' Union and the music department (17-19 April 2013), *Big Shot* (May 2014), *Mamma Mia!* (20-21 April 2015), and *Grease* (April 2016). These productions were fully staged and included a band comprised of college students and guest musicians. The 2013 production of *Big Shot* was an extraordinary achievement for Lauryn Gaffney, who created the show in its entirety including storyline, script and musical score while she was an undergraduate student of music and human development in St Patrick's College. *Big Shot* was subsequently performed at the prestigious San Diego Fringe Festival, (July 2015) where it won the 'Spirit of the Fringe' award. Other performances have taken place in London and elsewhere to great acclaim.

Semi-formal open mic sessions took place in the student canteen at regular intervals throughout the year. The sessions provided opportunities for aspiring singer songwriters, amongst them Moylan Brunnock, to perform original material or covers of popular songs in a highly supportive environment. The wide range of activities undertaken by the Irish traditional music society, Tradsoc is discussed in detail by Teresa O'Donnell in Chapter Five. The series of radio broadcasts for *Céilí House*[72] and the recordings on *ComhaltasLive* are amongst the most prominent and widely disseminated activities of Tradsoc.[73] Students also regularly performed Irish traditional music at college open days, conferring ceremonies, carol services and other similar events. These vibrant and engaging performances by college music students greatly enhanced public occasions and enriched the musical and cultural fabric of the College.

As St Patrick's College approached the completion of its one hundred and forty-one years as an independent entity in the autumn of 2016, it displayed no diminution in its engagement and commitment to music performance and no decrease in its creative imagination. Along with the numerous musical performances chronicled above, the following presentations were part of the College's final academic year. In October 2015 a new dance version of Prokofiev's celebrated *Peter and the Wolf* entitled *The Wolf and Peter* with choreography and direction by David Bolger was presented in the auditorium by CoisCéim Dance Theatre with pianist Conor Linehan. November witnessed 'Concert for Syria', organized by John O'Flynn and featuring performances by a wide variety of ensembles comprised of current and past students. In the same month St Patrick's College Repertory Company (SPARC) presented *Stages of the Rising*, featuring Patrick Pearse's drama, *The Singer and The King*, with music arranged and curated by Síle Denvir (Roinn na Gaeilge) while the world renowned Vogler Quartet performed music by Haydn, Shostakovich, and John Buckley in April 2016.[74]

Music has resonated across St Patrick's College for almost a century and a half. Performances in a variety of genres and styles have greatly enriched the daily life of the College over that period. Many of its graduates have made and continue to make outstanding contributions to the musical life of Ireland and beyond. The College brings its proud history and heritage of music performance into its new dispensation within Dublin City University.

---

[72] Recorded on location, *Céilí House* is one of RTÉ Radio's most popular programmes of traditional Irish music and song.
[73] *ComhaltasLive* is an internet video programme of Irish traditional music produced by Comhaltas Ceoltóirí Éireann.
[74] Formed in East Berlin in 1985, The Vogler Quartet is widely regarded as one of the finest string quartets of its generation.

Bibliography

Bosworth, Michael, 'Paul, Tibor (1909–1973)', in *Australian Dictionary of Biography, Vol. 15,* (Melbourne: National Centre of Biography, 2000).

Collins, Paul, & Larkin, David, 'Seymour, Joseph', in H. White & B. Boydell (eds.), *The Encyclopaedia of Music in Ireland,* (Dublin: UCD Press, 2013), pp. 927-928.

Cox, Gareth, 'Paul, Tibor', in H. White & B. Boydell (eds.), *The Encyclopaedia of Music in Ireland,* (Dublin: UCD Press, 2013), p. 826.

Dubiaga, Michael, 'Musician to Five Popes: Don Lorenzo Perosi', *Seattle Catholic,* (30 November 2005).
http://www.seattlecatholic.com/a051130.html.

Harrison, Bernard, *Catalogue of Contemporary Irish Music,* (Dublin: Irish Composers' Centre, 1982).

Howell, Christopher, *Forgotten Artists 24. Tibor Paul (1909-1973)*
http://www.musicweb-international.com/classrev/2017/Nov/Forgotten_artists_Paul.pdf.

Kellaghan, Thomas, 'Cregan, Donal Francis', in J. McGuire & J. Quinn (eds.), *Dictionary of Irish Biography,* Volume II, (Dublin and Cambridge: Royal Irish Academy and Cambridge University Press, 2009), pp. 987-988.

Kelly, Cyril, 'Déjà vu', *Comhnasc,* 18 (October 2015), pp. 10-11.

Kelly, James (ed.), *St Patrick's College, Drumcondra: A History,* (Dublin: Four Courts Press, 2006).

Lalor, Brian, (ed.), *The Encyclopaedia of Ireland,* (Dublin: Gill & Macmillan Ltd., 2003), 861-862.

McAuliffe Ryng, Mary, 'Peter Goodman: Ireland's First Music Inspector', *Oideas,* 51 (Spring 2005), 109-124.

McCay, Jennifer, 'Dublin Symphony Orchestra', in H. White & B. Boydell (eds.), *The Encyclopaedia of Music in Ireland* (Dublin: UCD Press, 2013), p. 331.

McManus, Francis, 'Fourteen Thousand National Teachers', *The Bell,* 1.2 (1940), 32-39.

Ó Ceallaigh, Tadhg, *Coláiste Phádraig/St Patrick's College Centenary Booklet, 1875-1975,* (Dublin: St Patrick's College, 1975).

O'Donoghue, Patrick, *Donal F Cregan, class '30.*
https://www.knockunion.ie/obituary/donal-f-cregan-class-30-85

O'Kelly, Pat, *The National Symphony Orchestra of Ireland 1948 - 1998* (Dublin: Raidió Telefís Éireann, 1998).

O'Kelly, Pat, (ed.), *The Fifth Dublin Festival of Twentieth Century Music,* (Dublin: The Music Association of Ireland, 1974).

Pine, Richard, *Music and Broadcasting in Ireland,* (Dublin: Four Courts Press, 2005).

Stakelum, Mary, 'Culwick Choral Society', in H. White & B. Boydell, (eds.), *The Encyclopaedia of Music in Ireland,* (Dublin: UCD Press, 2013), pp. 270-271.

Walsh, John, 'An era of expansion, 1945-1975', in J. Kelly (ed.), *St Patrick's College Drumcondra: A History,* (Dublin: Four Courts Press, 2006), pp. 158-183.

Newspapers and periodicals
Donegal Democrat
Evening Herald
Freeman's Journal
Irish Independent
Irish Echo
Irish Press
Meath Chronicle
Sunday Independent
The Bell

Archives
Charles Acton Collection, National Library of Ireland
RTÉ Documents Archive
St Patrick's College Archive

Interviews and email correspondence
Moya Ní Cheallaigh
Seán Mac Liam
Deirdre Seaver

Discography
Wha-Chung, Kyung, Previn, André & London Symphony Orchestra, *Violin Concertos,* (UK: Decca, SXL 6493, 1970).
Moore, Christy, *The Box Set 1964 - 2004.* (UK: Columbia – 514816 2)

Chapter Three: Music in Education and Humanities

Patricia Flynn and John O'Flynn

Introduction
When St Patrick's College first opened in Drumcondra in 1875 for the preparation of male teachers for Catholic primary schools, music was not included in its mandatory syllabus, although vocal and instrumental music were options taken up by many students following the appointment of Peter Goodman in 1883. Music became a compulsory subject for all students of the College in 1902.[1] While much has changed since then, including the introduction of degree courses in both education and humanities, the subject of music in one form or another has remained an essential requirement in teacher education programmes. The various types of courses that included music in their title however evolved and diversified over time within the College.

What was formalized in 1902 as essentially a singing programme based on the Curwen method gradually developed throughout the twentieth century to the point where three discrete categories of music courses were evident, each belonging to its own academic area and/or set of practices. The first category of music course at St Patrick's College and the one with the longest history at the institution became known as curriculum music. This was the term used to refer to the training of students in practical approaches to music teaching and learning in the classroom. Curriculum music always had links to broader pedagogical studies and was later informed by academic studies in education and in music education (as comes to be described below). It developed from the College's first mandatory music programme in 1902. Throughout much of the twentieth century, curriculum music's emphasis was on preparing students to fulfil the music syllabus requirements as outlined in successive official documentation, notable among which were: the *Revised Programme of Instruction* of 1900 and its various revisions up to and including 1921, the *National Programme of Primary Instruction* of 1922, the *Revised Programme of Instruction for Music in National*

---

[1] N. Kelly, 'Music in Irish Primary Education 1831-1922', *Proceedings of the Educational Studies Association*, (Galway: ESAI, 1979) p. 49.

Schools (1939); *An Curaclam Nua* (1971); and the *Revised Primary Music Curriculum* (1999).[2]

Music as a third-level subject in arts or humanities later became established in the College.[3] Long recognized in the history of European universities, music as an arts degree subject typically encompassed a musicological and music theory approach.[4] Traditionally, this included the study of harmony and counterpoint and the musicological study of western art music from both analytical and historical perspectives. While this 'classical' model still forms a basis for many degree programmes in music, it has developed from its medieval academic beginnings to embrace a much broader range of topics, approaches and methodologies. Third-level music studies now also incorporate performance, composition and music technology as well as a wider scope of musicological studies in traditional music, ethnomusicology, music education, popular music studies and film music among many other areas. Music as a degree subject in St Patrick's College was first offered within the BEd course in 1974 and later became a degree option in the BA (Humanities) programme in 1994; by the early twenty-first century, postgraduate music programmes up to doctoral level were also offered.

The third category of music course to emerge was that of music education. This developed throughout the latter decades of the

---

[2] *New Rules and Regulations (National Education), 1900-1*, Cd. 601, H.C. 1901 (3), lvii, p. 9; *Programmes of Instruction for National Schools for the School Year 1919-1920*, (Dublin: Office of National Education, 1919); Department of Education, *National Programme of Primary Instruction*, (Dublin: Educational Company of Ireland, 1922); An Roinn Oideachais, *Revised Programme of Instruction in Music for National Schools*, (Dublin: Stationery Office, 1939); An Roinn Oideachas, *Curaclam na Bunscoile*, Primary School Curriculum, (Dublin: Stationery Office, 1971); National Council for Curriculum and Assessment, *Primary School Curriculum, Arts Education: Music*, (Dublin: Stationery Office, 1999).

[3] Although music was not introduced as a full degree subject until the advent of the BEd programme in 1974, music options offered on the NT two-year diploma course included content and approaches that were comparable to first and second arts degree courses.

[4] Music was part of the *trivium* and *quadrivium* curriculum in the medieval university. S. Pendley, 'Trivium and Quadrivium', in E. Provenzo and A. Provenzo (eds.), *Encyclopedia of the Social and Cultural Foundations of Education*, (Thousand Oaks, CA: SAGE Publications, 2009), p. 829.

twentieth century in parallel with the evolution of education as an academic, theoretically informed and research-based discipline in its own right. As with the discipline of education, music education drew on a range of scholarly perspectives and approaches that included pedagogy, philosophy, psychology, sociology and the history of education – along with aspects of music studies.[5] Surprisingly perhaps, the academic study of music education at St Patrick's College did not initially form part of the BEd degree, but instead first appeared as a component of the BA music course. It could, however, be taken as a specialist option in the College's MEd programme, and postgraduate students at masters and doctoral level could carry out research studies in the academic field of music education.

While music and music education formed part of undergraduate and postgraduate degree programmes, curriculum music courses were primarily devised for the professional preparation of teachers. The distinction between music education and curriculum music reflected a major dichotomy that obtained in teacher education in the latter half of the twentieth century, namely between the training of teachers in areas to be taught, and teacher education as an intellectual formation through the study of education, arts and humanities disciplines. The initial aspiration for teacher education to be university-based often influenced which aspect of this dichotomy gained priority. At times, an arts formation for teachers was deemed most desirable; at other times, demands for a more skills-based, functional or technical approach to teacher preparation led to a reduction in time for the arts component and a stronger emphasis on pedagogy.[6] This pendulum swing occurred throughout the history of teacher education in St Patrick's College. Bríd Ní Shé illustrates this point in a comparison of music exam papers from the years 1930 and 1960 that were set for final year students on the

---

[5] Whereas music in compulsory education had initially been conceived in utilitarian terms, throughout the twentieth century it increasingly came to be considered from an aesthetic perspective. M. Mark, 'The Evolution of Music Education Philosophy from Utilitarian to Aesthetic', *Journal of Research in Music Education*, 30.1 (1982), 15-21.

[6] See for example, J. Coolahan, 'The development of educational studies and teacher education in Ireland', *Education Research and Perspectives*, 31.2 (2004), 30-47.

National Teacher (NT) diploma course.[7] These were external examinations set by the Department of Education.[8] In the 1930 exam paper there was no indication that the student might be preparing to be a teacher with the examination only assessing musical knowledge and skills. By 1960, six of the eight questions included an element addressing music teaching methods.

Change has been a consistent characteristic of the development of St Patrick's College, and often emerged in response to external influences and/or to wider political or cultural circumstances. These included: changing ideas of teacher education and the place of humanities subjects in such evolving conceptions; for music studies, the accommodation of a wider range of genres, practices, theoretical perspectives and methods; and the changing landscape of higher education and the place of music as a humanities subject within this. Among the instigators of change were the many statutory and professional body reports on education provision in Ireland (both for teacher education and for higher education in general) and the setting up of new statutory organizations whose remit extended to the accreditation of degree programmes.[9] Later, wider European initiatives for mobility across European higher education programmes also brought structural changes to degree programmes.

With the gradual expansion of the College into humanities as well as education and the changes in the higher education landscape that brought it into the university system, tensions often arose between the roles, needs and demands of the three different types of music courses described above. What was singular about the music department of St Patrick's College was that throughout the many changes over the institution's history, it continued to work in and have responsibility for all areas of music provision as they developed: the two academic areas of music and music education and the professional area of curriculum music.

---

[7] B. Ní Shé, 'The Initial Education and Training of Music Teachers for Primary Schools in the Republic of Ireland, Northern Ireland, England and Wales', Unpublished MEd Thesis, (Trinity College Dublin, 1994).

[8] Papers were set, examined and corrected by the Department of Education up to 1962, from which point College staff were allowed to set their own exam papers, subject to the approval of the Department of Education.

[9] Notably, the Teaching Council of Ireland and Quality and Qualifications Ireland, the state agency responsible for promoting quality and accountability in education and training services in Ireland.

The College underwent many organizational and structural changes as it evolved from a small single-mission college of teacher training, preparing students to be recognized by the Department of Education as qualified national teachers to a college of education and humanities providing university degree programmes at undergraduate and postgraduate levels. Staff numbers increased to meet this growing provision, and the College, which was historically a unitary organizational structure with staff of various disciplinary expertise contributing to the one programme, now began to devolve into smaller units or departments. These were later re-organized into two faculties - education and humanities. While music was located in humanities, the staff of the music department continuously engaged their teaching, scholarship, expertise and leadership across both areas, effectively bridging humanities and education through their work.

Before the BEd degree
Cultural nationalism
One of the early external forces on the College was the cultural nationalism that occurred prior to and following Irish independence in 1922. Education historian John Coolahan notes a shift in the curriculum at that time, following a call to place emphasis on the Irish language for courses in history, geography and music.[10] Coolahan comments that for many nationalists at the time, the main purpose of education in a free Ireland was the re-establishment of Gaelic culture. National schools were a key part of the policy to achieve the kind of cultural unity that was envisioned as part of nation building.

The national programme of primary instruction came into force on 1 April 1922. Its impact on music was largely through the inclusion of more songs in the Irish language and later, through the introduction of nationalist songs in English.[11] The 1922 programme recommended that 'in junior standards as a rule only Irish songs should be taught' with part-songs and suitable arrangements of Irish melodies to be taught in senior classes.[12] Music education historian Marie McCarthy observes that all official documents on music at the time were ideologically influenced by the Irish state's objective of re-instating the Irish

---

[10] J. Coolahan, *Irish Education History and Structure*, (Dublin: IPA, 1981), p. 38.
[11] M. McCarthy, *Passing it on: The Transmission of Music in Irish Culture*, (Cork: Cork University Press, 1999), p. 118.
[12] Ibid., p. 246.

language as the primary vernacular, noting the publication in 1933 by the Department of Education of the booklet *Téarmaí Ceoil* ['Musical Terms'] to support the teaching of music through the Irish language.[13] Meanwhile, Bríd Ní Shé describes how the booklet *Notes for Teachers*, first published in 1939 included a long list of about one hundred native songs in the Irish language and about fifty ballads in the English language, many of the latter with republican-nationalist texts.[14] Ní Shé outlines the modal nature and melodic intricacies of some of these prescribed songs, and the attendant skills and understanding that would be required of student teachers expected to sing them, more often than not from memory.[15]

The two-year diploma programme of the time was divided into three parts: professional studies, general educational studies and optional studies.[16] Vocal music was part of professional studies and was a compulsory two-year course (except for a small number of students for whom an exemption had been obtained). The syllabus and examinations were set by the Department of Education. The music syllabus at that time included three areas: theory of music, methods and practical music. For the third of these areas students had to demonstrate ability to memorize and transcribe six songs, to sight-sing a modulating passage from both staff notation and tonic solfa and to perform choral singing in unison, two and three parts.[17] Instrumental music was an additional optional subject alongside Latin and French. Students taking instrumental music were expected to perform pieces at an advanced level, with repertoire drawn from the canon of western art music and the inclusion of Irish pieces.[18] References to specifically Irish music in both the vocal and instrumental requirements were underpinned by the ideology of cultural nationalism. Arguably though, this accommodation of 'native' music in addition to the classical canon allowed for the representation of two valued traditions which continued in later degree level courses. As noted in Teresa O'Donnell's chapter in this volume, from the 1970s Irish music had its own section on the

---

[13] An Roinn Oideachais, *Téarmaí Ceoil*, (Dublin: Stationery Office, 1933).
[14] An Roinn Oideachais, *Notes for Teachers: Music*, (Dublin: Stationery Office 1939).
[15] Ní Shé, 'The Initial Education and Training of Music Teachers', pp. 189-90.
[16] An Roinn Oideachas, *Clar Léinn na gColáistí Oillúna*, (Dublin, Department of Education, 1930).
[17] Ibid., p. 14.
[18] Ní Shé, 'The Initial Education and Training of Music Teachers', p. 15.

history and analysis exam, and for a time also featured in the harmony and counterpoint course where students were introduced to techniques of accompanying Irish melody. It would be several decades later that ethnomusicology and popular music studies were included on courses offered by the music department.

Music and the University
As Daithí Ó Corráin sums up in Chapter One of this book, Cardinal Cullen, who was instrumental in setting up the College, was ultimately disappointed in his wish to make teacher training a function of the university through the then Catholic University of Ireland.[19] Instead, students who completed the two-year programme were recognized as qualified national teachers or NTs by the Department of Education. All denominational training colleges were put under the supervision of a Head Inspector of the Department of Education who had considerable influence over the curriculum.[20] Goodman, the College's first music lecturer, was the inspector who established music as a required subject to qualify as a national teacher.[21] The call for university-led degree courses for teachers in arts and pedagogy to cover all the subjects of the primary school curriculum continued after 1922.[22] While this was not realized until 1974, a relationship between teacher training colleges and the National University of Ireland (NUI) had developed during the 1960s.[23]

Courses provided within the general education studies section of teacher education programmes began to gain recognition by the NUI as 'academic' subjects qualifying for NUI's university first arts examination. Not all subjects were recognized, but the music course at St Patrick's College gained recognition in 1965.[24] These recognized academic subjects were marked by the absence of any professional

---

[19] T. Ó Ceallaigh, *St Patrick's College Centenary Booklet 1875-1975*, (Dublin: St Patrick's College, 1975).
[20] The Diploma qualification of NT was in fact awarded by the Department of Education after two years subsequent probationary teaching in a national school.
[21] Ní Shé, 'The Initial Education and Training of Music Teachers', p. 2.
[22] E. Neuman, 'An Evaluation of the Three-Year Course Leading to the Bachelor or Education (B.Ed.) Degree in St Patrick's College, Dublin', Unpublished report, (Dublin: Educational Research Centre, St Patrick's College, 1982), p. 16.
[23] Ibid., p. 17.
[24] Ní Shé, 'The Initial Education and Training of Music Teachers', p. 20.

element (arguably, such a dichotomy between academic and professional elements would not be as forcefully expressed in the contemporary higher education landscape). In the case of music, the course included harmony, counterpoint and melody writing; form, history and appreciation; and a performance component. The history and appreciation section for the second-year syllabus comprised a survey of European music 'from Bach to Debussy (1685-1900)' along with a course on the history and characteristics of Irish Music.[25] The 'form' component was similarly divided into analytic studies, this time ranging 'from Bach to Beethoven', and an examination of Irish dance music forms.[26]

If a student had matriculated and completed four recognized academic subjects in St Patrick's College they qualified to take the first arts examination of constituent NUI universities with equivalent departments and could go on to complete a BA after two years. Many students of the College who completed the NT qualification went on to complete the BA at University College Dublin (UCD). UCD organized evening lectures on a part-time basis to facilitate primary teachers and other cohorts of mature students.

Figure 3.1: Seán Hayes, lecturer and later, Head of Music at St Patrick's College, 1949-1985. Photographer unknown

---

[25] At the time, Irish music was considered as synonymous with Irish folk or traditional music. St Patrick's College, 'Syllabus / Mionchlár, An Dara Bliain [Second Year] 1974-75', p. 19.
[26] Ibid.

Music in the BEd Programme

A major development in the history of St Patrick's College was its recognition by the senate of the NUI in 1975 as a recognized NUI college, and the accreditation by NUI of its three-year BEd degree.[27] Seán Hayes was head of music at this time. From 1949 he had been sole lecturer in music but as a consequence of the new three-year BEd degree was joined by Colum Ó Cléirigh in 1971 and Caitlín Uí Éigeartaigh (Kathleen Hegarty) in 1972. Uí Éigeartaigh was the first published musicologist to work at the College.[28] The appointment of Seán MacLiam in 1977 brought the staff complement to four, although by that point Uí Éigeartaigh was employed on a part-time basis.[29] The three-year BEd degree followed the structure of the three-year arts degree in UCD. It differed however in the high proportion allocated to education studies in each year. In first year students took education (fifty per cent) and two arts subjects (twenty-five per cent per subject), and in each subsequent year students continued with education (sixty per cent) and one of the arts subjects (forty per cent) studied in first year.[30] Academic music courses followed the model used by UCD with examinations in three areas, namely, harmony and counterpoint, music history and analysis (including Irish traditional music) and a music practical – that is, individual performance studies. (Requirements for harmony and counterpoint are set out in Chapter Four, while the other course components of history and analysis and performance are discussed briefly here.)

History and analysis in first year included Baroque and Irish traditional music, in second year music of the Classical period and Irish traditional music, and in third year nineteenth- and early-twentieth-century art music.[31] A practical examination on a chosen instrument or

---

[27] Neuman, 'An Evaluation of the Three-Year Course', p. 19.

[28] Among other publications see C. Uí Éigeartaigh, 'Patrick Weston Joyce: the collector as editor', *Éigse Cheol Tíre/Irish Folk Music Studies*, 2 (1974-1975), 5-14. Uí Éigeartaigh's research on Irish traditional music is discussed in Chapter Five by Teresa O'Donnell.

[29] J. O'Flynn, 'Self-Assessment Report of the Music Department', (St Patrick's College, March 2011), p. 7.

[30] Neuman, 'An Evaluation of the Three-Year Course', pp. 356-365.

[31] Ollscoil na hÉireann, Coláiste Phádraig Baile Átha Cliath [National University of Ireland, St Patrick's College Dublin], Summer Examinations 1985: 'Music, First University Examination for B.Ed. Degree'; 'Music, Second University Examination for B.Ed.'; 'Music, B.Ed. Degree Examination'.

voice prepared through private classes was the final part of the exam and twenty per cent of the overall mark was allocated to this part of the music course.[32] It included a sight-reading test in each year, and keyboard harmony in second and third year. The latter included realizing a figured bass, with third year students additionally required to read from score a transposing instrument at pitch on the piano. Students participated in choir and from time to time also in special vocal and instrumental ensembles, although these activities were not officially integrated into the music department's courses until much later.

The inclusion of performance as a key element within the BEd music degree course was not without its challenges. While 'instrumental music' had been taught by part-time staff at the College since the late nineteenth century and continued up to the 1960s, this was largely confined to lessons on harmonium or piano.[33] For a while, full-time music lecturers including Seán Hayes and Caitlín Uí Éigeartaigh taught piano, while students learning orchestral instruments were facilitated through an arrangement with the Royal Irish Academy of Music. By the late 1970s Seán Mac Liam established a connection with the Dublin Municipal College of Music whereby BEd music students, including those studying piano, could take individual lessons with instrumental teachers based in its Chatham Row premises. A decade later, Marion Doherty developed a system of peripatetic instrumental and vocal tuition whereby students could receive individual lessons, in a variety of instruments and music styles, in the music department's rehearsal rooms. This system brought BEd (and later, BA) students into contact with some of Ireland's leading performers and teachers including, in more recent times, pianists Dearbhla Collins and Fionnuala Moynihan and mezzo-soprano Imelda Drumm.

The option to study music to degree level while qualifying as a primary school teacher was arguably a highly attractive option for many school leavers from the mid-1970s, particularly during the late 1970s and early 1980s when fees at colleges of education were minimal by comparison with those for universities and other higher education

---

[32] Neuman, 'An Evaluation of the Three-Year Course', p. 358.
[33] For example, Patrick W. Murphy and Finn O'Loughlin are listed as teachers of instrumental music at the College in the late 1940s, the former between 1946-1949 and the latter from 1948. Seán Neeson, 'The Organization of Music in the Schools', in A. Fleischmann (ed.), *Music in Ireland: A Symposium*, (Cork: Cork University Press, 1952), p. 60.

institutions. As documented in several chapters across this volume, many BEd graduates who 'majored' in music would go on to take roles as musicians and music leaders in schools and communities, with a significant number also impacting on national developments in music, media and the arts.

Curriculum music in the BEd and in professional postgraduate programmes
A curriculum music course was compulsory for all BEd students at the College. However, although the programme was now extended to three years, initially curriculum music was considerably reduced by comparison with provision within the two-year NT programme. Students were now obliged to study curriculum music only in first year. This reflected what appeared to be a swing in favour of academic studies, a change that arguably could not have come at a worse time from the perspective of equipping newly qualified teachers to teach music in schools. In the 'new' primary curriculum of 1971, music syllabuses were expanded to include singing, vocal technique, ear training, music and movement, notation, creative activities and integration with other school subjects. It was an ambitious curriculum requiring considerable musical skill and judgement on the part of the teacher. Initially, curriculum music courses in the College expanded to support these new demands, but the academic structure of the BEd degree could not accommodate the continuation of expanded curriculum music courses. The music department nonetheless found a way to allow students to continue with music in all three years by offering a special Diploma in Music. The diploma was outside the BEd qualification and was accredited by the College itself. It was an optional two-year course that was practically and professionally oriented, and was specifically designed to facilitate students who were not studying academic music but who wished to develop their own musicianship.

The diploma course comprised the following components: vocal, choral and group instrumental performance; song arrangement for classroom instruments; listening to music; and a range of music projects for the classroom. By 1980 fifty-seven per cent of students had registered for the diploma.[34] Following an internal review of the BEd in 1982, this course became an integral part of the degree, and was reconstituted as two distinct components: the mandatory course 'Expressive Arts: Music' for second-year students, and an elective in

---

[34] Neuman, 'An Evaluation of the Three-Year Course', table 4.68, p. 538.

music for third-year students. By the time that the *Revised Primary School Curriculum* was introduced in 1999, all BEd students at the College attended forty-eight hours of curriculum music in first year and twenty-four hours in second year, and those that wished to could opt to take a further forty-eight hours of music as an elective in third year. This extent of provision for curriculum music or professional music education studies was unparalleled in the history of the BEd and was exceptionally high by national and international comparisons (regrettably, provision for curriculum music would significantly decrease following the introduction of a revised four-year BEd programme at St Patrick's College in 2012).

There was a considerable expansion in student numbers around the time that the *Revised Primary School Curriculum* was published. In 1998 there were two hundred BEd students per year; by 2000 this had doubled to four hundred, largely as a response to an acute shortage of qualified teachers in the Irish education system at the time. On the retirement of Colum Ó Cléirigh in 1998, Patricia Flynn was appointed as music lecturer while Breda O'Shea (Bríd Ní Shé) was seconded to the College with specific responsibilities for curriculum music (The following year O'Shea joined the staff of Marino College of Education). Although by that time the student cohort for curriculum music had dramatically increased and numbers for the academic music course were steadily rising, the department's complement of three full-time music lecturers (Marion Doherty, Seán Mac Liam and Patricia Flynn) was the same that had obtained in 1972 (Seán Hayes, Colum Ó Cléirigh and Caitlín Uí Éigeartaigh). The number of music department members increased to four when John Buckley was appointed in 2001. This followed a further rise in the number of curriculum music students resulting from the reintroduction of an eighteen-month Graduate Diploma in Education for students who already held a primary degree (the Graduate Diploma had not been offered for much of the 1980s and 1990s due to a decreased demand for qualified primary teachers in those decades).

Considering the very large number of undergraduate students and the increasing number of academic and professional programmes that the department contributed to (discussed below) it was essential for the music department to depend on many part-time staff. Among several part-time music lecturers from the mid-1990s were Mary Stakelum and later, Rhona Clarke (who was subsequently appointed to the department on a full-time basis). In addition to the teaching contributions of full-time and part-time music staff, curriculum music also required a coordinator to oversee pedagogy, resources, timetabling and staffing for its various courses. Patricia Flynn undertook this role while continuing to contribute to the music degree programmes.

Those employed as part-time lecturers of curriculum music were experienced teachers and/or professional musicians and music scholars, many of whom made and continue to make significant contributions to education and the arts at community and national levels. Their number over the last two decades of the College's history included (in alphabetical order): Mary Amond O'Brien, Kathrine Barnecutt, Mairéad Berrill, Marie-Louise Bowe (Teaching Fellow, 2014-2015), Eileen Brogan, Lorraine Byrne, Aingeala De Burca, Loretta Desmond, Gordon Douglas, Julie Feeney, Sara Finer, Orla Flanagan (Teaching Fellow, 2015-2016), Maura Flynn, John Gearty, Evelyn Grant, Berna Hayden, Anna-Marie Higgins, Yvonne Higgins (Teaching Fellow, 2000-2001), Thomas Johnston, Éadaoin Kelly, Ailbhe Kenny, Aisling Kenny, Assumpta Kerins, Maria Kirrane, Denise Kerrigan, Helen Lawless, Caitríona McEniry, Clare McEvoy, Carrie Maher, Regina Murphy, Róisín Nic Athlaoich, Eimear Ní Mhaolmhuaidh (Teaching Fellow, 2003), Mary O'Flynn, Teresa O'Donnell, Anna Poires, Anne Purcell, Martina Sexton, Maria Westval, Laura Wickham and Niamh Williams.

Curriculum music content throughout the 2000s was based on the three strands of the 1999 music curriculum, namely, composing, listening and responding, and performing. In order to simulate classroom practice, students participated in workshops in song arrangement, group composition and movement to music; additionally, they were required to engage with music curriculum documentation and to formulate appropriate music lessons for teaching practice. The third-year elective course in music was led by Colum Ó Cléirigh for much of the 1980s and 1990s, with John Buckley taking over this role from 2001. The course devised by Buckley involved the input of full-time members of the music department and typically included the following elements: classical music in the classroom, music literacy (following the Kodály approach), choral conducting and working with school choirs, resourcing with world music, making and creating pieces for 'junk' (homemade) instruments, and music education, theory and practice. From 2009 the elective course also comprised a section on music technology in the classroom. Shorter music elective courses were also offered to students on the Graduate Diploma in Education programme.

The expansion of undergraduate and postgraduate music courses, 1994-2008

Music on the BA in Humanities programme

The BEd programme, which included both music as a degree-level subject and curriculum music as part of professional education studies, continued to be awarded by NUI until 1995, the final year of this arrangement. The year 1994 saw the introduction of a DCU-accredited BA programme in humanities. This represented a significant change for the College, which had maintained a long-lasting relationship with UCD since the mid 1960s, and followed an invitation by the then Minister for Education Mary O'Rourke to undertake a linkage agreement with Dublin City University. Completed in 1993, the linkage agreement proved to be very fruitful for St Patrick's College as it could now engage in further undergraduate, taught postgraduate and research masters and doctoral programmes. This had not been possible under the aegis of NUI. Two joint faculties were formed with DCU. The joint faculty of education included the departments of education (including the area of human development), special education, religious studies and biology from St Patrick's College, together with staff of the school of education studies in DCU. The joint faculty of humanities included what were now titled as the academic departments of English, French, Gaeilge, geography, history, mathematics and music from St Patrick's College together with the schools of communication and applied languages in DCU.[35] While there were no common programmes across the two linked institutions, the joint faculty of humanities held regular seminars with papers presented by staff of both institutions, organized and hosted in rotation by each institution.

Under the linkage agreement all degree programmes provided by St Patrick's College were accredited by Dublin City University. In 1994 a BA in Humanities programme was introduced at the College. The idea behind the BA degree was that it would be jointly taught with the students taking the humanities component of the BEd. Consequently it followed a similar structure to the BEd programme as well as to that of the traditional NUI model: three subjects taken in first year and two carried on to second and third years, all subjects with equal weighting in their respective years.

The first-year BA course comprised five areas: musical techniques; analysis, criticism and history; Irish traditional music; individual performance; and a study of two selected areas from a list of options.[36]

---

[35] St Patrick's College, *Student Information Handbook, 1994-1995*, (Dublin: St Patrick's College, 1994), p. ii.
[36] St Patrick's College, *BA Degree in Humanities/BA sa Léann Daonna*, (Dublin: St Patrick's College, 1994), p. 15.

This last unit was designed to provide lectures for BA students during spring teaching practice when it was not possible to have joint lectures with the BEd students (a similar situation and arrangement obtained for second-year students who would join the first-year BA cohort for the short courses offered). The available options changed from year to year and were a combination of lectures by invited guests and courses offered by full-time staff. This created a fertile and flexible space to try out new types of courses and to stretch the horizons of the students. It could take advantage of visiting international academics (including Fulbright Scholar Elizabeth Dyer from 2005-2006) or guest lecturers from other Irish institutions and explore musicological areas that were developing across university departments. Among many other areas, these short courses heralded the first lectures at the College on jazz, popular music, Irish opera, contemporary composition, music technology, comparative music education, and ethnomusicology. Some of these components later became established as an integral part of the BA music course. For example, approved minutes of a music department meeting dated 5 September 2005 included a discussion on timetabling and assessment for a course component titled 'Traditional and Popular Musics'.[37] This represents one of the earliest references in music department records to popular music which in the first semester of that academic year was taught by part-time lecturer Jennifer Byrne. However, there was no reference to popular music in minutes taken during the first departmental meetings of 2006-2007, with ethnomusicology now appearing in combination with traditional music (and apparently displacing popular music).[38]

BA students continuing with music in second-year studied musical techniques, analysis, criticism and history, music education, individual performance, Irish traditional music, and a combination of short occasional courses as in first year. This mirrored the second-year BEd music course in broad outline, but because the BA course comprised additional credits, orchestration (and later, free composition) was included under musical techniques. As previously noted, it could be regarded as somewhat anomalous that music education formed part of the BA course and yet was not an option within the BEd degree programme. The move to include music education on the BA was

---

[37] Music Department, St Patrick's College, Minutes of Meeting, 5 September 2005, p. 1.
[38] Music Department, St Patrick's College, Minutes of Meeting, 4 September 2006, p. 1.

devised to meet the needs of the particular career trajectories of BA students at the College at the time, many of whom went on to take postgraduate courses in either primary or secondary education. The third-year BA music course comprised further studies in the core areas of musical techniques; analysis, criticism and history; music education, Irish traditional music (with the later inclusion of lectures in ethnomusicology), and individual performance. Additionally, students carried out final year dissertation projects, which from 1994-2010 were primarily concerned with topics in music education (from 2010-2016 students had the option to carry out dissertations in areas of musicology or music ethnography).

Postgraduate degrees
The linkage agreement with Dublin City University provided for the accreditation by the University of postgraduate and doctoral programmes. This was a significant change to the College's earlier relationship with NUI, which had precluded such developments. Along with the BA in Humanities, the linkage agreement facilitated the growth of generic MEd and MA programmes at the College. As discussed in Chapter Eight these new developments in postgraduate programmes were shortly followed by an expansion of research activities across both academic faculties of the institution. For music, this would lead to the design and delivery of taught masters in humanities and in education as well as research degrees at MA and PhD levels.

A taught MEd in Music Education was developed and initially led by Seán Mac Liam, with the first cohort of students enrolled in 1998, just four years after the linkage agreement with DCU. This was the first Masters programme available in Ireland where students could specialize in the academic sub-discipline of music education. The course was offered on a part-time basis over two years to facilitate the engagement of primary and secondary teachers with full-time positions, and ran between the years 1998-2000, 2000-2002, 2004-2006 and 2009-2011 (a list of graduates from each of these cohorts can be found in Appendix E: Music and Music Education Dissertations and Theses, 2000-2016).[39] The MEd (Music Education) programme comprised six taught modules in first year, of which three were shared modules in education studies and three were modules specific to music education -

---

[39] Patricia Flynn and John O'Flynn jointly directed the 2009-2011 course.

the makeup of these could vary from course to course.[40] For the 2009-2010 course, the shared education modules were 'Current Issues in Education', 'Qualitative Research Methods in Education' and 'Quantitative Research Methods in Education' while the specialist music education modules were titled 'Music in Education', 'The Musical Mind' and 'Music, Society and Culture'. For the second year of the programme students took a module on research in music education and completed a minor dissertation on an original music education topic.

Figure 3.2: Seán Mac Liam with Teresa O'Donnell who was conferred with a PhD at the College on 9 November 2012. Photograph by Patricia Flynn

Seán Mac Liam also instigated the MA in Humanities (Music) programme which ran between years 2003-2005, 2005-2007, 2007-2009 and 2013-2015 (see Appendix E).[41] The two-year, part-time programme followed a similar structure to the MEd, with taught modules concentrated in the first year, and a research seminar plus options to specialize in a musicology dissertation or composition portfolio or performance recital during the second year of the course. (Students opting for composition portfolio or performance recital were also required to submit an accompanying research essay relevant to their creative output). From 2003-2009 taught elements of the first

---

[40] Units were the measurement used prior to the widespread breakdown of courses into modules.
[41] John O'Flynn directed the 2013-2015 course.

year course comprised three units in musicology, three units in musical techniques (with emphasis on modern and contemporary composition), one unit in music criticism and aesthetics, one unit on music technology and acoustics and one unit on research methodology. By 2013-2015, the first-year course structure reflected the modular system now in operation across St Patrick's College and comprised four fifteen-credit modules, each of which contained academic and applied elements. These modules drew on specialist topics that had been part of previous courses ('Introduction to Musicology, Criticism and Aesthetics' and 'Music and Modernity') as well as introducing new areas ('Music and National Identity' and 'Music in Performance'). The programme structure underwent further modifications in the years that followed and later emerged as a stand-alone MA in Music accredited by DCU.

Programme review and institutional change, 2008-2016
As head of the music department from 1985 until her retirement in 2008 Marion Doherty presided over a period of considerable development as well as stability for the department. Doherty made a notable impact in areas of choral and instrumental performance, and oversaw several programme innovations to the BEd and later, the BA music degree courses. This was a period that also saw the coordination of substantial provision for curriculum music by Patricia Flynn, the design and implementation of postgraduate courses in music and music education led by Seán Mac Liam, and the emergence of the department's reputation as a centre for composition through the additional appointments of John Buckley and Rhona Clarke.

John O'Flynn was appointed head of department in 2008 and remained in that position until the College was fully incorporated into DCU in October 2016. This was a period marked by extensive change for music programmes at the College. While much of that change was necessitated by external pressures as outlined below, the department was itself pro-active in this regard, and initiated a full review of its undergraduate degree courses from 2009. This began with some incremental changes, a noteworthy example being the timetabling of popular music studies in combination with established short courses in Irish traditional music and ethnomusicology under the umbrella title 'Traditional and Popular Musics' (which as previously noted was briefly used in the mid-2000s). Ethnomusicology, which had first been introduced as an additional course under the headship of Marion Doherty continued to by taught by Maria Escribano. Meanwhile, John O'Flynn delivered new components in popular music and in film music, while traditional music courses also evolved over this time (see Chapter

Five). This newly constituted 'Traditional and Popular Musics' course represented a cohesive area of study that complemented the long-established areas of 'Analysis, Criticism and History' and 'Musical Techniques'.

Following many staff meetings and consultations with external experts including Gabrielle McCann and Gerard Gillen, the review of music degree courses was completed and approved by the Standing Committee of the College's Academic Council in June 2011.[42] It reflected a holistic approach to course structure, content and assessment. The BA and BEd music degree courses now comprised the following three core elements over three years: musical techniques (with additional components in orchestration and free composition for BA students), musicology, and performance. Second- and third-year BA students additionally attended courses in 'Music, Human Experience and Culture'. These were built on earlier BA course components in music education studies but were broadened to include the psychology of music, the sociology of music and ethnography. Third-year BA students continued to carry out dissertations, now with options of specializing in musicology topics or carrying out music ethnography projects. While BEd and BA students shared most course units (later termed modules), there were subtle differences in the way that these respective units were considered. A course descriptor for the BEd music degree in the College's prospectus for the academic year 2010-2011 opened with the statement: 'This music course is designed to enable students to develop their musicality, and to deepen their understanding of music'. The exact same sentence opened the course descriptor for BA music, with the addition of the qualifying phrase 'from a range of musicological and social science perspectives'.[43]

The development of musicality was a core aim for both music degree programmes, as indeed it had been over the history of formal music studies at the College. As before, music students were expected to continue individual instrumental or vocal studies and to demonstrate progress through a formal exam recital at the end of each academic year. A system whereby the music department facilitated peripatetic

---

[42] Gabrielle McCann formerly coordinated the BMusEd degree at Trinity College Dublin while Professor Gerard Gillen, emeritus professor of music at NUI Maynooth, was external examiner for music at St Patrick's College from 2008-2011.

[43] St Patrick's College, *Prospectus 2011-2012*, Drumcondra (Dublin: St Patrick's College, 2011), p. 22.

teaching of individual performance had been established in earlier decades. A contentious issue for music students as well as for lecturing staff over the years was the costs incurred by students for individual lessons. This was a situation that obtained in spite of successive submissions requesting subsidies to alleviate the costs of individual lessons that were made to College management and also to the Higher Education Authority. On the positive side, the music department coordinated arrangements for lessons, provided practice rooms and put students in contact with a wide range of tutors, many of whom were prominent performers in Irish musical life. Two substantial innovations to performance components were brought about as a result of the 2011 music degree course review. The first was the establishment of a mid-year review system where music lecturers auditioned and provided pedagogical and programme advice regarding instrumental and vocal studies. The second innovation was the awarding of a proportion of credit for group participation in music, whether though choir and/or participation in a new mentorship system for student music groups initiated by John Buckley and John O'Flynn.[44] Students were encouraged to reflect on their participation in an end-of-year report in which they could also comment on their engagement with the lunchtime concert series and other public performances.

A major structural change to all programmes and courses at St Patrick's College was its alignment with the European Credit Transfer and Accumulation System (ECTS) following the Bologna declaration of 1999 and the eventual constitution of the European Higher Education Area (EHEA) in 2010. This necessitated several changes for music courses including the consolidation of a modular system that would enable transfer of ECTS (credits) to and from other EHEA institutions. Modifications to the ECTS system coincided with the music department's internal review process, and in some respects opened up possibilities for reimagining degree course structures that had not been the subject of review for decades.

---

[44] Students could also earn credit for participation and performance in other groups and societies across the College and DCU in areas such as musical theatre, liturgical folk music, hip-hop and open mic.

Figure 3.3: Rhona Clarke and Patricia Flynn with Louise Curtis who was conferred with a BEd at the College on 9 November 2012. Photographer unknown

The same could not be said about the impact of the introduction of a revised four-year BEd programme at St Patrick's College, which was jointly accredited by the Teaching Council of Ireland and the University. If the original three-year BEd of 1974 represented a swing in favour of studies in arts and humanities subjects, the four-year programme introduced in 2012 brought about a drastic reduction in available credits for these areas, to the extent that music and other humanities subjects could no longer be studied to degree level.[45] More surprisingly (and worryingly from the perspective of primary-level music education), the introduction of the four-year BEd signalled a substantial reduction in the time available for the study of curriculum music. In spite of these substantial cuts, members of the music department continued to design and implement music and curriculum music modules for students on the revised BEd programme, and moreover strove to connect education students to the wider activities of

---

[45] In the three-year BEd degree music could constitute sixty credits out of one hundred and eighty credits whereas out of the revised four-year degree's two hundred and forty credits, students could opt for a maximum of c. thirty credits in music modules (a proportion that gradually reduced following subsequent modifications brought about by the BEd Programme Board).

the music department through participation in choir, music groups and the organization of lunchtime concerts.

The demise of the music degree course within the BEd coincided with a restructuring of the College's BA in Humanities programme to align with a new joint honours BA (BAJH) accredited by DCU. The first cohort of BAJH music students enrolled in 2015, just one year before full incorporation into the university. The music course followed the existing BA (Humanities) course in most respects, but with additional credits now available for music in the first year of study,[46] and the semesterization of most modules.[47] The BAJH music course was based on three core areas that had their foundations in earlier BEd and BA degree programmes, namely: composition, theory, and applied techniques; topics in musicology; and performance/participation in music. The additional credits available to first-year students (in comparison with the music course of the BA in Humanites programme) resulted in increased studio workshop hours in areas of music technology, solfège, keyboard harmony and aural skills. 'Applied musical techniques' across all three years also referred to classical approaches to harmony and counterpoint, while 'composition' embraced orchestration skills and structured approaches to original composition. Building on the music department's internal review that was first implemented in 2011, 'Topics in Musicology' embraced analytic and historical studies of western art music, popular music studies, Irish art music, ethnomusicology and Irish traditional music studies (with an additional music psychology component in the second year of the course). This reflected the broad-based approach to musicology and parity of esteem for diverse music genres and practices that had gradually evolved at the music department of St Patrick's College over several decades.

As noted in Chapter Eight, the department's profile as a centre for musicology greatly increased at this time, not least through the

---

[46] Hitherto, BA in Humanities students selected three subjects in the first year of the programme; following the adoption of the BAJH course structure, just two subjects were selected during Year One.

[47] Semesterization is a term used here to describe changes from the predominant use of year-long courses/modules and end-of-year examinations to modules held and assessed over one semester (roughly, a period of fifteen weeks that includes lecture weeks, reading/study weeks and examination weeks).

organization of national and international conferences. In addition to contributions by full-time staff members John Buckley, Rhona Clarke, Patricia Flynn and John O'Flynn, components of musicology courses were also delivered by many emerging scholars at the time, including Majella Boland, Thomas Johnston, Aisling Kenny, Sheryl Lynch, John Millar and Jennifer O'Connor.

While the former BA (Humanities) music course held a distinct identity from its origins in 1994, it also shadowed the music course of the BEd degree which had been the flagship programme of St Patrick's College's since 1974. There were distinct advantages to this, not least the benefits of BA and BEd music cohorts studying, and in many cases also performing, together. Up until 2012 the BEd could be considered as the dominant fraction of that combination, not only in terms of student numbers, but also because, initially, timetabling for the BA (Humanities) programme had revolved around that of the BEd. A major consequence of programme revision for the four-year BEd was that students on that programme could no longer study music to degree level. This, along with the expansion of student numbers and available credits for music on the BAJH programme resulted in a major shift that saw that course emerge as the major offering of St Patrick's College's music department prior to incorporation into DCU. Up until 2016, the music department also continued to hold responsibility for the provision of curriculum music within professional education studies, representing an unbroken line of such provision since the first courses in vocal music were offered in the late nineteenth century.

Bibliography

An Roinn Oideachais, *Clar Léinn na gColáistí Oillúna*, (Dublin: Department of Education, 1930).

An Roinn Oideachais, *Revised Programme of Instruction in Music for National Schools*, (Dublin: Stationery Office, 1939).

An Roinn Oideachais, *Notes for Teachers: Music*, (Dublin: Stationery Office, 1939).

An Roinn Oideachais, *Curaclam na Bunscoile* (Dublin: Stationery Office, 1971).

Coolahan, John, *Irish Education History and Structure*, (Dublin: IPA, 1981).

Coolahan, John, 'The development of educational studies and teacher education in Ireland', *Education Research and Perspectives*, 31.2 (2004), 30-47.

Department of Education, *National Programme of Primary Instruction*, (Dublin: Educational Company of Ireland, 1922).

Kelly, James (ed.), *St Patrick's College, Drumcondra 1875-2000: A History*, (Dublin: Four Courts Press, 2006).

Kelly Noel, 'Music in Irish Primary Education 1831-1922', *Proceedings of the Educational Studies Association*, (Galway: ESAI, 1979).

Mark, Michael, 'The Evolution of Music Education Philosophy from Utilitarian to Aesthetic', *Journal of Research in Music Education*, 30.1 (1982), 15-21.

McCarthy, Marie, *Passing it on: The Transmission of Music in Irish Culture*, (Cork: Cork University Press, 1999).

National Council for Curriculum and Assessment, *Primary School Curriculum, Arts Education: Music*, (Dublin: Stationery Office, 1999).

Neeson, Seán, 'The Organization of Music in the Schools', in A. Fleischmann (ed.), *Music in Ireland: A Symposium*, (Cork: Cork University Press, 1952), pp. 59-64.

Neuman, Elizabeth, 'An Evaluation of the Three-Year Course Leading to the B.Ed. Degree in St Patrick's College', Unpublished report, (Dublin: St Patrick's College, 1982).

New Rules and Regulations (National Education), 1900-1, Cd. 601, H.C. 1901.

Ní Shé, Bríd, 'The Initial Education and Training of Music Teachers for Primary Schools in the Republic of Ireland, Northern Ireland, England and Wales', Unpublished MEd Thesis, (Trinity College Dublin, 1994).

Ó Ceallaigh, Tadhg, *St Patrick's College Centenary Booklet 1875-1975*, (Dublin: St Patrick's College, 1975).

Ollscoil na hÉireann, Coláiste Phádraig Baile Átha Cliath [National University of Ireland, St Patrick's College Dublin], Published examination papers (1988-1992).

O'Flynn, John, 'Self-Assessment Report of the Music Department', Unpublished report, (St Patrick's College, March, 2011).

Pendley, Shawn, 'Trivium and Quadrivium', in E. Provenzo and A. Provenzo (eds.), *Encyclopedia of the Social and Cultural Foundations of Education*, (Thousand Oaks, CA: SAGE Publications, 2009).

Programmes of Instruction for National Schools for the School Year 1919-1920, (Dublin: Office of National Education, 1919).

St Patrick's College, 'Syllabus/Mionchlár, An Dara Bliain 1974-75', (Dublin: St Patrick's College, 1974).

St Patrick's College, *Student Information Book 1992-1993*, (Dublin: St Patrick's College, 1992).

St Patrick's College, *Student Information Handbook 1994-1995*, (Dublin: St Patrick's College, 1994).

St Patrick's College, *BA Degree in Humanities/BA sa Léann Daonna*, (Dublin: St Patrick's College, 1994).
St Patrick's College, *Student Information Handbook 1995-1996*, (Dublin: St Patrick's College, 1995).
St Patrick's College, *Prospectus 2011-2012*, (Dublin: St Patrick's College, 2011).
Uí Éigeartaigh, Caitlín, 'Patrick Weston Joyce: the collector as editor', *Éigse Cheol Tíre/Irish Folk Music Studies*, 2 (1974-1975), 5-14.

Newspapers and periodicals
Freeman's Journal
Irish Independent

Archives
St Patrick's College Archive

Chapter Four: Composition and the College

Rhona Clarke

Introduction
Composition in its various guises, be it improvisation workshops, technical exercises or contemporary composition, formed an element of music courses at St Patrick's College since the mid-1960s. This chapter explores the various course components, teaching methods and modes of assessment for composition that featured in undergraduate and postgraduate degree programmes in Education and in Humanities over this time. Discussion of the latter includes mention of the internal and intercollegiate workshops set up by the College's music department to enable students to interact with live musicians and to hear their own work as well as the work of fellow students. The chapter follows changes in the content of music and curriculum music courses at the College over the last fifty or so years of its history, including those resulting from the inclusion of composition in the revised primary curriculum of 1999.[1]

As with many third-level institutions offering specialist music courses, composition at St Patrick's College began with applied techniques in common-practice harmony and counterpoint as a compulsory element.[2] In more recent decades, when some university music departments began to offer alternative modules to 'traditional' harmony and counterpoint, this element remained a core component of music courses at St Patrick's. The applied techniques courses explored harmony and counterpoint through writing for instrumental and vocal forces up to four parts. Technical skills were progressively developed throughout the two-year diploma and later, the three-year degree courses to include more complex harmonic language and textural skills. These comprised a variety of musical styles, from the sixteenth-century madrigal to eighteenth-century keyboard inventions to the harmonic language of the late nineteenth century. Conventional techniques were taught, not just with the objective of gaining useful skills for arranging and composing, but also to develop music theory and musical thinking and to foster better understanding in relation to listening and

---

[1] National Council for Curriculum and Assessment, *Primary School Curriculum, Arts Education: Music*, (Dublin: Stationery Office, 1999).
[2] The common practice period was an era of tonal classical music in Western Europe that spanned three centuries from approximately 1600 to 1910.

performing. Composing complements the skills and understanding learned by other experiences of music and allows the student to draw together their full breadth of knowledge in the subject while making independent decisions; it can also be informed by personal interests and tastes. From the year 2000 onwards and following the initiative of Head of Music Marion Doherty, composition in a contemporary idiom and using experimental styles was added to the course components.[3] This more flexible exploration of composition allowed for greater choice and also for more risk-taking on the part of students. Although the lectures demonstrated particular contemporary techniques, improvisation and experimentation were also encouraged.

From the early twenty-first century up to the time of incorporation into DCU, composition as research was undertaken at St Patrick's College by a number of established composers, including members of staff and postgraduate students who completed portfolios with commentaries leading to the awarding of PhDs. This resulted in a body of work written for various groupings of professional musicians in Ireland and abroad that included: solo, chamber ensemble, vocal/choral, electro-acoustic and orchestral music. Most of these works have been disseminated through performances, recordings and broadcasts.

Composition at the College flourished during the residency of The Fidelio Trio (2012-2015) during which time many new works performed by the ensemble were commissioned and funded by The Arts Council/An Chomhairle Ealaíon. [4] More generally, the music department forged several associations with composers and musicians outside the community of the College, notably through its collaboration with The Contemporary Music Centre (CMC).

Musical techniques

The fundamental principles of functional harmony were taught as an essential part of music courses at St Patrick's College. Musical techniques began as part of the two-year diploma course in 1965 under Seán Hayes,[5] and expanded with the establishment of the three-year BEd degree in 1974. This component was also a core feature of music studies within the BA in Humanities programme, continuing up to the

---

[3] This aspect of the techniques module was designed and taught by the author from 2000-2016.
[4] See Chapter Ten.
[5] The course may have begun earlier than 1965, but it was first recognized as an academic subject by the NUI in this year: National University of Ireland, *Calendar, 1965*, (Dublin: NUI), p. 203.

time of incorporation into Dublin City University in 2016. Methods of teaching for musical techniques were through lecture-workshops with end-of-year or end-of-semester examinations. For the most part, students were expected to complete twice-weekly exercises, ensuring constant feedback from lecturers.

An account of the two-year Diploma in National Teaching outlines requirements for the *Cúrsa Dhá Bhliain* [Two Year Course] which offered 'Special Music'.[6] The same document also confirms this as 'Music (special)' as distinct from 'Music (oral)'; these later became known, respectively, as academic music and curriculum music. Students of 'Special Music' were expected to apply understanding of: major, minor and chromatic scales; major and minor chords including dominant seventh chords; unessential notes; and simple modulation. They were further required to add three parts to a melody or a bass and to write *contrapointe simplí* [simple counterpoint] in two parts.

When the first three-year BEd programme was introduced in 1974, music was one of eight academic subjects from which two were chosen in the first year, with one subject continued for detailed study over the following two years.[7] The subject selected was 'pursued to a standard which was considered by the relevant university authorities to be appropriate to Primary Degree level' (see Chapter Three in this volume for a broader discussion of music in the BEd degree).[8] Harmony and counterpoint in first year included elementary four-part harmony, writing SAT over a given bass and BTA under a given soprano line, melodic writing in a given form with modulation, and elementary counterpoint.[9] In second year it entailed harmony and counterpoint in the Baroque style, including chorale harmonization, [10] three-part harmony and writing for keyboard. In third year this was extended to two papers, one in harmony that included a more advanced chorale and completion of a string quartet, and one in counterpoint that included fugue, writing for strings in imitative counterpoint and piano accompaniment. An understanding of the stylistic writing of the Classical and early Romantic eras was expected, and students at this

---

[6] *Cúrsa Dhá Bhliain* (n.d.), SPCA, A/8/4.2.
[7] The subjects were Biology, English, French, *Gaeilge*, Geography, History, Mathematics and Music.
[8] Irish National Teachers' Organisation, INTO Consultative Conference on Education Kilkenny (1990), *Pre-service Education: A Report by the Education Committee*, (Dublin: INTO), p. 4.
[9] SAT: soprano, alto and tenor parts; BTA: bass, tenor and alto parts.
[10] A hymn-tune in the tradition of the German Lutheran Church; hundreds of chorales were arranged for SATB choir by the composer J. S. Bach.

level were also required to show an understanding of chromatic harmony, secondary dominants, and diminished seventh and secondary seventh chords.

As noted above, a core aspect of musical techniques classes was the harmonization of chorales in the style of J.S. Bach; this type of question could be found in musical techniques examinations from the earliest years of the two-year diploma through to the BEd academic music course and the later BA music course. However, this particular approach is not in accordance with composer and theorist Arnold Schoenberg's ideas of teaching harmony: 'Harmonizing given melodies is in contradiction to the process of composition; a composer invents melody and harmony simultaneously'. [11] Nevertheless, the study of Bach's own harmonizations of chorale melodies is undoubtedly a **fundamental method of learning**, not just **of** functional harmony including modulations, but also **of** voice leading and the relationship between voices. The principles applied by Bach, especially when demonstrated in conjunction with the performance of examples (sung by the group or played at the keyboard by the lecturer) are transferable to other styles right up to contemporary idioms. In fact Schoenberg also states that 'One who cannot control four parts with a certain ability, either has not worked seriously or is entirely untalented and should give up music at once!'[12]

As the BA music course had more available credits than that of the BEd, the study of orchestration became an additional component of BA musical techniques modules. Up to 1999 orchestration was a year-long course with an examination paper at the end of the year. The examination was subsequently abolished in favour of an extended piece of coursework. In the first year, this entailed an arrangement of an existing short piano piece for strings; the addition of woodwind in second year and brass in third year ensured an incremental and cumulative building of skills in this area.

The teaching and learning of musical techniques at the College gave students a grounding in harmony and counterpoint (as well as orchestration for BA students) not only providing them with important skills for composing, arranging and analysing music, but also enhancing their problem-solving skills more generally.

Original composition at undergraduate level

---

[11] A. Schoenberg, *Structural Functions in Harmony*, revised edition (New York: W. W. Norton & Co. Inc., 1969) p. xv.
[12] Ibid. p. xvi.

Composition that explored contemporary and experimental styles was added to the BA music course in 2000. Taking place in the second semester of each year, this replaced a further component in orchestration, which hitherto had been a year-long module. One of the difficulties in teaching this type of composition was that there was no longer a 'common practice'. Various techniques were demonstrated including twelve-tone system, extended instrumental techniques and minimalist processes, using examples by the best-known exponents. As well as demonstrating some basic techniques, structured improvisation was encouraged: two or three of the lectures set certain parameters either for groups or the whole class to explore. An example of this was where a certain structure was given, for instance a thirty-second time-frame; students were then asked, using whatever instruments were available including voices, to play just once within this time. The response was mostly to play immediately for a couple of seconds leaving the remaining twenty-eight seconds as silence. Exploring this a second time, the students were more aware of the time span and also understood that the instruction to 'play once' did not necessarily mean just sounding one note. On a third exploration the students were asked to listen to material that the others played/sang and to respond to this in some way. Essentially, this activity was a derivation of John Cage's duration structures, which can be undertaken by any grouping from the least to the most experienced musicians. It explores structure, an awareness of real time, and the relationship between ideas and people that make up a musical performance. As the starting point is silence, any musical elements may be inserted.

However, while I often used the kind of activity above as a stimulus and a focusing exercise, the main focus was on the students producing individual, independent work: they selected the material and made the decisions as to what to do with that material. Put another way, 'Take an object/Do something to it/Do something else to it. [Repeat.]', as the celebrated artist Jasper Johns wrote in one of his sketchbooks.[13] Composition in this manner is constantly 'in progress' and may be modified over time as opposed to a weekly harmony or counterpoint exercise, which may simply contain obvious errors and so be deemed to be 'incorrect'. The processes involved in the teaching and learning of individual composition (as opposed to historical techniques) falls in line with the description of creativity as outlined by Ken Robinson: it involves the need to play, to take risks and also to apply critical judgment. In relation to originality, Robinson also states that 'if you're

---

[13] J. Johns, 'Take an object', The Museum of Modern Art [MoMA], https://www.moma.org/calendar/exhibitions/1549 [accessed 2 July 2018].

not prepared to be wrong, it's unlikely that you will come up with anything original'.[14]

One of the problems which arises in providing a variety of styles for demonstration in a group situation within a single semester is the difficulty of enabling students to achieve a high level of skills in any one style. Nevertheless, at least by providing a limited but varied palette, the students' vocabulary is enriched and the 'making-it-out-of-your-head' approach (that is, without putting something there first) is hopefully avoided. At postgraduate level and in conservatoire contexts, composition is generally taught on a one-to-one basis, so that content and examples are chosen with an individual in mind.

In working on their individual compositions, **BA students at St Patrick's College** were encouraged to use improvisation as a basis for gleaning musical ideas, thus avoiding the problem of the blank manuscript page and losing immediacy in the time it takes to write in standard notation. The use of recording or of graphic notation to 'grab' an idea immediately was also encouraged, as was the use of sequencing software on a computer. It is interesting to note that several students who were excellent at handling traditional techniques had problems with a more 'free' approach whereas the opposite sometimes came about - that is, students who were not *au fait* with standard techniques revelled in the creative process and produced original pieces of good quality. As with all tasks, the greater the freedom, the more daunting it becomes. Even for the most experienced composer some limitations, if not imposed from outside, need to be self-imposed. These limitations may be in relation to any or all the musical elements: time, duration, pitch, dynamics and so on.

In the first year of the BA music course, students were required to produce very short pieces based on specific techniques such as irregular metre or quartal harmony.[15] A short duo of approximately three minutes duration using contemporary musical techniques was the requirement for assessment for second years, while a three-minute trio or work for solo piano was required in the third year. It was suggested to students, depending on the styles in which they showed interest, that they look at particular exemplars – scores and recordings by well-known composers who worked with a sympathetic aesthetic. They were then encouraged to state an idea, be it rhythmic, melodic, or even graphic, perhaps based on a particular idiom for which they had a

---

[14] K. Robinson, *Out of Our Minds: Learning to be Creative*, (UK: Capstone Publishing, 2001), pp. 72-73.
[15] Chords built from the interval of a fourth as opposed to the more traditional chord formation, which is by superimposed thirds.

preference, and then develop that along the lines of Jasper John's statement above.

Composition workshops
Between 2000 and 2008 workshops were arranged in order to play BA students' original compositions. Head of Music Marion Doherty frequently played piano parts while other musicians, some of whom gave instrumental tuition to students at the College, were brought in to read the scores. Among the musicians involved were Anne O'Briain (flute), the Prey Trio, Petra Lexova and Antonin Prihoda (violins), and Colman Pearce (piano). [16]

In 2005 a conference titled 'Teaching the Unteachable, the Role of Composition in Music Education' was instigated by composer Eric Sweeney, Head of Music at Waterford Institute of Technology. This was held as part of Waterford New Music Week in association with the Council of Heads of Music in Higher Education (CHMHE). [17] An ensuing publication, *Teaching the Unteachable, Proceedings of the Symposium on Composing in Higher Education* edited by Patricia Flynn of St Patrick's College Music Department, was later published in 2007.[18] Arising out of this conference CHMHE set up an Intervarsity Composition Workshop. It was envisaged that the workshop would become an annual event hosted in rotation by different university music departments.

The first CHMHE Intervarsity Composition Workshop took place on 15 April 2008 at St Patrick's College with one student nominated by each of the following third-level institutions: DIT Conservatory of Music and Drama, Dundalk Institute of Technology, NUI Maynooth, Queen's University Belfast, Royal Irish Academy of Music, St Patrick's College Drumcondra and Waterford Institute of Technology. Compositions of three minutes duration were required for solo, duo or trio. Once again, professional performers were engaged, on this occasion Conor Shiel (clarinet), Mary McCague (piano), Erika Horsley (viola) and Martin Johnson (cello). These were the instrumental resources stipulated in advance, along with the possibility of an electro-acoustic element. Composer, Kevin Volans was invited to lead the

---

[16] Prey Trio: Susan Doyle (flute), Síle Daly (oboe), Deirdre O'Leary (clarinet).
[17] Founded in 1993, CHMHE's membership is made up of universities, colleges and conservatoires that offer music programmes in higher education in the Republic of Ireland and Northern Ireland. 'StudyMusicIreland', www.studymusicireland.ie/about_CHMHE.html [accessed 17 July 2018].
[18] P. Flynn (ed.), *Teaching the Unteachable*, (Waterford: Orpheus Press, 2007).

workshop performance, which he did with insightful and positive feedback throughout.

Although the CHMHE Intervarsity Composition Workshop failed to materialize into an annual event as first envisaged, from 2013 it resumed as part of the Fidelio Trio residency at the College. A call for scores for the last undergraduate composition workshop which took place on 11 April 2015 sought:

> ... submissions from undergraduate composers for scores written for piano trio (violin, cello and piano) with or without an electronic component. Duos from any of the above may also be considered. Only one work per College/ University will be selected for workshop performances ...

It was also required that the pieces should be no longer than five minutes (a movement or section of a longer work was acceptable) and that the student composer be present at the forum. In addition to the CHMHE event, the Fidelio Trio gave workshop performances of pieces by undergraduate second and third year BA students at St Patrick's College and also assisted in the composition sessions with music education students (discussed in more detail below).

In 2014 and again in 2015 the music department hosted an international composition forum for postgraduate composition students and early career composers; these were also facilitated through the Fidelio Trio Residency. The call for scores in both years received a tremendous response, with selections made by the Trio for pieces to be given a workshop reading. Only five or six scores were selected on each occasion, allowing adequate time for the rehearsal of, and commentary on, each piece. As facilitator of the forums, I witnessed much stimulating discussion on the compositions and performances, which offered a range of different styles using varied contemporary techniques. The composers came from Ireland, UK, Greece, US, South Africa and Japan and members of the Trio themselves led the conversations, offering positive criticism and suggestions for even clearer ways of communicating the composers' intentions.

Curriculum Music

Every student on the BEd programme, including those taking academic music, was required to study the component associated with practical skills of teaching music in the primary school classroom. The introduction of the new Primary School Curriculum in 1999 saw 'composing' placed as an equal strand alongside 'performing' and 'listening and responding'.[19] Students taking BEd, Postgraduate Diploma in Education and later, Professional Masters in Education programmes were introduced to musical composition, quite often for the first time; they were also provided with the ideas and methods to help children create their own music in the classroom. As coordinator of curriculum music, Patricia Flynn created an imaginative assignment for this component whereby students composed music in small groups using classroom percussion instruments; these could be combined with voices or other instruments which the students already played - tin whistle, flute, guitar and piano being the most common.

The students were encouraged to explore musical elements creating combinations of sounds and textures and were also required to make a graphic score of their piece. The stimulation might be in the form of a picture, a story, a poem or simply arise out of a musical idea. Each individual also wrote a rationale at the end of the process. Having read many of these, a common experience was that the students found the task daunting at first and then came to enjoy the process and found it a very valuable learning experience, often unleashing a creativity in music that they had not been previously aware was possible. A majority also stated that they would mirror the experience in a classroom situation.

Postgraduate studies at St Patrick's College on this aspect of the primary music curriculum included a number of MEd dissertations: 'The composing process in classroom music: an investigation into its theory and practice' (2004) by Yvonne Higgins, and 'Symbolising sound: an investigation into musical understandings revealed through visual representations of music at primary level' (2006) by Ailbhe Kenny. Both students were supervised by Patricia Flynn and were also alumni of the BEd programme of St Patrick's College. Regina Murphy, who was director of in-service education and also taught on the MEd programme, supervised the following two dissertations: 'A "write an opera" project in a school for children with physical and learning disabilities' (2000) by Siobhán Keane, and 'Scherzando: how primary teachers can be supported to engage in composing, particularly in the early years' (2012) by Sinéad Gaskin-O'Connell. The work of these four authors produced innovative research and findings in relation to different aspects of children's compositions and to the teaching of this strand as part of the revised Primary Curriculum (1999).

---

[19] NCCA, *Primary School Curriculum, Arts Education: Music.*

Postgraduate composition

The Music Department counted two composer members of Aosdána among its staff, John Buckley and Rhona Clarke.[20] Buckley is a former undergraduate student of St Patrick's College. Graduating in 1971 with a National Teacher Diploma, he later achieved an MA and also a PhD and DMus from the National University of Ireland. After studying under Seán Hayes at the College, Buckley subsequently studied with composers A. J. Potter and later James Wilson at the Royal Irish Academy of Music and with Alun Hoddinott in Cardiff. Other composers who are postgraduate alumni include Kevin O'Connell (PhD, 2007) and Colman Pearce (PhD, 2009), both of whom achieved their doctoral awards under the supervision of John Buckley.[21]

Sandie Purcell graduated in 2006 and Eoin Mulvaney in 2008, both with an MA by research in composition; they were supervised respectively by John Buckley and Rhona Clarke. In his second year as a research student, Eoin Mulvany was awarded the Jerome Hynes Young Composers Competition[22] (2006) and his work *PX2* for flute and piano was premiered at the National Concert Hall as part of its 'Rising Star' series.[23] In the case both of PhD and MA by research, a varied portfolio of original work was presented, comprising solo and chamber music with at least one orchestral work or work for large forces and a substantial analytical commentary. A number of students compiled portfolios of compositions, also with commentaries, as part of the taught MA in Humanities (Music). This fulfilled the dissertation element for the second year of this part-time course.

From its inception, the taught MA included a composition component in the module taught jointly by John Buckley and the author, namely, 'Music and Modernity'. The techniques here required students to write short pieces (1-2 minutes) based on major styles of the twentieth century such as serialism, minimalism, indeterminacy and experimental music. An instance of how this was taught might be taken from my own section of the module, which was restricted to the

---

[20] Aosdána is an Irish affiliation of creative artists engaged in literature, music visual arts, architecture and choreography.

[21] Both Kevin O'Connell and Colman Pearce are composer members of Aosdána.

[22] The competition is named in memory of the former Chief Executive of Wexford Festival Opera and former Deputy Chair of the Arts Council, Jerome Hynes (1959-2005). Open to composers under the age of 30, the award has been promoted by the National Concert Hall since 2006 and gives the winning composer an opportunity to collaborate with professional musicians on a commission for a chamber ensemble.

[23] *St Patrick's College Annual Report 2006-2007*, p. 28, SPCA, A/1/7.3.

American experimentalists. One of the lecture topics concerned Charles Ives's use of musical borrowings and a number of songs and instrumental works were explored during a three-hour lecture. Students were then asked to find existing musical material of any genre, and develop this, adding elements of their own, into a cohesive short piece. The results yielded a multiplicity of styles depending on the material chosen, which varied from 'Happy Birthday' to an Irish jig or borrowing from the standard classical repertoire. Another example of the integration of techniques on the MA was the inclusion of arrangements of folk songs for choir as an applied technique for the module 'Music and National Identity'. As a lecturer for this element, I encouraged the use of early twentieth-century harmony found in Bartók and Kodály taking the harmonic components from that suggested in the melodic lines. The use of imitative counterpoint and descant was also demonstrated.

Technology
Coinciding with the introduction of the BA in 1994, an electronic music studio was set up under the supervision of Seán Mac Liam. The idea was to provide notation and basic sequencing software to enable students to input and play back their work. It was primarily intended that tuition in this area would give BA students a dimension in addition to the modules they shared with the BEd students. The studio was upgraded in 2003 under Mac Liam while acting Head of Music and another refurbishment took place in 2015 under John O'Flynn. Eight, and later ten Apple Macs with Sibelius and ProTools software programmes facilitated students' exercises in techniques, arrangements for orchestra and original compositions. From 2003 tutorials were timetabled in order to provide students with a basis from which to explore the software.

During the two years 2004-2006, students had the option of taking harmony and counterpoint examination papers in the music studio, that is, they could provide their answers using music notation software. Despite some concerns that these students might have an advantage by being able to play the answer back, this was not shown to be the case in the results that ensued; also, very few students took this option and as a result it was subsequently abandoned. Under a different initiative, Mac Liam designed a module for the MEd programme which focused mainly on the use of music technology in education, with software packages suitable for the teaching and learning of notation, aural training and elementary harmony.

The MA also provided lectures involving technology, both for notation and sequencing purposes; this was not only to serve the composition components, but also to allow students to provide musical illustration for essays and dissertations.[24] Surprisingly perhaps, none of the students on the MA or PhD programmes pursued electro-acoustic composition. However, for the music technology element of the taught MA programme in 2014, which was delivered by Enda Bates, students produced short pieces demonstrating a command of sequencing software.[25] Similarly, a small number of BEd students who had elected to take the music specialism in their final year also chose to make an electro-acoustic piece.

Two theses based on technology's usefulness in the area of composition emerged at the College, with both of these supervised by Seán Mac Liam: Daniel Walsh's work leading to an MA by research titled 'The design and evaluation of prototype software for teaching and learning chord progression in music' (2004), and Amanda Geary's dissertation for the taught MA, 'Computer aided teaching and learning: a study of the use of music technology in melodic composition' (2005). Both of these research projects approached technology from the point of view of the music educator, finding and inventing tools for the teaching and learning of defined aspects of composition.

Premiere performances, commissions, and visiting composers

The earliest documented world premiere performed at St Patrick's College was a large-scale work by the eminent Irish composer A. J. Potter on 15 March 1966 (also discussed in Chapters One, Two and Six).[26] The work, *Lúireach Phádraigh* [St Patrick's Breastplate] is scored for male choir and symphony orchestra. Performers are cited on the website of the Contemporary Music Centre (CMC) as 'unnamed chorus', with the RTÉ Symphony Orchestra conducted by Tibor Paul.[27] In fact, the piece was commissioned by Raidió Éireann for the opening

---

[24] Sequencing software: software that can record, edit and play back music. It is not primarily used for notation.
[25] Enda Bates is an Irish composer; he is currently assistant professor and deputy director of the Music and Media Technologies programme in Trinity College Dublin.
[26] A. J. Potter, The Contemporary Music Centre, https://www.cmc.ie/music/luireach-phadraigh [accessed 26 June 2018].
[27] Tibor Paul (1909 – 1973) was a Hungarian-Australian conductor who was principal conductor of the RÉ (from 1966 RTÉ) Symphony Orchestra (1961 to 1967) and was also director of Music for that organization (1962-1967). Michael Bosworth, 'Paul, Tibor', in *Australian Dictionary of Biography,* Australian National University, http://adb.anu.edu.au/biography/paul-tibor-11352/text20277, published first in hard copy (2000) [accessed 20 January 2019].

of the newly built auditorium in St Patrick's College and composed for the College choir which was directed by Seán Hayes. A. J. Potter's personal archives show that there had been correspondence between Gerard Victory (deputy director of music at Raidió Éireann) and the composer, outlining the terms of the commission that included a stipulation that the text, which was to be in Irish, 'should be arranged through Fr. Cregan and Mr. Hayes' in advance. The latter refers to the then President of the College and the Head of Music respectively. The handwritten manuscript shows a celebratory, processional style with a three-part texture for the choir.[28]

The commissioning of A. J. Potter's *Lúireach Phádraigh* was exceptional for its time, and it was not until the early twenty-first century that the work of living composers would again feature in the activities of the College (although as John Buckley observes in Chapter Two, a substantial range of composition premieres and other new music performances were staged by external groups at the College Auditorium over this period). The third series of the College's biennial Seamus Heaney Lectures in 2004-2005 focused on the creative imagination, and one of the lectures was given by the renowned German composer Peter Michael Hamel, with the title 'Music Improvisation: Animation for a Flash of Inspiration'.[29] This lecture is included in the volume of essays *The Fire i' the Flint,* but as its editor Mary Shine Thompson points out: 'It is not possible to reproduce *on paper* the sensory – and intellectual– experience that Peter Hamel created'.[30] His lecture was a creative work in itself and included extemporization, both sung (including traditional Afghan and Indian Classical vocal material) and on piano, as he illuminated his own approach to and ideas about musical composition.

While the lunchtime concerts had always given a platform to the performance of new music, the arrival of the Fidelio Trio as musicians-in-residence enhanced this greatly.[31] During this time St Patrick's College hosted a number of significant premieres and workshops by composers including those of notable international standing.

The world premiere of Fergus Johnston's *Piano Trio*, commissioned by the Fidelio Trio and with funds from The Arts Council/An

---

[28] The Potter Archive, courtesy of Sarah Burn.
[29] See Chapter Eight for a discussion on the role of music throughout The Seamus Heaney Lecture Series.
[30] M. Shine Thompson, (ed.), *The Fire i' the Flint, Essays on the Creative Imagination*, (Dublin: Four Courts Press, 2009), p 3.
[31] For further information on the lunchtime concerts, see Chapter Two and Appendix B.

Chomhairle Ealaíon, was performed in the Mahony Hall at the Helix on 6 March 2013.[32] Another Fidelio Trio commission with Arts Council funding resulted in John Buckley's *Piano Trio* which received its world premiere on 3 November 2013 at the First Fidelio Trio Winter Chamber Music Festival in Belvedere House, St Patrick's College. On 3 February 2014 Joe Cutler, Head of Composition at Royal Birmingham Conservatoire gave an illustrated talk on his work. Five different pieces by Cutler were played by the Fidelio Trio and discussed with an audience comprising undergraduate music students.

MIMIK by the Mexican composer Arturo Fuentes was given its world premiere in the auditorium of St Patrick's College by the artists-in-residence on 9 July 2014, and two further world premieres were performed later that year at the Second Fidelio Trio Winter Chamber Music Festival. First heard on 5 December was Gerald Barry's *Fanfare* for solo oboe, played by the renowned British oboist Nicholas Daniel. Saoí of Aosdána, Seóirse Bodley was present on 7 December to hear the world premiere of his piano trio *Dancing in Daylight* at the same festival, and the title of his work was later used as the name of the CD recorded on the Métier label to document the residency of the Fidelio Trio.[33] With the subtitle *Contemporary Piano Trios from Ireland,* this CD included works by Seóirse Bodley, John Buckley, Fergus Johnston and *Piano Trio No. 2* by Rhona Clarke. The CD is dedicated to Patricia Flynn who initiated and helped oversee the project; it was co-funded by St Patrick's College Research Committee and by the DCU President's fund.

On 25 February 2015, eminent British composer Judith Weir, CBE visited the College for the Irish premiere of her *Piano Trio Two* (2004). Commissioned for the 2004 Spitalfields Festival, it was first performed by the Florestan Trio and had been recorded on CD (Delphian Records) by the Fidelio Trio. A pre-concert interview chaired by John Buckley, featured in-depth discussions with Weir about her extensive musical output and her role as Master of the Queen's Music. This title and tradition has been handed down since the time of Charles I, and the role includes advising the British sovereign on musical matters as well as composing for important ceremonial occasions.

---

[32] The event was organized by the music department of St Patrick's College.
[33] 'Saoí' is an honour bestowed by Aosdána 'for singular and sustained distinction in the arts'. Only seven members of Aosdána may hold this title at any one time. Former holders of the title include Samuel Beckett, Brian Friel, Seamus Heaney, Patrick Scott and Anthony Cronin.

Figure 4.1: John Buckley with Judith Weir (CBE), Master of the Queen's Music, 25 February 2015. Photograph by Paul Murphy

Also on the programme that evening was Buckley's *Piano Trio* from 2013. Both Weir's and Buckley's works are in themselves without title, but have titles for each of their three movements. Weir's trio centres on phrases from three Zen stories—'How Grass and Trees Become Enlightened'; 'Your Light May go Out'; 'Open your own Treasure House'—short anecdotes 'which resonate in the memory but do not reveal their secrets easily'.[34] For the movements of his piano trio, Buckley draws on imagery, both aural and visual, from mechanical devices: 'Shadows and Echoes'; 'Kaleidoscope'; 'Music Box'.[35]

Dorothy Ker, a UK-based New Zealand composer, spoke about her recent works in discussion and demonstration with the Fidelio Trio on 15 April 2015. Ker's talk took place immediately after a lunchtime concert featuring the world premiere of her piece *Onaia* at St Patrick's College and it illuminated some of the very unusual and subtle writing in that piece. Earlier that year, on the 21 January, the artists-in-

---

[34] Judith Weir, *Piano Trio Two*, programme note found on: http://www.musicsalesclassical.com/composer/work/14505 [accessed 2 July 2018].
[35] S. Bodley, J. Buckley, et al., *Dancing in Daylight: Contemporary Piano Trios from Ireland,* CD (UK: Métier 2015).

residence had given the first Irish performances of Benedict Schlepper-Connolly's *Ekstase II* and Mark Bowden's *Airs No Oceans Keep*. At the Third Fidelio Trio Winter Chamber Music Festival held from 4-6 December 2015, the Trio gave the Irish premieres of Sally Beamish's arrangement of Debussy's *La Mer* (for piano trio) and *Nocturnal after Benjamin Britten* by Benjamin Dwyer. The Trio had first performed the latter work in King's Place London in October of that year.

World premiere performances of several compositions by John Buckley were programmed during the years of the College lunchtime series. These included three works for solo flute performed by William Dowdall in separate programmes: *Winter Echoes* and *Sea Echoes* (flute with glissando head joint) in 2008, and *Les oiseaux rêvent dans les arbres* in 2011. *Dialogue* for solo cello was performed by Clíodhna Ní Aodáin in 2010 and *Fantasia and Variations* for flute ensemble performed by Flute Éire, directed by Julie Maisel, in 2012. Even prior to the series, in 1986 Gillian Smith gave the premiere performance of the piano version of Buckley's *And Wake the Purple Year;* the piece had been composed originally for harpsichord.

The third 'Women and Music in Ireland Conference' (10 May 2014), organized jointly by Jennifer Madsen O'Connor and the author, included a varied programme of talks and discussions on the subject of women in music in Ireland. Included in the schedule were talks on Irish composers Ina Boyle, Rhoda Coghill, and Joan Trimble. Nicola LeFanu, Professor Emeritus University of York, was present at the conference's lunchtime concert by the Fidelio Trio, which included her single movement *Piano Trio*. LeFanu was invited to give the keynote address at the Conference. Entitled 'Women and Composition: Fifty Years of Progress?' the speech outlined the historic neglect of music composed by women and the lack of recognition of some outstanding figures such as Ina Boyle (1889-1967), whose work was virtually unperformed during her lifetime. LeFanu also mentioned the progress that has been made by contributions of women such as composer Jane O'Leary:

> Through founding and directing an ensemble that has always been even-handed in its choice of composers, Jane and Concorde [36] have helped develop the careers of so many of Ireland's composers, as well as introducing work from overseas to Irish audiences.[37]

---

[36] Concorde is an ensemble founded and directed by Jane O'Leary devoted to the performance of contemporary music.

[37] Nicola LeFanu's keynote was kindly provided by the speaker in an email on 2 July 2018.

A panel discussion was held at the conference entitled 'Women as musicians and composers in Ireland and abroad: do the labels matter?' The panel included LeFanu and Patricia Flynn, the latter this time in her role as Chair of the Contemporary Music Centre, the body which represents and promotes Irish composers.

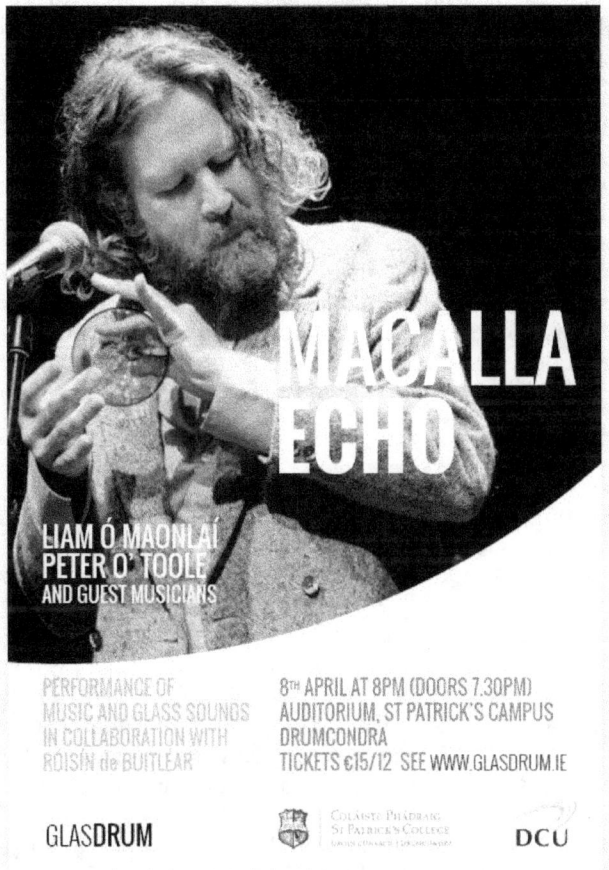

Figure 4.2: Poster for Macalla/Echo, 2016 with Liam Ó Maonlaí on 'Ortha' by Róisín de Buitléar. Photograph by Phillip Lauterbach

The final musical premiere before incorporation into DCU was at an event programmed under the auspices of GlasDrum, an organization set up to programme high quality arts and cultural experiences for the communities of Glasnevin, Drumcondra and beyond (see Chapter

Nine). GlasDrum members included John O'Flynn and Patricia Flynn from the music department, the college librarian, Orla Nic Aodha and art education lecturer Andrea Cleary. The event, titled 'macalla/echo' was held in the auditorium on 8 April 2016, and featured the Dublin premiere of a live collaboration between Liam Ó Maonlaí and his fellow Hothouse Flowers musician Peter O'Toole as they improvised on glass instruments made by Irish artist Róisín de Buitléar. [38]

Although the concern here has been to mention premieres within the history of the College, there were many other performances of works by living composers, both Irish and international, especially in recent decades. These included performances by students and amateur choirs as well as musicians working at the highest professional level. This practice by St Patrick's College of commissioning and performing new works has continued after incorporation, in particular for the annual Fidelio Trio Winter Chamber Music Festival. The university as patron is important in its own right, but the commissioning and performances of work by living composers also demonstrates to students that the discipline of musical composition is real, is a career option and is not just a theoretic practice. It continues to be the case that role models are at hand, both male and female, as exemplars of the discipline and it is hoped that this may continue well into the future of DCU.

Bibliography

Bosworth, Michael, 'Paul, Tibor', *Australian Dictionary of Biography*, http://adb.anu.edu.au/biography/paul-tibor-11352/text20277 [accessed 20 January 2019].

Flynn, Patricia (ed.), *Teaching the Unteachable: The Role of Composition in Music Education* (Conference Proceedings), (Waterford: Orpheus Press, 2007).

Irish National Teachers' Organisation, 'INTO Consultative Conference on Education, Kilkenny 16-17 November 1990, Pre-service Education: A Report by the Education Committee', (Dublin: INTO, 1990).

Johns, Jasper, 'Take an object', The Museum of Modern Art [MoMA], https://www.moma.org/calendar/exhibitions/1549 [accessed 2 July 2018].

---

[38] Rock band established in Dublin c. 1986; see M. Ní Fhuartháin, 'Hothouse Flowers', in H. White and B. Boydell (eds.), *The Encyclopaedia of Music in Ireland*, Volume I, (Dublin: UCD Press, 2013), p. 500.

National Council for Curriculum and Assessment, *Primary School Curriculum, Arts Education: Music*, (Dublin: Stationery Office, 1999).

National University of Ireland, *Calendar, 1965*, (Dublin: NUI).

Ní Fhuartháin, Méabh, 'Hothouse Flowers', in H. White and B. Boydell (eds.), *The Encyclopaedia of Music in Ireland*, Volume I, (Dublin: UCD Press, 2013), p. 500.

Robinson, Ken, *Out of Our Minds: Learning to be Creative*, (UK: Capstone Publishing, 2001).

Schoenberg, Arnold, *Structural Functions in Harmony*, revised edition, (New York: W. W. Norton & Co. Inc., 1969).

Shine Thompson, Mary (ed.), *The Fire i' the Flint: Essays on the Creative Imagination*, (Dublin: Four Courts Press, 2009).

St Patrick's College Annual Report 2006-2007, (Dublin: St Patrick's College, 2007).

Newspapers and periodicals
The Journal of Music

Archives
Contemporary Music Centre
Fidelio Trio Residency Archive
The Potter Archive
St Patrick's College Archive

Discography
Bodley, S., Buckley, J., Clarke, R., Johnston F., *Dancing in Daylight: Contemporary Piano Trios from Ireland,* CD (UK: Métier, MSV 28556,2015).

Chapter Five: 'All are welcome': Irish traditional music at St Patrick's College

Teresa O'Donnell

Irish traditional music has been interwoven into the cultural, social and academic fabric of St Patrick's College, Drumcondra from its establishment in 1875. Students, alumni and lecturers (from various academic departments) have celebrated Irish traditional music through formal and informal methods of transmission in campus life, the classroom environment and on national and international platforms. In this chapter, the term Irish traditional music is employed, in broad terms, to describe instrumental music and song of Ireland, but not solely based on the oral-tradition. This chapter focuses on three main areas: the first section discusses the collections of English and Irish language songs by Peter Goodman, lecturer in music and An tAthair Pádraig Breathnach housed in the Cregan library and which contributed to a national musical canon and highlighted the role of music in forging an Irish identity prior to independence. Music, together with the Irish language and Gaelic sports, served to cement an Irish identity in the pre and post-independence period. The second section considers graduates such as Seán Ó Siocháin, Liam Devally and Seán Ó Sé, who reflect this triduum of interest in Irish music, language and sport and have enriched contemporary Irish culture and society. In the final section, I explore various aspects of the Irish traditional music course for BEd and later BA students, including leading traditional music practitioners, such as Fintan Vallely and Matt Cranitch, who brought the living tradition into the lecture theatre.

The subtitle of this chapter, 'All are welcome', is taken from a short piece written by the committee of a newly formed traditional music society, Comhaltas Ceoltóirí Éireann (CCÉ) Coláiste Phádraig, in the 1978/9 Students' Handbook of St Patrick's College of Education Students' Union.[1] The fledgling society encouraged musicians, singers, dancers and non-musicians alike to join the society and attend events. CCÉ Coláiste Phádraig extended a particular welcome to students in their first year of college. This sense of welcome, of belonging to a group and connecting with others in the college, particularly in a non-structured social setting, captures the sense of community in which

---

[1] 'Comhaltas Ceoltóirí Éireann Coláiste Phádraig', *Students' Handbook of St Patrick's College of Education Students' Union* (1978/9), p. 22, C/21/viii, St Patrick's College Archive.

Irish traditional music has thrived in St Patrick's College for over 140 years. Music educator Marie McCarthy noted that, 'since participation in music is a maker and a marker of identity' and that educational and musical institutions are 'centres of cultural power', they draw together 'musical traditions of the past; they energize the present by reinventing and reincorporating tradition and in the process shape the future of individual lives, communities, and the cultural life of the nation'.[2] The current condition of traditional music at St Patrick's College is an outcome of the process of 'passing on' or reinvention navigated through a complicated web of ideological and cultural circumstances.

Cultural activism

Attitudes to culture, identity and, in particular, music in the twentieth century were shaped profoundly by the formation of various cultural nationalist movements in the closing decades of the nineteenth century.[3] Alarmed by the decline in Irish customs and with the aspirations of Irish self-government becoming a reality, Irish cultural endeavour embraced a renewal of nationalist fervour. This period witnessed the emergence of new organizations and doctrines articulated in the form of self-help movements. Each movement made a significant and distinctive contribution to fostering a new, shared identity for Irish people emphasising their membership of a noble Gaelic nation, albeit an idealized one.[4] Douglas Hyde's seminal paper, 'The Necessity for De-Anglicising Ireland' (1892), encouraged Irish people not to be influenced by English literature, music, games and fashions but, instead, 'to develop upon Irish lines' and to substitute Irish for every form of English culture.[5] He argued that anglicization had impinged on

---

[2] M. McCarthy, *Passing it On: The Transmission of Music in Irish Culture*, (Cork: Cork University Press, 1999), p. 5.

[3] The co-operation of disparate groupings, such as the Gaelic Athletic Association (1884), the Co-Operative Movement (1889), the Gaelic League (1893), Feis Ceoil (1897), An t-Oireachtas (1897) and the Irish Literary Theatre (1899) was essential in the revival and preservation of Irish sports, language, folklore and customs.

[4] The term 'self help movement' is used to describe cultural movements of this period such as the Gaelic League, the co-operative movement, etc. (as mentioned) by P. J. Mathews in *Revival: The Abbey Theatre, Sinn Féin, the Gaelic League and the Co-operative Movement* (Cork: Cork University Press, 2003).

[5] D. Hyde, 'The Necessity for De-Anglicising Ireland (1892),' quoted in B. Ó Conaire, ed., *Douglas Hyde: Language, Lore and Lyrics* (Dublin: Irish

music and noted that, if 'Ireland loses her music, she loses, what is, after the Gaelic language and literature, her most valuable and most characteristic expression.'[6] Music became increasingly politicized; it blossomed into a cherished emblem of nationalism, cultural protectionism intensified and the schism between art music and the traditional repertory was magnified.[7] As Harry White succinctly articulated, music travelled 'a clear path from antiquarian zeal, through Romantic appropriation and political association, to full-blown nationalist ideology'.[8]

The revival of Ireland's rich musical heritage, musical arrangements of the traditional repertory and the singing of Irish language songs became the accepted form of an identifiably Irish musical identity. National school teachers were vital in the transmission of Ireland's cultural heritage and various attempts were made to agitate for the inclusion of Irish music on the curriculum of the National School System. The teaching of Irish music was welcomed by the teaching profession, however, teachers encountered a number of challenges, namely the dearth of suitable repertoire and a lack of proficiency in the Irish language.[9] Peter Goodman, lecturer in music at St Patrick's from 1883 to 1892, addressed the absence of Irish music in national schools in his capacity as Inspector of Musical Instruction for the Board of National Education from 1892, and in the publication of two songbooks for use in national schools discussed below. Goodman believed it was the responsibility of the schools and training colleges to stimulate a music revival:

> An entire nation has to be made once more musical. The lost character of the Land of Song has to be re-established. Such is the work before the school teachers of Ireland. To prepare them for it must be the duty of the training colleges. Every school

---

Academic Press, 1986), p. 167. This speech was delivered to the National Literary Society in Dublin on 25 November 1892.

[6] Ibid.

[7] H. White, 'Nationalism, Colonialism and the Cultural Stasis of Music in Ireland,' in *Musical Constructions of Nationalism,* eds. Harry White and Michael Murphy (Cork: Cork University Press 2001), p. 266.

[8] Ibid.

[9] A Bilingual Programme was introduced in 1904 for schools in Gaeltacht areas (where the Irish language was spoken) and part-Gaeltacht areas where teachers were proficient Irish language speakers.

must be made to supply a choir, and if only the teacher be sufficiently competent, an excellent choir.[10]

Figure 5: Cover of *The Irish Minstrel*, No. 1.

Goodman drew from several collections of Irish airs by Thomas Moore, George Petrie, P.W. Joyce and F.W. Horncastle to produce three editions of *The Irish Minstrel: A collection of songs for use in Irish schools* Part 1 (1903), Part II (1904) and Part III (1906) which were sanctioned by the Commissioners of National Education. The first songbook contained a selection of thirty songs, including six Irish language songs. The front cover of both publications is noteworthy for its inclusion of an Irish harp, a large Celtic design decorative border and the bold statement, 'Go raibh Éire Ceolmhar Arís' [May Ireland be

---

[10] Peter Goodman, from 'The Report of the Board of National Education for the year 1896,' cited in *The Freeman's Journal*, 4 August 1897, p. 5.

musical again]. Part II was published in 1904 and featured 28 songs including, 'Dear Harp of my Country', 'Rich and Rare', 'Sweet Inisfallen', 'My Gentle Harp' and 'The Language of Éire' and Irish languages songs, 'Slán le Máigh' and 'An Abhainn Laoi'. Marie McCarthy acknowledged the importance of Goodman's publications, describing them as 'a symbol of official recognition of native Irish music in the curriculum of national schools'.[11]

Goodman's publications, together with numerous publications of Irish songs collected and edited by An tAthair Pádraig Breathnach (Fr. Patrick A. Walsh) (1848-1930), are available in the Cregan Library at St Patrick's. Though Breathnach was not attached to St Patrick's, the publications of both were useful teaching resources in the early twentieth century and marked the beginning of a boom in the publication of Irish song materials for schools. Breathnach's collections are the fruits of his travels to Irish speaking areas of the country where he transcribed the living tradition, acknowledged regional styles and captured the language as it was spoken. One of Breathnach's earliest collections, *Fuínn na Smól* (1900), consists of seven booklets of Irish language songs with tonic solfa notation suitable for children as well as adults, including, 'Éamonn an Chnuic', 'An Spailpín Fánach', 'An Dreoilín', 'Cill Chais' and 'Aillíliú na Gamhna'. In the foreword to the 1913 edition Breathnach thanked Áine Ní Raghallaigh for assisting him and 'rescuing from oblivion the lovely airs' in the book.[12] Author and Irish language activist, An tAthair Peadar Ó Laoghaire (1839-1920) predicted *Fuínn na Smól* 'will be real gold'.[13]

Like Breathnach, Ó Laoghaire was an advocate for the use of *caint na ndaoine* - the living speech of the people in printed matter, rather than a centralised Irish language as espoused by Eoin MacNeill and other members of the Gaelic League. Ó Laoghaire argued that the natural, everyday speech of the people captured the spirit of Irish people and the essence of the Irish language.[14]

---

[11] McCarthy, *Passing it On*, p. 89.
[12] P. Breathnach, 'Foreword,' *Fuínn na Smól*, (Dublin: Browne and Nolan, 1913), p. iii.
[13] 'Fuínn na Smól,' <https://www.ainm.ie/Tag.aspx?Type=opus&SubType=&Valyoo=Fu%C3%ADnn+na+sm%C3%B3l> [accessed 2 July 2018].
[14] This viewpoint is evidenced in Ó Laoghaire's publications, *Séadna* and *Mo Sgéal Féin* in which he brought the language of the people and the spirit of Irish nationalism into modern literature.

To our language through our music[15]

From the foundation of the Irish Free State in 1922, as for much of the previous century, nationalistic discourse pervaded every aspect of politics, society and culture. Music education was not a priority for the Irish Free State's Department of Education, other than through the singing of songs which could be used to integrate with other curricular areas, notably the Irish language. Official policy dictated that all songs be taught through the medium of Irish, particularly in the younger classes in national schools.[16] This policy was successful from 'an official standpoint' as teachers complied with official policy but many children had little grasp of the Irish language and the meaning of the songs. Further emphasis on this area of the curriculum resulted in neglect of other areas of the music curriculum.[17] Cognisant of the limited understanding of the Irish language in certain schools, Breathnach published *Songs of the Gael: A collection of Anglo-Irish songs and ballads: wedded to old traditional Irish airs* in 1915. The collection featured 200 songs in English and Irish and provided a more balanced approach to the teaching of Irish songs. Breathnach noted in the foreword of the first series of the 1922 revised and enlarged edition of the publication that the collection would provide '[p]romoters of Concerts and Feiseanna, teachers and pupils and singers alike...a cheap and accessible collection of songs that breathe the true spirit of Irish nationality and Irish home-life and Irish sentiment.'[18]

In 1924, Breathnach selected songs from his other publications, *Ceól ár Sínsear* (1913), *Songs of the Gael* (1915), *Ár gCeól Féinig* (1920), *Sídh-Cheól* (1924) to produce an impressive four-volume collection of songs, *Traditional Irish Airs*. The songs were arranged for two and three vocal parts with piano accompaniment by Annie Patterson (1868-1934), lecturer in Irish music at University College Cork.[19] As well as being a useful resource in the classroom, Breathnach's collections

---

[15] *The Teacher's Work*, 18 (November 1927), p. 119.

[16] National Programme Conference, *National Programme of Primary Instruction* (Dublin: Browne and Nolan, 1922); National Programme Conference, *Report and Programme of Second National Conference* (Dublin: The Stationery Office, 1926).

[17] McCarthy, *Passing It On*, p. 118.

[18] P. Breathnach, 'Foreword,' in *Songs of the Gael: A collection of Anglo-Irish songs and ballads: wedded to old traditional Irish Airs* (Dublin: Browne and Nolan, 1922), p. iii.

[19] Annie Patterson replaced Carl Hardebeck as lecturer in Irish music at University College Cork in 1924, a position she held until 1934.

became a rich source for arrangers; the Cregan library boasts a large collection of these arrangements based on songs from Breathnach's collections. For example, Liam de Noraidh (1888-1972) arranged 'Mar Mheath Uaim', 'An Dreóilín' from Breathnach's *Ceol Ár Sínsear* for three parts and Earnán de Regge arranged 'An Maidrín Ruadh' for three-part choir. An investigation of sheet music in the Cregan Library from the first half of the twentieth century reveals a wealth of choral and instrumental arrangements of Irish airs, original instrumental pieces and original English and Irish language songs by composers and arrangers such as Annie Patterson, Carl Hardebeck, John F. Larchet, Charlotte Milligan Fox, Éamonn Ó Gallchobhair, Liam de Noraidh, Fachtna Ó hAnnracháin and Seóirse Bodley.

The tradition of collecting Irish language songs was continued by Wexford graduate of St Patrick's College Stan Ó Briain (1906-67) who collected and edited four booklets of Irish language songs for school children, in unison and parts: *Ceol na Scol, Clasceadal na Scol* (1940), *Cór na Scol* and *Déanaimís Ceol* (1941), published by the Educational Company of Ireland. The first three booklets were produced in collaboration with Vincent O'Brien (director of music at Raidió Éireann, 1925-41) while the final booklet, with some 40 songs, was prepared by Ó Briain alone and required new lyrics or melodies at times. The songs which included 'Seoithín Seothó', 'Túirne Mháire' and 'Óró 'sé do Bheatha 'bhaile', were unaccompanied and presented in tonic solfa. Ó Briain was an accomplished tenor and pianist and studied voice in Basle, Switzerland. Nicholas Carolan described Ó Briain as belonging 'to a Gaelic League tradition of trained singers who sang in the Irish language'.[20] Ó Briain visited the Irish speaking area of An Rinn, Co. Waterford where he collected Irish language songs, including a version of ''Róisín Dubh' which Carolan opined to be closest to Seán Ó Riada's treatment of the air in the film score for George Morrison's 1959 film documentary, *Mise Éire*. Ó Briain taught at various schools in Offaly, Synge Street, Dublin and St Patrick's National School, Drumcondra and in 1962, pupils from St Patrick's National School, Drumcondra performed his operetta, *Amhrán na mBeach Fián* for national television. He devised mail-order music courses for teachers and taught music to teachers attending summer courses at Coláiste Chonnachta, Co Galway. Ó Briain held exhibitions of his paintings, wrote a music column for the *Irish School Weekly,* conducted choirs, adjudicated and sang regularly on Raidió Éireann in the 1930s and 1940s. He was a

---

[20] Information on Stan Ó Briain provided to the author by Nicholas Carolan, former director of the Irish Traditional Music Archive.

member of the Gaelic League, the Celtic Congress, the Irish America Society, president of the Irish-German Society and was involved in the resettlement of German children in Ireland after World War II.

Spotlight on graduates

Ó Briain, like many of his fellow graduates combined their educational and musical backgrounds with a lifelong dedication to cultural activism. In his 1975 booklet celebrating the centenary of St Patrick's College, the historian and former Head of the History Department, Tadhg Ó Ceallaigh wrote:

> Apart from the more obvious academic and educational fields, there are perhaps no areas of Irish cultural life which have not been influenced by St. Patrick's. For a hundred years the men who studied in the college have helped largely to keep alive the drama groups, the local historical societies, the sporting and athletic clubs and the Irish language societies throughout the country.[21]

I would now like to focus on four graduates of St Patrick's who have contributed significantly to Irish culture and society. All four have excelled in the field of music, appearing on radio and television broadcasts, and all promoted the use of the Irish language. Singer, broadcaster and Irish language activist, Seán Ó Síocháin (1914-97) was born Cill na Martra, Co. Cork and attended the preparatory college, Coláiste na Mumhan, Mallow before studying at St Patrick's College.[22] He taught at schools in Cork and Dublin, was a renowned singer of English and Irish language songs and ballads and performed regularly on radio programmes such as *Around the Fire*, *The Balladmakers*, *Saturday Night* and *Ireland is Singing*. Ó Siocháin toured extensively in the USA and sang with the Dublin Grand Opera Society. He was a member of Conradh na Gaeilge, Gael Linn and played football and hurling for various clubs, including Clann na nGael and St Patrick's Erin's Hope, as well as minor, junior and senior football for his home county. Ó Siocháin resigned his teaching post in 1946 to become assistant secretary of the Gaelic Athletic Association (GAA). He became

---

[21] T. Ó Ceallaigh, *Coláiste Phádraig St Patrick's College: Centenary Booklet 1875-1975* (Dublin: St Patrick's College, 1975), p. 29-30.
[22] In 1940, Coláiste na Mumhan moved from Mallow to Scoil Iosagáin in Ballyvourney, Co. Cork.

general secretary in 1964 (renamed director general in 1972) and remained in this position until his retirement in 1979.

The singer, RTÉ radio and television broadcaster, barrister and judge, Liam Devally (1933-2018) was born in Cahir, Co. Tipperary. Devally's family moved to Mullingar where he excelled as a boy soprano and won gold and silver medals at the Feis Ceoil in 1947 and 1954 respectively. He attended the preparatory college, Coláiste Einde, Galway where he became fluent in Irish and, after qualifying from St Patrick's, he began a career in broadcasting in 1953. As a member of the Irish Festival Singers, Devally toured the USA and Canada and appeared on the Ed Sullivan Show. He presented various music programmes for radio, including, *Morning Airs, Music for the Hour* which featured the RTÉ Light Orchestra and *Beirt Eile*, an Irish music and dance show which he co-hosted with Kathleen Watkins. Devally made a number of recordings, including *Songs of the Emerald Isle* which featured, 'Thugamar Féin an Samhradh Linn', 'The Croppy Boy', 'The Young May Moon' and 'The West's Awake'. He also featured on *Cabaret*, Gael Linn's 1960 LP recording with 'An Caipillín Bán'. Devally was called to the bar in 1974 and appointed to the Circuit Court in 1991. Renowned singer, Seán Ó Sé (b. 1936) entered St Patrick's College in 1953 having attended the preparatory college, Coláiste Íosagáin, Ballyvourney, Co. Cork. He auditioned for the college choir but Seán Hayes, Head of Music, refused him entry to the choir 'without giving any reason'.[23] Ó Sé explained that he was 'taken aback by his [Hayes's] decision. But, in later years, when we happened to bump into each other, Seán explained that he had rejected me simply because my voice was too distinctive for a choir. And he was right. Both of us had a good old laugh about it.' [24] Ó Sé has toured extensively and appeared on numerous radio and television programmes. He collaborated with Seán Ó Riada and Ceoltóirí Chualann and appeared on many recordings, including *An Poc ar Buile* (1962) and *Ó Riada sa Gaiety* (1969).

Fachtna Ó hAnnracháin (1920—2010), conductor, composer and part-time lecturer in music at St Patrick's from 1946 to 1947, was born in Skibbereen, Co Cork. He moved to Dublin on winning a scholarship to Coláiste Caoimhín and studied at St Patrick's. Ó hAnnracháin was the Director of Music at RTÉ (1947-62) and subsequently became head

---

[23] S. Ó Sé, *An Poc ar Buile: The Life and Times of Seán Ó Sé*, (Cork: Collins Press, 2015), p.44. Despite Ó Sé's assertion, the programme of the 'Cuirm Cheoil agus Drámaíocht na Macléinn' on 27 March 1955 indicates that he was part of the first tenor section in the college choir. SPCA C/21/9.

[24] Ibid., p. 44-45.

of Legal Services. He travelled throughout Europe to recruit musicians for the Raidió Éireann (RÉ) orchestras and played a crucial role in their development. The critic, Charles Acton noted that the Radio Éireann Symphony Orchestra under Ó hAnnracháin's directorship 'had a 20th century standard of superlative quality and a livelier repertoire in Dublin than orchestral concerts had in London'.[25] Ó hAnnracháin was active in commissioning arrangements of traditional music works by Irish composers. He adopted a policy of programming a composition by an Irish composer in concerts and engaged the uilleann piper, Leo Rowesome in numerous broadcasts. He arranged a selection of reels 'Meascra Ríleanna' for Gael Linn's first LP *Ceolta Éireann*, which was performed by the RÉ Light Orchestra (now the RTÉ Concert Orchestra). His arrangement of 'Dún do Shúile' for two-part choir with piano accompaniment, published by Oifig an tSoláthair [1954] is available in the Cregan library.

The College as a centre for traditional music
St Patrick's was the setting for a number of external events celebrating Irish traditional music and culture. In March 1970, the college hosted the final of the first All-Ireland Slógadh, an Irish language competition-based arts festival for young people. The festival was a great success and was attended by 500 people. Dónal Ó Moráin of Gael Linn noted that there 'is a tremendous interest among young people now in Irish music, debating and the language generally, thanks to the work over the years of many organizations'.[26] In 1975, 1,500 second and third level students from across the country took part in forty-one competitions in sean-nós singing, choral singing, group and solo instrumental playing, recitation, poetry, short story writing, contemporary song writing, ballets based on traditional themes and folk-dancing. The prize winners' concert (13 April) with Niall Toibín as master of ceremonies, was televised from St Patrick's on 13 May 1975. It featured budding traditional musicians such as ten year old Bairbre Ní Chiosáin, winner of the sean-nós competition for girls, the Cooley family from Galway and solo singer,

---

[25] *The Irish Times*, 7 November 1980. In a letter to Terence de Vere White, Charles Acton admitted that he 'would dearly like Ó hAnnracháin's job at the Radio and could do it far better in spite of what I know to be the peculiar difficulties of it) I have no musical degree, cannot speak Irish and presumably am the wrong religion ... I do feel I would make a greater success of the job'. Quoted in Richard Pine *Charles, The Life and World of Charles Acton 1914-99*, (Dublin: Lilliput Press, 2010), p. 236.
[26] *Irish Press*, 16 March 1970, p. 3.

Evonne Ní Bhraonáin.[27] From 28 July to 2 August 1980, the College was the venue for the annual International Celtic Congress, a festival which perpetuates the language, ideals and culture of the Celtic countries (Ireland, Scotland, Cornwall, Isle of Man, Brittany and Wales). The title for the 1980 conference was 'The Living Flame in our Country Today' and it was comprised of lectures, trips to local places of historic and cultural interest and music and dance events, including nightly sessions, and culminating in a gala concert by Na Casadaigh.

Irish traditional music course
The appointment of Caitlín Uí Éigeartaigh (Kathleen Hegarty) in 1972 as a fulltime lecturer until 1977 in all aspects of the music course heralded a new era for Irish traditional music at St Patrick's College. Prior to Uí Éigeartaigh's appointment, lectures in traditional music were incorporated into the teaching of curriculum music and on the academic strand of the National Teachers (NT) programme. With the introduction of the three-year BEd degree in 1974, St Patrick's College became a recognized college of the National University of Ireland. Seán Hayes, Head of Music at St Patrick's (1949-85) who delivered lectures in traditional music during his tenure was eager to introduce an academic course for traditional music and tasked Uí Éigeartaigh with designing and teaching a syllabus. The course covered topics such as the use of modes in traditional music, performance style, ornamentation and regional styles, dance tunes and songs, the music of Turlough O'Carolan and of the collectors, and collections of unpublished manuscripts. Students were assessed through an end-of-year written examination. In the final year of the degree, students were required to compose a melody in a traditional style and provide a piano accompaniment to a traditional air. An innovative component of the final examination was the requirement of individual students to examine and record on index cards, the mode, form, source and other details of a selection of unpublished tunes from the Forde and Pigott manuscripts provided by Uí Éigeartaigh.[28]

During her tenure at St Patrick's College, Uí Éigeartaigh was actively involved in the Folk Music Society of Ireland (Cumann Cheol Tíre Éireann), of which she was honorary secretary and regularly wrote in the society's newsletter, *Ceol Tíre*. The issue of folk (traditional) music in education was regularly discussed at meetings of the society and in open forums. At one such gathering on 26 October 1974, composer

---

[27] *Cork Examiner*, 4 April 1975, p. 9.
[28] Caitlín Uí Éigeartaigh, interview with author, 18 August 2018.

Seóirse Bodley, chair of the society, suggested those in attendance consider the subject under two headings; the teaching of folk music and the use of folk music as material for general music teaching (in the teaching of sight singing, as espoused in the Kodály method). Seán Hayes (Music Department, St Patrick's) explained the principles of the Kodály method to the meeting and opined that it 'could be adapted in this country'.[29] Another notable contributor to the discussion was Frank Corcoran, music inspector with the Department of Education. Corcoran outlined the position of traditional music in secondary schools, endorsed 'the teaching of local traditions and songs' in schools and averred that improvements could only be achieved through specialist training and the provision of appropriate teaching materials.[30] The dearth of pedagogical materials in traditional music was being addressed at primary level at this time. In the mid-1970s, three important collections of Irish language songs for use in primary schools were published, namely, *Cas Amhrán* (1975), *Éigse an Cheoil* (1975) and *Cuisle an Cheoil* (1976).[31] These songbooks were a useful resource for teachers and widely used by students and teachers providing a rich source of common heritage for class instruction. The songs were presented in staff notation and tonic solfa and are noteworthy for the standardization of spelling and grammar and the selection of particular regional versions of songs over others. *Éigse an Cheoil* and *Cuisle an Cheoil* are noteworthy for the inclusion of chords to traditionally unaccompanied songs.

From 1977 to 1985, Uí Éigeartaigh lectured in traditional music only on a part-time basis. An investigation of examination papers of this period reflects her commitment to raising the status of traditional music as an academic subject. Papers from the 1980s reveal an emphasis on the music of harpers, in particular Carolan, the collections

---

[29] Caitlín Uí Éigeartaigh, 'Teaching Folk Music', *Ceol Tíre* 5 (October 1975), pp. 3-5, (p. 4).

[30] Ibid.

[31] *Cas Amhrán* was edited by Mícheál Ó hEidhin (1938-2012), music inspector with the Department of Education and an accomplished concertina and piano accordion player. The book contains an illustrated collection of over 100 songs in staff notation and tonic solfa, including 'Peigín Leitir Móir' and 'An Poc ar Buile'. *Éigse an Cheoil* presents 12 Irish language songs, including, 'An raibh tú ar an gCarraig?', 'Caoineadh na hAoine' and 'Im'aonar seal'. *Cuisle an Cheoil* contains 56 songs with staff notation, tonic solfa, chord symbols, explanatory notes and includes, 'Úna Bhán', 'Seán Ó Duibhir an Ghleanna' and 'An Draighneán Donn'.

of Bunting and Petrie and ornamentation, in first and second year courses. Towards the end of the 1980s, there was a marked simplification and generalisation of exam questions which coincided with Uí Éigeartaigh's departure from the college. In 1986, second year students were asked to list the most common types of ornamentation in current use among traditional players and provide examples or suggest suitable types of ornamentation for a jig provided to be played on the concertina. Second year students in 1987 were requested to list examples of gapped scales in traditional music or to suggest suitable ornamentation for a reel provided to be played on the fiddle and in 1988, first year students were requested to outline the development of traditional folk song in Ireland. This brief overview of the written examination papers underscores the fact that the subject was taught and assessed as an academic subject, with a limited practical component and most importantly that the course content was simplified after Uí Éigeartaigh. There was however, one exception to this experience, namely in 1991 when a graduate of the BEd programme was awarded a degree with academic music 'having performed Irish traditional music on the flute for the practical part of the examination'.[32]

The late 1990s marked a significant development in the study of traditional music at St Patrick's with the appointment of leading exponents to lecture on the subject. From 1999 to 2001, Armagh-born writer, researcher and traditional musician, Fintan Vallely lectured on the traditional music course. Vallely has toured extensively, made numerous recordings, was music correspondent and reviewer with *The Irish Times* (1994-2000), columnist with *The Sunday Tribune* (1996-2002) and has lectured in traditional Irish and international folk musics at Maynooth University, Trinity College Dublin and Dundalk Institute of Technology. Drawing from his wealth of experience as a pedagogue and practitioner in addition to publications, such as, *Timber: The Concert-Flute Tutor* (1986) and in particular *The Companion to Irish Traditional Music* (1999 and 2nd edn. 2011), he devised a six-week course for BEd and BA students from first to third year, specializing in traditional music. Vallely described the course as an

> ... uncomplicated introduction to the rudiments of traditional music ... definitions, explaining the components of traditional

---

[32] B. Ní Shé, 'The Initial Education and Training of Music Teachers for Primary Schools in the Republic of Ireland, Northern Ireland, England and Wales', Unpublished MEd thesis, (Trinity College Dublin, 1994), p. 29.

music, song and dance, descriptions of instruments and their playing styles and discussing the Irish and English language song repertoire, sean-nós, macaronic and modern pop songs.[33]

In consultation with Marion Doherty, then Head of Music, Vallely devised a post-graduate diploma/MA course on traditional music for qualified teachers; unfortunately this did not come to fruition.

Donegal born fiddler player, Eithne Vallely (née Ní Chiardh) succeeded Fintan as lecturer on the traditional music course. Like Fintan, her cousin by marriage, Eithne is an accomplished musician and experienced teacher and hails from a family steeped in traditional music and renowned for their fiddle playing. Eithne studied Celtic Studies at UCD and taught music and Gaeilge/Irish at various secondary schools. In 1966, she and her husband, Brian (John B.) Vallely set up the Armagh Pipers' Club and published a series of tutors for uilleann pipes, tin whistle, fiddle and children's songs. For many years, she advocated for the inclusion of traditional music in primary education, particularly in the North of Ireland. To this end she and her husband published a three-year course of traditional music entitled, *Sing a Song and Play It: A Book of Irish music and song for children* (three volumes) with an accompanying handbook for teachers in 1976. The songs selected include a broad spectrum of Irish and English language love songs, lullabies, animal songs and occupation songs. Complementing this rich selection of songs is the provision of information on collections, composers, instruments and musicians, musical theory, instructions on how to play the tin whistle, translations of songs, and activity work for children. All of this provides a cultural context for the songs.

Other notable part time/guest lecturers on the traditional music course at St Patrick's College include, Nicholas Carolan, founding director of the Irish Traditional Music Archive; Micheál Ó Súilleabháin composer, pianist, founder of the Irish World Academy of Music and Dance, University of Limerick; Niall Keegan, flute player and Associate Director at the Irish World Academy of Music and Dance and Cork fiddle player, and Matt Cranitch, an authority on the regional fiddle style of Sliabh Luachra. The appointment of Mary Nugent and Mary Louise O'Donnell as lecturers on the Irish Traditional Music Course in 2005 brought a more structured approach to delivering the Irish music module at undergraduate level to BEd and BA students. Mary Nugent is a flute player and lecturer at the Marino Institute of Education and has

---

[33] Fintan Vallely, interview with author, Dublin, 26 June 2018.

produced accompaniment parts for *Alive-O* and *Beo Go Deo* series, the primary school religious education programme in English and the Irish language respectively. Harpist and researcher, Mary Louise O'Donnell was completing a PhD on 'Custodians of Culture: A Social, Political, Musicological and Cultural History of the Irish Harp and its Patronage from 1790 to 1845' at the University of Limerick at this time. She brought her research on all aspects of the harp into the lectures. Nugent and O'Donnell devised a comprehensive and exciting programme of eight lectures for each year of the BEd and BA degrees; Year 1 focused on traditional instruments, dance tunes and regional styles, year 2 centred on Ireland's vocal tradition and year 3 investigated innovation in the tradition from the 1950s, the history of the harp, music collections and the legacy of Seán Ó Riada.

From 2007 until 2012, the author, Teresa O'Donnell lectured on this module (as well as curriculum music). First year students were introduced to the characteristics of Irish dance music, traditional instruments; regional styles, styles of accompaniment, the music and musicians of Sliabh Luachra and contemporary developments in traditional music. The second year course focused on Ireland's vocal tradition; macaronic songs, the ballad tradition, characteristics of sean-nós singing and exponents of sean-nós such as Joe Heaney and Iarla Ó Lionard, songs of rebellion (1778-1916), songs of Thomas Moore, the legacy and influence of Mary O'Hara and contemporary singers and groups such as Mary Black, Karan Casey, Christy Moore, The Voice Squad and Liadán. Third year students attended lectures on innovation and developments in the tradition (The Pogues, Afro-Celt Sound system, Planxty, Bothy Band, Kíla), collections and collectors (from Neal to O'Neill), the history of the harp in Ireland (wire-strung harping tradition, 1792 Belfast Harp Festival and contemporary practice), the folk music revival and the music of Seán Ó Riada. The module was assessed by an end of year examination and an essay.

From 2009, the course was incorporated into a module which included ethnomusicology and popular music. In line with recommendations from the European Credit Transfer and Accumulation System contact hours for this course were reduced; this reflected an overall reduction in hours for all types of music and for the music course in general. Nonetheless this diminution of hours and subsequent revision of the course gave a parity of esteem to traditional music, as well as to other musics not previously studied as part of the BA or BEd music courses. In 2014, the traditional music course was incorporated into the mainstream module, 'Topics in Musicology', available to BA and BEd students specializing in music. Under the new system, third year students, for example, study traditional music alongside narrative in music and contemporary art music within the discipline of musicology under the following headings: Contemporary Developments in Irish Traditional Music, Celtic Connections, Irish Traditional Music in the Global Context, Musicians among the Irish diaspora, The Parameters of Style in Irish Traditional Music and the Irish Traveller Song tradition. This module continues to operate in the DCU BA joint honours programme whereby students have 22 hours on Irish Traditional Music topics, 11 hours in Year 1 and 11 hours in Year 2. At the time of writing the lecturer of this module is Thomas Johnston, an uilleann piper, tin whistle player and a former Music Generation Research Fellow. Johnston's and Patricia Flynn's report, *Possible Selves in Music: The Transformative Potential for Children and Young People of Performance Music Education* underpinned by principles of diversity, was a landmark research document, which provided a fresh approach to performance music education and was published by Music Generation in 2016.

Lecturers in other academic departments at St Patrick's College have also been actively involved in promoting and performing traditional music in the college, school classrooms and on the public platform, and this has invariably been linked to the Irish language. Máire Ní Bhaoill, of the School of Language, Literacy and Early Childhood Education promotes the use of Irish-language songs through various academic courses. Her PhD (Elphinstone Institute, Aberdeen) investigated traditional singing among children in Ireland. Donegal sean-nós singer, Máire Ní Choilm lectured in Roinn na Gaeilge/Irish Department for many years and has won prizes at the Pan Celtic festival, Fleadh Cheoil na hÉireann and An tOireachtas. Her Irish language album, *Nuair a théid sé fán chroí* was released in 2010 and featured fifteen tracks, nine of which were unaccompanied. A number of the songs celebrate the rich musical heritage of Tory Island. Sean-nós singer and harper, Síle Denvir of Roinn na Gaeilge/Irish Department has appeared on numerous television and radio programmes and has performed regularly at concerts and events at St Patrick's organized by the Music Department and the Tradsoc, a society established by students of the college for the celebration and promotion of traditional music.

Music is at the heart of our endeavour[34]
A number of attempts were made with varying results to establish a students' society solely dedicated to the promotion and enjoyment of traditional music. More frequently, however, traditional music existed

---

[34] John Buckley, interview with author, 28 June 2018.

as part of the College's Cumann Gaelach (Irish language society). In 1978, Comhaltas Ceoltóirí Éireann (CCÉ) Coláiste Phádraig was established. The society organized weekly sessions, céilís/céilithe, concerts, tin whistle classes and participated in Gael Linn's Slógadh festival/competition, An tOireachtas and Comhaltas Pléaracha, and visited a number of CCÉ branches around the country. In the 1980/81 *Students' Handbook of St Patrick's College of Education Students' Union*, Máire de Baróid, secretary of the society, encouraged all students to become involved in the organization's activities, declaring that no level of proficiency in music, song or dance was required, '[a]ll you need is a little bit of interest.'[35] Annual reports of CCÉ Coláiste Phádraig were predominantly written in the Irish language and always appeared alongside reports of An Cumann Gaelach. Interestingly, there is no further mention of a traditional music society in subsequent student handbooks but traditional music has always been entwined in the college's activities and has survived as a living art, in sessions, in the social life of students and in concerts organized by the music department.

Music lecturer John Buckley discusses the music department's lunchtime concert series elsewhere in this publication; nevertheless, it is important to note that the series also provided a valuable platform for traditional musicians. Buckley has been steadfast in his support of, and commitment to promoting traditional music in cultural and social settings at St Patrick's and I have selected three concerts from the series to illustrate this. On 16 February 2011 a group of traditional musicians performed as part of a concert of third year music students which featured songs from musicals, contemporary and traditional Irish songs and jazz. The Irish traditional group included Ellen Hynes (fiddle), Barbara Kirk (flute), Martina Gorman (accordion), Darragh Healy (accordion), Donal McCague (fiddle), Síle Ryan (fiddle), Gemma Cooper and Ellen Hynes (dancers). Lecturers from academic departments also participated in the lunchtime concert series - Thomas Johnston (uilleann pipes and whistles) of the Music Department, Síle Denvir (harp and vocals) of Roinn na Gaeilge performed alongside Kieran Munnelly (flute and vocals) and Eoin Ó Beaglaoich (concertina) on 12 February 2014. Líadan, the award-winning all-female traditional group performed as part of the lunchtime concerts series on 18 February 2015.

---

[35] 'Comhaltas Ceoltóirí Éireann Coláiste Phádraig', *Students' Handbook of St Patrick's College of Education Students' Union* (1980/1), p. 48. SPCA C/21/viii.

Musicians from St Patrick's College have featured regularly as soloists or as part of groups on Comhaltas Ceoltóirí Éireann's ComhaltasLive weekly internet videos.[36] On 20 November 2014, thirteen musicians from St Patrick's recorded two jigs, 'The Frost is All Over' and 'The Young Fair Maidens'. John Buckley interviewed after the performance explained that music has always been at the heart of life in St Patrick's, as an academic subject and in all aspects of college life. He estimated that between sixty and eighty traditional musicians perform at various events during the academic year and described their style of playing as 'vibrant and polished', 'hugely exciting and infectious in its enthusiasm'.[37] A number of students have performed solos on *ComhaltasLive*, for example, harper and concertina player, Aoife Ní Argáin, and fiddle players, Caoimhe Kerins and Éadaoín Ní Mhaicín, all prizewinners at Fleadh Cheoil na hÉireann. Students from St Patrick's College have also performed on RTÉ Radio 1's *Céilí House* on numerous occasions, including 2010, 2013 and most recently on 9 December, 2017. The popular Saturday night radio programme with Kieran Hanrahan celebrates traditional music and song in a community setting rather than in a radio or television studio.[38]

DCU Tradsoc was founded in 2016 when St Patrick's College was incorporated into DCU and currently has approximately ninety members. Though this time period lies outside the remit of this book, it is important to acknowledge the current efforts of the society and the commitment of the college and wider DCU family to traditional music. Members rehearse on a weekly basis during term time, perform at a regular session at the Cat and Cage pub in Drumcondra, occasionally at the Ivy House Pub, Drumcondra and join Tradsoc UCD's weekly session

---

[36] ComhaltasLive was devised by Willie Fogarty and first introduced in March 2003.

[37] Mary O'Donnell (Donegal), John Traynor (Monaghan), Mark Swain (Westmeath), Sarah Meehan (Dublin), Evan Cunniffe (Roscommon), Niamh Molloy (Galway), Paul O'Sullivan (Wexford), Deirdre Barry (Mayo), Cliona Henry (Sligo), Kate Byrne (Leitrim), Emer McCague (Monaghan), Catherine McGinley (Donegal), Éadaoin Ní Mhaicín (Mayo). ComhaltasLive #456:1 Students of St Patrick's College
https://comhaltas.ie/music/detail/comhaltaslive_456_1_students_of_st_patricks_college/ [accessed 16 June 2018].

[38] Céilí House was first heard on RTÉ radio in the 1950s and was presented by Seán Ó Murchú. Musicians travelled to the RTÉ studios in Dublin and Cork to record the programmes until the mid-1980s when it was decided to travel around Ireland, and later further afield, and record musical gatherings.

in Club Chonradh na Gaeilge every second Wednesday. The society has made numerous recordings from An Seomra Chaidrimh, St Patrick's College; one of its first recordings was on 1 December 2016 when eighteen members of the society performed two reels, 'Janine's Fancy' and 'Farrell O'Gara' for CCÉ's 'ComhaltasLive'.[39] Daire Keogh, Deputy President of DCU spoke after the performance observing that DCU TradSoc allowed students of engineering, science, innovation or accountancy to come together and make music. He described the society as 'a great expression of DCU and all that's best in the university.' The recording was organized by two prominent members of the society, Éadaoin Ní Mhaicín (All-Ireland Champion on fiddle, harp, piano and lilting) and Paul O' Sullivan (piano).

Concluding comments
The transmission of Irish traditional music over the past one hundred and forty years has reflected changes in contemporary Irish culture, navigating a path from choral and instrumental arrangements of Irish airs from printed collections to providing a learning environment for the academic study of the subject. Through the College's cross-fertilisation of both academic and performance pursuits, Irish traditional music holds an equal role with classical, popular and other musical genres. Further, as part of the performance element of the BA, students may perform traditional music for their practical exam. St Patrick's has been a creative and welcoming hub for Irish traditional music and has actively celebrated the lived experience of the tradition as evidenced by the activities of the DCU Tradsoc and other events.[40]

---

[39] Áine Duffy, Mark Swain, Patrick Flood, Sam Ó Ceallaigh, Niamh Downes, Mary Grace, Pádraig Clancy, Meabh Mulligan, Saoirse Conway, Hannah Rhattigan, Niamh Molloy, Éadaoin Ní Mhaicín, Nicole Martin, Hannah Whelan, Grace Doolan, Niamh Leahy, Ruth Dolan and Paul O' Sullivan. https://comhaltas.ie/music/detail/18_musicians_from_dcu_trad_society_in_dublin/ ComhaltasLive #507_2:18 Students of St Patrick's College [accessed 21 June 2018].

[40] These included travelling to the Celtic Connections festival in Glasgow (2018), organizing and performing at an intervarsity traditional music session, Seisiún na n-Ollscoileanna in Club Chonradh na Gaeilge, Harcourt Street, Dublin (January 2018) and taking part in ANAM 2018, a two-day cultural event of music, poetry, drama, film and workshops celebrating North Dublin's culture and creativity, with events spread across DCU's three campuses, St Patrick's Campus, All Hallows and Glasnevin. Interview with Nicole Martin, chair of

Many of the voices that shaped Irish traditional music at St Patrick's have excelled in the fields of academia, performance and education and have enriched contemporary Irish culture and society. They have expanded the relationship between the wider music community and brought their experiences of Irish traditional music to a global, cross-cultural audience and most importantly, into the classroom setting for future generations.

Bibliography

Breathnach, Pádraig, *Fuínn na Smól*, (Dublin: Browne and Nolan, 1900 and 2nd edn. 1913).

Breathnach, Pádraig, *Ceol ár Sínsear*, (Dublin: Browne and Nolan, 1913).

Breathnach, Pádraig, *Songs of the Gael: A collection of Anglo-Irish songs and ballads: wedded to old traditional Irish airs*, (Dublin: Browne and Nolan, 1915).

Breathnach, Pádraig, *Ár gCeól Féinig*, (Dublin: Browne and Nolan, 1920).

Breathnach, Pádraig, *Traditional Irish Airs*, (Dublin: Browne and Nolan, 1924).

Breathnach, Pádraig, and Ó Lochlainn, Colm, *Sídhe-Cheól*, (Dublin: Browne and Nolan, 1924).

Cuisle an Cheoil, (Baile Átha Cliath: Oifig an tSoláthair, 1976).

Éigse an Cheoil, (Baile Átha Cliath: An Roinn Oideachas, 1975).

Goodman, Peter, *The Irish Minstrel: A Collection of Songs for use in Irish schools,* Part I, (Dublin: Falconer, 1903).

Goodman, Peter, *The Irish Minstrel: A Collection of Songs for use in Irish schools,* Part II, (Dublin: Falconer, 1904).

Goodman, Peter, *The Irish Minstrel: A Collection of Songs for use in Irish schools,* Part II, (Dublin: Gill, 1906).

Mathews, P. J., *Revival: The Abbey Theatre, Sinn Féin, the Gaelic League and the Co-operative Movement*, (Cork: Cork University Press, 2003).

McCarthy, Marie, *Passing it On: The Transmission of Music in Irish Culture*, (Cork: Cork University Press, 1999).

National Programme Conference, *National Programme of Primary Instruction*, (Dublin: Browne and Nolan, 1922).

DCU TradSoc, fiddle player and third-year BA student (music and Gaeilge), 4 July 2018.

National Programme Conference, *Report and Programme of Second National Conference*, (Dublin: The Stationery Office, 1926).

Ní Shé, Bríd, 'The Initial Education and Training of Music Teachers for Primary Schools in the Republic of Ireland, Northern Ireland, England and Wales', Unpublished MEd thesis, (Trinity College Dublin, 1994).

Nugent, Mary and Hegarty, Patricia, *Music to honour God's name: accompaniment for liturgical music from Alive-O and Beo go Deo*, (Dublin: Veritas Publications, 2000).

Ó Ceallaigh, Tadhg, *Coláiste Phádraig St Patrick's College: Centenary Booklet 1875-1975*, (Dublin: St Patrick's College, 1975).

Ó Conaire, Breandán (ed.), *Douglas Hyde: Language, Lore and Lyrics*, (Dublin: Irish Academic Press, 1986).

Ó hEidhin, Mícheál, *Cas Amhrán*, (Gaillimh: Cló Chois Fharraige, 1975).

Ó Sé, Seán, *An Poc ar Buile: The Life and Times of Seán Ó Sé*, (Cork: Collins Press, 2015).

Pine, Richard, *Charles: The Life and World of Charles Acton 1914-99*, (Dublin: Lilliput Press, 2010).

Uí Éigeartaigh, Caitlín, 'Teaching Folk Music', *Ceol Tíre*, 5 (October 1975), pp. 3-5.

Vallely, Eithne and Vallely, J.B., *Sing a Song and Play It: A Book of Irish music and song for children*, three vols., (Belfast: Appletree Press, 1976 and 1980).

Vallely, Fintan, *The Companion to Irish Traditional Music*, (Cork: Cork University Press, 1999 and 2nd edn. 2011).

Vallely, Fintan, *Timber: The Concert-Flute Tutor*, (Clare: Longnote, 1986).

White, Harry, 'Nationalism, Colonialism and the Cultural Stasis of Music in Ireland', in H. White & M. Murphy (eds), *Musical Constructions of Nationalism: Essays on the History and Ideology on European Musical Culture 1800-1945*, (Cork: Cork University Press 2001), pp. 257-272.

Newspapers and periodicals
Cork Examiner
Freeman's Journal
Irish Press
The Irish Times
The Teacher's Work

Archives
St Patrick's College Archive
Special Collections and Archives, DCU Library

Discography
Ó Riada, Seán & Ceoltóirí Chualann, *Ó Riada sa Gaiety*, (Ireland: Gael-Linn, CEFCD 027, 1988).
Ó Sé, Seán, Ó Riada, Seán & Ceoltóirí Chualann, *An Poc ar Buile*, (Ireland: Claddagh, CEFCD 197, 2010).
Various artists, *Ceolta Éireann*, (Ireland: Gael-Linn, CEF OO1, 1958).
Various artists, *Cabaret Gael-Linn Ag An Georgian Room*, (Ireland: Gael-Linn, GL 10, 1966).
Various artists, *Songs of the Emerald Isle*, (UK & Ireland: Music for Pleasure, DL 1104, 1987).

Chapter Six: Vocal and Choral Music

John O'Flynn

Introduction

No one can watch a choir successfully singing fine choral music without seeing that no other activity, social or artistic, creates the same intense feeling of delight, physical, mental, spiritual and moral, evokes such a complete manifestation of the whole personality, generates such vivid enthusiasm and ambitious striving, affords such opportunity for spontaneous yet harmonious communal effort, or results in such complete self-expression.[1]

The human voice represents a primary source for musical experience and development. This capacity for vocal music can be recognized at an individual level, especially when considering the artistry of an accomplished singer. It is arguable though, as the above quote from Donnchadh Ua Braoin, Head Organising Inspector of Musical Instruction in Ireland from 1931-1947 suggests, that singing's potential for developing musicality and wider human and cultural understanding is more intensely felt when voices combine together to train and develop, and ultimately communicate and perform choral music. Choral singing may also contribute to our health and well-being, and can further act as a catalyst in social bonding for various groups, including students attending professional and academic programmes at universities and other tertiary institutions.[2] The terms 'vocal' and 'choral' are of course closely related. While in contemporary usage 'choral' usually relates to the activities of choirs, 'vocal music' was the equivalent term used throughout the late-nineteenth and early-twentieth centuries. At that time, 'vocal music' was also the term used to describe mandatory programmes of instruction for music in teacher training colleges as well as in national schools. This differs from current usage, where 'vocal music' is more generally applied to works for solo voice(s) as opposed to 'choral music'.

---

[1] D. Ua Braoin, 'Music in the Primary Schools', in A. Fleischmann (ed.), *Music in Ireland: A Symposium*, (Cork: Cork University Press, 1952), p. 39

[2] S. M. Clift & G. Hancox, 'The perceived benefits of singing: findings from preliminary surveys of a university college choral society', *The Journal of the Royal Society for the Promotion of Health*, 121.4 (2001); J. O'Flynn, 'Strengthening choral community: the interaction of face-to-face and online

This chapter explores aspects of vocal and choral music at St Patrick's College throughout its significant history. It considers vocal music training at the College from the end of nineteenth century through to the early decades of the twentieth century, at a time when classroom singing and ear training became established in the Irish national school system. It continues by noting developments in music syllabuses of the Irish Free State (later, the Irish Republic) from 1922 until the 'new' Primary School Curriculum of 1971, with several 'snapshots' of vocal training and choral performance at the College over the same period.[3] The record of these respective periods is appraised in light of the promotion of choral music more generally in Ireland up to this time. As shall be discussed, vocal music courses and choral activities at the College were linked with various stages in the evolution of school music curricula, as well as with broader socio-cultural developments in Ireland.

The chapter's remaining sections examine the role of choral music in the cultural life of the College from the early 1970s to the mid-2010s. This covers the period from when the institution opened its doors to female as well as male students to its branching out academically to include humanities as well as education programmes in the 1990s through to its incorporation into Dublin City University in 2016. This was a time of considerable expansion and diversity for choral music at the College in respect of student population, conducting styles, choral genres, performance outlets, in-service education, and national and international representation. The chapter concludes by considering the legacy of choral music at the College.

1883-1922[4]

As noted in Daithí Ó Corráin's historical overview in Chapter One of this book, the first few decades of music at St Patrick's College coincided with the consolidation of Curwen's method of vocal music instruction, and with the National Board of Education's 'payment by results' system of 1882-

---

activities amongst a college choir', *International Journal of Community Music*, 8.1 (2015); H. I. Tonneijck, A. Kinébanian & S. Josephsson, 'An exploration of choir singing: Achieving wholeness through challenge', *Journal of Occupational Science*, 15.3 (2008).

[3] An Roinn Oideachais [Department of Education], *An Curaclam Nua. Teachers' Handbook*, Parts I and II, (Dublin: Browne and Nolan, 1971).

[4] While the College was established in 1875, its first professor of music, Peter Goodman, would not be appointed until 1883, the same year that music on the national curriculum was elevated in status from 'extra' to 'ordinary and optional'. M. Ryng, 'A really good man: Peter Goodman and his contribution to music in Irish primary education', *British Journal of Music Education*, 19.2 (2002), p. 146.

1899.⁵ A key figure in this regard was Peter Goodman who served as the first professor of music at St Patrick's College 1883-1892 before his subsequent appointment as Inspector of Musical Instruction and later promotion to Examiner in Music by the Board of Commissioners of National Education in Ireland. Goodman's significant contribution to music in Irish primary education can be appraised in overwhelmingly positive terms.⁶ The establishment of the Curwen method heralded the importance of tonic solfa and to a lesser extent, staff notation as a means towards sight singing and aural development in Irish national schools as well as in teacher training colleges. This was an influence that would extend until and beyond the advent of the 'new' primary curriculum of 1971.⁷ Although a rigid adherence to the Curwen approach had waned by that time, it is worth noting here how from the mid-1980s St Patrick's College would become actively involved in the national promotion of the concept of music education developed by Hungarian composer Zoltán Kodály (1882-1967) which in turn had revised and adapted musical and pedagogical aspects of Curwen's nineteenth-century method.⁸

Among the significant advances proposed under the approach developed much later by Kodály in the 1930s and 40s were a more holistic conception of music learning that gave due recognition to folk and traditional music, and the pedagogical maxim of 'fluency before literacy' - the principle that singing by ear was developmentally prior to sight-singing in either tonic solfa or staff notation.⁹ Similar ideas had in fact been foreshadowed in Ireland and elsewhere during the first decades of the twentieth century, an era which can be considered as a relatively progressive one for national education. ¹⁰ Goodman's influence as Inspector of Musical Instruction was certainly evident in the Revised Programme of 1900 which for the first time identified music (singing) as a compulsory school subject, with an emphasis on learning 'national' and

---

⁵ Curwen's method drew on the earlier approach developed by Sarah Glover (1776-1867). See K. Simpson, *Some great music educators: a collection of essays*, (London: Novello, 1976). On music and 'payment by results' see M. McCarthy, *Passing it On: The Transmission of Music in Irish Culture* (Cork: Cork University Press, 1999), p. 79.
⁶ Ryng, 'A really good man', pp. 146, 148.
⁷ McCarthy, *Passing it On*, p. 80.
⁸ See Yvonne Higgins's chapter, 'The Kodály Connection' in this volume.
⁹ E. Szőnyi, *Kodálys principles in practice*, (London: Boosey & Hawkes, 1973).
¹⁰ See M. McCarthy, 'Ireland: Curriculum development in troubled times', in G. Cox & R. Stevens (eds.), *The Origins and Foundations of Music Education* (London: Bloomsbury, 2016), pp. 56-57.

religious songs deemed appropriate to domestic culture.[11] Although sight-singing through tonic solfa was prioritized, the 1900 programme also allowed for 'singing by ear' for pupils in infant classes. Most significantly perhaps, and as outlined in Ó Corráin's chapter, the early 1900s witnessed the most extensive music in-service programme provided for Irish primary teachers up to that point[12] (Indeed, this was an enterprise not matched in scale until the early twenty-first century with the implementation of the 1999 Revised Primary Curriculum by a designated specialist music team under the NCCA's Primary Curriculum Support Programme).[13]

How were pre-service teachers prepared to teach singing in the early twentieth century? In keeping with the national school curriculum, vocal music was compulsory over the two years of the teacher training programme. The term 'written' appeared as a separate component in some of the first examination result sheets, although this later became subsumed under the vocal category as 'theory'. The following syllabus for vocal music appeared in the College's thirty-first annual report for the session 1913-1914:

VOCAL MUSIC (*Theory*)

Staff Notation: - Treble stave; major scales and key signatures; diatonic intervals; simple time signatures; transcription from one time to another; easy transposition; musical terms

Or,

Tonic Sol-fa: - The common scale, its chordal structure; mental effects; diatonic intervals; pitch of keys; two, three, and four-pulse measures; simple time names; musical terms.

---

[11] *New Rules and Regulations (National Education)*, 1900-1, Cd. 601, H.C. 1901 (3), lvii, p. 9. Goodman had himself collected, arranged and published several songbooks for these purposes. See Ryng, 'A really good man', p. 155.

[12] Goodman's extensive efforts in providing music in-service are chronicled in Ryng, 'A really good man', pp. 151-153. Meanwhile, Áine Hyland concludes more generally that the implementation of the Revised Programme in the early twentieth century had mixed results, with at best lukewarm reception from primary teachers. Á. Hyland, 'The process of curriculum change in the Irish national school system', *Irish Educational Studies*, 6.2 (1986-87), pp. 28-29. See also T. Walsh, 'The Revised Programme of Instruction, 1900-1922', *Irish Educational Studies*, 26.2 (2007).

[13] National Council for Curriculum and Assessment, *Primary School Curriculum*, (Dublin: The Stationery Office, 1999).

VOCAL MUSIC (*Practical Test*)

To sol-fa from the examiner's pointing on the modulator simple passages without transition; to sing an easy sight test from the tonic sol-fa or from the staff notation. [14]

While the College's annual report for 1913-14 observed a modest success in implementing the music syllabus – notwithstanding the noting of quite varied results among students – it failed to consider the efficacy of the syllabus itself, particularly with regard to the prior musical background of students and the course's privileging of music theory to the neglect of music pedagogy.[15]

In addition to reflecting national developments in education, the music programmes offered at St Patrick's College at the turn of the nineteenth and twentieth centuries were linked to wider cultural movements, notably the development of church music through the Cecilian reform movement and through the Gaelic revival which would progressively become more nationalist in outlook during the early decades of the twentieth century.[16] The first of these movements and its influence on music at St Patrick's College is considered briefly below, while Teresa O'Donnell's chapter in this volume includes a discussion on the Gaelic revival as it related to publications of Irish songs for schools (including those compiled by Peter Goodman).

From the first appointment in 1883 through to incorporation into DCU in 2016, music professors (later designated as lecturers) at St Patrick's College included active choral conductors, many of whom doubled as church musicians. Goodman was an accomplished church organist, conductor, and composer of liturgical music, and his advocacy of the Curwen method was strongly related to the educational mission of the Irish Cecilian reform movement of which he was a leading figure.[17] Choral

---

[14] *Thirty-First Annual Report of St Patrick's Training College, Drumcondra*, For the Session 1913-14, (Dublin: Browne and Nolan, 1915), p. 10.

[15] Ibid., p.12

[16] The Cecilian movement for the reform of Catholic liturgical music originated in Germany in 1868 and was prominent in Ireland between 1878-1903: K. Daly, *Catholic Church Music in Ireland, 1878-1903: The Cecilian Reform Movement*, (Dublin and Portland, ON: Four Courts Press, 1995). The Gaelic revival was a movement centred on the revival of the Irish language [*Gaeilge*] and culture c. 1890-1921, with various secular, religious and socio-political roots: J. Hutchinson, *Dynamics of Cultural Nationalism: The Gaelic revival and the Creation of the Irish Nation State*, (London and New York: Routledge, 2012).

[17] Ryng, 'A really good man', pp. 147-148.

music was paramount in Goodman's vision for what he considered as a necessary revival of music in Ireland, and he identified a critical role for the vocal music programmes of teacher training colleges. To fulfil this national ambition, Goodman declared that '[e]very school must be made to supply a choir, and if only the teacher be sufficiently competent an excellent choir'.[18]

Cork-born Joseph Seymour, professor of music at the College from 1891-1910, was another prominent member of the Cecilian Society. In addition to his prolific activities as organist and choral director, Seymour was a highly successful composer of sacred and secular choral music, and was editor of a Latin church music series for the London-based publisher Curwen. He also wrote several pieces for children's choirs, including a May Day operetta based on Irish airs and an arrangement of the song, 'The Bells of Shandon'.[19]

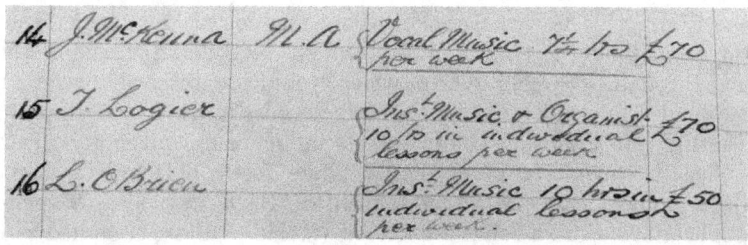

Figure 6.2: Extract from 'Returns from St Patrick's College for Masters' for the year ending 31 August 1916, with details of vocal and instrumental professors employed by the College.[20]

Two other prominent organists and choirmasters from this period who taught music at St Patrick's College were Theodore Logier and English-born Samuel Spencer Myerscough. The latter taught for a relatively short period between 1910-13 while Logier spent several decades as 'external professor' of music at the College following his appointment at the young

---

[18] P. Goodman quoted in 'Board of National Education Annual Report', *Freeman's Journal* (4 August 1897), p. 5.
[19] P. Collins & D. Larkin, 'Joseph Seymour', in H. White & B. Boydell (eds.), *The Encyclopaedia of Music in Ireland*, Volume II, (Dublin: UCD Press, 2013), pp. 927-8; M. Humphreys & R. Evans (eds.), *Dictionary of Composers for the Church in Great Britain and Ireland*, (London: Mansell, 1997), p. 303.
[20] 'Staff Lists 1892-1926', SPCA, A/15/i.

age of twenty-two in 1884.[21] He led choral activities in addition to teaching aspects of the vocal music syllabus and also conducted the boys' choir of St Patrick's N.S. Drumcondra. A competition report published in the *Freeman's Journal*, 3 July 1897 on Dublin Corporation's Public School Competition for Singing noted the participation of that choir conducted by Logier; also mentioned in the same report were Peter Goodman who was present in his capacity as music inspector, and Joseph Seymour whose arrangement of 'The Bells of Shandon' was sung by the winning choir of St Mary's Place, conducted by Vincent O'Brien.[22]

From the end of the nineteenth century, students at the College could also elect to study harmonium, a facility that could be linked with a national resurgence of Catholic church music as much as with the accompaniment of singing in schools. Initially, more than two thirds of students opted to study the instrument, but this number gradually dwindled to less than a tenth of students by 1918.[23] It is not altogether clear if lessons on harmonium ceased after Louis O'Brien was released from his duties in 1921, as Theodore Logier continued to teach instrumental music up to 1946, less than one year before his death.[24] What is likely however is that there was a gradual decline in the popularity of the instrument in the post-independence period. That said, those graduates of the College who studied harmonium over the previous two decades would arguably have made a significant impact on the growth of plainchant and hymnody in local schools and parish churches across the country. As noted in the afore-mentioned College report for 1913-14: 'Such teachers are a great acquisition in country districts. They are usually able to train a choir of school children and to accompany them at the ordinary devotions in the Church'.[25] A foot-pumped harmonium, manufactured by Alexandre et Fils of Paris remains in the main music room of what is now St Patrick's Campus, DCU (See Figure 6.2 below).

---

[21] Theodore Logier (1862-1944) was the grandson of German-born Johann Bernhard Logier (1777-1846), an internationally renowned piano pedagogue and a founding figure of the Royal Irish Academy of Music in Dublin.

[22] 'Vocal Music in Primary Schools', *Freeman's Journal*, 3 July 1897, p. 6.

[23] A note on the College's timetable for 1899 states: 'About seventy students get lessons on the harmonium and practice each day for about three-quarters of an hour', SPCA, C/37.

[24] 'St. Patrick's Training College, Tabulated Results July Examinations 1904 to 1918', SPCA, C/31; The dismissal of O'Brien is noted in D. Ferriter, '"For God's sake send me a few packets of fags": the College, 1922-45', in J. Kelly (ed.), *St Patrick's College, 1875-2000*, (Dublin: Four Courts Press, 2006), p. 135.

[25] *Thirty-First Annual Report of St Patrick's Training College, Drumcondra*, p. 12.

Figure 6.2: Harmonium manufactured by Alexandre et Fils, Paris, c. 1851.[26] Photograph by John O'Flynn

1922-1971

The music education historian Marie McCarthy sums up musical development during the early decades of independent Ireland as follows:

> Musical development, both in formal education and in the culture at large, was influenced by a number of factors during the early decades of independence: a state cultural policy that focused almost exclusively on the revival of the Irish language to the neglect of arts education in general, the prevailing Catholic ethos, the expansion of mass media, and the organisation of music at the national level. The first two reproduced the values of nationalist ideology while the latter two, although at times committed to a nationalist agenda, tended to broaden the vision for music in Ireland.[27]

---

[26] The Paris address given on manufacturer's nameplate suggests the date of production to be c. 1851. The French harmonium used a pressure system that blew air through internal metal reeds. See also L. Benderius, 'The Future Role of the French Harmonium', Unpublished MA dissertation, (University of Gothenburg, 2015), pp. 6-13.

[27] McCarthy, *Passing it On*, p. 109.

Overall, the above statement points to a general lack of coherence over the period. Ó Corráin's chapter in this volume adumbrates the first part of McCarthy's assessment, pointing to timetabling limitations for music in primary schools as well as to successive syllabuses that initially brought about little change from the pre-independence period. The main exception to this – and the primary reason for the diminished status of music education - was the increased emphasis placed on the Irish language and a resultant reduction in time for other curricular areas. By 1930, all subjects taught at St Patrick's College, including music, were taught in Irish (this could also be viewed as a development that may have enhanced the status of music as Irish was the *lingua franca* of the College at the time).[28]

Post-independence Ireland was also marked by its conservative religiosity. As with Diarmuid Ferriter's chapter in the 2006 volume *St Patrick's College, 1875-2000*, Ó Corráin's chapter for this book points to the stark realities of student life in a Catholic college that was virtually enclosed right up to the 1960s.[29] At the same time, there was, in the words of Frainc Ó Murchadha who attended the College from 1946-1948, 'a lively social atmosphere', especially during weekends. Ó Murchadha would reflect:

> I was fortunate in being involved in most of the College activities, the choir, the Cumann Gaelach ... the St Vincent de Paul Society, the hurling team. Many of us who were there at that time regarded those two years as the happiest years of our lives.[30]

In a similar vein, Seán Ó hAodha [Seán Hayes], who studied at the College from 1938-1940 and later was appointed music lecturer in 1949, comments on the relief afforded to students through the option of evening choral rehearsals: '... the boys were delighted to come along. It was such a great break from study'.[31]

Furthermore, and to quote once again the second part of Marie McCarthy's statement above, the students of St Patrick's College – or at

---

[28] D. Ferriter, '"For God's sake"', p. 140.
[29] The most biting criticism of this regime would come from the author John McGahern who studied at the College from 1953-1955. E. Ó Súilleabháin, 'Cuimní Cinn ar CPD: Céad Bliain de Ré na bhFear leo féin' (1975), SPCA C/46.
[30] E. Ó Súilleabháin, 'Cuimní Cinn ar CPD'.
[31] Seán Ó hAodha, cited in B. Ní Shé, 'The Initial Education and Training of Music Teachers for Primary Schools in the Republic of Ireland, Northern Ireland, England and Wales', Unpublished MEd thesis, (Trinity College Dublin, 1994), p. 16.

least those who participated in choir - would benefit from 'the expansion of mass media, and the organisation of music at the national level'. Even before the advent of national broadcast media, members of the choir had opportunities to perform externally, such as during their annual forays to the Gaiety theatre in Dublin. More significantly, the college choir would achieve a national platform following the establishment of Ireland's first state radio service, 2RN in 1926. As detailed in John Buckley's chapter on performance in this volume, from the late 1920s until 1951, the College's all-male choir performed challenging programmes of Irish and international repertoire.

It is ironic to note that while the choir appeared to excel during this period, the majority of students at the College struggled with the mandatory vocal music course. An examiner's report dated as '1930s' in the college archive reveals a critique by John Redmond of what he perceived to be a technical approach in the College's programme for vocal music, a programme that had remained largely unchanged from that developed in 1897. Redmond, who was music professor at the College from 1918-1920 and subsequently its Supervisor of Schools until 1949 (while continuing to teach vocal music and conduct the college choir) observed that most students had no prior music education before entering St Patrick's College. Reflecting what might now be termed as a praxial approach, he advocated that more time be given to experiences of song singing and to the methods of teaching a singing class in addition to instruction in music literacy. In the same vein, he also suggested a more holistic approach to 'ear-tests', preferring that these be based on song material rather than on technical tasks.[32]

Here, Redmond communicated two of the most critical factors in implementing any curriculum course to prospective teachers: first, that teachers understand and are convinced by its underlying pedagogy, and second, that the content of the course is engaging and relevant for student learners and, in turn, for their future pupils. Redmond may have had a role in the *Revised Programme of Instruction for Music in National Schools* published in 1939 which included the following syllabus components: vocal technique, ear training, attention and memory, notation and sight-reading and songs.[33] It was supported by limited in-service provision for teachers, and by a revised syllabus of instruction in the training colleges, developments which by 1952 were interpreted to

---

[32] J. J. Redmond, 'Vocal Music', Notes on Examination Performance, 1930s, SPCA C/29/5.
[33] Department of Education, *Revised Programme of Instruction in Music for National Schools*, (Dublin: Stationery Office, 1939).

have yielded largely positive results by retired music inspector Donnchadh Ua Braoin.[34]

Choral music appeared to have thrived at St Patrick's College from the 1920s under the leadership of John Redmond, and from 1949 under that of Seán Hayes who in 1971 was promoted as the College's first Head of Music. A programme titled 'Cuirm Ceoil agus Dráma na Macléinn' [Students' Music and Drama Presentation] dated 19 March 1939 opened with four arrangements of Irish songs for male choir by B. Ua Briain: 'An Maidrín Rua', 'An Londubh 'gus an Chéirseach', 'Ó Cé h-é seo?' and 'Bó na Leath-Adhairce'.[35] Following the play *An Paistín Fionn* (Seosamh Mac Grianna's translation of the comedy *The Whiteheaded Boy* by Lennox Robinson) the choir continued with a predominantly Irish programme. This comprised 'Sean-fheara-Chonnacht' by S. Réamonn (John J. Redmond), a vocal trio that included a young Seán Hayes singing Annie Patterson's arrangement of 'Ó Suilleabháin ag Fagáil na Sléibhte', and the full choir performing 'Cailín na Gruaige Doinne' arranged by J. Mac Daid, and Arvin Samuelson's TTBB arrangement of the Scottish folksong 'Road to the Isles'.[36] The programme's emphasis on Gaelic song and on the Irish language undoubtedly reflected the cultural Zeitgeist and indeed the College's own Irish-language policy from 1930.

A similar format for a music and drama concert by students appeared in a programme dated nine years later in 1948, just one year before Redmond's retirement. [37] It opened with *An Dochtúir Bréige*, Fionán Ó Loinsigh's translation of Molière's farce, *Le Medecin malgré lui* and continued with the following choral programme:

'Ag an mBoithrín Buí' (Cóirithe ag an Ollamh Réamonn)
'Passing By' (Focail le Herrick, Ceol le Edward C. Purcell)
'Péarla an Bhrollaigh Bán' (Cóirithe ag an Ollamh Réamonn)
'Just for Today' (Focail le Seaver, Ceol le Hewitt)
'Bíonn Cuimhne Fuar Agam' (Oft in the Stilly Night: Moore—Tórna)
'Carraig Donn' – Ceathairéad: S. Crémer, S. Ó Súilleabháin, T. Ó Garbhaigh, S. Ó Muircheartaigh
'The Comrades' Song of Hope' (Adam)
Amhrán Náisiúnta

As with the 1939 concert programme, a priority for Irish-language material, including the national anthem, was evident here. At the same

---

[34] D. Ua Braoin, 'Music in the Primary Schools', pp. 38-39.
[35] 'Cuirm Ceoil agus Dráma na Macléinn', 19 March 1939, SPCA C/21/9.
[36] A choral arrangement divided into two tenor and two bass parts.
[37] 'Cuirm Ceoil agus Drámuíochta na Macléinn', 7 March 1948, SPCA C/21/9.

time, it can be observed that the proportion of English-language material had increased, and included one piece by Handel. John Redmond is credited as conductor as well as choral arranger for two pieces on the programme, and among the vocal quartet singing an arrangement of 'Carraig Donn' we find the name of Seán Crémer (Creamer) who is also credited as the event's student music organizer or 'reachtaire ceoil'. This would be the same Seán Creamer who later became a music inspector for primary schools, and who was renowned as a choral conductor. Among many notable achievements he established the National Children's Choir in 1985. Another graduate of distinction from the mid-twentieth century was Alfred (Alf) McGowan who taught in East Wall, Dublin and conducted several award-winning choirs, including St Joseph's Choral Society, the male voice choir of the Municipal School of Music, Chatham Row and the Teachers' Choir based in Club na Múinteoirí, Parnell Square.[38]

A student programme from 1955, now with Seán Hayes as choral conductor, revealed a similar format to those described above, albeit with some significant additions.[39] It featured a production of Lady Gregory's *Éirí na Gealaighe* [The Rising of the Moon], among which cast was Eoghan Ó Súilleabháin, later to become an Irish lecturer at the College, credited as 'ceoltóir sráide' [street musician]. The same event saw a set of tunes performed on fiddle by Criostóir Mac Gearra, revealing perhaps a growing appreciation of traditional music in the wake of its national revival in the 1950s.[40] As can be ascertained below, the choral programme now included pieces in three languages - Irish, English and Latin - and across several choral styles (arrangements of Irish and Welsh folksongs, sacred and secular music from the Renaissance period and an African-American spiritual). In contrast to earlier concerts, composer dates were added in the case of the more historical pieces, suggesting a more musicological approach to programming:

'Cantate Domino' (J. Hassler, 1564-1612)
'Seán Ó Duibhir an Ghleanna' – gléasta ag an Ollamh S. Ó hAodha
'Cumha Eoghan Ruaidh Uí Néill' (E. de Regge)
'All Through the Night' gléasta ag Barnes[41]
'Now is the Month of Maying' (T. Morley, 1557-1603)
'Domine Non Sum Dignus' (T. La Vittoria 1548-1611)

---

[38] *Irish Independent*, 23 August 1957, p. 3; T. J. O'Connell, *100 Years of Progress: The Story of the Irish National Teachers' Organisation, 1868-1968*, (Dublin: INTO, 1968), p. 475.
[39] 'Cuirm Ceoil agus Drámaíochta na Macléinn', 27 March 1955, SPCA C/21/9.
[40] Comhaltas Ceoltóirí Éireann was established a few years earlier in 1951.
[41] First name not known.

'Swing Low Sweet Chariot' - gléasta ag G. Bantock, Amhránuí Aonair Pádraig Ó Gadhra
'Och, Och, Éireagh Leigeas Ó' (C. Hardebeck)
'Torramh an Bharaile' - gléasta ag an Ollamh S. Ó h-Aodha
'Amhrán na bhFiann'

In keeping with a now-established College tradition, several of the Irish-language pieces were TTBB choral arrangements made by the students' music lecturer and choral conductor, Seán Hayes (Ó h-Aodha).[42] Cork-born Hayes had studied at the College from 1938-1940 and in 1947 was awarded an honours BMus degree from UCC. During his tenure at St Patrick's College he also worked part-time as a professor of liturgical music at the Royal Irish Academy of Music, and was later organist and choirmaster at the nearby All Hallows Seminary.[43]

As documented in Chapters Two and Four, a milestone moment in the history of the college choir was its première performance of the extended piece *Lúireach Phádraig* [St Patrick's Breastplate] composed by A. J. Potter in late 1965. It was performed with the RTÉ Symphony Orchestra under the baton of Tibor Paul in the College's newly built auditorium on March 15 1966. This joint celebration of the College's patron saint and its modern building development was reflected in Potter's piece which adapted the original Irish text of St Patrick's Breastplate in a contemporary setting that juxtaposed modernist and modal musical ideas.

A surviving audio recording of the piece demonstrates, firstly, Potter's ability to write a substantial and challenging piece for a mixed ability male youth choir which for this piece was divided into a three-part TTB arrangement and secondly, Seán Hayes's thorough preparation of the choral parts for performance, as evidenced by the students' clear and in-tune vocal lines above a full symphony orchestra. Also clearly audible was the students' enthusiasm for the text and indeed for the historic occasion.[44]

1971-2008

1971 was a significant year for St Patrick's College and more generally for education in Ireland. It heralded the publication of a new curriculum for primary schools, with several innovations evident in the music syllabuses for the four biennial age groups, at least in theory. Group instrumental

---

[42] TTBB: choral arrangement of Tenor 1, Tenor 2, Bass 1 and Bass 2.

[43] 'Seán Hayes' (adjudicator biography), *31st International Cork Choral and Folk Dance Festival*, May 2 to May 6, 1984 (published programme), p. 13.

[44] Audio-recording of *Lúireach Phádraig* by A. J. Potter, Potter Archive (The Potter Archive is currently located in A. J. Potter's former home in Greystones, Co. Wicklow and is curated by musicologist Sarah Burn).

music making was introduced and a greater emphasis on listening than heretofore was advocated; at the same time singing would remain at its core, and songs in the Irish language continued to be prioritized.[45] As previously noted, 1971 also marked the admission of female students in addition to male students at St Patrick's College, and the expansion of the music department to include two new full-time appointments: Colum Ó Cléirigh from 1971 and Caitlín Bean Uí Éigeartaigh just one year later. In 1974 the three-year BEd degree programme in St Patrick's College was introduced.

Taking over from Seán Hayes as choral director, Colum Ó Cléirigh introduced several new avenues for choral performance at the College, most notably, the staging of musicals/light opera which continued well into the twenty-first century under a succession of musical directors (these are listed in John Buckley's chapter on performance), an enhanced annual carol service and participation in choral festivals and competitions – in particular, at the Cork International Choral Festival (Ó Cléirigh's substantial work and impact in advancing Zoltán Kodály's approach to vocal and choral music is detailed in Yvonne Higgins's chapter in this volume). The other major change of this time was of course that the college choir would now be a mixed choir, more often than not singing in SATB arrangement.[46] Reflecting on the academic year 1971-1972 former student John O'Carroll recalls Cantóirí Choláiste Phádraigh 'as a fledgling SATB choir'. O'Carroll also remembers Ó Cléirigh's cultural entrepreneurship in bringing the college choir for the first time to the Cork International Choral Festival in 1972 'with the moral and financial support of the President, Dr Cregan and the INTO'.[47]

A further development occurred in 1977 with the appointment of Seán Mac Liam. In 1976, the year prior to his appointment, Mac Liam had conducted the UCC Madrigal Group at the international choral festival in Cork; two of his own choral pieces had also been performed there: 'The Self-Unseen' by the newly formed Madrigal '75 in 1975, and 'In Tenebris' by the UCC Madrigal Group in 1976.[48] Early in 1978 Mac Liam established a select choral group at St Patrick's College that in later years would

---

[45] By this time the term 'vocal music' could no longer encapsulate the breadth of the music curriculum, at least in theory. Moreover, it was only rarely used in relation to choirs, the term 'choral music' now being more widely applied.
[46] SATB: choral arrangement comprising soprano, alto, tenor and bass parts.
[47] John O'Carroll, email correspondence with the author, 19 May 2017.
[48] A digital archive of festival programmes for the Cork International Choral Festival 1954-2015 is available on the website of Cork City Libraries: http://www.corkcitylibraries.ie/music/corkinternationalchoralfestival/ [accessed 17 February 2019]. See also R. Fleischmann, *The Cork International Choral Festival 1954-2004: A Celebration*, (Herford, Germany: Glen House Press, 2004).

expand into a larger chamber choir. This was the first time that the College had an auditioned choir comprising staff as well as students, and also the first time that it had more than one choir; in 1977 these were known as Cantóirí Choláiste Phádraig (in some contexts also referred to as the College's choral society) and St Patrick's College Madrigal Choir. Mac Liam's madrigal/chamber choir at St Patrick's would perform regular concerts at the College up until 1985 (see Chapter Two, pp. 45-46).

Notwithstanding the many innovations in choral performance from the 1970s onwards, Cantóirí Choláiste Phádraig and other vocal groups continued to contribute to masses and to other liturgical events throughout the College's academic calendar. A highlight during the 1970s was the choir's participation in a celebratory mass marking the centenary of the College's foundation, led by Archbishop Dermot Ryan.[49] This took place on 2 December 1975 and was broadcast on RTÉ Radio. One year later Colum Ó Cléirigh would compose an original setting of the mass that was subsequently sung for the next few years at the College's annual mass to mark the commencement of the academic year.[50] Its modal and traditional character suggests some influence from Seán Ó Riada whom Ó Cléirigh would have known during his time studying at UCC. Ó Cléirigh's mass was scored for unison choir in melismatic style with occasional polyphonic textures, including a rhythmic drone-ostinato and some short homophonic sections in three or four vocal parts. The year 1980 marked the first performance of an extended sacred work by St Patrick's College Choral Society with a performance featuring *The Creation*, Part I by Haydn. It took place in the chapel under the baton of Colum Ó Cléirigh. Audio-visual footage of the event taken by Paul Murphy, senior technician at the College provides evidence of the high choral standards achieved at the time.[51]

Ó Cléirigh had a lifelong association with the Cork International Choral Festival from its beginnings in 1954.[52] He brought choirs from St Patrick's College there for no less than ten festivals over two decades, from the first trip in 1972 until the festival of 1992 (See Appendix C for full details of participation by college choirs at the festival from 1972-2015). Optional entry pieces for the years 1972-1976 were largely in keeping with the kind

---

[49] A cassette tape recording of this event is held in the college archive, SPCA, I/K.
[50] Handwritten sketch on six pages, signed and dated by Ó Cléirigh as 'Márta [March] 1976'. Ó Cléirigh Archive, courtesy of Peter McDermott.
[51] A digitized version of this and other video recordings by Paul Murphy were kindly compiled and sent to the editors during the preparation of this volume.
[52] Ó Cléirigh recalls being 'absolutely dumbstruck' by the 1954 festival that took place while he was studying at UCC. He sang in the choir Cór Cois Laoi which was conducted by Pilib Ó Laoghaire: Ó Cléirigh interviewed in Fleischmann, *The Cork International Choral Festival*, p. 196.

of music selected by earlier choral conductors at the College, namely, arrangements of Irish language songs, Renaissance and classical motets, and choral pieces by English composers. After a gap of eleven years, Cantóirí Choláiste Phádraig returned to participate in six festivals in succession, from 1987 to 1992. By this time Ó Cléirigh had introduced the choir to 'alternative' twentieth-century choral works and especially those of Kodály; it can also be noted here how choral instruction at the College had now fully adapted Kodály's choral method, that is, learning and rehearsing pieces through tonic solfa.[53] In 1989 Cantóirí Choláiste Phádraig achieved first place in the National Competition for Youth Choirs with two showcase choral pieces: the sixteenth-century French chanson 'Il est bel et bon' by Pierre Passereu and Charles Villiers Stanford's serene composition, 'The Bluebird'. As Colum Ó Cléirigh was invited to adjudicate at the 1991 festival, Cantóirí Choláiste Phádraig participated that year under the direction of Darragh McGonigle, a former choir member.[54] It would not be until the Cork Choral Festival of 2008 that a student once again conducted the choir, on that occasion Ruth O'Leary.

The contributions of Colum Ó Cléirigh and Seán Mac Liam to choral music at the College were further enhanced by those of Marion Doherty who was appointed as Head of Music in 1985. In 1987 Doherty had set up her own youth choir, Enchiriadis in the North Dublin town of Malahide where she and her family lived, soon followed by a junior Enchiriadis choir, and by 1994 Enchiriadis Treis, a 120-strong adult choral society that went on to win many national awards. The original Enchiriadis choir had a long association with St Patrick's College that began with a joint concert with the college choral society in May 1995 featuring Antonio Vivaldi's *Magnificat* and *Gloria*.[55] Enchiriadis also became well known locally for providing music at Christmas Eve midnight mass ceremonies in the chapel during the 1990s and early 2000s. They also performed there at a special mass marking the departure of the Vincentian Order from the College on 13 June 1999, singing motets by Victoria, Marenzio and Duruflé.[56]

---

[53] Darragh McGonigle (BEd 1986-1989), email correspondence with the author, 12 June 2018. McGonigle recalls: 'We used solfa when learning most pieces, particularly pieces that would have had modulations'.
[54] Previously, Seán Hayes had been a member of the adjudication panel for the 1984 festival. Further associations between the festival and St Patrick's College included the commissioning of new works by John Buckley (1981, 1996) and Rhona Clarke (1994, 2008) and the chairing of the seminar on contemporary music by Rhona Clarke between 2009-2015.
[55] *St Patrick's College Annual Report 1994-1995*, n. p., SPCA, A 1/7.
[56] 'Aifreann chun críoch riaradh Choláiste Phádraig Droim Chonrach – 1875 -1999 ag Cuallacht na hUinseannach a chinneadh', SPCA, E/15.

Marion Doherty conducted the college choir from the mid-1990s, occasionally substituted by Brian McKay and later, Yvonne Higgins while Doherty was pursuing doctoral studies in choral conducting at the University of Iowa (Yvonne Higgins also conducted the chamber choir Viva Voce). [57] In April 2000, the college choir took part in five competitions at the Bangor Choral Festival in Co. Down, achieving second place in both the madrigal and youth choir sections.[58]

Arguably, Doherty's major contribution to the development of choral music at the College was that for the first time since 1980, full-length sacred works came to be performed by the choral society. Her considerable experience as a conductor as well as an instrumentalist (primarily on harpsichord and viola) was invaluable at a time when increasing numbers of orchestral players could be found among cohorts of BEd and BA students. Two notable concerts in this respect were first, a concert with Fauré's *Requiem* and Vivaldi's *Gloria* in December 2000, and one year later, a performance of Haydn's *Missa in Tempore Belli* and Britten's *Ceremony of Carols* (with harpist Denise Kelly). For the second of these concerts, the College's annual report for 2001-2002 noted that all vocal soloists were current college students, and that the concerts were recorded and later pressed on CD.[59] From time to time Doherty also engaged early career vocal soloists who had previously graduated with a BEd degree from the College;[60] these included Kathleen Tynan (soprano), Declan Kelly (tenor) and Eoin Power (bass-baritone).[61]

In November 2004 the college choral society collaborated with Cantairí Avondale (conducted by Mary O'Flynn) and Enchiriadis youth and junior choirs (conducted respectively by Cathal Clinch and Aideen O'Brien) to present a programme of choral music over two nights that included Bernstein's *Chichester Psalms* and Fauré's *Requiem*. [62] A concert in December 2006 showcased the advances that Doherty had made with orchestral as well as with choral music during her tenure, and her

---

[57] The chamber choir Viva Voce included graduates and staff members of St Patrick's College. Among other performances, it participated in the College's annual carol service up to 2008.

[58] *St Patrick's College Annual Report 1999-2000*, p. 25, SPCA, A 1/7.

[59] *St Patrick's College Annual Report 2000-2001*, p. 27; *St Patrick's College Annual Report 2001-2002*, p. 32, SPCA, A 1/7. Copies of the CDs are held in the College archive, SPCA, I.K.

[60] Marion Doherty, interview with the author, 14 April 2019.

[61] All three BEd graduates studied with Professor Paul Deegan at the Royal Irish Academy of Music. Deegan himself attended St Patrick's College c. 1959-1960 and qualified with an NT diploma prior to developing a celebrated career as a singer and singing teacher. Interview with the author, 22 April 2019.

[62] *St Patrick's College Annual Report 2004-2005*, p. 29, SPCA, A 1/7.

encouragement of student conductors. It took place in the main auditorium and featured a mainly instrumental programme that included Beethoven's *Symphony No. 1* conducted by Gavan Ring and Britten's *A Ceremony of Carols* (this time with Andreja Malir on harp) conducted by Ruth O'Leary.[63]

Figure 6.3: Marion Doherty, Head of Music at St Patrick's College 1985-2008. Photographer unknown

Doherty graduated from the University of Iowa with a Doctor of Musical Arts in Choral Conducting and Pedagogy in December 2007, and just over one year later retired from her post as Head of Music. Her contribution to choral music at the College would continue however through the development and delivery of the course, 'Choral Conducting in Education and in the Community'. This modular in-service diploma was designed for primary and post-primary teachers as well as for community musicians. Its teaching faculty included an array of widely experienced conductors: alongside Marion Doherty were Colman Pearce, Mary O'Flynn, Orla Flanagan, Brian McKay and Marian Mullen. The first cohort to take the course included Róisín Nic Athlaoich, a part-time music lecturer at the College, and Darragh McGonigle and Ruth O'Leary (both of whom had enjoyed some conducting experience during their undergraduate studies at the College).

From 2008
2008 marked the year that the author (henceforth referred to by name) began to conduct the college choir following his appointment as Head of

---

[63] *St Patrick's College Annual Report 2007-2008*, p. 30. SPCA, A 1/7.

Music. John O'Flynn continued with many of the choral traditions established by his predecessors (having previously sung in choirs conducted by both Colum Ó Cléirigh and Seán Mac Liam while he was a student at the College), notably, directing the annual carol service, and resuming the college choir's participation in the Cork International Choral Festival. In a sense, O'Flynn also reverted to the model of in-house concerts as programmed by John Redmond and later by Seán Hayes in the middle decades of the twentieth century. Between 2009-2016 the college choir's showcase concert became part of the spring semester lunchtime concert series organized by John Buckley. [64]

During the first few years that he directed the choir, O'Flynn strove to increase participation which had diminished by comparison with previous decades, particularly among male students. Among other strategies he introduced repertoire in popular style that had been developed for youth choirs. For example, the choir's lunchtime choral concert in February 2009 was themed 'Gospel, Folk and Musicals' and comprised the following programme:

'Didn't my Lord Deliver Daniel'	arr. R. Emerson
'The Turtle Dove'	arr. L. Spevacek
'Songs of a Starry Night'	arr. E. Crocker
'My Johnny's a Soldier'	arr. C. Bennett
'Moon River'	H. Mancini, arr. E. Lojeski
'The Rhythm of Life'	D. Fields / C. Coleman, arr. R. Emerson
'Shenandoah'	arr. L. Spevacek
'Hush my Babe'	J. Koudelka, arr. B. Bacaon
'Send Down the Rain'	J. Eilers
'Sinner Man'	arr. R. Emerson

In later years and as the capacity of the choir was perceived to grow, the programming for lunchtime concerts reflected a greater emphasis on standard and contemporary choral repertoire, including pieces by Dowland, Weelkes, Bach, Mendelssohn, Berlioz, Saint-Saëns, Rutter, Stanford, Kodály, Duruflé, Seiber and John Buckley. In addition to lunchtime concerts the choir also continued to contribute to college-wide events, including the annual mass for the commencement of the academic year and the December carol service. From time to time St Patrick's College Choir also participated in and was broadcast on *Lyric FM*'s 'Carols for Christmas' series. During this period the choir had a pro-active student committee, and was further supported by choral members who accompanied the choir for its many engagements, including Davina Baker

---

[64] Clare McEvoy conducted the choir for the lunchtime concert in spring 2016.

(BEd 2007-2010), Judith McGann (BA 2008-2011), Mark Sheekey (BEd 2008-2011), Anna Bourke (BEd 2009-2012), and the Czech Erasmus students Anna Pragrová and Markéta Krucka.

Figure 6.4: Members of St Patrick's College Choir at the Mahony Hall The Helix, 14 December 2011. Photograph by Eoin Campbell

Following the return of an annual Kodály summer school to the College in July 2009 - presented by the Kodály Society of Ireland and hosted by the music department - O'Flynn established an association with the then Hungarian ambassador to Ireland, Mr Ferencs Jári. In 2010 invitations were extended for the college choir to participate in two special events. The first of these was an Irish-Hungarian concert programmed as a non-competitive event for the Cork International Choral Festival where the college choir presented a joint concert at St John's Art Centre with Amica Voce, the Dublin-based Hungarian choir.[65]

The second and more substantial invitation that year was for the college choir to participate in the Hungarian-Irish Music Festival that took place in July in the city of Győr. The University of Western Hungary hosted twenty-five students from the College, accompanied by O'Flynn

---

[65] Two items on the programme featured the renowned mezzo-soprano Imelda Drumm in performance with St Patrick's College Choir and Davina Baker (BEd 2007-2010) on piano: *Haiku Seasons* by John Buckley and 'Laudate Dominum' from *Vesperae Solennes de Confessore*, K339 by Mozart.

and by the president of St Patrick's College at that time, Dr Pauric Travers. During the festival the choir performed two outdoor concerts in popular and folk styles (with instrumental sets of traditional music performed also by choir members) in the city's main square, a concert of sacred music at Győr Cathedral, and a recital of sacred and secular music at a church in the nearby village of Hédervár. Later, in December 2010 Ambassador Jári and Mrs Melinda Jári hosted a recital given by the choir and selected chamber music groups from the College at the Hungarian Embassy in Dublin.[66]

O'Flynn brought choirs to the Cork International Choral Festival between the years 2009-2015 (see Appendix C for details). [67] With participation by BEd, BA and Erasmus students, the choir was particularly successful in the national competition for youth choirs, ranked first in 2012 and second place through 2013, 2014 and 2015. The winning programme for 2012 comprised the madrigal 'Hark All Ye Lovely Saints' by Weelkes and the evocative 'Calmes des Nuits' by Saint-Saëns. From 2013-2015 the choir also participated in the festival fringe event 'Afternoons in the Atrium' at Cork's Clarion Hotel. These semi-formal performances staged for festival tourists and local audiences provided the choir with opportunities to perform mixed-repertoire programmes as well as representing a welcome balance to the formal competitions.

In addition to conducting the main college choir until 2016, from 2012-2015 O'Flynn also conducted a female chamber choir that took the name St Patrick's College Alumni Choir. [68] It was set up at the request of graduates who were among the choir that had visited Hungary in 2010 and also included several staff members, two of whom – Ruth McManus and Susan Hegarty of the College's geography department – had previously sung with Viva Voce. The alumni choir performed a mix of sacred and secular repertoire, with at least one College event each semester. In December 2012 this included participation in the staging of John Cage's *MusiCircus* under the artistic direction of The Fidelio Trio. Externally, the alumni choir participated at the Mayo International Choral Festival in 2013, and at charity events in Mater Dei Institute of Education in 2014 and Marino Institute of Education in 2015.

---

[66] The extensive choral activities and social life of St Patrick's College Choir around this time are the subject of the previously cited article from 2015 in the *International Journal of Community Music*: J. O'Flynn, 'Strengthening choral community'.

[67] The exception to this was during the spring semester of 2011 when Rhona Clarke conducted the college choir.

[68] Amy Ryan conducted St Patrick's College Alumni Choir during the spring semester of 2016.

Figure 6.5: Members of St Patrick's College Choir at the Clarion Hotel Cork, 8 May 2013. Photograph by Hertz Oliveira da Silva

Concluding comments

The legacy of choral music at St Patrick's College continued after incorporation into DCU. In October 2016 and at the request of DCU Music Society chairperson Ben Davis (a member of the final BA cohort to graduate from the College), the college choir was renamed the DCU Music Society Choir, albeit with the same mix of humanities, education and international students as before and with O'Flynn continuing as conductor. This 'transitional' choir had the honour of representing its original institution at a special event held in The Helix on 17 November 2016 to mark the incorporation of St Patrick's College along with Mater Dei Institute of Education and the Church of Ireland College of Education into DCU. In keeping with the patterns of programming for college choirs of previous decades, the two showcase pieces chosen for that event were the anonymous Catalan madrigal 'Dindirrindin' and the student anthem 'Cohors Generosa' by Kodály.

Choral music was an integral aspect of life at St Patrick's College, from the appointment of its first music lecturer in 1883 to incorporation into DCU in 2016. Throughout this time, choral music was closely linked with issues of music education. This was especially the case during the earlier history of the College when 'vocal music' referred both to school music syllabuses and to choral performance. More importantly perhaps, student participation in college-based choral activities for more than one hundred and thirty years has led to the establishment of innumerable choirs in schools and communities across the country. From the College's foundation, choral music was also linked to religious ceremonies, and further constituted a significant aspect of campus (and off-campus) experience for many students over the years.

The College has a long line of choral directors. Peter Goodman and Joseph Seymour, both leading figures in the Cecilian reform movement, can be credited with establishing high standards for choral music at the College at the turn of the twentieth century. These were upheld and developed in changing socio-political contexts by John Redmond in the post-independence period and by Seán Hayes for much of the mid-twentieth century. Colum Ó Cléirigh, Seán Mac Liam and Marion Doherty all made significant contributions to the expansion and diversification of choral activities at the College from the 1970s to the early twenty-first century, with John O'Flynn continuing that trajectory up to 2016.

The number of students who sang in the choirs of St Patrick's College over the years would likely run into thousands. Although they sang during different historical periods, under various conductors and for a range of religious and secular functions that evolved in line with the College's history, they nonetheless constitute a continuous legacy. Arguably, this is a legacy that above all is built on aspirations towards shared artistic goals - in experiences both within and beyond the life of the College.

Bibliography

An Roinn Oideachais, *Revised Programme of Instruction in Music for National Schools*, (Dublin: Stationery Office, 1939).

An Roinn Oideachais, *An Curaclam Nua*. Teachers' Handbook, Parts I and II, (Dublin: Browne and Nolan, 1971).

Benderius, Lisa, 'The Future Role of the French Harmonium', Unpublished MA dissertation, (University of Gothenburg, 2015).

Clift, S. M., & Hancox, G., 'The perceived benefits of singing: findings from preliminary surveys of a university college choral society', *The Journal of the Royal Society for the Promotion of Health*, 121.4 (2001), 248-256.

Collins, Paul (ed.), *Renewal and Resistance: Catholic Church Music from the 1850s to Vatican II*, (Bern: Peter Lang, 2010).

Collins, Paul, and Larkin, David, 'Joseph Seymour', in H. White & B. Boydell (eds.), *The Encyclopaedia of Music in Ireland*, Volume II, (Dublin: UCD Press, 2013), pp. 927-8.

Daly, Kieran, *Catholic Church Music in Ireland, 1878-1903: The Cecilian Reform Movement*, (Dublin and Portland, ON: Four Courts Press, 1995).

Ferriter, Diarmuid, '"For God's sake send me a few packets of fags": the College, 1922-45', in J. Kelly (ed.), *St Patrick's College, Drumcondra: A History*, (Dublin: Four Courts Press, 2006), pp. 133-157.

Fleischmann, Ruth, *The Cork International Choral Festival 1954-2004: A Celebration*, (Herford, Germany: Glen House Press, 2004).

Humphreys, Maggie and Evans, Robert (eds), *Dictionary of Composers for the Church in Great Britain and Ireland*, (London: Mansell, 1997).

Hutchinson, John, *Dynamics of Cultural Nationalism: The Gaelic Revival and the Creation of the Irish Nation State*, (London and New York: Routledge, 2012).

Hyland, Áine, 'The process of curriculum change in the Irish national school system', *Irish Educational Studies*, 6.2 (1986-87), 24-45.

McCarthy, Marie, *Passing it On: The Transmission of Music in Irish Culture*, (Cork: Cork University Press, 1999).

McCarthy, Marie, 'Ireland: Curriculum development in troubled times', in G. Cox & R. Stevens (eds.), *The Origins and Foundations of Music Education*, (London: Bloomsbury, 2016), pp. 52-66.

National Council for Curriculum and Assessment, *Primary School Curriculum, Arts Education: Music*, (Dublin: Stationery Office, 1999).

New Rules and Regulations (National Education), 1900-1, Cd. 601, H.C. 1901 (3).

Ní Shé, Bríd, 'The Initial Education and Training of Music Teachers for Primary Schools in the Republic of Ireland, Northern Ireland, England and Wales', Unpublished MEd thesis, (Trinity College Dublin, 1994).

O'Connell, T. J., *100 Years of Progress: The Story of the Irish National Teachers' Organisation, 1868-1968*, (Dublin: INTO, 1968).

O'Flynn, John, 'Strengthening choral community: The interaction of face-to-face and online activities amongst a college choir', *International Journal of Community Music*, 8.1 (2015), 73-92.

Ó Súilleabháin, Eoghan, 'Cuimní Cinn ar CPD: Céad Bliain de Ré na bhFear leo féin' (1975), Saint Patrick's College Archive, C/46.

Ryng, Mary, 'A really good man: Peter Goodman and his contribution to music in Irish primary education', *British Journal of Music Education*, 19.2 (2002), 145-156.

Simpson, Kenneth, *Some Great Music Educators: A Collection of Essays*, (London: Novello, 1976).

St Patrick's College Annual Report 1994-1995, (Dublin: St Patrick's College).

St Patrick's College Annual Report 1999-2000, (Dublin: St Patrick's College).

St Patrick's College Annual Report 2000-2001, (Dublin: St Patrick's College).

St Patrick's College Annual Report 2001-2002, (Dublin: St Patrick's College).

St Patrick's College Annual Report 2005-2005, (Dublin: St Patrick's College).

St Patrick's College Annual Report 2006-2007, (Dublin: St Patrick's College).

Szőnyi, Erzsébet, *Kodálys Principles in Practice*, (London: Boosey & Hawkes, 1973).

Tonneijck, Hetty, Kinébanian, Astrid, & Josephsson, Staffan, 'An exploration of choir singing: Achieving wholeness through challenge', *Journal of Occupational Science*, 15.3 (2008), 173-180.

Thirty-First Annual Report of St Patrick's Training College, Drumcondra, For the Session 1913-14, (Dublin: Browne and Nolan, 1915).

Ua Braoin, Donnchadh, 'Music in the Primary Schools', in A. Fleischmann (ed.), *Music in Ireland: A Symposium*, (Cork: Cork University Press, 1952), pp. 37-44.

Walsh, Thomas, 'The Revised Programme of Instruction, 1900-1922', *Irish Educational Studies*, 26.2 (2007), pp. 127-143.

White, J. P., & Heller, G. N. (1983, October). 'Entertainment, enlightenment, and service: a history and description of choral music in higher education', *College Music Symposium*, 23. 2 (1983), pp. 10-20.

Newspapers and periodicals
Freeman's Journal
Irish Independent

Archives
Cork International Choral Festival, Cork City Library Digital Archive
The Potter Archive
St Patrick's College Archive

Interviews and email correspondence
Paul Deegan
Marion Doherty
Peter McDermott
Darragh McGonigle
John O'Carroll

Chapter Seven: The Kodály Connection

Yvonne Higgins

Introduction
This chapter traces the connections between the music department of St Patrick's College, Drumcondra and the Zoltán Kodály Institute of Music Pedagogy in Kecskemét, Hungary. It describes how, initially, one lecturer's interest in the Zoltán Kodály concept of music education, forged a relationship between the two institutions that spanned many years, impacting on music education in Ireland.

The chapter reports on the first and second International Zoltán Kodály Music Seminars hosted by the music department at St Patrick's College during the 1980s and records the formation of the Irish Kodály Society following these seminars. Following a period when Kodály courses were held in the Church of Ireland College of Education, Rathmines, the chapter continues with a description of the Kodály Society of Ireland's 'Active Music-Making Summer Courses' held at St Patrick's College between 2009 and 2016. The remainder of the chapter discusses the impact of the Kodály approach to music education at St Patrick's College and on the Irish primary music curriculum (1999). It recounts how students of the music department who, as a result of Kodály-related experiences during their formation as teachers, embarked upon studies at the Kodály Institute in Hungary before returning to lead and contribute in various roles to music education in Ireland and further afield.

This chapter draws upon available hard copy and digital sources of documents and correspondence relating to the seminars and summer courses. In addition, it draws upon first-hand experience of these seminars and courses through interviews conducted with individuals involved in their organization.

The Kodály approach to music pedagogy
The Kodály approach to music pedagogy is an internationally recognized system of music education based on a philosophy and approach to music teaching instigated by the twentieth-century Hungarian composer, ethnomusicologist and music educator Zoltán Kodály (1882-1967). Through his work as an ethnomusicologist Kodály, together with his friend and colleague Béla Bartók (1881-1945), uncovered an ancient layer of Hungarian folk song. Scholarship of this repertoire led him to the realization that pentatony was a key feature of

that music.[1] This heritage informed both Bartók's and Kodály's composition style and influenced Kodály's thinking on Hungarian music education.[2]

At the heart of the Kodály approach is a belief that 'music belongs to everyone', an ideal that resonated with Hungarian socialist policies of the late 1940s and 1950s and proved useful when arguing for the place of music in the education system.[3] This belief was particularly relevant for, and underpinned the work of the music department at St Patrick's, in seeking to meet the needs of all children in the Irish primary school system. Kodály's initial concern for music education came about as a result of his dismay at the music literacy levels of students entering the *zeneakademia*, the highest-level music school in Hungary in the early 1900s.[4] A second concern was students' ignorance of their own Hungarian musical heritage. Kodály sought to 'give back' this musical heritage to the people of Hungary and to cultivate a musically literate Hungarian society.[5] He advocated singing as the best means of active participation in music making, and as a means through which to create a literate musical culture: 'The best approach to musical genius is through the instrument most accessible to everyone: the human voice'.[6] The development of music reading and writing skills through singing were key tenets and were a prerequisite for learning to play an instrument. Music reading and writing was understood to include an ability to think in sound in relation to notation, referred to as 'innerhearing':

> Developing the inner ear to the highest degree is indispensable; one should be able to transfer notation immediately into sound

---

[1] The use of pentatonic scales (i.e. five-note scales containing only the intervals of major 2nd and minor 3rd)

[2] L. Eősze, M. Houlahan, & P. Tacka, 'Kodály, Zoltán', *Grove Music – Oxford Music Online*, https://doi.org/10.1093/gmo/9781561592630.article.15246 [accessed 28 April 2019].

[3] E. Szőnyi, *Kodály's Principles in Practice: An Approach to Music Education through the Kodály Method*, trans. J. Weissman, 5th edn, (Budapest: Corvina, 1990). Kodály's concept of music for all was devised almost two decades before its formal implementation in the Hungarian school system. It was partially realized through the Hungarian Youth Choral Movement instigated by Kodály's former students.

[4] L. Choksy, *The Kodály Method: Comprehensive Music Education from Infant to Adult*, (Englewood Cliffs, NJ: Prentice-Hall, 1974).

[5] M. Houlahan & P. Tacka, *Kodály Today: A Cognitive Approach to Elementary Music Education,* (Oxford: Oxford University Press, 2008).

[6] Szőnyi, *Kodály's Principles in Practice*, p. 11.

and vice-versa in the mind, without recourse to an instrument.[7]

Kodály insisted that children should begin music learning as early as possible, acquiring their 'musical vernacular' through singing songs in their Hungarian 'musical mother tongue'. It was upon this aural store of melodies garnered through musical play and movement in the nursery school that formal teaching could draw when musical concepts were presented 'consciously'. Children, he believed, should be taught with only the most musically valuable material. 'For the young, only the best is good enough'.[8] Through the use of Hungarian children's games and folk songs, followed by folk songs of other countries he sought 'to make masterpieces of world music literature [i.e. Western classical music] public property, to convey them to people of every kind and rank'.[9] This notion of learning through the senses and through direct participation resonates with the ideas of Pestalozzi - another advocate of music instruction for all who emphasized the importance of singing.[10] The principle of 'sound before symbol', that is experiencing music aurally before the introduction of notation, underpins the Kodály approach.

Whilst he did not personally devise a syllabus or a defined sequence of learning, colleagues and former students under his guidance and encouragement developed pedagogical materials and methodologies. The Kodály approach was unique in its reliance on a vast repertoire of folksong analysed and organized for teaching purposes in a sequential order in which particular musical elements were to be presented in a delineated learning sequence. This sequence was dictated by the frequency with which music elements occurred in the folk song repertoire and took account of the developmental level of learners.[11] Singing was the means through which musical imagination and thinking could be developed.[12] In addition to the use of folk song repertoire, the Kodály approach drew upon a rich European heritage of pedagogical strategies related to music teaching and learning.[13] These

---

[7] Ibid., p. 15.
[8] Ibid., p. 11.
[9] Z. Kodály, *The Selected Writings of Zoltán Kodály*, ed. F. Bónis, trans. L. Halápy & F. Macinicol, (London: Boosey & Hawkes, 1974).
[10] Johann Heinrich Pestalozzi (1746-1827) was an educational and social reformer whose thinking influenced Friedrich Froebel (1782-1852) and John Dewey (1859-1952).
[11] Application of Kodály's principles requires analysis of a country's folksong repertoire in order to sequence learning.
[12] L. Dobszay, 'The Kodály Method and Its Musical Basis', *Studia Musicologica Academiae Scientiarum Hungaricae*, 14.1/4 (1972), 15-33.
[13] Eősze, Houlahan, & Tacka, 'Kodály, Zoltán'.

included relative solfa solmization, related hand signs, rhythm solmization, and simplified or proto-notations (for example, stick-notation and 2/3-line staves).[14] Kodály emphasized relative solfa as a means of expressing tonality and giving meaning to notation. He also placed special importance on the early introduction of part-singing. In a speech at the Academy of Music in Budapest (1953), Kodály summarized the characteristics of a good musician and therefore what music education should entail:

> ... a cultured ear, a cultured intelligence, a cultured heart, and a cultured hand. These four need to be developed simultaneously and kept in constant equilibrium.[15]

Following the sharing of Hungarian music education practices at the International Society for Music Education Conference in Budapest in 1964, Kodály's philosophy and the system of music education he instigated became known among its proponents outside of Hungary as 'The Kodály Method'. Within Hungary, however, Kodály's legacy is viewed more as a set of guiding principles for music education based upon 'a philosophy on the role of music in society, in the life of the child, youth and adult'.[16]

The beginning of the 'Kodály connection'

The 'Kodály connection' in the chapter title refers to the relationship that developed between the music department of St Patrick's College of Education, Drumcondra, (referred to within this chapter as St Patrick's College) and The Zoltán Kodály Pedagogical Institute of Music in Kecskemét in Hungary.[17] It was initiated by Colum Ó Cléirigh, senior lecturer in the music department of St Patrick's College and Péter Erdei, Head of the Kodály Institute. Whilst there is documented evidence of Irish interest in Kodály as a composer as well as in his concept of music education before this connection was established, Ó Cléirigh was pioneering in that he brought the Kodály concept of music education to national attention.[18]

---

[14] Stick notation, a type of 'proto' or simplified notation, refers to a basic or 'short-hand' version of rhythm notation using standard rhythm notation without note heads.

[15] Szőnyi, *Kodály's Principles in Practice*, p. 15.

[16] Ibid., p. 8.

[17] The Institute is now part of the Liszt Academy of Music in Budapest.

[18] In 1978 Albert Bradshaw presented a Kodály course 'of interest to all teachers of music, primary and post-primary alike' in UCC: *Cork Examiner*, 20 January 1978, p. 8; Bradshaw also co-presented a Kodály course at TCD in 1979 with

Donal Colum Ó Cléirigh completed his music studies in University College Cork (UCC) in 1964, having been awarded a scholarship to the University by Tipperary South Riding County Council.[19] He studied under Professor Aloys Fleischmann and started his lifelong association with the Cork Choral Festival.[20] Ó Cléirigh had regularly brought choirs from St Patrick's College to compete at the Festival during the 1970s and it was there in 1982 that he met Péter Erdei, Director of the Kodály Institute. Erdei had been to Cork to adjudicate at the festival on the 100th anniversary of Zoltán Kodály's birth.[21] Ó Cléirigh had already become interested in Kodály's concept of music education and had travelled to Kecskemét to attend a Kodály Summer Seminar in 1980.[22] Following his meeting with Erdei, Ó Cléirigh attended the 1982 Summer Seminar in Kecskemet and a 'Kodály connection' between the two institutions that was to span several decades was forged. This connection was to contribute to thinking in music education at St Patrick's College and impact more widely on Irish music education and choral life.

In addition to its responsibilities for music as an academic subject, the music department at St Patrick's College was tasked with preparing all BEd students to teach music as one of ten curriculum subjects of the primary school curriculum.[23] Given the diversity in the students' levels of musicianship and the limited number of contact hours, this was an on-going challenge. Innovative, effective ways to enhance students' musical understanding and music teaching skills were always of interest.

American composer/educator Seán Deibler. Among the attendees was John Buckley, co-editor of this volume.

[19] 'Lecturer made a lasting contribution to Irish Musical Life', *The Irish Times*, 27 May 2017.

[20] Cork International Choral Festival, 'Tribute to Colum Ó Cléirigh RIP' (2017) www.corkchoral.ie/tribute-to-colum-o-cleirigh-rip [accessed 2 February 2019].

[21] The festival had a much earlier connection with Kodály. Professor Aloys Fleischmann of UCC commissioned a choral piece by the composer for the first of its contemporary music seminars in 1962. Owing to Kodály's ill-health, his SATB work 'Ode to Music' was not completed in time for the 1962 seminar, but instead was performed at the 1963 Seminar. 'Work of Zoltán Kodály Analysed at Seminar', *The Cork Examiner*, 8 May 1963.

[22] Interview with Lilla Gabór, December 2018; email correspondence from Albert Bradshaw, 4 February 2019. Bradshaw was surprised to find Ó Cléirigh, a fellow music educator in Dublin, at his first lecture on 'Kodály Adaptation in Ireland' during the seminar.

[23] An Roinn Oideachais, *An Curaclam Nua*. Teachers' Handbook, Parts I and II, (Dublin: Browne and Nolan, 1971).

Figure 7.1: Colum Ó Cléirigh conducting at Galway Cathedral in 1974.[24] Photographer unknown

Having experienced Kodály principles and pedagogies at first hand, Ó Cléirigh recognized teaching strategies and approaches that would both benefit Irish student primary teachers and be appropriate for them to use with their future pupils in line with the demands of the curriculum.[25] Furthermore, he appreciated the breadth of possible applications of the Kodály approach in developing high levels of musicianship amongst Irish vocal and instrumental performers. As a consequence, following his attendance at the 1980 seminar and subsequent visits to Kecskemét, he succeeded in organizing for the music department to host a Kodály music seminar. As a result of his determination, two international Kodály seminars were held in St Patrick's College in 1983 and 1985.

The First International Zoltán Kodály Seminar at St Patrick's College, 1983

The plan to host an international seminar at St Patrick's in the 1980s was an ambitious one that was fraught with challenges. These ranged

---

[24] A caption written by Ó Cléirigh on the back of the original photo reads 'Conducting Amassed Choirs 1200, Secondary School All Ireland Festival Chorus of Thanksgiving at Galway Cathedral. I wrote it for choir, organ and orchestra. 1974'. Ó Cléirigh Archive, courtesy of Peter McDermott.

[25] Whilst the 1971 Irish primary curriculum for music did not adopt a Kodály approach, its emphasis on singing and its guidelines relating to song repertoire selection resonated to some degree with Kodály thinking.

from issues relating to the promotion of the seminar amongst potential Irish and international participants to the funding of such an elaborate initiative. [26] In an effort to ensure that the initial seminar would proceed, Ó Cléirigh sought the support of many well-known figures in the Irish academic and music communities. By lending their names to the cause, the seminar's profile was raised and its place was assured. It was for this reason that, in addition to an organizing committee, the First International Kodály Seminar in 1983 boasted a Seminar President and five Vice–Presidents. Professor Anthony Hughes, Professor of Music at University College Dublin was the Seminar President. The seminar vice-presidents were Aloys Fleischmann, Emeritus Professor of Music at University College Cork; Seán Hayes, Head of Music at St Patrick's College; Seán Creamer and Brian Ó Dubhghaill, both Department of Education music inspectors and Cáit Lanigan Cooper, Director of the Goethe Institute Choir.[27]

Fears in relation to the financing of the seminar were abated when Fr Sam Clyne, on behalf of the Vincentian Community, offered to make up any shortfall from Vincentian funds. [28] Tuition fees for Irish participants were 'only Ir. £110' whilst overseas participants could avail of tuition and full board or tuition and bed and Irish breakfast for $473 and $323 respectively. All overseas participants were offered accommodation in what was described as 'a new and comfortable student hostel on the College Campus', with limited space for Irish participants. Meals were to be served in the college restaurant.[29]

An information sheet, printed on official college-headed notepaper announced the seminar.[30] Committee members appealed for financial support locally, nationally and from corporate and public bodies including, for example, Bord Fáilte and Córas Iompar Éireann. [31] Appeals for support were made to friends, colleagues and relatives employed in various locations and positions. The seminar programme and finance records evidence the generosity and support of many patrons and sponsors from the academic, religious, local and corporate

---

[26] Information about the 1983 seminar was disseminated by the seminar secretary that year through letters published in the 'Letters to the Editor' columns of several Irish regional newspapers (for example, *Tuam Herald*, *Sligo Champion* and *Cork Examiner*): Interview with Deirdre Seaver, March 2019.
[27] Interview with Deirdre Seaver, October 2018.
[28] Ibid.
[29] Seminar Information Sheet, 1983, Ó Cléirigh Archive.
[30] Ibid.
[31] Ó Cléirigh's personal archive contains copies of letters sent to a number of financial institutions and corporate bodies appealing for financial support. Recipients were offered opportunities to sponsor concerts, public lectures or travel expenses.

worlds.[32] Such was the success of its promotion, that by the time it was advertised to participants the seminar had received sanction from the Department of Education as an intensive course for which primary teacher attendees could be released from school with pay for the last four days of the primary school year.[33]

The organizing committee for the 1983 seminar was a *meitheal* comprised of Ó Cléirigh's friends, colleagues and past and present students.[34] For the most part they were primary teachers, some of whom were recent graduates of St Patrick's College, and current students. The format of both seminars (1983 and 1985) was modelled on the biennial international Kodály seminars in Kecskemét, the first of which was held in 1970. The aims outlined for the first seminar in Dublin were:

- to offer a model of musicianship training that employs all musical skills, develops a conscious sense of style, trains the ear and memory;
- to show several models for the practical use of the Kodály music educational concept;
- through analysis and performance of XX [20th] century music (Bartók, Kodály, etc.) participants will have a unique chance to see theory, performance and pedagogy in their true unity.[35]

The core component of the course was the daily solfège class, where participants studied musical elements through ear-training, musical reading and writing, singing in parts, memorization and the use of relative solfa solmization. In addition, participants attended daily conducting and methodology classes (5 hours each per week) folk music classes (3 hours per week), choir (4 times per week) and optional chamber music classes. Irish traditional music, both vocal and instrumental, had a special place in folk music classes and, together with Irish dancing, was a topic addressed in public lectures and a feature of social gatherings. Folk music classes were analytic in presentation and drew on Hungarian ethnomusicology.

On the basis of a musicianship test, participants were placed into class groups where instruction was differentiated to target the needs of

---

[32] For example, financial records note a donation of £100 from Archbishop Dermot Ryan.

[33] Interview with Deirdre Seaver, October 2018; Seminar Information Sheet, 1983.

[34] *Meitheal* is an Irish-language term meaning a working party made up of family, friends and neighbours.

[35] Seminar Information Sheet, 1983, Ó Cléirigh Archive.

each group. Materials used were drawn for the most part from the *Kodály Choral Library* published by Boosey and Hawkes, and were supplemented by additional materials as necessary.[36] Three faculty members of the Kodály Institute in Kecskemét were invited to teach on the 1983 seminar: Ildikó Herboly Kocsár, Mihály Ittzés and Katalin Kiss. Kiss taught the beginners solfège and conducting classes, Herboly took the intermediate levels and Ittzés taught the advanced level.[37]

Public lectures played an important part in attracting participants to the seminar and in fostering connections. Aloys Fleischmann spoke on choral music in Ireland after which Anthony Hughes, UCD chaired an open forum and discussion. Composer John Buckley, who later lectured in the music department, spoke on 'Approaches to Listening to Contemporary Music'. Declan Townsend, Head of Music Theory at the Municipal School of Music in Cork, presented on the application of Kodály, Ward and Orff methods of teaching music in Irish schools whilst Caitlín Uí Éigeartaigh, lecturer at St Patrick's College music department, presented on Irish music. Other familiar names from the wider music community listed in the programme included Mícheál Ó Suilleabháin and Geoffrey Spratt from UCC and Albert Bradshaw, Head of Music at Mount Temple Comprehensive School. Bradshaw had completed studies in the Kodály approach both in the United States and in Hungary.[38]

Lecturers from within St Patrick's College who contributed included Éanna Mac Cába, an accomplished uilleann piper from *Roinn na Gaeilge* [the Irish Department], and Peter O' Driscoll, Head of Drama who led a practical demonstration on the Ward method.[39] In addition to establishing a connection between the music department of St Patrick's College and the Kodály Institute in Kecskemét, the 1983 and 1985 seminars, through their series of concerts and public lectures, drew upon and strengthened ties between the music department and a host of Irish musicians, teachers, and academics.

The seminar was advertised widely by word of mouth and in print media, attracting people from diverse musical backgrounds and geographic locations.[40] In addition to primary teachers and music department students of St Patrick's College, seminar participants

---

[36] Z. Kodály, *Kodály Choral Method Series*, ed. P. Young, (London: Boosey and Hawkes, 1965).

[37] The Vincentian community welcomed the Hungarian faculty to St Patrick's College at a lunch in Belvedere House.

[38] 1983 Seminar Programme, Ó Cléirigh Archive.

[39] Interview with Peter O'Driscoll, December 2018.

[40] For example, there is a reference to 'a massive Kodály course' in music critic Charles Acton's column in *The Irish Times*: 'Embarrassment of Riches', *The Irish Times*, 17 June 1983, p. 8.

included post-primary music teachers, post-primary pupils and third-level lecturers.[41]

An eclectic and exciting range of concerts enriched participants' experiences of the seminar, and these were advertised in the national press, with some also reviewed.[42] Leading Irish musicians performed, including pianist Charles Lynch. Known for his keen interest in twentieth century piano repertoire, Lynch gave the Irish premiere of 'The Night's Music' from Bartok's *Out of Doors* suite in an evening recital in the College Auditorium.[43] Four Irish choirs gave performances at the 1983 seminar: Cantairí Óga Atha Cliath conducted by Brian Ó Dubhghaill; The Park Singers conducted by Seán Creamer; The Palestrina Choir from St Mary's Pro-Cathedral conducted by Ite O'Donovan; and the Goethe Institute Choir conducted by Cáit Lannigan Cooper.

Pianists Gillian Smith and Frank Kelly each performed at lunchtime recitals whilst organist Gerard Gillen and harpist Denise Kelly gave a joint recital in the College Chapel. Soprano Kathleen Tynan, who graduated with a BEd from St Patrick's College in 1980 was accompanied by Paula Best on harpsichord at an evening concert on 27 June. A surprise international addition to the evening was a performance by the Golden Triangle Chorus from Pennsylvania, USA, funded by the national tourism agency Bord Fáilte. A separate concert featured the finalists of the Raidió Teilifís Éireann (RTÉ) Young Musician of the Year 1983 Competition. In keeping with the focus on Irish folk music, Len Graham gave an illustrated lecture titled 'Aspects of the Ulster Song Tradition' whilst the Sliabh na mBan Set Dancers, directed by Connie Ryan performed at the opening concert. Ó Cléirigh invited supreme court judge, The Honorable Mr Justice N. St. John McCarthy S.C. to officially open the Seminar at a concert in the College Auditorium on June 26, 1983. [44]

A popular addition to the programme of events was a demonstration class given by primary teacher Mary O'Flynn who applied Kodály methodologies with a group of her students from Holy

---

[41] The list of course participants for 1983 indicates that whilst the majority of those attending appear to have been based in Dublin, participants came from eleven counties within the Republic of Ireland and one from Northern Ireland. Among the post-primary students in attendance was singer Eleanor McEvoy. One participant from Finland attended. Ó Cléirigh Archive.

[42] For example: 'Next Week in the Arts: Music', *The Irish Times and The Weekly Irish Times*, 16 July 1983, p. 14; 'What's on Today', *Sunday Independent*, 26 June 1983.

[43] 'Symphonies added Bonus', *Irish Independent*, 5 July 1983.

[44] Letter to the Honorable Mr Justice N. St. John McCarthy S.C. detailing enclosed readings on Kodály. Ó Cléirigh Archive.

Spirit Girls National School in Ballymun. O'Flynn had worked closely with John Buckley who composed several choral pieces for her choirs, and was no stranger to the Kodály approach. As a result of this demonstration class, some of her pupils were encouraged to apply for, and were later awarded scholarships to study at the College of Music in Dublin.[45]

The 1985 Seminar
The Second International Zoltán Kodály Music Seminar held in St Patrick's College in 1985 followed the model of the earlier seminar of 1983. Ó Cléirigh once again assembled a committee, many of whom had been involved in the 1983 seminar committee.[46] Mihály Ittzés, Katalin Kiss and Ildikó Herboly Kocsár, who had taught on the 1983 seminar, returned to teach on the 1985 seminar. The success of the previous seminar led to a need for four new faculty members: Ida Erdei, faculty member of the Kodály Institute; Bo Aurehl, founder and conductor of the Stockholm Youth Choir and graduate of the Kodály Institute; Albert Bradshaw; and John O'Flynn, a graduate of St Patrick's College and a recently returned graduate of the Kodály Institute.[47] The 1985 seminar included a range of participants who would later emerge as leading figures in Irish musical life, including: the musicologist Barra Boydell; Celia Donoghue, who had an extensive career as a producer for Lyric FM; John Fitzpatrick, who later became director of the Cork International Choral Festival; jazz vocalist and actor Honor Heffernan; and choral conductor Bernie Sherlock. [48] Once again, classes were augmented by a series of concerts, public lectures and demonstration classes. Mihály Ittzés presented a formal lecture on Zoltán Kodály on 1 July. Irish contributors comprised representatives from a range of Irish music practices and settings, and included Professor Hormoz Farhat, TCD; Professor Anthony Hughes, UCD; Veronica Dunne, Dublin College of Music; Bebhinn Ní Mheara, Cork School of Music; and schoolteachers Harry Carpendale and Lillian Kavanagh. [49]

In addition to the College Auditorium and Chapel, concerts and liturgies featuring works by Hungarian composers took place in venues as varied as the National Concert Hall, the Hugh Lane Gallery and St

---

[45] Interview with Mary O'Flynn, October, 2018.
[46] Interview with Regina Murphy, February 2019. Two members of the organizing committee, Patricia Hegarty and Yvonne Higgins, subsequently studied at the Kodály Institute in Kecskemét. Hungarian student member, Balázs Kocsár later became an eminent conductor.
[47] Programme for The Second International Zoltán Kodály Music Seminar, 1985 (incomplete copy), Ó Cléirigh Archive.
[48] Interview with John O'Flynn, December 2018.
[49] Interview with Regina Murphy, February 2019.

Mary's Pro-Cathedral.[50] In preparation for the 1985 seminar, committee members had approached conductors and musicians, some of whom had participated in the 1983 seminar, to ask that Hungarian repertoire be included in performances taking place during the seminar.[51]

Figure 7.2: Front cover of programme for the Second International Zoltán Kodály Music Seminar in 1985. Photographer unknown

These external concerts further raised the profile of Kodály seminars at St Patrick's College in the print media. Barra Boydell, for example, wrote a very favourable review of a lunchtime concert in the Hugh Lane Gallery on 30 June to mark the opening of the 1985 seminar, in which Aisling Drury Byrne performed Kodály's *Sonata for Solo Cello* and Leonora Carney played piano works by Bartók and Liszt.[52] At the National Concert Hall on 2 July, Bryden Thomson conducted the RTÉ Symphony Orchestra in a lunchtime concert which included pieces by Liszt. Ite O'Donovan conducted the Pro-Cathedral Choir singing

---

[50] 'Next Week in the Arts: Music', *The Irish Times and The Weekly Irish Times*, 29 June 1985, p. 12.; Barra Boydell, 'RTESO at the NCH', *The Irish Times and The Weekly Irish Times*, 13 July 1985, p. 20.
[51] Interview with Deirdre Seaver, March 2019.
[52] Barra Boydell, 'Hungarian Music Recital at Hugh Lane Gallery', *The Irish Times*, 1 July 1985, p. 12.

Kodály's *Missa Brevis* at Sunday morning mass in St Mary's Pro-Cathedral on 7 July, while Hungarian conductor Zoltán Rozsnyai included Bartók and Liszt in his programme for the RTÉ Symphony orchestra with pianist Valentina Kamenkivo on 9 July.

The concert for the official opening of the 1985 Seminar was held in the College Auditorium on 29 June. This was also the venue for pianist Gillian Smith and violinist Brian McNamara who gave a recital of works by Tartini, Delius, Prokofiev and Schubert on 3 July. The Park Singers conducted by Seán Creamer performed works by Kodály, Bartók, and Miklós Kocsár in the College Chapel on 7 July. Also in the chapel, on the evening of 15 July, Aisling Heneghan gave a harpsichord recital.[53] An Irish trio, Airs & Graces performed in the College Auditorium on 14 July. The trio comprised Denise Kelly (harp), Moya O'Grady (cello) and Joan Merrigan (soprano). The seminar programme listed these concerts together with concerts featuring Hungarian and Irish composers, encouraging participants to engage with the musical life of Dublin city and strengthening ties between the department and national cultural institutions. The official closing concert of the seminar, which included choir and soloists, was held on 16 July.[54] The following autumn the inauguration of the Irish Kodály Society (IKS) was celebrated at a concert and reception at St Patrick's College.

After the 1985 seminar Ó Cléirigh continued to encourage music department students to study at the Kodály Institute in Kecskemét but his attention and energies now reverted to applying Kodály principles to his own teaching and choral work. Members of the college choir remember learning how to read their parts through the use of solfa, rhythm syllables, and handsigns.[55] Ó Cléirigh brought further choirs from St Patrick's College to participate in the Cork International Choral Festival. Between 1987 and 1992 echoes of the music making at the 1983 and 1985 seminars could be heard in the choir's repertoire which included Kodály favourites such as 'Esti Dal', 'Túrót Eszik a Cigány' and 'Ave Maria'. On Ó Cléirigh's suggestion, the new head of music at St Patrick's College, Marion Doherty attended the International Summer Seminar in Kecskemét in 1987. To explore Kodály pedagogies further

---

[53] Fergus Linehan, 'Backdrop: A Weekly Column on the Arts and Entertainment', *The Irish Times and The Weekly Irish Times*, 13 July 1985, p. 14.

[54] Just after the seminar ended, committee members Deirdre Seaver and Michael O'Leary were married in the College Chapel. For the occasion, and in gratitude for all that they had contributed to the organization of both seminars, Colum Ó Cléirigh formed a choir comprising seminar participants, which was conducted by Bo Aurehl and accompanied by Ó Cléirigh on organ.

[55] Interviews with BEd graduates Fiona Roche (October 2018) and Muireann Joy (February 2019).

she arranged to teach music to a fourth class in St Patrick's Boys National School for a period. This informed her use of Kodály principles in her work with curriculum music students at the College. Later, whilst visiting Hungary with her choir Enchiriadis Treis, Doherty returned to Kecskemét to observe music classes at the Zoltán Kodály Iskola.[56] To support music literacy skills among academic music students in St Patrick's College she arranged for Institute graduate and accomplished conductor Brian McKay to teach a six-week intensive Kodály-based course. She continued to use Kodály pedagogies in her own choral work and supported Ó Cléirigh's work with students.[57]

In 1993 one of the participants of the 1985 seminar, Bernie Sherlock, returned from studies at the Kodály Institute eager to form a Kodály Society and promote Kodály principles through re-establishing the summer seminars. The new Kodály Society of Ireland (KSI) could be viewed as a legacy of the 1983 and 1985 Kodály International Music Seminars in St Patrick's College and of the Irish Kodály Society set up by Colum Ó Cléirigh.[58] Regina Murphy and John O'Flynn, both of whom were involved with the seminars in the 1980s were KSI committee members from 1993-1997 while Marion Doherty served on the committee between 1997-1998. Between 1993 and 2008 Kodály summer courses took place in the Church of Ireland College of Education in Rathmines, Dublin.

'Active Music Making: The Kodály Approach' Seminars at St Patrick's College, 2009-2016

The 'Kodály connection' with the music department at St Patrick's College was rekindled when, in July 2009, the Kodály summer course returned to the home of the original international seminars. This followed an approach made by Daniel Walsh, KSI Chair, initially to John O'Flynn who was appointed head of music at the College in 2008. Hungarian ambassador, Ferenc Jári, and his wife Melinda Jári attended a reception hosted by the college president, Pauric Travers to mark this residency. The course culminated in a choral and chamber music recital in the College Chapel on the evening of Friday 10 July. [59] Between 2009 and 2016 a number of music department students were awarded KSI

---

[56] A special music school in Kecskemét catering for primary and post-primary levels.
[57] Interview with Marion Doherty, March 2019.
[58] Regina Murphy was on the 1983 and 1985 seminar committees. Bernie Sherlock, Kris Kinder and Daniel Walsh were seminar participants in 1985. John O'Flynn was involved in seminar organization in 1983 and taught on the 1985 seminar.
[59] *St Patrick's College Annual Report 2008-2009*, (Dublin: St Patrick's College, 2009).

scholarships to attend, among them composer Paul Gilgunn and primary teacher Rachael Byrne who subsequently studied at the Institute in Kecskemét.[60] By the time of its return to St Patrick's College, the format of the Kodály Music Summer Seminar had become more aligned with that of summer courses designed for the continuing professional development (CPD) of primary teachers. The seminar, now titled 'Active Music Making: The Kodály Approach' was incorporated into the suite of CPD Summer Courses offered across a range of subjects by St Patrick's College. The courses were supported through funding from the In-career Development Unit of the Department of Education and Science.[61] Eight 'Active Music Making' Kodály courses were held for a week each July between 2009 and 2016. Despite the shortened duration of the courses, they maintained their intensive focus.

Between 2009 and 2016, the courses were directed by Daniel Walsh, Chairperson of the Kodály Society. A key factor in the on-going success of the courses was the continued invitation extended to Hungarian experts in Kodály pedagogy. Three of the original faculty of the 1983 and 1985 seminars, Ildikó Herboly Kocsár, Albert Bradshaw and John O'Flynn returned.[62] Hungarian Institute faculty members who taught on the course over a number of years include Zoltán Pad, Sarolta Platthy, Kata Kortvési and László Nemes, Director of the International Kodály Institute of the Liszt Academy. Borbála Szirányi and Brigetta Kovacs joined the faculty on the course in 2013 and 2015 respectively.[63] Lilla Gabór was a faculty member each year since 2014.[64] Renowned Hungarian soprano, Éva Andor, was the vocal coach in 2009.

A marked difference between the original seminars in St Patrick's College and the Active Music Making Kodály summer courses 2009-2016 was the increasing number of Irish Kodály Institute graduates now available to contribute to these courses.[65] The 1983 and 1985 seminars were perhaps contributory factors to this dissemination of the

---

[60] Interview with John O'Flynn, December 2018. See Paul Gilgunn's contribution in Chapter Eleven.
[61] Interview with Daniel Walsh, KSI Chairperson.
[62] Ildíko Herboly Kocsár from 2009 to 2013, Albert Bradshaw in 2011, 2012 and 2016, and John O'Flynn in 2010.
[63] Kodály Society of Ireland Summer Course Timetable (KSISCT) 2009–2016, courtesy of Daniel Walsh.
[64] Lilla Gabor was one of the Hungarian teachers with whom Ó Cléirigh formed a lasting friendship at the Kodály Institute in Hungary in the summer of 1980. Interview with Lilla Gabór, July, 2018.
[65] Between 2009 and 2016 Irish faculty included John O'Flynn, Bernie Sherlock, Orla Flanagan, Róisín Blunnie, Mary Nugent, Amy Ryan, Ciara Coleman and Grace Bergin.

Kodály philosophy of music education in Ireland and the subsequent uptake of Kodály studies among Irish students.

Figure 7.3: Éva Andor and John O'Flynn at St Patrick's College, 10 July 2009. Photograph by Paul Murphy

As was customary, a solfège assessment was held on the first morning of the courses, in order to assign participants to the class group best suited to meet their needs. Each day started with 'common singing', open to participants of all class levels, followed by daily solfège classes (7 hours per week), teaching methods (4 hours), conducting classes (5 hours) and choir rehearsal (5 hours). Folk music classes were not included, perhaps as a consequence of the reduced time. In the late afternoons elective activities were offered. Participants could choose from chamber music activities, led initially by Danusia Oslizlok (2009) and later by Margaret O'Sullivan Farrell (2010-2016), or individual singing lessons. [66] A separate contribution to the chamber music offering between 2013 and 2015 resulted from the three-year residency of the Fidelio Trio at St Patrick's College music department.[67] The Trio joined Margaret O'Sullivan Farrell in leading chamber music activities.

One of the features of the 1983 and 1985 seminars that helped to bring the seminars and the Kodály approach to national attention was the programming of public lectures and concerts. By comparison, the extra-curricular offerings of the 'Active Music Making' summer courses

---

[66] Singing teachers over this period were Éva Andor, (2009), Victoria Massey (2010), Colette McGahon (2011-13), Stephen Wallace (2014) and Kodály Institute graduate, Clare McEvoy (2015-16).
[67] See Chapter Ten of this volume.

were more modest. Concerts were planned for course participants rather than for a wider public audience and usually took place as lunchtime recitals, with the exception of the Fidelio Trio evening performances, and workshops or exhibitions held in Dublin city centre. End-of-course Friday evening concerts were open to family and friends. 'In-house' recitals over this time comprised performances by chamber music and vocal teachers, including singers Victoria Massey, Colette McGahon and Clare McEvoy, and pianist Margaret O'Sullivan Farrell. Music performance students from conservatoires and other institutions were also invited to give special recitals. Participants were further invited to attend choral workshops with renowned international and national groups that comprised Mornington Singers and Chanticleer in 2009, and a four-choir concert directed by guest conductor Doreen Rao in 2016. [68]

Another point of difference between the early seminars and the later summer courses was the profile of participants. For the 1983 seminar, participants were predominantly practising teachers at primary, secondary or third level, in that order. [69] In contrast, participants of the summer courses from 2009-16 represented a wider cross-section of Irish society. Whilst teachers at primary and secondary level continued to participate, the majority of the summer course attendees were third-level music students whose courses reflected the diversity of music programmes currently on offer in Ireland. [70] In addition, course participants included many individuals who were interested in developing musicianship skills but who were not involved in music or in teaching by profession. From time to time, course participant lists included individuals who had retired.

In common with the earlier seminars, teaching methods classes taught by the Hungarian faculty during the summer courses addressed strategies for developing rhythm, melody and polyphonic skills; the use of folksongs, canons and Kodály singing exercises as teaching tools; and approaches to teaching twentieth-century music. A new and complementary pedagogy developed by Klára Kokas was introduced in 2011 by Kata Kortvési. This Hungarian pedagogy, rooted in the Kodály philosophy of music education, uses moving to music as experiential music appreciation and promotes creative collaborative improvisation. [71] Drawing on Kokas's work, Kortvési's workshops explored improvisation skills and creative musical games. This addition resonated with wider theories of embodiment in music learning, and accorded with the introduction of composing as a separate strand of

---

[68] KSISCT 2009 – 2016.
[69] List of Participants, 1983, Ó Cléirigh Archive.
[70] Interview with Daniel Walsh, February 2019.
[71] K. Kokas, *Joy through music and movement*, (Budapest: Akkord, 1999).

activity and the inclusion of movement as a response to listening to music in the Irish primary school music curriculum. [72] Additionally, Irish teachers and lecturers shared insights from their application of Kodály principles in Irish contexts on the 2009-2016 summer courses. Presentations on Kodály-based music learning in early years settings featured annually. [73] Input focusing on Kodály approaches within primary and secondary school contexts was also presented. For example: Wendy Stephens shared her experience of applying Kodály principles to her work in early years over a number of years (Lorraine O'Connell also gave several presentations on early years music education); Mary Nugent, Mairéad Ní Chondúin and Ciara Coleman spoke on applications of Kodály approaches at primary level, while Lorraine O'Connell, Albert Bradshaw and Róisín Blunnie explored aspects of the post-primary syllabus through Kodály pedagogies. [74]

The summer schools between 2009-2016 included sessions that explored contemporary educational questions in and through music, such as inclusion, assessment, and music in the community. [75] Siobhán Keane, for example, presented 'Encouraging inclusion through the medium of music' in 2011; Regina Murphy spoke on 'Evaluation and teaching outcomes' in 2015; Siobhán Ní Chonaráin presented on 'Comhaltas Ceoltóiri Éireann and its contributions as a community-based cultural movement' in 2013. Daniel Walsh presented on 'Instrumental teaching with Kodály concepts and other tools' in 2014. Alex Ruthmann from NYU Steinhardt, who was visiting St Patrick's College in 2012, was invited to speak on the use of technology in music education in a session titled 'New Media: Inspiring Practices for Music Education'. That same year, Irish composer Peter Moran led a session titled 'Composition in the Classroom'. This reflected the interest in developing creative practices in Irish classrooms in response to curricular change. Unsurprisingly, choral singing continued to enjoy a special place on the 2009-2016 courses. In addition to the participants' choirs, approaches to developing young people's and children's choral singing were explored in presentations by Máire Mannion in 2010, László Nemes in 2014, and Clare McEvoy in 2015. Whilst time had wrought changes in political and educational spheres in the intervening years between the original international seminars and the later 'Active Music-Making' Kodály summer courses at St Patrick's College, the focus on joyful experiential learning and discovery through actively making music with others, especially through singing, endured.

---

[72] F. Varela, E. Rosch & E. Thompson, *The Embodied Mind: Cognitive Science and Human Experience*, (Cambridge, MA: MIT Press, 1993).
[73] KSISCT 2009-2016.
[74] Ibid.
[75] Ibid.

Influence of the 'Kodály connection' on Irish music education at St Patrick's College and beyond

The impact of that chance meeting in 1982 between Ó Cléirigh and Péter Erdei at the Cork Choral Festival on the musical lives of students of St Patrick's College and on Irish music education was far-reaching. Many music department students who were participants on the 1983 and 1985 seminars continued Kodály studies in Kecskemét and went on to take up leadership roles in music within St Patrick's College and beyond.[76]

The first Irish students who undertook the full-time programme of study at the Kodály Institute in 1983 - John O'Flynn and Micheál Houlahan - were also BEd graduates of St Patrick's College. O'Flynn lectured in music education in Mary Immaculate College in Limerick from 1999 and subsequently returned to the music department of St Patrick's as head of music in 2008.

Houlahan, one of the students on the 1983 seminar organizing committee, is a professor and currently chairs the music department at Millersville University in the United States. Together with his co-author Philip Tacka, he has published extensively on Kodály approaches to music education. Breda O'Shea, who had been a member of the organizing committee for both the 1983 and 1985 seminars, was one of the first Irish female students on the programme at the Institute in 1984.[77] O'Shea lectured in the music department at St Patrick's College and later in Marino Institute of Education and at Froebel College of Education, Blackrock.

Other Kodály Institute graduates who have lectured or contributed to courses at the music department in St Patrick's College and continue to hold leadership roles in music and music education include Orla Flanagan (Trinity College Dublin), Yvonne Higgins (Institute of Education, DCU), Brian McKay (Artistic Director, Zezere Arts Festival, Portugal), Mary Nugent (Marino Institute of Education), Lorraine O'Connell and Clare McEvoy (Technological University, Dublin) Amy Ryan (Trinity College Dublin and Royal Irish Academy of Music), Mary Stakelum (Institute for Education, Bath Spa University) and Donagh Wylde (Wylde School of Music, Wexford).[78]

---

[76] List of Irish participants who attended the Kodály Institute as full-time students, provided by Péter Erdei, December 2018.

[77] Edel Thomas also began full-time studies at the Kodály Institute in 1984.

[78] Two teaching fellowship positions in the music department were held by Kodály Institute graduates: Yvonne Higgins (2000-2001) and Orla Flanagan (2015-16).

Leadership in choral singing

The Kodály concept had a profound effect on choral life in Ireland. Conductors of some of the best choirs in Dublin studied in Kecskemét.[79] Ó Cléirigh contributed to and supported choral practice in Ireland, adjudicating at, participating in, and attending Irish choral festivals. Irish choral conductors with Kodály connections to Kecskemét and to courses or seminars at St Patrick's College include Róisín Blunnie, (DCU Lumen Chorale, Laetare), Orla Flanagan (Mornington Singers), Patricia Hegarty (Tourdion Chamber Choir, St Mologa's School Choir, Balbriggan), Yvonne Higgins (Viva Voce Chamber Choir, St Patrick's BNS Drumcondra Harmony Boys Choir), Muireann Joy, (Scoil Mhuire Killorglin Children's Choir, Killorglin Youth Chamber Choir, Killorglin Girls' Choir), John O'Flynn (DCU Music Society Choir), Breda O'Shea (Ceiliúradh Choir), Amy Ryan (Cuore), Claire Sheedy (Fingal Children's Choir), Bernie Sherlock (New Dublin Voices, Culwick Choral Society, TU Chamber Choir), and Donagh Wylde (Enniscorthy Choral Society). They have led and continue to lead children and adults in school, college and community settings in choral singing, a core component of the Kodály approach.

Kodály influences on the Irish primary music curriculum

Perhaps the clearest impact of the Kodály seminars held in the 1980s at St Patrick's College is in the influence of Kodály thinking on the music curriculum for Irish primary schools.[80] Whilst not explicitly or exclusively drawing upon the Kodály approach, many of the principles that underpin the *Irish Primary Curriculum, Music* programme of 1999 align closely with Kodály philosophy.[81] An emphasis on singing, for example, as a means of developing musical skills and understanding is evident in the performing strand of the music curriculum which dwells on:

> ... the importance of using the voice, the first and most accessible instrument for the child, both for the sheer enjoyment of performance and as a means through which musical skills may be expanded.[82]

---

[79] Interview with Péter Erdei, December 2018.

[80] Ó Cléirigh was a member of the Curriculum Committee for Arts Education, established by the National Council for Curriculum and Assessment (NCCA) with responsibility for preparing the music curriculum. Regina Murphy was Arts Education Officer. Dympna Mulkerrins, another NCCA committee member had attended the 1983 seminar. Interview with Regina Murphy, February 2019.

[81] NCCA, *Primary School Curriculum, Arts Education: Music*, (Dublin: Stationery Office, 1999).

[82] Ibid., p. 6.

Guidance on the selection of song repertoire in the curriculum mirrors progression in song singing materials used in the Kodály approach. In the Irish curriculum, children progress from singing game songs and folk songs of Irish origin and those of other countries in junior classes, to the inclusion of simple part-singing and learning art songs at the upper end of primary school. It is, perhaps, in the approaches taken to developing children's music literacy skills that the Kodály influence is most noticeably evident. In common with the Kodály approach, the music curriculum is based on the philosophy of sound before symbol and on:

> ... the belief that musical knowledge is best acquired through moving from the known ... to the unknown ... from the simple to the complex, and from an experience ... to a conscious understanding of that experience ... .[83]

The foundation for sight-reading skills in the 1971 primary music curriculum was ear-training that was based on singing and representing intervals. In the *Primary Curriculum, Music* (1999), the development of musical literacy is closely linked with the song-singing programme, especially in the early stages.

Strategies and tools synonymous with the Kodály approach are included in the Teacher Guidelines chapter that advises on approaches to music literacy.[84] They are also used to illustrate and clarify the literacy learning outcomes in the performing strand of the music curriculum document. Whilst these approaches are not mandatory, and teachers are free to use others and/or generate their own, the Irish music curriculum suggests that children be afforded opportunities to read and represent melodic and rhythmic patterns through the use of teaching tools that are used in Kodály pedagogy to enable children to read and write music using standard notation (for example, solfa names, hand-signs, finger staves, rhythm syllables, stick notation, 2/3-line staves). The guidelines also provide advice on the development of musical memory and inner-hearing, key musical skills in the Kodály approach. In line with international trends, the *Irish Primary Curriculum, Music* (1999) introduced significant changes to the teaching of music.[85] These innovations are complemented by

---

[83] Ibid., p. 8.
[84] NCCA, *Primary School Curriculum: Music Teacher Guidelines*, (Dublin: The Stationery Office, 1999), pp. 89-103.
[85] As examples, the inclusion of composing as one of three separate strands of activity, and an emphasis on children's responding to music in a variety of ways.

established Kodály principles and approaches that were explored in the seminars of the 1980s and that continued through in-service summer courses up to the time of writing.

The implementation of the primary music curriculum to schools in 2004 was not without a 'Kodály effect'.[86] Regina Murphy was a member of the design team that organized training and input for the music team members (the training included a presentation on the Kodály approach). The music team comprised Irish primary teachers seconded on the basis of their musical expertise and experience. Four members of the original Primary Curriculum Support Programme (PCSP) for music were graduates of the Kodály Institute - Patricia Hegarty, Yvonne Higgins, Mary Nugent and Dympna O'Byrne. Hegarty, Higgins and O'Byrne were also graduates of St Patrick's College. Two other members, Christine Ferguson and Miriam O'Sullivan were graduates of the College who had attended Kodály summer courses.[87] One of the 'key messages' drawn from the primary music curriculum and presented to participants on the in-service days was that 'music is for all teachers and all pupils'. This clearly resonated with Kodály's slogan, 'Let music belong to everyone'.

Concluding Comments

The thread from that chance meeting between Colum O Cléirigh and Péter Erdei at the Cork Choral Festival in 1982 continues to be woven into the fabric of music education in Irish schools and in teacher education today. It was whilst working to support students learning at third level that Kodály first became interested in developing a national system of music education in Hungary spanning from early childhood to university and conservatoire. It was Ó Cléirigh's interest in choral music together with a wish to improve the music teaching skills of his student teachers at St Patrick's College that led him to study the Kodály concept. Whilst Kodály's work as a composer and educator was already known in Ireland, Ó Cléirigh's vision for and enthusiastic promotion of the Kodály approach, and the 1983 and 1985 International Kodály Seminars contributed to Kodaly's concept of music education coming to

---

[86] The Primary Curriculum Support Programme (PCSP) was the body appointed to facilitate the introduction of the Irish Primary Curriculum (1999) to Irish schools. The PCSP model of continuing professional development was based upon each subject area, including music, having a design team and a team of subject 'trainers' who, collaboratively developed and presented courses designed to introduce each subject to Irish teachers over two in-service days at national level. http://ppds.pdst.ie/pdsparchive/about/php [accessed 19 January 2019].

[87] Ferguson had been a committee member for the 1983 and 1985 seminars and had attended a Kodály Summer Seminar in Kecskémet in the interim.

national recognition. The music department at St Patrick's College succeeded in hosting two international seminars, fostering connections between the Department and the Kodály Institute on the one hand, and drawing upon and strengthening ties with Irish teachers, musicians and academics on the other. Neither institution continues to exist independently, yet between these two, a musical connection was forged whose reach, both directly and indirectly, touched and continues to enhance the lives of many Irish adults and children.[88]

Bibliography
An Roinn Oideachais, *An Curaclam Nua*. Teachers' Handbook, Parts I and II, (Dublin: Browne and Nolan, 1971).
Choksy, Lois, *The Kodály Method: Comprehensive Music Education from Infant to Adult,* (Englewood Cliffs, NJ: Prentice-Hall, 1974).
Dobszay, László, 'The Kodály Method and Its Musical Basis', *Studia Musicologica Academiae Scientiarum Hungaricae*, 14.1/4, (1972), 15-33.
Eősze, Laszló, Houlahan, Mícheál, & Tacka, Philip, 'Kodály, Zoltán', *Grove Music – Oxford Music Online,* https://doi.org/10.1093/gmo/9781561592630.article.15246 [accessed 28 April 2019].
Houlahan, Mícheál & Tacka, Philip, *Kodály Today: A Cognitive Approach to Elementary Music Education,* (Oxford: Oxford University Press, 2008).
Kodály, Zoltán, *Kodály Choral Method Series*, ed. P. Young (London: Boosey and Hawkes, 1965).Kodály, Zoltán, *The Selected Writings of Zoltán Kodály,* ed. F. Bónis, trans. L. Halápy & F. Macinicol, (London: Boosey & Hawkes, 1974).
Kokas, Klára, *Joy through music and movement,* (Budapest: Akkord, 1999).
National Council for Curriculum and Assessment, *Primary School Curriculum: Music*, (Dublin: The Stationery Office, 1999).
National Council for Curriculum and Assessment, *Primary School Curriculum: Music Teacher Guidelines,* (Dublin: The Stationery Office, 1999).
St Patrick's College Annual Report 2008-2009, (Dublin: St Patrick's College, 2009).

---

[88] On 28 January 2019 at an event at the Embassy of the Republic of Hungary in Dublin, the Kodály Society of Ireland (KSI) announced the launch of the Colum Ó Cléirigh Scholarships, 'named in honour of the late Irish music pedagogue'. The purpose of the scholarships is to provide an opportunity for third-level music students to avail of fully subsidized tuition at a KSI summer course.

Szőnyi, Erzsébet, *Kodály's Principles in Practice: An Approach to Music Education through the Kodály Method*, trans. J. Weissman, 5th edn, (Budapest: Corvina, 1990).

Varela, Francisco, Rosch, Eleanor & Thompson, Evan, *The Embodied Mind: Cognitive Science and Human Experience*, (Cambridge, MA: MIT Press, 1993).

Newspapers and periodicals
Irish Independent
Sunday Independent
Cork Examiner
The Irish Times
The Irish Times and The Weekly Irish Times

Archives
Kodály Society of Ireland
Ó Cléirigh Archive
St Patrick's College Archive
Zoltán Kodály Institute of Music Pedagogy

Interviews and email correspondence
Albert Bradshaw
Marion Doherty
Lilla Gabór
Péter Erdei
Muireann Joy
Regina Murphy
Lorraine O'Connell
Peter O'Driscoll
Mary O'Flynn
John O'Flynn
Fiona Roche
Deirdre Seaver
Daniel Walsh

Chapter Eight: Engagement and Research

John O'Flynn

> Service to community is considered central to the work of the Music Department.[1]
>
> The Department is committed to providing leadership in, and advocacy for music education at a national level. As the largest department of music on the north side of Dublin, it realizes its importance in contributing to the cultural life of the area and beyond.[2]
>
> The Department recognizes research to be one of its key areas of activity, and encourages staff to follow individual research interests as well as to explore the potential for collaborative projects.[3]
>
> The Department is committed to the supervision of research in areas cognate to the expertise of staff, namely, Composition, Music Education and Musicology.[4]

Introduction
This chapter records and reflects on various forms on engagement and research undertaken by music staff as well as by postgraduate students at St Patrick's College from the 1970s to the 2010s. While focussing on this more recent period of the institution's history, it is recognized that engagement and research also concerned previous figures at the College, going back as far as Peter Goodman's significant contributions to national music curriculum design and to the publication of song collections from the end of the nineteenth century onwards.

As the above statements from the 2011 Self-Assessment Report of the Music Department suggest, engagement and research were recognized as key areas of activity for music staff at the College.[5] While

---

[1] Self-Assessment Report of the Music Department (St Patrick's College, March 2011), p. 45.
[2] Ibid.
[3] Ibid., p. 32.
[4] Ibid., p. 37.
[5] The music department underwent a formal review administered by the College's Quality Assurance Unit in March 2011. The peer evaluation team comprised Professor Máirín Nic Eoin (St Patrick's College), Professor Marie

the two areas are treated separately in chapter layout, several points of overlap between engagement and research will emerge throughout the discussion.

Engagement can be broadly imagined in terms of contribution to, and impact on communities and wider society, on the part of individuals and groups. It can refer to community-based projects, curriculum development and professional publications as well as to research studies linked to broader societal and cultural issues. Increasingly, the engagement activities of university faculty can also extend to international networks and concerns.[6]

Historically, engagement has tended to be viewed by some academics as less prestigious than either 'pure' research or college/university teaching.[7] A useful concept in countenancing such views is that of outreach which can be regarded and developed as a bridge between, on one side, disciplinary expertise and professional interests and on the other side, community and societal concerns.[8] Service, engagement and outreach are ideas that perhaps translate more readily into action in the case of lecturers who are also involved in music and education networks. This might explain the extensive record of competition and festival adjudication on the part of many of those who were based at the music department of St Patrick's College over the years; both Seán Hayes and Colum Ó Cléirigh adjudicated at the Cork International Choral Festival, and most staff of the department were involved at some stage as *moltóirí cheoil* [music adjudicators] for *Cór Fhéile na Scoileanna Baile Átha Cliath*, the non-competitive music festival for children established in Dublin in 1967.[9]

While performance and composition are undoubtedly key ways of engaging people with music – and this has certainly been the case at St Patrick's College - these activities are for the most part excluded from the present discussion. This is because histories of performance, composition, choral music, and the Fidelio Trio residency at St Patrick's College constitute the subjects of dedicated chapters elsewhere in the volume. This chapter's exploration of engagement begins with a brief

---

McCarthy (University of Michigan) and Dr Gareth Cox (Mary Immaculate College, University of Limerick).

[6] R. Friesen, 'Faculty member engagement in Canadian university internationalization: A consideration of understanding, motivations and rationales', *Journal of Studies in International Education*, 17.3 (2013).

[7] K. Ward, Kelly, *Faculty Service Roles and the Scholarship of Engagement. ASHE-ERIC Higher Education Report*, (San Francisco: Jossey-Bass, 2003), pp. 5-6.

[8] Ibid., p. 7.

[9] See http://www.corfheile.ie/about-us.html [accessed 11 January 2019].

survey of in-service music courses that took place at the department from the 1970s to 2016 (the College's extensive promotion of the Kodály approach to music education is discussed separately by Yvonne Higgins in Chapter Seven). It then considers involvement by college staff in music curriculum development and in the writing and publishing of educational music texts and CDs for both primary and post-primary levels from the 1990s until the mid-2000s. This is followed by a consideration of two community-based music education projects with strong ties to the music department, one taking place from 1986-1987, the other carried out almost four decades later in 2012.

Various types of engagement with initiatives in higher education, arts and humanities are next explored. First documented here is the contribution by music department members to college-wide committees, including participation in organizing committees for the celebrated Seamus Heaney Lecture Series. This is followed by mention of staff members' connection with the Music Association of Ireland, and the music department's substantial involvement in higher-level music education through membership of CHMHE, the Council of Heads of Music in Higher Education. The chapter goes on to document how music department staff made significant contributions to other national organizations and agencies including the Society for Music Education in Ireland, the Society for Musicology in Ireland, the Contemporary Music Centre, Music Generation, and in more recent years, to the local arts organization GlasDrum.

The remainder of the chapter focuses on research, while still concerned with engagement. It continues by considering the significance of taught MA and MEd programmes and the diverse dissertations by graduates of those courses. Also discussed here is the range of guest research seminars that ran as part of the taught masters courses. This is followed by a survey of research MA and PhD dissertations and theses in areas of musicology, performance, composition and music education, noting the impact of some of these research projects (Appendix D provides a chronological list of relevant dissertations and theses from 2000-2016).

The chapter continues by reporting on funded research projects supervised by music department staff, including research on music provision by local authorities, the department's long-term research collaboration with Music Generation and an applied research project funded by Fáilte Ireland/Irish Tourism (the last of these is discussed in detail in the next chapter by Áine Mangaoang). It closes by combining themes of engagement and research through a review of music and music education conferences hosted by the music department, both national and international. While the subject of the chapter embraces engagement and research by music staff members, this is for most part confined to projects that were based in or that were otherwise institutionally linked to St Patrick's College. Accordingly, the bibliography provided at the end of the chapter constitutes a selection only of publications and other research outputs by staff members up to and including 2016.

In-service education

Reports published by the INTO in 1980 and later in 1993 underlined a consistent need throughout the last three decades of the twentieth century for in-service training in many aspects of the primary curriculum; unsurprisingly perhaps, music was identified as one of the key areas requiring attention.[10] The INTO's Consultative Conference on Education in 1989 focussed on arts education, and one of its recommendations specifically addressed the area of in-service education:

> A properly-structured programme of in-service education is needed to enable serving teachers overcome the inadequacy many of them feel in teaching the Arts Subjects. The deployment of underused facilities and resources in Colleges of Education and Universities could be of enormous value in such a programme.[11]

While the perception of 'underused facilities and resources' might be challenged by those working in third-level institutions at the time, the INTO report identified a need for greater collaboration between various sectors in provision for in-service education. As shall be touched on below, it would be several decades before national programmes of in-service education were established in Ireland; at the same time, the impact of many local initiatives over the intervening period was substantial, as indeed was that of a number of colleges, education centres and voluntary organizations. Staff at the music department of St Patrick's College were intermittently involved in organizing and contributing to music in-service courses for primary and post-primary teachers from the 1970s. Summer courses for primary teachers typically

---

[10] Irish National Teachers' Organisation, *Inservice Education and Training of Teachers* (Report and Recommendations of the Education Committee of the Irish National Teachers' Organisation), (Dublin: INTO, 1980); Idem, *The Professional Development of Teachers: Issues in Inservice Education*, (Dublin, INTO: 1993). 51% of teachers surveyed for the 1993 report identified music, in particular 'song singing', as an area requiring in-service training (pp. 84-85).
[11] Irish National Teachers' Organisation Consultative Conference on Education, *The Arts in Education*, 26-27 May 1989, (Dublin: INTO, 1989), p. 15.

took place during the first week of July and their content was focussed on singing and song repertoire and to a lesser extent on the use of classroom instruments.

From 1975 in-service music courses were offered through the adjacent Drumcondra Teachers' Centre, later renamed as the Drumcondra Education Centre. For the first decade of its existence many of the Centre's courses took place in Room B118, the main music room of the College, and some of these involved music department staff. That decade was a time of considerable growth and development for music in-service. To take the academic year 1983-1984 as an example, no fewer than three music courses were organized by the Centre during term time: in autumn 1983 an evening course on music literacy for post-primary teachers delivered by Seán Mac Liam; in spring 1984 an evening course on descant recorder for primary and post-primary teachers led by Cathal Fleming and the renowned recorder player and flautist Doris Keogh; and also in spring 1984 an evening course specifically designed for primary teachers in the Ballymun area delivered by primary music inspector Seán Creamer, a graduate of the College.[12] All of these courses took place in Room B118.

The music department also hosted music courses organized by other parties. The summer course 'Enjoying Music' was regularly co-delivered by primary teacher Gerard Fox and composer John Buckley (prior to the latter's appointment to the College). This was a course that placed emphasis on listening to and engaging with orchestral music and opera in recorded and live formats. For example, the course offered in July 1988 included a concert that took place at the College as well as a group excursion to a lunchtime concert programmed at the National Concert Hall. Another innovation of this course was its inclusion of East Asian and South Asian music into its selection of listening activities.[13]

As detailed in Yvonne Higgins's chapter in this volume, the Kodály seminars organized by Colum Ó Cléirigh at the music department in 1983 and 1985 were much more substantial than previous music in-service courses insofar as they involved intensive schedules over two full weeks, were delivered by international as well as Irish tutors, and included participants from a variety of education and music sectors. Critically, the Kodály summer schools strove to develop the musicianship of course participants as much as they offered approaches to teaching music in schools.

---

[12] Drumcondra Teachers' Centre Annual General Report, May 1984, SPCA, A/19/6.2. The description of the course led by Seán Creamer states: 'The course is designed for teachers experiencing <u>difficulty</u> in teaching music' [original emphasis].

[13] Drumcondra Teachers' Centre Annual Report, 1989, SPCA, A/19/6.2.

In-service courses initiated by Marion Doherty, Head of Music from 1985, placed greater emphasis on classroom instrumental learning than heretofore, with the recorder as the preferred instrument for group performance. Doherty also set up evening recorder classes, and from 1987-1989 organized courses in chamber music. These took the format of adult participants coached in groups by prominent instrumental performers. From 1985-1989 the music department also provided evening classes as part of the College's in-service BEd, a degree qualification programme designed for primary school teachers who had taken the NT diploma prior to the introduction of the pre-service BEd in 1974.

Annual summer courses organized by the music department throughout the 1990s and early 2000s reflected the many curricular changes taking place throughout this period, a notable development being the introduction of group composition into music syllabuses of the Revised Primary Curriculum of 1999. Although expert-led workshops supporting the music curriculum revisions had been provided nationally through the Primary Curriculum Support Programme, music remained high on the list of curricular areas identified as requiring further professional development.[14] By this time, general music in-service courses were regularly offered by the INTO and through local education centres. Those taking place at St Patrick's College music department over the same period tended to offer more specialist options. Several of these were organized in collaboration with Fuaim (the Association for the Promotion of Primary-Level Music Education) set up in 1997. Fuaim ran many workshops, courses, symposia and conferences until the mid-2000s. Among the highlights of the organization's partnership with the music department were the 'Write an Opera' teachers' summer course in 1999 under the artistic direction of composer John Browne and pedagogical leadership of Mary Ryng McAuliffe, and in March 2000 'Linking Together', a practice-based weekend course led by a national and international team that included Patricia Flynn from the music department. More than one hundred participants attended the course, and the programme featured workshops on composing for the classroom, homemade instruments, graphic notation and African drumming.[15]

---

[14] Irish National Teachers Organisation, *Creativity and the Arts in the Primary School* (Discussion Document and Proceedings of the Consultative Conference on Education 2009), (Dublin: INTO, 2010), p. 84.
[15] The 'Write an Opera' model was developed by The Royal Opera House, London. Details of the 'Linking Together' course can be viewed at http://www.esatclear.ie/~fuaim/March00.htm [accessed 11 January 2019].

Music department members would continue to organize and present summer courses for primary teachers up until 2008. In August 2007 research fellow Ailbhe Kenny presented the course 'Tuned In – Music in the Primary Classroom' with input also from Marion Doherty and external facilitators Brian Fleming and David Darcy. Kenny also co-ordinated 'Sounding Off: Creative Approaches to Music in School' in July 2008, this time working with Patricia Flynn, Marion Doherty and Brian Fleming. As already noted in Chapter Six, the year 2008 also heralded the introduction of the modular in-service certificate/diploma 'Choral Conducting in Education and the Community' led by Marion Doherty. From 2009 the annual Kodály Summer School returned to St Patrick's College. It was presented by the Kodály Society of Ireland in association with the music department up to and including the course that took place in July 2016.

Curriculum development and resources
Throughout the 1990s Seán Mac Liam occupied a leading role in post-primary music curriculum development in Ireland. Mac Liam was Education/Research Officer (Music) for the National Council for Curriculum and Assessment (NCCA) while still based at the music department of St Patrick's College. In his NCCA role he carried out research on international music education literature and curricular resources, and in 1990 authored the Junior Certificate Music Syllabus that replaced the existing music syllabus for the Intermediate Certificate examination. This was followed in 1991 by a publication of guidelines for teachers.[16] Mac Liam next led curriculum reform for music in the Leaving Certificate examination, an initiative that was in no small part prompted by the low uptake for the subject in the senior cycle of post-primary education.[17] By 1997 a new Leaving Certificate music syllabus with supporting teacher guidelines had been developed.[18] From this point Mac Liam liaised with a curriculum

---

[16] An Roinn Oideachais, *The Junior Certificate Music Syllabus*, (Dublin: Oifig an tSoláthair, 1990); idem, *Junior Certificate Music Guidelines for Teachers*, (Dublin: Oifig an tSoláthair, 1991).

[17] The document 'Position Paper on the Standing of Leaving Certificate Music' (Unpublished research into subject popularity and assessment undertaken for the National Council for Curriculum and Assessment 1990, updated 1992) is cited by Mac Liam in 'Turascáil Bliantúil an Choláiste/Annual College Report Samhradh/Summer 1992', n. p., SPCA, A/1/17.

[18] Mac Liam's contribution is officially noted in the teacher guidelines: 'In particular, the role of Seán Mac Liam (NCCA Education Officer for Music) is acknowledged for his work in developing and editing the Teacher Guidelines for Music'. An Roinn Oideachais, *Leaving Certificate Music Draft Guidelines for*

support team comprising four post-primary teachers appointed by the Department of Education. Looking back over the preceding years and addressing issues of accessibility and cultural relevance he would reflect:

> Leaving Cert music had become quite an elitist subject ... The levels of attainment in technical requirements were unrealistic and grades were low. There was a loss of confidence in the subject and taking music for the Leaving was getting a bad press. We needed to make it more accessible to students from a range of musical backgrounds so we have tried to plug into real life by being sensitive to aspects of local and national culture and to pitch it at a level which will see grades improve.[19]

As with the Junior Certificate Music Syllabus that had preceded it, the new course was simultaneously intended to be more music-centred and more student-centred than the syllabus it had replaced:

> The emphasis is on the 'ing, drawing attention to the experiential nature of the task. In the past the emphasis was all too often on imparting information about music as opposed to an educational experience in music.[20]

In addition to advocating for the centrality of performing, listening and composing in official curriculum policy, Mac Liam can also be credited with introducing approaches to the use of music technology in schools.

Since their introduction in the 1990s, the Junior and Leaving Certificate music syllabuses have undergone a number of reforms and have moreover been the subjects of many debates.[21] However these syllabuses are appraised, Mac Liam was at the forefront of a major pedagogical shift in post-primary music education in Ireland that ultimately paved the way for greater participation in music, not only in post-primary schools, but also in the increasing range of third-level music courses offered by colleges, conservatoires and universities.

Teachers, (Dublin: National Council for Curriculum and Assessment and Department of Education, 1997), p. 5.

[19] Seán Mac Liam quoted in J. Bourke, 'Do-Re-Mi', *The Irish Times*, (14 January 1997), https://www.irishtimes.com/news/education/do-re-mi-1.21869 [accessed 12 January 2019].

[20] Ibid.

[21] See for example, H. White, '"A Book of Manners in the Wilderness": The Model of University Music Education and Its Relevance as Enabler in General Education in Ireland', *College Music Symposium*, 38 (1998).

In addition to producing official teacher guidelines, Mac Liam compiled and published classroom resources following publication of the Junior Certificate Music Syllabus. *Music – Major and Minor* was a dual-volume publication by Folens, Dublin in 1991. [22] Book One comprised a resource book and CD of songs and recorded works for listening, while Book Two was a textbook on listening and composing skills.

Other music department staff became involved in writing school music textbooks following a demand after publication of the Revised Primary School Curriculum in 1999. *The Right Note*, published by Folens in 2006/2007 was a four-stage series for primary schools with textbook, teacher's manual, CDs and activity book prepared for each level. Full-time and part-time music staff who wrote for the series included Niamh Williams (junior and senior infants), Anne Purcell and Patricia Flynn (1st and 2nd class) and John Buckley and Yvonne Higgins (3rd and 4th class).[23] A similar series with the title *Upbeat* was co-written by Regina Murphy, a member of the education department with expertise in music education.[24] Like Seán Mac Liam, she had previously worked for the NCCA, in Murphy's case for the area of arts education in the primary curriculum.[25] At the time of writing, both music textbooks, *The Right Note* and *Upbeat* continued to be used in primary schools. In addition to writing music education textbooks and supplementary CDs, between 2001-2003 John Buckley presented a series of educational broadcasts for Lyric FM with the title 'ABC Sharp'. The series, which introduced children to classical music repertoire, was later issued as a two-volume CD.[26]

Arts-in-education projects

In 1986 the Arts Council introduced a new Arts Education Projects scheme 'which encouraged long term collaboration between artists and schools on projects which they would design according to their own

---

[22] S. Mac Liam, *Music – Major and Minor*, Books 1 & 2, (Dublin: Folens, 1991).
[23] Various authors, *The Right Note*, (Dublin: Folens, 2006-7).
[24] R. Murphy & M. Espeland, *Upbeat*, (Dublin: Carroll Education Limited, 2005).
[25] Colum Ó Cléirigh was also a member of the Curriculum Committee for Arts Education, established by the National Council for Curriculum and Assessment (NCCA) in the years prior to the publication of the *Revised Primary School Curriculum* in 1999.
[26] Three series of twelve programmes each were broadcast in 2001, 2002 and 2003. The double CD and booklet issued in 2001 were based on Series 1: *ABC Sharp*, (Ireland: RTÉ, 246 CD, 2001).

interests and concerns'.[27] Among the ten awards made for the school year 1986-87 was an innovative project involving the composer John Buckley with pupils and staff of Holy Spirit Girls' National School (G.N.S.) in Ballymun, North Dublin. Although it would be some time before Buckley eventually joined the music department at St Patrick's College, the project design involved close links between the College and Holy Spirit G.N.S. Spaces for music workshops were made available to the composer and to the project's primary participants - about seventy 5th class pupils. Twelve BEd students and staff members Marion Doherty (music), Eoin Butler (visual art) and Peter O'Driscoll (drama) collaborated with Buckley and the school-based team comprising principal teacher Mary O'Flynn and 5th class teachers Caitriona O'Shea and Marian Hackett.

John Buckley chose the general theme of water for the six-week project. During the first four weeks the pupils found, recorded and catalogued water-related sounds (of waves, seagulls, rain, taps, sprinklers and so on) in addition to making instruments. Under Buckley's guidance they learnt how to produce different grades of roughness/smoothness in hand-made maracas to effect large, medium and small wave sounds. The pupils also engaged with experimental techniques using metal percussion, for example, discovering the 'refracted' qualities of sound when triangles or finger cymbals were dipped in water immediately after being struck. Further experimental practices included the rhythmic use of speech, pitch-bending vocalise, effecting muted sounds on piano strings with rubber bands, and the creation of a piece-specific graphic notation agreed by the composer and his young co-composers. The last two weeks of the project were oriented towards the performance of an original work titled 'Drip, drop, drip' which was thirteen minutes in duration and incorporated visual art, drama and dance in addition to music.

Arguably, this was a project considerably ahead of its time (it would not be until 1999 that ideas of free (group) composition were officially endorsed in the Irish primary curriculum). As John Buckley commented in an RTÉ radio documentary following the project, 'nothing like it had been done before'. The ground-breaking nature of the arts-in-education engagement was more emphatically expressed by head of music Marion Doherty who stated: 'I felt as if there were walls falling down around me'.[28]

---

[27] The Arts Council/An Chomhairle Ealaíon, *Thirty-Fifth Annual Report and Accounts for the Year Ended 31st December 1986*, (Dublin: The Arts Council, 1988), p. 32.

[28] 'Drip, drop, drip', presented by Dermot Rattigan and produced by Tim Lehane, RTÉ Radio 1, 7 November 1988.

Twenty-five years after the collaboration with Holy Spirit G.N.S. in Ballymun, music staff and doctoral students at St Patrick's College became involved in another community-based music project, on this occasion involving the dual goals of engagement and research. From March to July 2012, an early years music project was piloted by community arts organization Common Ground in partnership with Early Childhood Ireland and The Base in Ballyfermot. Over the four-month period of the project professional musicians Eamon Sweeney and Thomas Johnston (part-time lecturer in traditional music and curriculum music at St Patrick's College) held regular music workshops with pre-school children and childcare workers in parts of Dublin 8 and Dublin 10. Early Childhood Ireland was represented by Michelle Finnerty who at the time was undertaking PhD studies on the theme of children's musical cultures in Ireland.[29]

At the core of the project was the young children's participation in a wide range of music genres and practices through play, as well as their engagement with professional musicians. In addition to providing high quality musical experiences for two cohorts of 2-4 year olds in inner city community settings, the project also aimed to inform policy in relation to arts provision for pre-school children. The music department of St Patrick's College was centrally involved in researching and documenting the pilot programme, first through the engagement of Mairéad Berrill as researcher – Berrill was then completing PhD studies at the music department - and second through membership of the project steering group by John O'Flynn and Maura O'Connor, respectively representing the areas of music and early childhood education.[30] The eventual report was co-published by Common Ground and St Patrick's College in spring 2013.[31] It took place at roughly the mid-point of the first year of the Fidelio Trio Residency at the College, a project that became the music department's most extensive involvement with an arts-in-education scheme in its history (this is explored in detail in Chapter Ten).

---

[29] Finnerty had dual registration as a doctoral student in St Patrick's College and in UCC with joint supervision respectively, by John O'Flynn and Mel Mercier.
[30] Michelle Finnerty also sat on the steering group representing Early Childhood Ireland as well as the music department of UCC where she lectured.
[31] *Tiny Voices: An Early Years Music Research Project*, (Dublin: Common Ground and St Patrick's College, 2013).

Engagement with humanities, music development and higher education

Over the years, members of the music department contributed to college-wide committees and activities, in addition to carrying out specific functions in the area of music. To give just one example, from 1979-1982 Seán Hayes co-chaired an evaluation steering committee that oversaw a substantial internal review of the three-year BEd programme.[32] As the College expanded in terms of student numbers as well as the range of programmes offered, so too did a need for more complex academic and administrative structures.

The Universities Act of 1997 included a directive for Irish universities and linked colleges to establish an academic council within each institution.[33] The Academic Council of St Patrick's College, by then a college of DCU, was constituted that same year. All lecturers were automatically elected as its members, while heads of department served on the College's inter-departmental management committee. Additionally, staff could be nominated to serve as members of college-wide committees that were answerable to Academic Council. Among the music staff participating in such groups were Patricia Flynn (Quality Assurance, Research) and John O'Flynn (Research, Teaching & Learning). Both Seán Mac Liam and Patricia Flynn were promoted to college-wide leadership roles that they carried out in addition to their music department activities, the former as Programme Chair for the BA in Humanities, the latter as Co-ordinator of Research.

Three music department members would contribute to the Seamus Heaney Lecture Series. The series was established in 2000 and among other aims strove to 'address significant issues in Education and the Humanities, with a view to promoting discussion and, as appropriate, informing and shaping debate on national policies'.[34] The series had a different organizing committee for each year that it ran. John Buckley was co-proposer and coordinator (with Mary Shine Thompson) for the third series that took 'the creative imagination' as its theme. Its proceedings were subsequently published as an edited volume. This

---

[32] E. Neuman, 'An Evaluation of the Three-Year Course Leading to the Bachelor or Education (B.Ed.) Degree in St Patrick's College, Dublin' (Dublin: Educational Research Centre, St Patrick's College, 1982).

[33] http://www.irishstatutebook.ie/eli/1997/act/24/enacted/en/html, accessed 13 February 2019.

[34] Pádraig Ó Duibhir, 'Proposals for future series of Seamus Heaney Lectures', document circulated to the Academic Council of St Patrick's College, 14 February 2014.

included an afterword by Patricia Flynn with the title 'Words and music: a dialogue of maker and materials'.[35]

The fourth Heaney lecture series in 2007 was addressed to drama and theatre in the modern world. It included the lecture 'Like a bell with many echoes: drama and opera' by John Buckley. The lecture was illuminated with insights into the chamber opera *Words Upon The Window Pane* that Buckley had composed in 1991 after the play by Yeats.[36] The Sixth Heaney Series took place in 2011 and was organized by a committee that included John O'Flynn. Its theme, 'Hearing Heaney' was centred on the life and works of the poet, and partly because it could be considered as a celebratory series, it also included elements of music programming for some of the events. Arguably, the highlight of this series was the reading-recital 'The Poet and the Piper' that took place on 14 March. At it Heaney read his own poems in dialogue with music performed by the renowned uilleann piper Liam O'Flynn.[37] 2011 was the same year that Seamus Heaney was conferred with an honorary doctorate by Dublin City University. The formal ceremony took place in the very auditorium of St Patrick's College where months earlier he had performed at one of his last public poetry readings.

Over the years members of the music department at St Patrick's College were also actively involved in initiatives at national and international levels. Seán Hayes served for many years on the Dublin Diocesan Commission on Liturgical Music, established following the Second Vatican Council (the Twenty-first Ecumenical Council of the Roman Catholic Church) held from 1962-1965. Kathleen Hegarty (Caitlín Uí Éigeartaigh) was an active member and honorary secretary of the Irish Folk Music Society from its foundation in 1971.[38] Throughout much of the 1980s and 1990s Colum Ó Cléirigh was Irish representative of the British-based Association for the Advancement of Music in Education, in addition to affiliations he established with the

---

[35] P. Flynn, 'Words and music: a dialogue of maker and materials', in M. Shine Thompson (ed.), *'The Fire i' the Flint': Essays on the Creative Imagination: The Third Seamus Heaney Lectures*, (Dublin: Four Courts Press, 2009).

[36] The lecture was subsequently published in P. Burke (ed.), *Mirror Up To Nature: The Fourth Seamus Heaney Lectures*, (Dublin: Carysfort Press, 2010).

[37] The reading-recital took its name from a longstanding collaboration between the poet and traditional musician, culminating in a CD album: Seamus Heaney and Liam O'Flynn, *The Poet and the Piper* (Claddagh Records, CCT21CD, 2003).

[38] '*Ceol Tíre*: Newsletter of the FMSI, 1973-89', https://www.itma.ie/features/printed-collections/ceol-tire [accessed 14 April 2019].

International Kodály Society. Ó Cléirigh also gave many years service to IFUT (the Irish Federation of University Teachers); he was a long-standing member of IFUT Council and also served two terms as trustee for the Federation. In later years, John O'Flynn was chairperson of the St Patrick's College branch of IFUT (2011-2014), going on to serve on IFUT's National Executive (2014-2016).

Prior to and following his appointment to the College, John Buckley served on various boards, including the Irish Music Rights Organization, Music Network, the Dublin Festival of Twentieth-Century Music, the Association of Irish Composers and the *Toscaireacht* of Aosdána (Rhona Clarke was elected to the *Toscaireacht* in more recent years).[39] Buckley also contributed in various ways to the aims of the Music Association of Ireland (MAI).[40] The MAI was established in 1948, and actively promoted classical music in the country. Marion Doherty acted as MAI chair for a short period in the early 1990s before going on to join the committee of the Kodály Society of Ireland in 1997.[41] From 1994-2008 Doherty represented the music department on the Council of Heads of Music in Higher Education (CHMHE), an intervarsity group that

> ... has specific administration functions in the co-ordination of entrance tests for music at third level, in publishing information on music courses in Ireland, and in organising an annual undergraduate musicology competition as well as occasional seminars and open days.[42]

Doherty served as chair of CHMHE from 2005-2008, during which time she initiated and hosted the first intervarsity composition forum for undergraduate music students.[43] Following his appointment to St Patrick's College in 2008 John O'Flynn took on the role of CHMHE

---

[39] Aosdána is an Arts Council-supported affiliation of creative artists in Ireland, and is self-regulated through an elected committee or *Toscaireacht*.

[40] T. O'Donnell, 'Music Association of Ireland', Unpublished PhD thesis (St Patrick's College, Dublin City University, 2012). See also Benjamin Dwyer, *Constellations: The Life and Music of John Buckley*, (Dublin: Carysfort Press, 2011), p. 169.

[41] Patricia Flynn was later a MAI board member during the final years of the association from 2005-2006.

[42] G. Cox, 'Council of Heads of Music in Higher Education (CHMHE)' in H. White and B. Boydell (eds.), *The Encyclopaedia of Music in Ireland, Volume 1*, (Dublin: UCD Press, 2013), p. 255.

[43] See Rhona Clarke's chapter in this volume.

honorary secretary until 2011. He continued as chair of the Council until 2015 from which point he would serve as web liaison officer. During his time in these various officer roles he hosted three CHMHE intervarsity composition forums during the Fidelio Trio Residency 2012-2015, and also collated and edited text for CHMHE's revised website www.StudyMusicIreland.ie which was launched in June 2016.[44]

O'Flynn was founding chairperson of the Society for Music Education (SMEI) in Ireland from 2010-2013[45]. An affiliate of the International Society for Music Education, the SMEI was publicly constituted at a research symposium and meeting held in St Patrick's College in November 2010, and was officially inaugurated by Gary Ó Donnchadha, Deputy Chief Inspector at the Department of Education and Skills.[46] O'Flynn was further involved in activities of the Society for Musicology in Ireland (SMI) and was elected to its national council in 2015.

Established in 1985 the Contemporary Music Centre (CMC) is the national archive and resource centre for contemporary music from the island of Ireland. Its remit is to document, develop and promote Irish composition on an all-Ireland bias. It has represented a considerable number of composers based in St Patrick's College including staff members Rhona Clarke and John Buckley as well as past postgraduate students Kevin O'Connell, Vincent Kennedy, Eoin Mulvany and Colman Pearce. From the perspective of research and engagement, work carried out by Patricia Flynn served to build close and long-lasting ties between the College and the CMC. Among several enterprises, Flynn was principal investigator of the Irish Composers Project in partnership with Dundalk Institute of Technology, Maynooth University, the CMC and An Foras Feasa.[47] This was a project involving the digitization of a considerable corpus of archival scores, recordings and other media held by the CMC, and was conceived and developed for future use by musicians, musicologists and other researchers. Flynn was appointed as chair of CMC's board of directors in 2015. In other research and

---

[44] http://www.studymusicireland.ie [accessed 13 January 2019].

[45] O'Flynn was also founding chair of Fuaim (the Association for the Promotion of Primary-Level Music Education), established in 1997, and was also a member of the Executive Committee of CERC (Colleges of Education Research Consortium) from 2005-2011 while based, respectively, at Mary Immaculate College, Limerick and at St Patrick's College.

[46] See https://www.smei.ie/about-us/ [accessed 13 January 2019].

[47] See http://doras.dcu.ie/21513/1/49_SCAN.pdf [accessed 13 January 2019]. Now based solely at Maynooth University, An Foras Feasa (the Institute for Research in Irish Historical and Cultural Traditions) was at the time an interinstitutional funding organization.

engagement projects she nurtured close institutional ties with Music Generation, the music development agency initiated by Music Network in 2010 and co-funded by U2 and the Ireland Funds, the Department of Education and Skills and a national network of local music education partnerships (the music department's partnership with Music Generation is discussed below).[48] Patricia Flynn was also founding chair of local arts organization GlasDrum which was established in early 2015. Members of its arts programming committee also included Áine Mangaoang and John O'Flynn from the music department, college librarian Orla Nic Aodha and Andrea Cleary, lecturer in visual art education. Engaging local communities with high quality arts events was and remains core to GlasDrum's mission; details of its music programming and other events are outlined and discussed in sections of the next two chapters.

Postgraduate Research
Postgraduate degree programmes arrived relatively late to St Patrick's College although a professional Graduate Diploma in Education had been offered since 1971. Shortly after DCU accredited the College's MEd programme in 1996, the MEd (Music Education) ran for the first time in 1998. Later in 2003 the first taught MA in Music course was offered as an option within a generic MA in Humanities programme, although all of the music modules were discipline-specific.

The content for the music department's two taught postgraduate programmes – the MEd (Music Education) and the MA in Humanities (Music) - is discussed in some detail in Chapter Three. Here it can be noted how both programmes equipped a considerable number of students to carry our minor dissertations in their chosen field in either music or music education (See Appendix D for a complete list of all dissertations and theses from 2000-2016). In the case of the taught MA, independent work on dissertations was preceded by research seminars organized by the programme director. This brought postgraduate students in contact with leading figures in various aspects of music research. In recent years these included Julian Horton, Jaime Jones and Harry White (UCD) Lorraine Byrne Bodley, Adrian Scahill and Antonio Cascelli (Maynooth), Kevin O'Connell (RIAM), Mark Fitzgerald and Adrian Smith (DIT), Danijela Kulezic-Wilson (UCC), Ioannis Tsioulakis (QUB) and Sara Cohen (Liverpool). Among the visitors to the MEd in Music Education programme were leading international scholars Keith Swanwick (London), Magne Espeland (Stord/Haugesund, Norway) and Marie McCarthy (Maryland, later Michigan).

---

[48] https://www.musicgeneration.ie/about/ [accessed 13 January 2019].

A wide range of dissertation topics across the taught MA and MEd is evinced in Appendix D. While most MEd dissertations were directly concerned with primary and post-primary music curricula, a wide range of research methods was employed, from quantitative survey to action research to school-based ethnography. The majority of MEd students selected research topics that were situated in and that arguably impacted on the schools where they practised. At the same time, many BEd graduates of the College and other qualified teachers opted for the taught MA in Music, reflecting the interrelationships between humanities and education that permeated the music department and indeed the College as a whole. The MA course also attracted established and aspiring composers and performers in addition to those working in arts administration and related fields. A cursory view of Appendix D reveals a very broad range of topics and approaches that embraced music analysis, music in culture, music history, music technology, music education, performance, music editing and composing.

St Patrick's College awarded its first research degrees in music (at both MA and PhD levels) from the mid-2000s. MA theses from 2004 and 2006 and the first PhDs from 2007 reflected two major strengths of the music department at that time: music education and composition. Daniel Walsh, supervised by Seán Mac Liam, was awarded an MA for his research on applications of music technology in education. Meanwhile, the supervision of Maria Westvall's PhD (awarded 2007) by Patricia Flynn reflected the international music education networks that Flynn and other colleagues at St Patrick's College had begun to establish in the 2000s. In her final year of PhD studies Westvall was awarded a research fellowship from Örebro University, Sweden to carry out a related postdoctoral project there. Supervised by John Buckley, theses by Sandie Purcell (2006) and Kevin O'Connell (2007) for MA and PhD respectively, broke new ground for both college and university insofar as their work presented the first occasions where creative practice was appraised as research, (although a precedent had already been established in the taught MA programme which gave options to specialize in dissertation, performance portfolio or composition portfolio).

Subsequent PhDs would include a portfolio of original compositions by Colman Pearce (2009), and a range of theses that addressed issues of national significance for music and music education, from Teresa O'Donnell's history of The Music Association of Ireland (2012) to Mairéad Berrill's development of group music-making pedagogies in post-primary schools (2014) to Michelle Finnerty's exploration of children's musical cultures through ethnography (2016).

Funded Research Projects

At the turn of the twenty-first century St Patrick's College widened its ambition in respect of research activity and funding. As Ciarán Sugrue notes: 'A significant declaration on the part of the College was made by the submission of a proposal when the government introduced the PRTLI research programme in 1999'.[49] Sugrue refers here to the Programme for Research in Third Level Institutions that was part of the state's strategy for research and development from 2000-2006. In addition to core PRTLI funding, other public funding streams led to research applications by College departments and individual staff members, including Patricia Flynn in the music department. In 2006 Flynn successfully attracted funding to lead a collaborative project that for the first time aimed to provide an overview of music provision among local authorities in Ireland. The project came under the Arts Council Local Partnership Scheme 2006-2008 and was jointly funded by The Arts Council, St Patrick's College and local councils in Sligo (county and borough) and Wexford. Ailbhe Kenny was appointed as research fellow for the project which culminated in the report *Knowing the Score*, published by the College in 2009.[50] A foreword by leading arts consultant Marc Jaffrey describes the project thus:

> This report illuminates a vital strand of activity currently happening in Irish society. It pinpoints the unique role of Local Authorities and its Arts Officers in joining up the ambitions for the role of arts in Irish society. It provides strong evidence for the immediate value of this work, from commissioning new work and supporting artists in their professional development to improving the quality of daily life for local citizens and driving more effective music education. It gives insight into why this is effective and recommendations to improve and exploit its potential going forward.[51]

The above quote by Jaffrey emphasizes the value of *Knowing the Score* not only for its clear set of research findings, but also with regard to its potential for future collaborations ('joining up the ambitions') and ultimately for societal impact.

---

[49] C. Sugrue, 'Three Decades of College Life, 1973-1999: The Old Order Changeth?', in J. Kelly (ed.), *St Patrick's College, 1875-2000: A History*, (Dublin: Four Courts, 2006), p. 256.
[50] A. Kenny with P. Flynn, *Local Authorities & Music: Knowing the Score*, (Dublin: St Patrick's College, 2009).
[51] M. Jaffrey, 'Foreword', *Knowing the Score*, p. vii.

Patricia Flynn's subsequent research projects at the College were also collaborative in orientation; a consistent thread was the aim of establishing further connections between music education research and practice and to reflect the diversity of music education in Ireland. In 2010 she established the web resource 'Irish Music Education' with Ailbhe Kenny, music education lecturer at Mary Immaculate College, Limerick. Under the aegis of Irish Music Education, Flynn also facilitated the establishment of the Music Educators' Orchestra, an ensemble for teachers and other adult amateur musicians that rehearsed in the main music room (B118) of St Patrick's College. Conducted by composer Peter Moran, the orchestra performed mainly contemporary programmes, including works by Moran and by orchestral members, and was highly active between 2011-2015.

From 2013 the music department's partnership with Music Generation would result in its most extensive external research project to date. Its board of directors commissioned Patricia Flynn to act as principal investigator for a project exploring the diversity of 'performance music education' across the eleven music education partnerships that had been established in local authorities throughout Ireland at that point.[52] Thomas Johnston was appointed as research fellow at the music department with responsibility for the project. Using a multi-modal approach Johnson carried out surveys, interviews, site visits and documentary analysis across all eleven music education partnerships between 2013-2016.

In addition to capturing the diversity of performance music education and its organization within Music Generation's remit, the project also proposed a new model for arts-in-education research. Going beyond the evaluation of specific activities in and for themselves, the analysis employed a mainly 'grounded' theoretical approach that explored the wider experiential and developmental impact of the various phenomena surveyed. This approach would lead to the eventual subtitle for the published research report, *Possible Selves in Music*.[53]

---

[52] The full project title was 'Developing Diversity in Performance Music Education'. The term 'performance music education' is used by Music Generation to describe its focus on children and young people's access to training and participation in musical performance: 'It can happen in many contexts such as through mainstream education, in a community setting or through a music school'.
https://www.musicgeneration.ie/content/files/PerformanceMusicEducation.pdf [accessed 14 January 2019].

[53] P. Flynn & T. Johnston, *Possible Selves in Music: The transformative potential for children and young people of performance music education based on principles of diversity*, (Dublin: Music Generation, 2016).

Links between Music Generation and the music department of St Patrick's College were further strengthened in 2013 through the advertising of a doctoral fellowship in the area of performance music education. The successful candidate was Yvonne Higgins who in early 2014 embarked on PhD studies in the area of music literacy and choral performance. [54]

In 2015-16, during the final academic year of St Patrick's College prior to its incorporation into DCU, the music department hosted the applied research project 'Mapping Popular Music in Dublin' (MPMiD) with funding from Fáilte Ireland/Irish Tourism. The idea for the project - which forms the subject of the next chapter by Áine Mangaoang - arose from the research interests of John O'Flynn who had previously carried out ethnographies of various styles of music in Ireland. Research participation for MPMiD extended to large numbers of musicians, fans and music industry personnel. Insofar as it blurred the lines between research and engagement, it was continuous with the earlier funded projects *Knowing the Score* and *Possible Selves in Music*.

Combining research and engagement: music and music education conferences at the College, 2001-2016
The first scholarly conference to be hosted by the music department of St Patrick's College was titled 'The Drumcondra Music Education Conference: Music Challenges in the 21st Century'. It took place from 28-29 September 2001 and was presented in association with Fuaim, the association promoting primary-level music education. Scheduled over two days the conference programme included fourteen research papers, an invited panel discussion and four workshops. [55] Paper presenters included music department lecturers Seán Mac Liam and Patricia Flynn, and among the workshop leaders were Carrie Maher and Mary Nugent who were part-time lecturers at the College, respectively, in curriculum music and in Irish traditional music. The conference also represented an important platform for the first cohort of MEd in Music Education students at the College, including Siobhán Keane, Assumpta Kerins and Yvonne Higgins.

The Drumcondra Music Education Conference was organized several years after the Music Education National Debate (MEND) convened by Frank Heneghan at the Dublin Institute of Technology

---

[54] The working title for Higgins's doctoral research was 'Imagining Sound from Notation: A Study of Children's Musical Thinking in Choral Settings'.
[55] http://www.esatclear.ie/~fuaim/Conference%20Programme.htm [accessed 14 January 2019].

over three stages from 1994-1996.[56] MEND's national and international line-up and volume of proceedings have been unsurpassed to date in an Irish context. While the Drumcondra conference in 2001 was a much more modest event, it arguably constituted a coming of age for music education as a scholarly discipline in Ireland insofar as it comprised a complete programme of peer-reviewed papers and workshops presented by local academics and practitioners. Many of those present would later go on to found the Society for Music Education in Ireland (SMEI) almost one decade later.

On 24 March 2009 the college hosted a national music symposium in association with Music Generation. Its title, 'Knowing the Score: Local Authorities and Music' revealed one of its primary functions: to disseminate the findings of the research project and publication described above. Arts officers, teachers and local authority councillors from around the country attended the symposium. Along with keynote speeches and small specialist working groups, the event also included the performance of *Ardee Dances* by Rachel Holstead and a performance of Nick Page's *Nursery Rhyme Cantata* by the children's choir Aspiro.[57]

Two years later, on 26 May 2011 the music department hosted a one-day postgraduate seminar titled 'Popular Music in Ireland'. Jointly chaired by John O'Flynn and Barbara Bradby (TCD) its programme comprised a range of PhD papers on aspects of popular music production, distribution and consumption in Ireland. While not the first popular music conference held in Ireland, the seminar was unique in bringing together a range of studies focusing wholly on local and domestic popular music scenes.[58] Shortly afterwards, on 2 June 2011 Patricia Flynn and Ailbhe Kenny organized a one-day conference titled 'What counts as music education?'. It brought together practitioners,

---

[56] F. Heneghan, 'Music Education National Debate: A Review of Music Education in Ireland, Incorporating the Final Report of the Music Education National Debate (MEND - Phase III)', Unpublished report, (Dublin Institute of Technology, 2001),
https://www.musicnetwork.ie/content/files/MEND09d.pdf, [accessed 15 January 2019].

[57] *Ardee Dances* by Rachel Holstead was first commissioned by Louth County Council in 2005 under the Percent for Art Scheme. It was performed at the 'Knowing the Score' symposium by Gerry O'Connor (fiddle), Elizabeth Wallfisch (violin) and the Irish Baroque Orchestra.

[58] The first popular music conference to take place in Ireland was the Biennial Conference of the International Association for the Study of Popular Music (UK and Ireland Branch) in July 2004. It was hosted by the music department of Mary Immaculate College, University of Limerick and chaired by John O'Flynn.

administrators and scholars from diverse music and music education fields. Proceedings comprised a panel discussion, invited presentations, a workshop and performance of *Always Considering Kitchen Sinks* by composer Karen Power, and the official launch of the Teachers' Orchestra [later renamed the Music Educators' Orchestra].[59]

Figure 8.1: Poster for The Music Education Gathering 2013. Design by Mick McCabe

---

[59] See P. Flynn (ed.), 'What Counts as Music Education? The Proceedings of the Voicing Conference 2011', (Dublin: St Patrick's College, 2012).

The Music Education Gathering 2013 was the title given to the third annual conference of the Society for Music Education in Ireland which that year took place at St Patrick's College from 1-3 November. It came under the umbrella of The Gathering 2013, a government-led culture and tourism initiative that aimed to bring large numbers of the Irish Diaspora 'home' throughout the same calendar year. The SMEI adapted this initiative to its conference theme that had three main strands: to look back at the afore-mentioned Music Education National Debate and other national and international initiatives: to reflect on current trends; and to contemplate future aspirations and challenges for music education in Ireland and beyond.

The ambition and scale of the conference was evidenced by the participation of no less than six international keynote speakers of renown: David Elliott (US/Canada), Marie McCarthy (US/Ireland), Mícheál Ó Súilleabháin (Ireland), Keith Swanwick (UK), Sheila Woodward (US/South Africa) and Harry White (Ireland), with all apart from Woodward having previously contributed to MEND in the mid-1990s. With in excess of one hundred and fifty participants, the conference brought together a wide range of national and international research papers, practical workshops, symposia, showcase performances and keynote debates. It was also programmed locally to coincide with the inaugural Fidelio Trio Winter Chamber Music Festival that took place over the same three days (this is discussed briefly in Chapter Ten).

Figure 8.2: Keith Swanwick delivering a keynote address at The Music Education Gathering 2013. Photograph by Barbara Flynn

If the Drumcondra Music Education Conference of 2001 was a coming-of-age event for music education scholarship in Ireland, it could be argued that the Music Education Gathering 2013 provided an international showcase for the significant developments that had occurred in the interim. It consolidated the reputation of SMEI as an umbrella organization for the promotion of music education in Ireland. Locally, it represented the strong sense of collaboration that existed between many of the organizers working in the complementary areas of music and music education at the College, including Patricia Flynn, Yvonne Higgins, Thomas Johnston, Regina Murphy and John O'Flynn.

The next conference hosted by the music department was the third 'Women and Music in Ireland Conference' jointly organized by Rhona Clarke and Jennifer Madsen O'Connor. It took place on 10 May 2014 and its featured keynote speaker was composer and professor emeritus at York University, Nicola LeFanu (see Chapter Four for further details). Later that year the music department hosted the 2014 autumn meeting of the European Chamber Music Teachers' Association (ECMTA). The weekend of workshops and master classes for chamber ensembles was scheduled to coincide with the Fidelio Trio Winter Chamber Music Festival from 5-7 December. More than twenty international delegates attended, along with advanced student ensembles from eight European countries as far afield as Portugal and the Russian Federation, as well as from the RIAM, DIT, the Irish World Academy at UL and St Patrick's College.

It was not until its final year of existence that the music department of St Patrick's College hosted the annual plenary conference of the Society for Musicology in Ireland.[60] In keeping with SMI custom, the conference took place over three days, from 10-12 June 2016. It was preceded by a symposium to launch the executive report and city music map developed as part of the Mapping Popular Music in Dublin project based at the music department between 2015-2016.[61]

The SMI conference attracted over 120 delegates representing all tertiary institutes with music departments in Ireland (north and south) as well as presenters from overseas institutions and independent

---

[60] The conference committee was made up of Rhona Clarke, Áine Mangaoang, Barry O'Halpin and John O'Flynn (chair) from St Patrick's College along with Róisín Blunnie (Mater Dei Institute) and Michael Murphy (Mary Immaculate College, UL).

[61] Á. Mangaoang & J. O'Flynn, *Mapping Popular Music in Dublin: Executive Report*, (Dublin: St Patrick's College, Dublin City University, 2016); *Dublin Music Map*, (Dublin: Fáilte Ireland and St Patrick's College, Dublin City University, 2016).

scholars. Its twenty-four panels of research papers included a wide range of themes including: nineteenth-century music; vocal and choral music; film music and sound design; traditional music; music education and community music; performance-based musicology; music, language and literature; twentieth-century music; contemporary composition in Ireland; popular music scenes; music philosophy and criticism; and music and cultural politics. Such a response to the original call for papers was testament to the broad range of topics and approaches that musicology had come to embrace by the second decade of the twenty-first century. This plurality along with the conference organizers' ambition to communicate parity of esteem to various music genres and scholarly approaches was linked to two further items in the programme: the plenary session 'Research in Musicology and in Related Music Studies' and the keynote delivered by Georgina Born, professor of music and anthropology at Oxford University, 'Music and Sound Art - From Interdisciplinarity to Ontological Politics'. Additionally, two concerts were programmed during the conference: a recital of song cycles by Schumann and Finzi given by Gavan Ring (baritone) and Fionnuala Moynihan (piano), and a jazz gig performed by the Paul McIntyre Trio.[62]

In retrospect the conference could be viewed as a celebratory event for the music department of St Patrick's College, a significance that was evidenced by the extent of staff and student participation. In addition to conference papers given by a number of graduates and postgraduate students, four lecturers and two researchers based at the department also contributed individual presentations and/or chaired paper sessions or plenary symposia.[63]

Concluding comments
This chapter has documented and considered engagement and research carried out by music staff at St Patrick's College for the last half-century or so of its history. The music department had a significant record in contributing to music in-service provision for primary and other education sectors from the 1970s to the 2010s. Individual staff members played critical roles in music curriculum development throughout the 1990s, as well as in the production of textbooks, CDs

---

[62] All of the performers mentioned here held a connection with the music department. Gavan Ring was a BEd graduate of the College and subsequently was a part-time singing teacher there, Fionnuala Moynihan was coach and accompanist for practical exams, and Paul McIntyre was a part-time lecturer for the MA in Music.
[63] John Buckley, Rhona Clarke, Patricia Flynn, Thomas Johnston, Áine Mangaoang and John O'Flynn.

and other educational materials for primary and post-primary schools. From time to time, the music department also became directly involved in music initiatives at community and local levels. Additionally, staff members made many contributions to national organizations and agencies that promoted music and music education scholarship and development.

The chapter has illustrated how in many instances the lines between research and engagement were blurred across various initiatives and enterprises. The music department's scholarly profile would greatly increase from the early 2000s through the organization of national and international conferences in music education, music development, popular music studies, chamber music and musicology. The same period witnessed a series of funded research projects based at the music department, all of which were directly engaged with community and societal concerns. Arguably, the strong links that emerged between engagement and research in various projects carried out by music lecturers, researchers and others were reflective of the department's dual interests in music and music education, and in the shared concerns of humanities and education at the College.

Bibliography

The Arts Council/An Chomhairle Ealaíon, *Thirty-Fifth Annual Report and Accounts for the Year Ended 31st December 1986*, (Dublin: The Arts Council, 1988).

An Roinn Oideachais, *The Junior Certificate Music Syllabus*, (Dublin: Oifig an tSoláthair, 1990).

An Roinn Oideachais, *Junior Certificate Music Guidelines for Teachers*, (Dublin: Oifig an tSoláthair, 1991).

An Roinn Oideachais, *Leaving Certificate Music Draft Guidelines for Teachers*, (Dublin: National Council for Curriculum and Assessment and Department of Education, 1997)

Bourke, Jackie, 'Do-Re-Mi', *The Irish Times*, (14 January 1997).

Buckley, John, 'Like a bell with many echoes: drama and opera', in P. Burke (ed.), *Mirror Up To nature: The Fourth Seamus Heaney Lectures*, (Dublin: Carysfort Press, 2010), pp. 83-97.

Buckley, John & Higgins, Yvonne, *The Right Note – 3rd & 4th Class*, (Dublin: Folens, 2007).

Cox, Gareth, 'Council of Heads of Music in Higher Education (CHMHE)', in H. White and B. Boydell (eds.), *The Encyclopaedia of Music in Ireland, Volume 1*, (Dublin: UCD Press, 2013), pp. 254-255.

Dwyer, Benjamin, *Constellations: The Life and Music of John Buckley*, (Dublin: Carysfort Press, 2011).

Flynn, Patricia, 'Words and music: a dialogue of maker and materials', in M. Shine Thompson (ed.), *'The Fire i' the Flint': Essays on the Creative Imagination: The Third Seamus Heaney Lectures*, (Dublin: Four Courts Press, 2009), pp. 173-186.

Flynn, Patricia (ed.), 'What Counts as Music Education? The Proceedings of the Voicing Conference 2011', (Dublin: St Patrick's College, March 2012).

Flynn, Patricia and Johnston, Thomas, *Possible Selves in Music: The transformative potential for children and young people of performance music education based on principles of diversity*, (Dublin, Music Generation, 2016).

Friesen, Rhonda, 'Faculty member engagement in Canadian university internationalization: A consideration of understanding, motivations and rationales', *Journal of Studies in International Education*, 17.3 (2013), 209-227.

Heneghan, Frank, 'Music Education National Debate: A Review of Music Education in Ireland, Incorporating the Final Report of the Music Education National Debate (MEND - Phase III)', Unpublished report, (Dublin Institute of Technology, 2001), https://www.musicnetwork.ie/content/files/MEND09d.pdf [accessed 15 January 2019].

Irish National Teachers' Organisation, *Inservice Education and Training of Teachers* (Report and Recommendations of the Education Committee of the Irish National Teachers' Organisation), (Dublin: INTO, 1980).

Irish National Teachers' Organisation, *The Professional Development of Teachers: Issues in Inservice Education*, (Dublin: INTO, 1993).

Irish National Teachers' Organisation, *Creativity and the Arts in the Primary School* (Discussion Document and Proceedings of the Consultative Conference on Education 2009), (Dublin: INTO, 2010).

Irish National Teachers' Organisation Consultative Conference on Education, *The Arts in Education*, (Dublin: INTO, 1989).

Kenny, Ailbhe with Flynn, Patricia, *Local Authorities & Music: Knowing the Score*, (Dublin: St Patrick's College, 2009).

Seán Mac Liam, *Music – Major and Minor*, Books 1 & 2, (Dublin: Folens, 1991).

Mangaoang, Áine & O'Flynn, John, *Mapping Popular Music in Dublin: Executive Report*, (Dublin: St Patrick's College, Dublin City University, 2016).

Mangaoang, Áine & O'Flynn, John, *Dublin Music Map*, (Dublin: Fáilte Ireland and St Patrick's College, Dublin City University, 2016).

Murphy, Regina & Espeland, Magne, *Upbeat*, (Dublin: Carroll Education Limited, 2005).

National Council for Curriculum and Assessment, *Primary School Curriculum, Arts Education*, (Dublin: Stationery Office, 1999).

Neuman, Elizabeth, 'An Evaluation of the 3 year Course Leading to the BEd Degree in St Patrick's College', Internal report, (Dublin: St Patrick's College, 1982).

O'Donnell, Teresa, 'Music Association of Ireland', Unpublished PhD thesis, (St Patrick's College, Dublin City University, 2012).

Purcell, Anne & Flynn, Patricia, *The Right Note – 1st & 2nd Class*, (Dublin: Folens, 2006).

Sugrue, Ciarán, 'Three Decades of College Life, 1973-1999: The Old Order Changeth?, in J. Kelly (ed.), *St Patrick's College, 1875-2000: A History*, (Dublin: Four Courts, 2006), pp. 225-265.

Tiny Voices: An Early Years Music Research Project, (Dublin: Common Ground and St Patrick's College, 2013).

Ward, Kelly, *Faculty Service Roles and the Scholarship of Engagement. ASHE-ERIC Higher Education Report. Jossey-Bass Higher and Adult Education Series*, (San Francisco: Jossey-Bass, 2003).

White, Harry, '"A Book of Manners in the Wilderness": The Model of University Music Education and Its Relevance as Enabler in General Education in Ireland', *College Music Symposium*, 38 (1998), 47-79.

Williams, Niamh, *The Right Note – Junior & Senior Infants*, (Dublin: Folens, 2006).

Newspapers and periodicals
The Irish Times

Archives
St Patrick's College Archive

Interviews and email correspondence
Ailbhe Kenny

Discography
Buckley, John, Pearce, Colman & National Symphony Orchestra of Ireland, *ABC Sharp*, (Ireland: RTÉ 246 CD, 2001).

Heaney, Seamus & O'Flynn, Liam, *The Poet and the Piper*, (Ireland: Claddagh Records, CCT 21 CD, 2003).

Chapter Nine: Music and Tourism: Mapping Popular Music from St Patrick's College

Áine Mangaoang

Introduction

In February 2015, St Patrick's College Drumcondra (SPD) became the epicentre for the first applied research project mapping Dublin's contemporary popular music landscape. The Mapping Popular Music in Dublin (MPMiD) project charted the popular music experiences of fans, musicians, and music personnel in Ireland's capital city. Led by Principal Investigator John O'Flynn and Postdoctoral Research Fellow Áine Mangaoang, the project was funded for twelve months by Fáilte Ireland – the National Tourism Development Authority – and was based at the Department of Music at St Patrick's College, Dublin City University.

This chapter presents a brief background to and overview of the MPMiD project, before focusing on three aspects: one methodological – map-making workshops, and two associated outcomes – a new *Dublin Music Map*, and a grass-roots community initiative, GlasDrum. The chapter then considers how St Patrick's College itself played a vital role in the shape, nature, and outcomes of the MPMiD project. I trace how St Patrick's College as an institution, its location, and most crucially, its people all played a role in the conversations and collaborations that formed through the research. I highlight how the frequent opportunities for inter-departmental discussions afforded by the College went a considerable way in fostering the convergence of ideas across disciplinary boundaries, bringing musicologists and popular music scholars together with cartographers, geographers, and historians.

SPD's geographical situation in Drumcondra allowed for the project to engage with the changing nature of the local Northside community and its present relationship with popular music. Located off the Drumcondra Road, the campus houses a range of 'hidden' architectural delights, from the ornate seventeenth-century Belvedere House to the 1960s smooth, concrete chapel designed by Andrew Devane. As the project progressed through musical and research events hosted by the college, MPMiD quickly revealed a near neglect of formalized cultural and musical venues and spaces in Drumcondra. This served, in part, as a catalyst for the founding of a new arts and cultural collective stemming from colleagues based at St Patrick's College. The resulting organization GlasDrum has gone on to encourage some local residents and visitors to engage with, and extend, their own musical maps of Dublin. In short, through accounts of primary moments in this research project, this chapter demonstrates how the unique environment of the College became a meaningful actor in the project. Such a perspective of St Patrick's College, told through the lens of a one-year popular music and tourism research project, highlights the significance in affective agency offered by research and education institutions.

Background to the project
Music, identity, place

Music offers powerful human experiences. It can shape lives through meaning making, bring people together in communities and fuel a sense of shared, as well as disparate socio-cultural identities. The heart of an industry (or several industries), music is both an active commercial product alongside an important facet of social life. Music sociologist Tia DeNora describes how music revolves around cognitive, emotional and embodied social processes whereby personal and cultural identities are remembered, constructed, negotiated, and performed socially.[1] For music journalist and academic Simon Frith, music helps 'construct our sense of identity through the direct experiences it offers of the body, time and sociability, experiences which enable us to place ourselves in imaginative cultural narratives'.[2] Music has the capacity to evoke personal memory, and entangled with this process is how individuals interpret and understand songs and artists.

Music and media scholar David Hesmondhalgh tells us that people's attachment to music is as strong as it is because it feels extremely linked to the private self and emotions, while it is also 'often the basis of collective, public experiences, whether in live performance, mad dancing at a party, or simply by virtue of the fact that thousands and sometimes millions of people can come to know the same sounds and performers'.[3] Meanwhile anthropologist Georgina Born asserts that individuals can have multiple musical identifications that are manifest in diverse and potentially contradictory musical tastes and practices. Born explains how music can 'variably *both* construct new identities *and* reflect existing ones. Sociocultural identities are not simply constructed in music; there are 'prior' identities that come to be

---

[1] T. DeNora, 'Music as a technology of the self', *Poetics*, 27. 1 (1999).
[2] S. Frith, 'Music and identity', in S. Hall, S. & P. du Gay (eds.), *Questions of Cultural Identity*, (London: Sage, 1996), p. 124.
[3] D. Hesmondhalgh, *Why Music Matters*, (Oxford: Blackwell Publishing, 2013), pp. 1-2.

embodied dynamically in musical cultures, which then also form the reproduction of those identities'.[4]

Music's distinct potential to evoke nostalgia makes it particularly ripe for tourism industries to harvest. Add to this the fact that music and place are inextricably linked. In recent years there has been a significant rise in music tourism – the act of consciously travelling to places associated with particular music, musicians and/or genres – across many parts of the world. Music tourism directly impacts economies, bringing many tangible benefits and associations for certain places (for example creating employment opportunities, building new audiences, commodification, revitalization, increased investments in music, cultural and related services, and so on). Places of music production and musical expression form the apex of most music tourism pilgrimages. From the Beatles' Liverpool and Elvis Presley's Graceland to Ibiza's electronic dance music and New Orleans jazz, music is intertwined with the identity, marketing and promotion of certain cities, sites, and places, and increasingly is used to attract tourists and visitors as part of a growing trend in global tourism.[5] The connection between music and tourism has received increasing attention from academia and media alike. However prior to the MPMiD project, these connections remained relatively underexplored in an Irish popular music context. As a form of cultural and experiential tourism, music tourism is comparable to other kinds of leisure and travel activities, yet it offers some distinctive socio-cultural qualities in an Irish, and specifically in a Dublin perspective.

Music tourism in Ireland
Ireland's history is steeped in music, articulated not least in the use of a musical instrument – namely, the Irish harp – as a political symbol of Ireland for centuries before it was formally adopted in independent Ireland's coins and coat of arms in 1922. Since the 1990s, Ireland was frequently presented in media publications as a place of music, both at home as well as to an ever-growing global diaspora.[6] Nevertheless, despite this, the few existing scholarly studies on music and tourism in Ireland to date have tended to focus on Irish traditional music or

---

[4] G. Born & D. Hesmondhalgh (eds), *Western Music and its Others: Difference, Representation and Appropriation in Music*, (Berkeley: University of California Press, 2000) pp. 31-32. Born was keynote speaker at the SMI Annual Plenary Conference held in SPD, June 2016.

[5] J. Connell & C. Gibson, *Sound Tracks: Popular Music, Identity and Place*, (London: Routledge, 2003) p. 221.

[6] J. Connell & C. Gibson, *Music and Tourism: On the Road Again*, (Clevedon: Channel View Publications, 2005).

general overviews of music in Ireland. A 2001 study by Clancy et al. found that there was a widespread consensus among music industry personnel that Ireland had an established brand reputation as both an attractive location and a source of successful musicians and artists, providing benefits to Ireland as a preferred location for international music industry players. Ireland's strong reputation as a 'place' for music — and in particular popular music, was seen by the authors as providing access to international markets because of a 'number of interrelated characteristics,' including:

> ... cultural traits of friendliness combined with respect for privacy, a perception of Ireland as a fashionable centre for all aspects of the entertainment industries, the country's reputation as being particularly rich in the arts including literature for example, [...] the image of Ireland as a non-imperialist State, Ireland's cultural position—including its language — somewhere between American and British musical culture, and Ireland's standing as a tax-friendly environment for composers.[7]

At the same time, Bernadette Quinn and others have written about the socio-economic impact of music making, arts policies, and music festivals on tourism in Irish towns and villages.[8]

At the very least, tourism brings welcome economic benefits by supplying extra audiences for arts and cultural events. Fáilte Ireland actively promotes cultural tourism through their marketing material, publications and best practice case studies. For those who curate cultural experiences, organize concerts or produce arts events, tourism can be a means of supporting and developing arts, particularly in regional areas where local populations may be small in number. In addition to growing foreign markets, domestic tourism is also on the rise in Ireland. Dublin, in particular, is undergoing targeted promotion as a tourist destination to two market segments that offer significant

---

[7] P. Clancy et al., 'Industry clusters in Ireland: An application of Porter's model of national competitive advantage to three sectors', *European Planning Studies*, 9.1 (2001), p. 16.

[8] See B. Quinn, 'Rethinking Arts Festival Policy in Ireland', *European Journal of Cultural Policy*, 3.3 (1996); Idem, 'Symbols, practices and mythmaking: cultural perspectives on the Wexford Festival Opera', *Tourism Geographies*, 5.3 (2003); A. Kaul, *Turning the Tune: Traditional Music, Tourism, and Social Change in an Irish Village,* (New York: Bergham, 2009).

growth potential — the 'social energizers' and the 'culturally curious'.[9] Fáilte Ireland and Central Statistics Office figures reported that in 2014, 4.1 million overseas visitors came to Ireland. 2015 statistics from Fáilte Ireland revealed that eighty-seven per cent of overseas holidaymakers cited Ireland's interesting history and culture as very important when choosing it for a holiday. Indeed in a 2014 survey, when overseas holidaymakers were asked what activities they carried out in Ireland, eighty-three per cent included listening to live music in a pub. According to the participants of the survey in question, this makes the act of listening to live music in a pub a prime experience for international tourists visiting Ireland. Thus, it would appear that listening to live music lies at the very heart of what it is to authentically experience Ireland.

Dublin: city of music tourism?
There is a fast growing market for music fans as tourists, and Dublin has become such a location for a range of music enthusiasts — most notably U2 fans.[10] At the start of the MPMiD project in early 2015, Dublin's popular music history, heritage and tourism offerings were confined to the following three formalized contributions: first, the 'U2: Made in Dublin' exhibition at the Little Museum of Dublin which was established in 2011; second, 'Rock 'n' Stroll: Dublin's Music Trail', a public, self-guided tour established and published as a map around 1995; and third, various U2 walking tours of Dublin. The latter were private, paid tours run by two separate businesses: 'Dublin Differently'

---

[9] According to Fáilte Ireland, the social energizer demographic is identified as young couples and adult groups looking for excitement, new experiences, and a fun, social holiday in somewhere different. The culturally curious demographic are usually over 40 years old, choose their holiday destinations carefully, and are independent 'active sightseers' looking to visit new places. *Fáilte Ireland Global Segmentation*, http://www.failteireland.ie/International-sales/International-sales.aspx

[10] For more details on how Dublin's U2 tourism experiences affect processes of identity-work on personal, cultural, and embodied levels, see L. Bolderman and S. Reijnders, 'Have you found what you're looking for? Analysing tourist experiences of Wagner's Bayreuth, ABBA's Stockholm and U2's Dublin', *Tourist Studies*, 17.2 (2017), 164-181. It is also worth noting that at the time of writing, planning permission has recently been granted to applicants U2 for the construction of a U2 visitor centre on Dublin's Grand Canal Quay. See Gordon Deegan 'U2 gets green light for band's visitor centre planned for Dublin's docklands', *Irish Independent*, 23 January 2019
https://www.independent.ie/business/commercial-property/u2-gets-green-light-for-bands-visitor-centre-planned-for-dublins-docklands-37742234.html

established in 2013 by Seán McBride, and 'The U2 Experience' established in the early 2000s by Dave Griffith. Midway during the MPMiD project in July 2015, the brand new 'Irish Rock 'n' Roll Museum Experience' opened. This proved to be quite timely, as private businesses noticed and duly acted upon a perceived gap in tourism initiatives based on Dublin's and Ireland's popular music heritage.

The primary public popular music tourist offering in Dublin until 2015 was thus the 'Rock 'n' Stroll: Dublin's Music Trail'. Established by Dublin Tourism and Fáilte Ireland in c. 1995, the free, self-guided trail was advertised as a musical tour that enabled the visitor to walk in the footsteps of Dublin's world famous musical artists. Detailed 36-page *Rock 'n' Stroll* booklets describing each of the plaques – that took the shape of vinyl records – were once sold at Dublin Tourist Offices, but these ceased circulation some years ago. These booklets acknowledged the assistance of *Hot Press* magazine in compiling the guide, along with the artists included in the trail and their agents, the Arts Council, Dublin Corporation and various premises along the trail where plaques were erected. As recently as July 2013, Fáilte Ireland advertised the 'Dublin Rock 'n' Stroll iWalk' as 'a new musical tour of Dublin' available as a free downloadable podcast from the Visit Dublin website. The website announced that you can walk 'in the footsteps of Dublin's world famous artists: U2, Sinéad O'Connor, Enya and Glen Hansard. A Spotify playlist has also been developed to accompany this tour so that visitors can enjoy the music while they are on the move'. Yet clicking on the listed link brought up no such musical tour, and several searches were unsuccessful in locating this podcast. Indeed, the trail continued to be advertised on various Dublin and Irish tourism websites, and on request at Visit Dublin and other tourism offices in 2015, one could still receive a one-page photocopy of the 'Rock 'n' Stroll Trail' map to carry out the walking tour at leisure. However, the 'Rock 'n' Stroll Trail' had not been updated since the early 2000s, and by March 2015, almost half of the plaques were missing, including the very much in-demand U2 plaque that paid homage to the site of U2's earliest gigs at the now long-gone Dandelion Market venue on St Stephen's Green. The remaining – and arguably less sought-after – plaques are still visible on various Dublin locations today, illustrating the gap in popular music heritage provision and in its maintenance.

Mapping popular music from St Patrick's College
The MPMiD project sought to map popular music experience in Dublin with the aim of informing cultural policy makers and industry analysts by providing the first comprehensive and scholarly overview of popular music in Dublin. The project was thus designed to contribute to

strategies that enhanced Dublin's reputation as a 'place' for popular music experience, and that contributed to civic and national strategies working to position Ireland's capital as a future UNESCO designated 'city of music' in addition to its earlier designation as a 'city of literature' in 2010.[11]

Using mixed methodologies (qualitative and quantitative), the researchers surveyed popular music experience in the Dublin urban area during the 2015 calendar year, including targeted heritage/tourism events. This was followed by an ethnography of selected events – live music and/or music tourism/heritage events – scheduled over eight months and comprising a series of observations and sets of semi-structured interviews. Primary data collection was central to the MPMiD project, and as such a key component of this exploratory research was to map the range of popular music experience from the perspective of fans, musicians, residents, and tourists. To that end we deployed a range of methods including reviews of other studies and secondary literature; participant observation at a range of concerts, festivals, gigs, and other popular music-related events (ninety-seven individual or separate performances at thirty-five different Dublin venues and spaces in total); an e-survey open to all members of the public (yielding 366 responses); in-depth consultations and semi-structured interviews with select individuals (forty-four) working within Dublin's popular music industries.

Reaching a range of potential project participants
Advertising the project through posters and word of mouth, participants for our study were further gathered through social media and snowball sampling.[12] The researchers launched a MPMiD blog and social media presence in June 2015. After the e-survey was launched in July 2015, various media corporations covered our project including features in *The Irish Times* 'On The Record' blog, an article in the online *Dublin Inquirer*, radio interviews with the researchers (*Dave Fanning Show* on RTÉ 2FM and the *John Barker Totally Irish* show on 98FM), and guest posts on *The Blackpool Sentinel* and *LibFocus* blogs.

---

[11] UNESCO Creative Cities Network was launched in 2004, and at the time of writing includes 180 UNESCO Creative Cities globally. While not (yet) a formally recognized 'City of Music,' Dublin received official recognition as a UNESCO 'City of Literature' in 2010.

[12] Snowball sampling involves identifying research participants who can in turn refer researchers to other potential participants. In the case of music ethnography, it's an effective method of making contact via off- and online social networks.

Various music forums also shared the link to the e-survey (*Metal Ireland, Thumped, The Journal of Music*), which led to a wider reach that was reflected in the responses received to our e-survey.

However, as the data from the e-survey began to be submitted – varied and rich in detail as it was – it became clear that this form of response might leave out some potential participants, particularly the non-digital native population. The researchers looked into other methods of gathering data for the project, taking inspiration from Sara Cohen's 2014 work on using sketch mapping in interviews with musicians as a way to visualize musical life in Liverpool. Sketch mapping, or mental mapping, is a methodology used by researchers in geography and related disciplines to collect a broad range of data – both geographic and non-geographic. As a participatory research method usually using simple tools like pen and paper, sketch mapping aims to gather knowledge across a range of scales ranging from one's immediate surroundings to wider communities, cities, or parts of the world, while also capturing insights into attitudes, emotions, and feelings about the places that are being mapped. The uniquely collegial and cosy atmosphere of the St Patrick's College staff room proved crucial in offering numerous opportunities for inter-departmental discussions over lunch break. Chance conversations with cartographer, geographer, and historian colleagues enabled philosophies and methods of contemporary mapping to be discussed and debated over coffee. Thus the research team decided to add an additional stream to the data collection – to actively seek out responses through public music map-making workshops. The College proved to be a fundamental site in inspiring this method, and also in testing it out. Students and colleagues volunteered to participate in pilot mapping exercises while the researchers tested out two kinds of map typographies: one map template that featured a street-less Dublin identifiable by the Liffey and some major city landmarks so that individual pathways could be drawn in as desired, and one cognitive map that took a blank-page approach, offering participants a more freestyle, mind-map approach.[13]

In order to reach members of the public who might not have had access to our e-survey for a range of possible reasons, and to include a more diverse and egalitarian approach to data collection to access different information, the researchers organized two drop-in music-mapping workshops that were free and open to the public. Participants from one workshop recommended or connected us with other interested individuals, and this proved advantageous for reaching out to members of specific scenes or groups which were otherwise difficult to

---

[13] The template map was kindly illustrated by local architect Frank Hughes.

access. In total, forty-one maps were collected. While we did not formally categorize areas of Dublin according to north/south division, of the two publicly advertised mapping workshops, one took place at the College and yielded over half of the final number of maps, and the other was held in a Southside venue, at the NDRC Digital Exchange on Crane Street, Dublin 8.[14] The music-map-making workshop at St Patrick's College was held in the open-plan ground-floor area of the new Cregan Library as part of Culture Night in September 2015. By hosting the first, public music-map workshop on St Patrick's College attractive campus, in conjunction with the nationwide Culture Night initiative, the researchers helped enact – on some scale – Culture Night's ambitious aims. Such goals included encouraging more people to visit cultural venues in their locality, try new cultural activities, make it easier for people to play a role in their local cultural scene(s), and ultimately help create a sense of community and belonging through the arts and cultural activities.[15] The workshop was well-attended by SPD colleagues, students and local residents ranging in ages from four to seventy-four years old, and resulted in twenty-four individual, hand-drawn music maps.

The findings
The hand-made maps give rich, emotionally charged insights into personal geographies of the participants' musical experiences and memories of the city. Several notable themes emerged from the music-mapping workshop held in St Patrick's College. As with the e-survey, participants were invited to recall their favourite popular music-related memories in and of Dublin. To that end, musical events that marked a 'rite of passage' were often evoked, for example one's first ever gig attendance, first time seeing and hearing a particular idol live, first record purchase in a store (that may no longer exist), or first time playing with a band, or selling out a venue. Overall, the research confirmed, for the first time, that Dublin was perceived as a centre for popular music experience according to the overwhelming majority of research participants. In addition, a majority of respondents believed that Dublin held an identifiable popular music 'sound' or 'sounds.'[16] The

---

[14] For the purpose of this chapter I focus on the mapping workshop held at St Patrick's College that constituted over half of the project's map data. The other music-map workshops took place at NDRC (National Digital Research Centre) Digital Exchange during the Hard Working Class Heroes Festival, 1-3 October.
[15] See Culture Night website: https://culturenight.ie/information/.
[16] This strand of the research is given detailed consideration in the co-authored journal article by J. O'Flynn and Á. Mangaoang, 'Sounding Dublin: Mapping

findings revealed the many and diverse ways in which popular music is valued and enjoyed in Dublin, from gig attendance, media engagement, music-making, museum visiting or tour participation, alongside entertainment, aesthetic, narrative, memory, social, and other 'extra-musical' reasons.[17] For the remainder of this chapter I briefly highlight two aspects that the map-making process itself brought out from the participants, particularly details that did not feature as prominently, if at all, in the e-survey.

Compared to the online e-survey, the creatively cognitive act of map-making elicited different responses on individuals' memories and experiences of Dublin as a site for music. First, eight per cent of e-survey respondents specifically highlighted Dublin's buskers and street musicians as being among their favourite musical memories or sonic signature of the city. This figure was even more strongly represented on individuals' musical maps of Dublin, with busking or buskers featuring on over twelve per cent of participants' maps. The difference in these figures may be slight, but nonetheless indicates at least two possibilities: that individuals taking part in the mapping workshops held a higher appreciation for busking, or that the act of physically tracing one's route around the city through the active practice of map-making ignited different and/or additional sensorial details to filling out an e-survey.

Second, the act of map-making brought out a further multimodal layer of detail from participants that was not evoked at all in responses to the e-survey. A small minority of map-makers highlighted specific places on their maps where they met their partner, significant other, or future spouse; this was signalled by hand-written text or sketched love-hearts and arrows, or a combination of both. The embodied action of physically mapping out one's musical relationship with Dublin inspired, ignited and initiated friendships and even romantic relationships. As these maps illustrated to the researchers, Dublin's popular music events offered attendees crucial spaces for self-discovery and socializing. In all, the mapping process among our research participants went a considerable way towards revealing hidden narratives of popular music experience and memory in the city.

Popular Music Experience in the City', *Journal of World Popular Music*, 6.1 (2019).

[17] For a more detailed account of the project's findings, see Á. Mangaoang and J. O'Flynn, *Mapping Popular Music in Dublin Executive Report*, (Dublin: St Patrick's College, 2016), available for free download online via the project website: https://mappingpopularmusicindublin.wordpress.com.

The mapping workshops enabled us to connect with a wide range of members of the public, and to map their popular music experiences of the city – experiences that might be overlooked in other cultural surveys of the city. These maps overwhelmingly demonstrated how popular music is indeed active in Dublin, shaping people's lives, as detailed by the numerous references to concerts and festivals experienced with friends, family, and loved ones. In these maps our participants measured the value of popular music through charting the role of Dublin's music in shaping their personal journeys, relationships, and memories. To experience popular music in Dublin, according to our map-makers, is 'to consider music as a collective accomplishment.'[18]

From mapping to map
One of our recommendations made in the project's final report for Fáilte Ireland was for increased communication and collaboration between Dublin's tourism agencies and the city's music communities. While processing the direct experience of music-mapping and the data gathered from the workshops, we realized we had more than enough information to create an exemplar of a new *Dublin Music Map*. At the project's eleventh hour, and once again following consultation with colleagues from the geography and art departments of St Patrick's College, and with additional funding from Fáilte Ireland and St Patrick's College Research Committee, the researchers created and published 10,000 copies of a new *Dublin Music Map*. Following the data from our extensive ethnography, the final map included links to an array of Dublin's performance spaces, traditional Irish music sessions, club, dance and cabaret venues, music archives, museums, independent record stores and music instrument shops, Dublin music landmarks and historical sites (see Figures 9.1 and 9.2 below).

This additional project output of a participant-generated, research-informed music map succinctly summarized one of the project's recommendations: namely, shining a light and bringing together the wide range of music-led offerings that Dublin's fair city does in fact offer. To further enhance the map's aim of supporting Dublin's popular music networks, yet while still fitting on a physical map that could be actually used, we included a brief annual calendar of Dublin music festivals and major events to encourage participation by local, national and international visitors. Each and every single map location was subjected to detailed discussion among the production team, as decisions about which section of the city should, and could, be included within the map itself.

---

[18] N. Prior, '"It's a Social Thing, Not a Nature Thing": Popular Music Practices in Reykjavík, Iceland', *Cultural Sociology*, 9.1 (2014), p. 3.

Figure 9.1: *The Dublin Music Map* (2016), cover.[19]

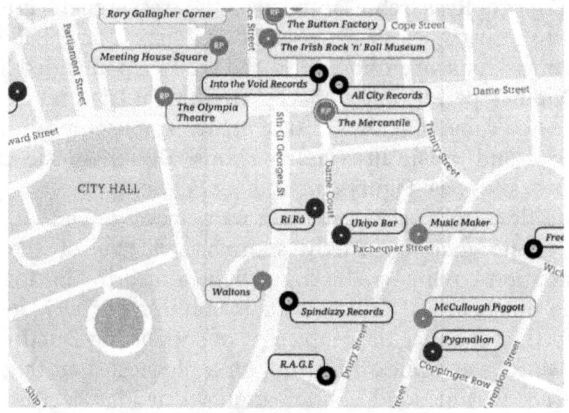

Figure 9.2: *The Dublin Music Map* (2016), inset detail.

---

[19] The *Dublin Music Map* is authored by Áine Mangaoang and John O'Flynn, designed by Simon Roche, and illustrated by Maria Hildrick. The map is available in hard copy from select Visit Dublin and Fáilte Ireland branches located around Dublin, and as a free PDF download via the MPMiD project website: https://mappingpopularmusicindublin.wordpress.com.

The resulting 2016 *Dublin Music Map* stretches into neighbourhoods beyond Dublin (south) city centre, which had been the primary focus of the *Rock'n'Stroll* map produced twenty years earlier. Themes that emerged from the data were all put to the test as we made decisions about how to frame the map, where to create borders, how much Northside versus Southside should proportionally be included, and whether to include the researchers' own personal, civic or political perspectives. As academic Peter Turchi wrote, 'to ask for a map is to say "tell me a story."'[20] Yet this process showed us firsthand just how easy – or even understandable – it may be to erase the stories that do not 'fit' in to whatever neat and convenient, constructed categories we might have.

Inspiring creative action from St Patrick's College and out to Dublin's Northside community
Among many findings, the research revealed a near neglect of formalized cultural and musical offerings in the Drumcondra area of Dublin, other than the numerous events hosted by the College itself. The MPMiD project term coincided with the emergence of GlasDrum, a not-for-profit voluntary organization that aimed to facilitate arts and cultural events in Glasnevin, Drumcondra and beyond. It was founded through the coming together of a small group of St Patrick's College colleagues and arts professionals living in the locality. MPMiD's music-mapping workshops and other public engagement activities resonated with the objectives of like-minded individuals from GlasDrum who recognized the lack of arts and cultural events programmed within and for the local community.

GlasDrum was formally constituted in October 2015 and for its first project co-presented the 3rd Fidelio Trio Winter Chamber Music Festival, taking place at Belvedere House, with the College's music departments in 2015. [21] In April 2016, the inaugural event to be programmed exclusively by GlasDrum was *Macalla* ['Echo'] a unique collaboration between Irish glass artist Róisín de Buitléar and one of Ireland's best known musicians and songwriters of Hothouse Flowers fame, Liam Ó Maonlaí. The musical performance on de Buitléar's glass instruments was led by Ó Maonlaí with Peter O'Toole (also of the

---

[20] P. Turchi, *Maps of the Imagination: The Writer as Cartographer*, (San Antonio: Trinity University Press, 2004), p. 11.
[21] GlasDrum's founding committee included SPD colleagues Andrea Cleary, Patricia Flynn (Chair), Orla Nic Aodha, Áine Mangaoang and John O'Flynn, with Martin Byrne (Honorary Secretary), Evonne Ferguson, Irma McLoughlin (Honorary Treasurer), Rachel O'Flanagan, and Róisín Murphy.

Hothouse Flowers), traditional harpist and singer Síle Denvir (from the College's Roinn na Gaelige) and other guest musicians. It took place in the very heart of the College, in its wood-panelled auditorium. Following the concert, twenty-five of de Buitléar's glass sculptures were exhibited in the new Cregan Library for the month of April, where local schoolchildren and members of the public could enjoy the artworks at their leisure as well as in specially guided tours. This unique live music experience and subsequent exhibition brought in crowds from the Northside of Dublin and beyond, introducing and inviting many Dubliners into St Patrick's College for the very first time.

From the outset, GlasDrum identified a need and a niche, and responded by creating a new, grassroots arts community that stemmed from St Patrick's College before moving beyond the walls and reaching out into the local neighbourhood. The success of this initial event thus laid the foundations for subsequent GlasDrum initiatives that continued to connect St Patrick's College with the wider community. This notably included 'New Sounds in an Old Place', a series of live gigs that showcased some of the best up-and-coming Irish bands and musicians in the intimate and atmospheric surroundings of St John the Baptist Church.[22] A previously 'hidden' location on Drumcondra's Church Avenue and the oldest church in the district dating back to 1743, St John's provided an ideal venue for the innovative series and served to bring new audiences to Drumcondra for high-quality, live music concerts. As a result of the activities of GlasDrum - partially reignited by the MPMiD project at St Patrick's College - Dublin's musicmaking and music venue map had now stretched further into the city's Northside communities.[23]

Locating Dublin's 'hidden' musical pathways: concluding comments

'We are enamoured with maps of the world.'[24]

---

[22] At the time of writing, artists featured in 'New Sounds in an Old Place' concert series included Soulé, Maria Kelly, John Cummins, Malojian, Sorcha Richardson, Ailbhe Reddy, Roe, Saint Sister, Ryan Vail, Paul Noonan, Slow Moving Clouds, Mary Barnecutt, Loah, Kitt Philippa, Ye Vagabonds, Joshua Burnside and Elephant.

[23] This is not to suggest that there are no other Northside venues; notably, the Helix, located on DCU's main campus, is a large conference centre that hosts large-scale music concerts and other events.

[24] A. Treske, *The Inner Life of Video Spheres*, (Amsterdam: Institute of Network Cultures, 2013), p. 38.

The events organized by GlasDrum to date have been instrumental in putting the north inner-city suburb of Drumcondra on Dublin's contemporary music map. Ruth Finnegan's ethnographic study, *The Hidden Musicians: Music-making in an English Town* theorizes local and urban contexts of making music in everyday life. She details the collective and active practices of music on the ground in the English town of Milton Keynes, identifying 'musical pathways' through which musicians develop, perform identity and gain a sense of collective belonging within an urban community. Finnegan's framework is particularly relevant in the context of MPMiD's approach, but also in the various offshoots that have followed, from GlasDrum initiatives to the production of the new *Dublin Music Map*. Finnegan offers a useful model for exploring the non-musical and social implications of music-making, where musical 'pathways' are valuable vehicles for social interactions, as well as the emotional lives of those who make music. For Finnegan, 'whether in deeply intense fashion or more light-touch action, music provides a human resource through which people can enact their lives with inextricably entwined feeling, thought and imagination.'[25] Though writing specifically about her fieldwork in Milton Keynes, Finnegan's remarks on the extra-musical and social values of music making could easily be applied to Dublin.

This chapter has offered an overview of Dublin's popular music tourism landscape through the lens of an applied research project. The MPMiD project and associated events held in St Patrick's College demonstrate how popular music in Dublin serves as a form of social cohesion – binding people and places, providing soundtracks to relationships, and shaping significant memories. Like Finnegan's 'hidden musicians' of Milton Keynes, MPMiD revealed how much of Dublin's musical landscape is organized and supported by an array of musicians across the narrow binaries of 'amateur' and 'professional.' Far from having a peripheral role in society, the project's findings reveal how popular music in Dublin is a central feature for many of our project's informants, valued for its special ability to bring people together in shared experiences of communion.

The mapping workshops, conceived of and launched from the College, were critical in gaining insights into the practices and pathways of everyday popular music experience in Dublin. In a 2012 article in *Social Semiotics*, Sara Cohen – adapting Finnegan's concept – employs the term 'hidden' to include: 1) venues that are literally hidden to the unknowing eye; 2) areas of the city that are largely ignored in cultural

---

[25] R. Finnegan, *The Hidden Musicians: Music-Making in an English Town*, (Cambridge: Cambridge University Press, 1989), p. 355.

branding; 3) less spectacular venues, musicians or events that have tended not to be documented or archived; and 4) music subcultures that are ideologically excluded from dominant narratives. The physical process of map-making, as piloted at St Patrick's College, proved to be essential in gaining insight into the more hidden aspects of Dublin's musical landscape, as well as the unseen values of music experienced by our project participants. Additionally, the work of grassroots organizations like GlasDrum, through bringing musical events to previously hidden venues such as St John the Baptist Church in Drumcondra, demonstrate the extent to which any willing participant can indeed re-write existing maps and chart the course towards their own musical pathways. From the act of mapping to producing a new tourist-oriented music map of Dublin, the process further revealed how the relationship between music and place is constantly in flux, for indeed any musical map of a city becomes dated as soon as the ink has dried.

Overall, this chapter illustrates the unique place of St Patrick's College in relation to the recent past of Dublin's popular music map, through initiatives stemming from research projects like MPMiD and local community groups like GlasDrum. As the research project host, the College itself became a vital and meaningful actor in MPMiD. Such a perspective of St Patrick's College highlights the significance in affective agency offered by research and educational institutions in and of themselves. And lastly, it points to the enduring role of St Patrick's College in providing a place, space, and most importantly, people who will continue to shape – and sound – the future of Dublin's popular music and cultural heritage landscape.

Bibliography

Born, Georgina & Hesmondhalgh, David (eds), *Western Music and its Others: Difference, Representation and Appropriation in Music*, (Berkeley: University of California Press, 2000).

Bolderman, Leonieke & Reijnder, Stijn. 'Have you found what you're looking for? Analysing tourist experiences of Wagner's Bayreuth, ABBA's Stockholm and U2's Dublin', *Tourist Studies*, 17.2 (2017), 164-181.

Clancy, Paula, O'Malley, Eoin, O'Connell, Larry & Van Egeraat, Chris, 'Industry clusters in Ireland: An application of Porter's model of national competitive advantage to three sectors,' *European Planning Studies*, 9.1 (2001), 7-28

Cohen, Sara, 'Urban musicscapes: mapping music-making in Liverpool', in L. Roberts (ed.), *Mapping Cultures: Place, Practice,*

Performance, (Basingstoke: Palgrave Macmillan, 2014), pp. 123–43.

Cohen, Sara, 'Live music and urban landscape: mapping the beat in Liverpool', *Social Semiotics*, 22.5 (2012), 587-603.

Connell, John & Gibson, Chris, *Sound Tracks: Popular Music, Identity and Place*, (London: Routledge, 2003).

Connell, John, & Gibson, Chris, *Music and Tourism: On the Road Again*, (Clevedon: Channel View Publications, 2005).

DeNora, Tia, 'Music as a technology of the self', *Poetics*, 27.1 (1999), 31-56.

Frith, Simon, 'Music and identity', in S. Hall & P. du Gay (eds), *Questions of Cultural Identity*, (London: Sage, 1996), pp. 108-126.

Finnegan, Ruth, *The Hidden Musicians: Music-Making in an English Town*, (Cambridge: Cambridge University Press, 1989).

Hesmondhalgh, David, *Why Music Matters*, (Oxford: Blackwell Publishing, 2013).

Kaul, Adam, *Turning the Tune: Traditional Music, Tourism, and Social Change in an Irish Village*, (New York: Bergham, 2009).

Mangaoang, Áine, & O'Flynn, John, *Mapping Popular Music in Dublin: Executive Report*, (Dublin: St Patrick's College, 2016).

O'Flynn, John, & Mangaoang, Áine, 'Sounding Dublin: Mapping Popular Music Experience in the City', *Journal of World Popular Music*, 6.1 (2019), 32-61.

Prior, Nick, '"It's a Social Thing, Not a Nature Thing": Popular Music Practices in Reykjavík, Iceland', *Cultural Sociology*, 9.1 (2014), 81-98.

Quinn, Bernadette, 'Rethinking Arts Festival Policy in Ireland', *European Journal of Cultural Policy*, 3.3 (1996), 91-107.

Quinn, Bernadette, 'Symbols, practices and mythmaking: cultural perspectives on the Wexford Festival Opera', *Tourism Geographies*, 5.3 (2003), 329-349.

Treske, Andreas, *The Inner Life of Video Spheres: Theory for the YouTube Generation*, (Amsterdam: Institute of Network Cultures, Network Notebooks #06, 2013).

Turchi, Peter, *Maps of the Imagination: The Writer as Cartographer*, (San Antonio: Trinity University Press, 2004).

Newspapers and periodicals
Irish Independent

Chapter Ten: The Fidelio Trio Residency

John O'Flynn

Introduction
The internationally renowned Fidelio Trio, originally comprising Darragh Morgan (violin), Robin Michael (cello) and Mary Dullea (piano) were appointed as artists-in-residence at the Music Department, St Patrick's College Drumcondra in September 2012 in a scheme that was jointly funded by The Arts Council of Ireland and the College. It continued until July 2015, with Adi Tal taking on the role of cellist for the ensemble from October 2014.

The residency developed around the four interrelated strands of Music in Education and in Community, Performance and Musicology, Composition and Orchestration, and Promoting Chamber Music. In addition to the programming of concerts at St Patrick's College, at DCU and beyond, the Trio engaged in interactive workshops with student teachers, undergraduate and postgraduate music students, primary and secondary school pupils, teachers, amateur musicians and other community groups. The Fidelio Trio's appointment to this unique position as artists-in-residence at the College involved three stimulating years with performances of established piano trio repertoire, new commissions and world premieres by leading contemporary composers, and workshops and master classes mentoring young composers and performers. All of these events were facilitated through the Trio's collaboration with the College's music department, a partnership that was further enhanced by the establishment in 2013 of the annual Fidelio Trio Winter Chamber Music Festival at Belvedere House, St Patrick's College. The festival continued beyond the end of the residency's term in September 2015 and after the College was legally incorporated into Dublin City University in October 2016.

For the College's music department, the residency brought about an intensification of links with external institutions and organizations that included the Arts Council/An Chomhairle Ealaíon, the Contemporary Music Centre, RTÉ Lyric FM, Music Generation, the Helix, the Ark Cultural Centre for Children, the Council of Heads of Music in Higher Education, the European Chamber Music Teachers' Association, the Society for Music Education in Ireland, Mater Dei Institute of Education and numerous primary and post-primary schools.

This chapter continues by contemplating early twenty-first-century policies and actions towards the interface of arts and education, including the setting up of a number of artist residencies in Irish colleges of education, of which The Fidelio Trio residency was the first of its type. The rest of the chapter describes and appraises the various strands of the

Fidelio residency. It draws on hard copy and digital sources of programmes for workshops, concerts, conferences and other events that took place in the College and occasionally elsewhere over the period 2012-2016 (during the term of the residency and extending to include subsequent chamber music festivals).[1] The discussion also refers to relevant correspondence and to documented evaluations of workshops held during the residency. In addition to providing an outline history with milestones for both the residency and the festival, the chapter contemplates the former's efficacy as a model for engagement with professional musicians in higher education. Accompanying this chapter at the end of book is an appendix that details an extensive list of events which took place during the residency and in the two subsequent years of the winter chamber music festival (Appendix E).

The arts-education interface

In January 2013 a new *Arts in Education Charter* was jointly announced by education minister Ruairí Quinn and arts minister Jimmy Deenihan.[2] Several months later, in May 2013 a national online arts-in-education digital platform was launched at Dublin Castle.[3] These developments followed more than a decade of consultations between Ireland's Department of Education and Science (DES) and the Department of Arts, Heritage and the Gaeltacht (DAHG); they were also preceded by the 2007 policy document jointly published by the DES and the Arts Council, *Artists ~ Schools Guidelines: Towards Best Practice in Ireland*.[4] What might have been the reasons for these developments, given that arts education was long established in the Irish system, and given that the Arts Council had indirectly supported artist placements in education from the mid-1980s? (From 1985 a small number of local authorities began to provide an arts service, gradually increasing to the point where in 2007 every county and city council had a designated arts office.)[5] Indeed, even prior to the 1980s there were many instances of artists working in schools and in other educational establishments: John Buckley's chapter on performance in this volume shows how throughout the 1960s the RÉSO programmed symphony concerts in universities and colleges, and it has further been noted how RTÉ commissioned a work

---

[1] The author currently maintains this archive of printed and electronic records at the School of Theology, Philosophy, and Music, All Hallows Campus, DCU.
[2] https://www.education.ie/en/Press-Events/Press-Releases/2013-Press Releases/ PR12-01-04.html [accessed 5 January 2019].
[3] http://artsineducation.ie/en/about/ [accessed 5 January 2019].
[4] Department of Education and Science and the Arts Council, *Artists ~ Schools Guidelines: Towards Best Practice in Ireland*, (Dublin: DES, 2009).
[5] A. Kenny with P. Flynn, *Knowing the Score: Local Authorities and Music*, (Dublin: St Patrick's College, 2009), p. ix.

by A. J. Potter to be performed jointly by the symphony orchestra and St Patrick's College Choir in 1966. These and similar activities took place long before terms such as 'community' and 'outreach' became axiomatic in the policies of orchestras and other arts organisations.

One major reason why the DES, DAHG and Arts Council worked together to develop new policies and guidelines in the 2000s was that while schools and other educational institutions had by then a considerable history of interaction with artists, in most of these contexts the mere fact of interaction between artists, teachers and students did not necessarily lead to meaningful collaboration or sustainable impact. Much of the national and international literature evaluating artist residences up to this point found that while many projects based in schools, higher education institutions and communities often recorded a perceived value in terms of artistic experience, they could simultaneously be appraised as lacking in respect of sustainability and transferability.[6] One of the key strategies to address this lacuna was identified in the *Arts in Education Charter* as follows:

> The Arts Council will work with the Department of Arts, Heritage and the Gaeltacht and the Department of Education and Skills to increase the number of artists' residencies in Colleges of Education.[7]

The rationale behind this statement of intent in the *Arts in Education Charter* was not merely to increase the number of artist residencies; rather it was intended to produce a positive cascade effect whereby structured arts experiences for student teachers had potential to lead to multiple arts experiences for the many school pupils they would later teach. Prior to this initiative the Arts Council had funded several musician and writer residencies in university departments across the country, including residencies in the English and Gaeilge [Irish] departments of St Patrick's College from 2010; moreover, artists in residence had been a standard feature of many British university

---

[6] For example: M. Cox, '"What Next?" Exploring the Potential Long-term and Short-term Educational Benefits of Music Composition Projects in Irish Primary Schools', Unpublished MA dissertation, (Mary Immaculate College, University of Limerick, 2006); B. Hanly, 'The Good, the Bad, and the Ugly - Arts Partnerships in Canadian Elementary Schools', *Arts Education Policy Review*, 104.6 (2003). J. Harland et al., *The Arts-Education Interface: A Mutual Learning Triangle*, (Slough, Berkshire: National Foundation for Educational Research, 2005); M. Ross, 'Evaluating Education Programmes of Arts Organisations', *Music Education Research*, 5.1 (2003).

[7] Department of Arts, Heritage and the Gaeltacht and Department of Education and Science, *Arts in Education Charter*, (Dublin: DES, 2012), p. 17.

departments from as early as the 1970s. What was unique about the Fidelio Trio Residency - which began in St Patrick's College in September 2012, just a few months before the publication of the *Arts in Education Charter* - was its combination of music and music education components. This was reflective of the dual mission of a music department that was located in a college of education and humanities.

The initiative came from Gaye Tanham who at the time headed the division for young people, children and education at the Arts Council. In 2011 Tanham invited the author (henceforth referred to by name) to devise a proposal for a three-year music residency that would be jointly funded by the Arts Council and the College. In the years following the resultant establishment of the Fidelio Trio residency at St Patrick's College in 2012, and in keeping with the aforementioned national strategy within the *Arts in Education Charter*, residencies in diverse arts platforms were set up in Mary Immaculate College, Limerick, Marino Institute of Education, Dublin and at the Froebel Department of Primary and Early Childhood Education, Maynooth University. A second, three-year arts-in-education residency led by the dance company CoisCéim took place at St Patrick's College between 2013-2016. All in all, these residencies were deemed to make a significant impact on arts education nationally; as early as 2014 the Implementation Group of Arts in Education Charter would report:

> The response to the [Arts Council] Residencies has been very impressive and has nurtured a higher sense of awareness among teacher education students of the potential value and modes of pupil involvement in arts education.[8]

Residency design
The Fidelio Trio residency was designed to accord with the Arts Council's strategy towards developing artist residences in colleges of education as set out in the *Arts in Education Charter*. The proposed model to emerge from the music department of St Patrick's College was specific to that department's dual responsibility for academic music studies and pre-service courses in music education (curriculum music). A principal aim of the residency was for the appointed artists to engage with all student teachers passing through the College during the term of the residency. It was also designed to enhance artistic experiences and music learning for those pursuing undergraduate and postgraduate music programmes, as well as reaching out to broader communities of students, teachers, musicians and others in the College and beyond.

---

[8] Implementation Group of Arts in Education Charter, 'Newsletter November 2014: Work in Progress', https://www.chg.gov.ie/app/uploads/2015/09/arts-in-education-newsletter.pdf, [accessed 5 January 2019].

While the *Arts in Education Charter* had made no specific mention of higher education other than its reference to colleges of education, the proposal to emerge from St Patrick's College was based as much in arts and humanities as it was in education, and was further premised on the view that all students in higher education could potentially benefit from engagement with artist residencies. Such a perspective would later come to be embraced in May 2014 at a national symposium on engagement between the arts and higher education sectors. This took place at the Croke Park Conference Centre, Dublin and was organized by the DAHG. Its programme would include a joint presentation on the Fidelio Trio residency presented by the ensemble's leader Darragh Morgan and residency director John O'Flynn (see Appendix E).[9]

The process of residency selection and design took several stages between 2011-2012. First, in consultation with Gaye Tanham and with the College's music department, the genre of piano trio was selected for its breadth of repertoire and for its potential to subdivide occasionally into duo and solo workshops and performances.[10] The residency was originally designed around the four interrelated strands of performance, education/community outreach, ensemble workshops, and composition workshops. Following the appointment of the Fidelio Trio and the rollout of the residency programme these became reimagined as Music in Education and in Community, Performance and Musicology, Composition and Orchestration, and Promoting Chamber Music. From its outset and throughout the residency, contingency was also made for a 'fifth element', allowing for unexpected directions and developments, both artistic and pedagogical.

The residency design drew on international experience, bearing in mind the observation that many earlier classical music residencies yielded 'the narrowest of effects' by comparison with other arts platforms and with other music styles.[11] It also contemplated more general criticisms of 'parachute art' or art that 'is dropped in without regard for the particularities of a community'.[12] At the same time, it considered that for some students and school pupils the 'parachute effect' had the potential to make significant impact and to motivate them towards future engagement with music, whether as listener, performer,

---

[9] https://www.chg.gov.ie/09052014-symposium-underlines-importance-of-links-between-arts-and-higher-education-sectors/ [accessed 7 January 2019].
[10] It was agreed that other music styles, for example Irish traditional or singer-songwriter, should be represented in any subsequent artist residencies at the music department.
[11] J. Harland et al., *The Arts-Education Interface*, p. ix.
[12] P. Duncum, 'Engaging Public Space: Art Education Pedagogies for Social Justice', *Equity & Excellence in Education*, 44:3 (2011), p. 353.

composer or combinations of these.[13] Some general principles were adapted from previous studies of teacher professional development in contexts of residencies. These included a need to enhance student teachers' knowledge and appreciation of music, and to demonstrate possible connections between the residency and the school music curriculum, as well as between music and other areas of the curriculum.[14]

Also considered at the design stage and at subsequent stages over the three years was the need to reflect, reappraise and review the residency as it evolved. One of the key recommendations to emerge from *Live Music in the Classroom*, a research report on the Vogler Quartet's residency in Co. Sligo between 1999-2004 was:

> [F]or future reference, further emphasis could be placed on the formal revision and re-articulation of aims, objectives and roles on a regular, shared basis, regardless of how clear they are at the beginning.[15]

The Fidelio Trio's workshops with music education students were initially designed in keeping with the 'listening and responding' strand of the 1999 Revised Primary Curriculum. However, after one year and following the input of music education lecturers coordinated by Patricia Flynn, this model was adapted to reflect a 'relational art practices' approach; in addition to listening and responding to piano trio performances, student teachers would perform their own group compositions for feedback from the visiting artists.[16] This had the result of facilitating greater interaction between artists, students and lecturers.

---

[13] N. Jeanneret & G. DeGraffenreid, 'Music education in the generalist classroom', in G. McPherson & G. Welch (eds.), *Music Learning and Teaching in Infancy, Childhood, and Adolescence: An Oxford Handbook of Music Education*, Volume 2 (2018), p. 178.

[14] L. Silverstein, 'Artist residencies: evolving educational experiences', in B. Rich, J. Polin & S. Marcus (eds.), *Acts of Achievement: The role of performing arts centers in education*, (New York: The Dana Foundation, 2003), p.14.

[15] Vogler Partners Steering Group, *Live Music in the Classroom: An Analysis of the Primary Curriculum Support Programme of the Vogler Quartet in Sligo Residency*, (Sligo: The Arts Office, Sligo County Council, 2006), p. 55. The primary curriculum support programme was designed by Breda O'Shea, a former music education lecturer at St Patrick's College.

[16] R. Irwin & D. O'Donoghue, 'Encountering pedagogy through relational art practices', *International Journal of Art & Design Education*, 31.3 (2012). This echoes findings in the literature on music residencies in schools that suggest that '..."making art" needs to be the core experience for students': P. Freer, 'Toward

For other components of the residency – notably in the interrelated areas of musicology, composition and chamber music performance – the Fidelio Trio residency could be said to have broken new ground. It took place at a time when many universities and higher education institutes were only beginning to acknowledge artistic practice as research (although this was an idea that had currency for some time in progressive conservatories and art colleges).[17] The idea of linking live performance to musicology lectures was in part based on the lecture-recital model that had started to emerge in musicological conferences in Ireland and elsewhere; this was an aspect of the residency design that would later impact on a review of the music department's MA in Music programme. Pianist for the Fidelio Trio, Mary Dullea, who was also at that time Director of Performance at the University of Sheffield, contributed to the 'Music in Performance' module for the revised MA programme at St Patrick's College. Meanwhile, two members of the music department, the composers John Buckley and Rhona Clarke were ideally placed to work with the Trio on those aspects of the residency relating to composition, in addition to other areas. All in all, the residency design strove to explore relationships between performance, composition, musicology and pedagogy in higher education.

Timetabling for the residency took its cue from the academic calendar of the College and from the busy international schedule of the London-based Fidelio Trio. Accordingly, a plan was set up for a residency based on an average of six weeks throughout each academic year. As can been seen from the detailed schedules set out in Appendix E this roughly divided between the first and second semesters of each year with several events recurring such as the annual chamber music festival in November/December and the Trio's contribution to in-service music courses in July. Most concerts and workshops took place across the campus of St Patrick's College, with additional residency events scheduled off-campus.

The residency was officially launched in Room B118, Music Department on 19 October 2012 (although Darragh Morgan and Mary Dullea had performed for Culture Night a few weeks earlier, representing the College's first participation in that national event). Martin Drury from the Arts Council and Daire Keogh, President of St

---

the purposeful engagement of students with artists', *Teaching Artist Journal*, 5.4 (2007).

[17] See for example, D. Wright, D. Bennett & D. Blom, 'Artist academics: Performing the Australian research agenda', *International Journal of Education and the Arts*, 10.17 (2009), http://www.ijea.org/v10n17/index.html, [accessed 7 January 2019].

Patrick's College spoke at the launch while the Trio performed movements from piano trios by Beethoven and Arensky.

Concerts, conferences, festivals and communities
Performance was core to all strands of the residency, and reaching new audiences as well as performing established and new repertoire was a vital aspect of the Trio's investment in the project (see the chapters by John Buckley and Rhona Clarke in this volume for further discussion respectively on concert programming and composition commissions during the residency). A major outlet for performance was the College's long-running lunchtime concert series taking place in B118 ('the Music Room'), which at the time was curated by John Buckley. The Trio presented a total of ten lunchtime concerts throughout the three-year residency term. As can be gleaned from Appendix E, in the first two years a small number of these comprised solo or duo recitals by members of the ensemble. Evening concerts were also occasionally scheduled and took place either in the auditorium of St Patrick's College or at the Mahony Hall, The Helix.[18] Other college venues explored by the Trio included B103 for Culture Night 2013 and earlier, in April 2013, the lecture hall D210 (subsequently named the McGahern Room). Their performance on that occasion was in the context of the annual John McGahern Evening hosted by the College's English Department.[19] In addition to engaging with occasional events hosted by other academic disciplines, members of the Trio also participated in the annual carol service; during the 2012 service Darragh Morgan and Mary Dullea played reflective arrangements of Irish airs, while for the 2014 event the full ensemble performed the second movement of Fauré's *Piano Trio in D Minor* as well as joining St Patrick's Alumni Choir for Brahms's seasonal lullaby 'Wiegenlied'.

The musicians' engagement with the College community and with its unique heritage and architecture would develop significantly through the establishment of the annual winter chamber music festival at the historic Belvedere House in 2013. Violinist and ensemble leader Darragh Morgan first came up with the idea, recognizing the venue's unique acoustic properties and its overall ambience for chamber music performance. While Belvedere House's beautiful Library Room had long been in use as a reception area for distinguished guests of the College, since its acquisition by the Vincentian Order it had not been used as a

---

[18] The President's Office of Dublin City University funded the hire of the Mahony Hall for these events.
[19] The Fidelio Trio made a guest performance at the John McGahern Evening that year alongside Claire Keegan, creative writing fellow in the English Department and Nuala Ní Dhomhnaill, writer-in-residence at the College's Roinn na Gaeilge [Irish Department].

centre of cultural production, nor had it been made accessible to the public.

The first winter chamber music festival took place from 1-3 November 2013. It was programmed to coincide with the Music Education Gathering 2013 (doubling as the 3rd Annual Conference of the Society for Music Education in Ireland) a unique symposium that brought together the largest forum of international and national researchers and practitioners of music education held in Ireland since the mid-1990s. There was considerable crossover in audiences for the festival and conference, leading to a meaningful cross-fertilisation of ideas for some attendees. For example, many of those present would apprehend a humanistic resonance between Professor Sheila Woodward's keynote talk 'The Educative Role of Music in the South African Freedom Struggle' and immediately afterwards, a performance of Messiaen's *Quatuor pour la fin du temps* [Quartet for the End of Time] by the Fidelio Trio with clarinettist Robert Plane.

The second annual chamber music festival in December 2014 was programmed in parallel with the autumn gathering of the European Chamber Music Teachers' Association (ECTMA) which was organized in Ireland for the first time. Staging these events together highlighted the residency's mission to promote chamber music, among its other strands. In addition to four public concerts, a range of guest speakers provided insights into chamber music instruction and activities in Ireland.[20] The ECMTA meeting also featured master classes, thematic work groups and a members' forum.[21]

By the time of the third festival in December 2015, the period of the funded residency had come to an end. Nonetheless, the festival would continue to be hosted by St Patrick's College Music Department, in that year with the financial support of the president's office of Dublin City University. As noted in Áine Mangaoang's chapter in this volume, 2015 was also the year that local arts group GlasDrum was constituted. Among its directorate were Patricia Flynn and John O'Flynn of St Patrick's College Music Department.

---

[20] Speakers over the weekend included Raymond Deane, Miriam Roycroft, Ferenc Szucs, John O'Flynn, Christopher Marwood, Sharon Rollston and John O'Kane.

[21] Delegates included professors from conservatoires and music academies in Lithuania, Estonia, Finland, Germany, Spain, Portugal, Russia, Cyprus and the UK. Advanced students from as far away as the Tatar city of Kazan also travelled to the gathering.

Figure 10.1: The Fidelio Trio at the 3rd Winter Chamber Music Festival in the Library Room of Belvedere House, December 2015. Photograph by Frances Marshall

Fittingly perhaps, the fourth festival in 2016 was jointly presented by music faculty at DCU and GlasDrum, and once again enjoyed funding from the Arts Council.[22] This is an arrangement that has continued up to the time of writing. Arguably, the successful staging of the festival in recent years can be regarded as providing continuity on several counts: first, as a way of bringing forward aspects of the residency model co-developed by the artists and the former music department of St Patrick's College; second, as a means for music staff at the university, as well as DCU as a whole, to maintain artistic links with the world-renowned ensemble; and third, as a process whereby the Fidelio Trio, music at DCU and GlasDrum can collaborate to continue bringing world class chamber music events to audiences in North Dublin.

---

[22] In October 2016 St Patrick's College ceased as an entity following full incorporation into DCU. Former music department members of the College were assigned to the University's newly established School of Theology, Philosophy, and Music.

Figure 10.2: Poster for the 4th Fidelio Trio Winter Chamber Music Festival, 2016. Design by Alastair Keady, Hexhibit

Chamber music in education and in community

While all strands of the Fidelio Trio residency were related to music in higher education, the education and community strand was specifically engaged with student teachers at St Patrick's College. It also reached out to primary and post-primary pupils and to music education in the wider community. The bulk of the Trio's workshop commitments throughout the residency were through the mandatory curriculum music courses taken by students of the BEd and Postgraduate Diploma in Education programmes. As previously noted, the mode of engagement here would gradually change from that of 'receiving art' to a more relational arts model. That is to say, students would perform and discuss their group composition pieces with the artists, in addition to more traditional workshop formats where the artists performed whole pieces or extracts of works, followed by semi-structured question and answer sessions.

A survey investigating the responses of 116 second-year BEd students to the residency workshops was conducted in March 2014.[23] The questionnaire comprised thirteen questions in polar ('yes/no') or in multiple-choice formats, with the option to provide additional comments in each field. While it is beyond the scope of this chapter to interpret the data in any detail, it can be reported that overall, students were highly positive in their responses to the workshops, notwithstanding the cohort's quite varied levels of prior exposure to classical music and to chamber music in particular. One of the questions posed, 'Did you find the Fidelio lectures/workshops you attended interesting?' revealed a 101/15 divide in favour of 'yes'. More tellingly, a range of qualitative responses showed how students appreciated the artists' creative engagement in addition to their musicality and virtuosity. The following is a compilation of individual statements separated by line breaks:

> I really enjoyed their performance. The fact that they were listening to our performance made it exciting.
>
> They gave us interesting comments on our compositions. Also they were excellent musicians.
>
> Obviously being professional musicians at such a high standard was useful to us when they gave us feedback on our compositions.
>
> It was good to get feedback on our composition from musicians of that calibre.
>
> Interesting because they are something different, they're very helpful and give clear precise, informative advice. Enjoyable to watch them perform.

The majority of students were also positive in response to the question, 'Did you find the Fidelio lectures/workshops you attended helpful in terms of the BEd course?' although the breakdown of 'yes/no' in this instance was 85/31. Few of those who responded in the negative supplied qualifying statements, but those who did pointed to a perceived lack of connection between the workshops and professional education studies. One student, for example, stated: 'No. I wouldn't be able to apply what they covered in the workshop to a classroom environment.' In contrast, several students seemed to make imaginative leaps between

---

[23] The independent arts consultant Anne Marie Herron designed and administered the questionnaire survey. Herron was at that time contracted by the Arts Council to liaise with artist residencies at the colleges of education.

what they experienced in the workshops and their future practice as teachers:

> They gave advice as to how we could use any piece of music in creative ways with children.

> We were shown ways to use music in the classroom in ways I had never thought of before.

> It encouraged me to invite musicians into the classroom.

The above examples strongly suggest the impact that artist-residencies can have in specific contexts of teacher education, with multiple opportunities for 'parachute-effect' moments in the here-and-now as well as in future professional contexts. And it is perhaps worth bearing in mind here that the total number of education students who attended Fidelio Trio workshops between 2012-2015 would have been in excess of 1,500.

The residency schedule also included workshops specifically designed for primary and post-primary school pupils. Most of these workshops took place in the music department of St Patrick's College, with participating schools mainly from north and central Dublin catchment areas. Their organization was one of many roles undertaken by the residency's administrators, Annette Slattery (2013-2014) and Barry O'Halpin (2014-2015).[24] In contrast to the approach taken in much contemporary programming of classical music for children, the Trio did not mediate the performance of their repertoire for these workshops through simplified storylines or other reductive means, but instead challenged children to engage with whole movements of pieces. In many cases, children were primed for live music experiences through preparation by their class teacher or music teacher. In looking back at one of the earliest such workshops in December 2012, primary school teacher (and later, MA in Music graduate) Rachael Byrne would observe: 'As a teacher, I am constantly looking for opportunities to offer my pupils meaningful experiences within the curriculum and The Fidelio Trio's performance workshop achieved that in a special way for the children.'[25] More than two years later, Helen Brennan, music teacher at Larkin Community College noted her students' appreciation of the

---

[24] These were arts administration internships advertised under the Department of Employment Affairs and Social Protection's JobBridge scheme.

[25] Rachael Byrne, 'Testimony statements on the impact of the Fidelio Trio Residency' compiled by Barry O'Halpin, May 2015. Byrne was a BEd student from 2008-2011 and returned for the MA course between 2013-2015.

workshop that they attended in February 2015.[26] She listed proximity to the musicians, hearing varied repertoire and seeing/understanding instrumental techniques as the aspects most appreciated by them. Brennan's report could equally describe audience members' response to a chamber music recital in more formal contexts, and this is testimony to the Fidelio Trio's artistry and their commitment to the schools' workshops.

Programming for the Fidelio Trio residency also overlapped annually with the spring schedule of The Ark, the dedicated cultural centre for children in Temple Bar, Dublin. Planning for these events involved close collaboration with music programmer Aisling O'Gorman. In contrast to the workshops scheduled for St Patrick's College, those presented at The Ark were conceived under a general theme linked to other arts activities. Additionally, the Trio performed early evening recitals at The Ark for teachers, and the centre's partnership with the residency was further strengthened at those events by guest talks given by music lecturers from St Patrick's College.[27]

The Fidelio Trio also played a key role in music in-service provision at St Patrick's College over three years. In July 2013 they presented workshops at a summer course focusing on music in primary schools.[28] The ensemble made a special contribution to chamber music classes as part of the annual Kodály Summer School presented by the Kodály Society of Ireland (KSI) and hosted by the College's music department. This was and continues to be a course that attracts primary and post-primary teachers as well as other adult musicians of diverse backgrounds and abilities. The contribution made by the Fidelio Trio to this course over three consecutive years was summed up as follows by Daniel Walsh, KSI Chairperson at the time:

> The members of the trio maintained high musical standards while remaining personable, encouraging and patiently advising musicians in a practical way at a level that was appropriate to their needs. They added enormous value to our course. We also enjoyed wonderful formal and informal artistic performances that uplifted the mood and attitudes of people and helped

---

[26] Helen Brennan, 'Testimony statements on the impact of the Fidelio Trio Residency' compiled by Barry O'Halpin, May 2015.
[27] In April 2013 John O'Flynn delivered a talk on musicians and artists working in schools while in March 2014 John Buckley gave a presentation on the subject of classical music in the primary school.
[28] The course was designed in association with Regina Murphy, Director of In-Service Education at St Patrick's College, and included components in West African drumming, samba and chamber music.

towards the positive, supportive environment we create for musicians to develop their musicianship.[29]

Walsh's appreciation here underlines the residency's mission to promote chamber music *per se* in addition to the promotion of music in education and in communities more generally. The residency's very first workshop at St Patrick's College, held in October 2012 in conjunction with the DIT Conservatory of Music and Drama had a focus on string learning in conservatoire and community settings. Almost a year later, in September 2013 a second workshop for young orchestral players was programmed at the College, this time with the participation of members of St Ultan's Senior Primary School Orchestra and their teachers. The generalist primary teachers in attendance were also instrumentalists who provided coaching for their pupils. Among their number was Emma Heverin (BEd 2007-2010) who played clarinet. The Trio continued to promote chamber music among young players when they conducted a series of workshops with Louth Music Partnership Strings in July 2014.

Integrating music studies: performance, musicology and composition

The penultimate section of this chapter contemplates the Fidelio Trio's substantial involvement with the music degree courses offered at St Patrick's College, and considers the residency's impact on facilitating dialogue across the traditionally demarcated areas of performance, musicology and composition (As previously indicated, the Trio's broader impact in respect of performance and composition is discussed in chapters by Rhona Clarke and John Buckley for this volume, with a full list of residency performances and premieres detailed in Appendix E).

Between 2012-2015 all students taking the BA music course at St Patrick's College benefitted from a range of scheduled lecture-workshops involving co-participation by the Fidelio Trio. The Trio became a valued resource for lecture-workshops in orchestration and composition, as well as contributing to the delivery of musicology lectures, specifically on aspects of nineteenth- and early-twentieth-century music and film music. Several cohorts of BEd students taking a specialist music option would also have encountered the Trio in some of their historical musicology lectures. Students taking the taught MA in Music course additionally benefitted from interactions with the ensemble. As graduate John Bonner (MA 2013-2015) recalls:

---

[29] Daniel Walsh, 'Testimony statements on the impact of the Fidelio Trio Residency' compiled by Barry O'Halpin, May 2015.

Their participation in the module on Music and Modernity was most impressive, demonstrating many new compositional and performing techniques for both strings and piano.[30]

In the same testimony, Bonner also recalls occasional master classes offered to MA students by Mary Dullea on piano and Darragh Morgan on violin.[31] From time to time members of the trio would also mentor undergraduate music groups across different genres; for the staging of John Cage's *MusiCircus* in December 2012, the Trio included folk duo Richard Molloy and John Maher (both BEd students 2010-2013) and Irish traditional harpist Aoife Ní Argáin (BEd 2011-2014).

The Trio's interaction with BA composition and orchestration lecture-workshops given by Rhona Clarke was considerable, from the basics of understanding the scope and range of solo instrumental writing in first year to the composition of short works for piano trio by the third and final year of the BA course. During one visit to the music department of the nearby Mater Dei Institute of Education in December 2014, the Trio engendered a musical vitality when demonstrating orchestral techniques to fourth year students on the BRelEd and Music programme, as course leader Róisín Blunnie recounts:

> The Trio brought a fourth-year orchestration lecture to life by providing live music examples of the highest calibre to illustrate stylistic and theoretical concepts relevant to the course content, as well as offering compositional advice and insights into score preparation from the performers' perspective(s).[32]

As Blunnie's statement above eloquently attests, the Trio's presence at composition and orchestration lecture-workshops facilitated a dynamic integration of performative, compositional, theoretical and musicological facets of music learning in higher education. Students fortunate enough to have had opportunity to hear their compositions for piano trio performed by the world-renowned ensemble would have included all third-year BA students at St Patrick's College, and undergraduate students from other university music departments and conservatories who were nominated by their institutions to take part in an annual Intervarsity Composition Forum. This was organized by the residency in association with CHMHE, the Council of Heads of Music in

---

[30] John Bonner, 'Testimony statements on the impact of the Fidelio Trio Residency' compiled by Barry O'Halpin, May 2015.
[31] Ibid.
[32] Róisín Blunnie, 'Testimony statements on the impact of the Fidelio Trio Residency' compiled by Barry O'Halpin, May 2015.

Higher Education. Student Composer Rachel Corcoran from Waterford Institute of Technology had this to say following her participation at the third forum in April 2015:

> Got back there a while ago, from what I can easily say was one of the best learning experiences and compositional highlights of my life so far. Getting an original composition played multiple times ... and then workshopped by the Fidelio Trio was an amazing experience. [33]

Given their pivotal role in the development of the piano trio genre, it is perhaps not surprising that works by Beethoven, Schubert, Schumann and Brahms featured more than any other composers in historical musicology lectures during the term of the Fidelio Trio residency; most of these were designed and delivered by Patricia Flynn and by John Buckley. To present an example, the study of Brahms' *Piano Trio No. 3 in C minor* formed part of the musicology module for third year BA students. Having studied the score in detail with John Buckley, students were highly receptive to lecture room engagement with the Fidelio Trio at the end of semester. Through exemplification, analysis, commentary, interaction and above all performance, the Fidelio Trio transformed the piano trio from an academic study to the actual living experience, leaving a deep and profound impact on the musical understanding of the students.

Early twentieth century works came to be explored more circuitously in a series of BA film music lectures devised by John O'Flynn. For these O'Flynn selected European film titles that featured musicians and/or composers as filmic subjects, both in the literal narrative sense as well as through the implied sonic presence or imprint of particular composers. Two films chosen for this purpose were *Un Coeur en Hiver* which among other works by Ravel features his monumental piano trio, and *The Unbearable Lightness of Being*, the soundtrack for which is dominated by the highly individual chamber music of Leoš Janáček. [34] The substantial point to make in the context of this chapter is how the presence and openness of the Trio to perform during film music lectures ultimately impacted on O'Flynn's approach to film musicology. [35]

---

[33] Rachel Corcoran, 'Testimony statements on the impact of the Fidelio Trio Residency' compiled by Barry O'Halpin, May 2015.

[34] *Un Coeur en Hiver*, dir. Claude Sautet, 1992; *The Unbearable Lightness of Being*, dir. Philip Kaufman, 1988.

[35] The impact of the Fidelio Trio on the film music course would further lead to a conference paper in 2014: J. O'Flynn, 'Juxtaposed Intertextuality? The re-presentation of chamber music by Ravel and Janáček in two "European" films of

Members of the Trio were further active in suggesting new material for the course. This resulted in a series of lectures featuring the extensive film music output of Michael Nyman, and included some of Nyman's hand-filmed 'silent' films with original scores for piano trio. Two of these 'shorts' – *Poczatek* and *Yellow Beach* - were screened during lectures with simultaneous sounding of Nyman's scores performed by the Fidelio Trio.[36]

Concluding comments
The Fidelio Trio residency at St Patrick's College was unique in many respects. Jointly funded by the Arts Council and the College, it was at the vanguard of innovations for artist residencies in colleges of education and universities in Ireland, and in fact preceded official policy to develop strategies towards further engagement between the arts and higher education sectors. The residency stimulated approaches to listening, composing and performing for more than 1,500 student teachers at the College. It further proposed a model for the meaningful integration of performance, composition and musicology in the experiences of those studying music to degree level, and also served to stimulate course review and new research directions for academic staff.

For the artists, the residency afforded space and time to extend programming and develop new repertoire, to collaborate with national and international composers, and to commission new works in the context of a newly established annual chamber music festival under the artistic direction of the Trio. The festival and residency also extended the ensemble's already substantial audience base to include: student teachers and teachers; college and university staff; local communities, university students, school pupils and other young people and children; lifelong music learners; and other newly converted supporters of chamber music.

Collaboration with national and local organizations was key to the success of the residency, and also proved beneficial in raising the national and international profile of music at St Patrick's College. In the years preceding incorporation into DCU, the residency also stimulated classical music programming at The Helix as well as promoting musical collaborations with colleagues based at Mater Dei Institute of Education.

---

the late twentieth century', 12th Annual Plenary Conference of the Society for Musicology in Ireland, (University College Dublin, 8 June 2014).
[36] Nyman combined hand-held filming technique with the re-composition of existing documentary footage. In a reversal of traditional audio-visual hierarchies in film, the screenings can be regarded as accompaniments to the original music. Both pieces are included in the Fidelio Trio CD released in 2012, *Michael Nyman, Chamber Music Vol. 1: Piano Trios 1992-2010.*

The sheer number and range of concerts, workshops and other events led by the ensemble, as documented in this chapter and supported by the schedules outlined in Appendix E, bear testament to the Fidelio Trio's innovation, commitment and engagement. It provides a record of arts-in-education engagement that has been unsurpassed to date in any other music residency in Ireland. Over the course of the residency and beyond its term, the Fidelio Trio came to be regarded as honorary members of St Patrick's College Music Department and were integral to the cultural life of the College.

Bibliography

Cox, Michelle, '"What Next?" Exploring the Potential Long-term and Short-term Educational Benefits of Outreach Music Composition Projects in Irish Primary Schools', Unpublished MA dissertation, (Mary Immaculate College, University of Limerick, 2006).

Department of Arts, Heritage and the Gaeltacht and Department of Education and Science, *Arts in Education Charter*, (Dublin: DAHG and DES, 2012).

Department of Education and Science and the Arts Council, *Artists ~ Schools Guidelines: Towards Best Practice in Ireland*, (Dublin: DES and the Arts Council, 2009).

Duncum, Paul, 'Engaging Public Space: Art Education Pedagogies for Social Justice', *Equity & Excellence in Education*, 44:3 (2011), 348-363, http://dx.doi.org/10.1080/10665684.2011.590400 [accessed 5 January 2019].

Freer, Patrick, 'Toward the purposeful engagement of students with artists', *Teaching Artist Journal*, 5.4 (2007), 269-278.

Hanly, Betty, 'The Good, the Bad, and the Ugly - Arts Partnerships in Canadian Elementary Schools', *Arts Education Policy Review*, 104.6 (2003), 11-20.

Harland, John et al., *The Arts-Education Interface: A Mutual Learning Triangle*, (Slough, Berkshire: National Foundation for Educational Research, 2005).

Irwin, Rita & O'Donoghue, Dónal, 'Encountering pedagogy through relational art practices', *International Journal of Art & Design Education*, 31.3 (2012): 221-236.

Kenny, Ailbhe with Flynn, Patricia, *Knowing the Score: Local Authorities and Music*, (Dublin: St Patrick's College, 2009).

Neryl, Jeanneret & DeGraffenreid, George, 'Music education in the generalist classroom', in G. McPherson & G. Welch (eds.), *Music Learning and Teaching in Infancy, Childhood, and Adolescence: An Oxford Handbook of Music Education*, Volume 2 (2018), pp. 178-195.

Ross, Malcolm, 'Evaluating Education Programmes of Arts Organisations', *Music Education Research*, 5.1 (2003), 69-79.

Silverstein, Lynne, 'Artist residencies: evolving educational experiences', in B. Rich, J. Polin, and S. Marcus (eds.), *Acts of Achievement: The role of performing arts centers in education*, (New York: The Dana Foundation, 2003), pp. 10-22.

Vogler Partners Steering Group, *Live Music in the Classroom: An Analysis of the Primary Curriculum Support Programme of the Vogler Quartet in Sligo Residency*, (Sligo: The Arts Office, Sligo County Council, 2006).

Wright, David, Bennett, Dawn & Blom, Diane, 'Artist academics: Performing the Australian research agenda', *International Journal of Education and the Arts*, 10.17 (2009), http://www.ijea.org/v10n17/index.html [accessed 7 January 2019].

Archives
Fidelio Trio Residency Archive
St Patrick's College Archive

Discography
Fidelio Trio, *Michael Nyman, Chamber Music Vol. 1: Piano Trios 1992-2010*, (UK: MN Records, MNRCD 120, 2012).

Chapter Eleven: Graduate Perspectives

Introduced by John Buckley

Until the introduction of BA programmes in the early 1990s, all students of St Patrick's College encountered the music department or its earlier manifestations, to one degree or another. From the beginning of the college in 1875 student teachers were required to engage with methodologies and appropriate materials relating to the teaching of music in the primary school. Prior to 1993, two possibilities for musical study were available to students, at least from the 1950s onwards: the obligatory study of classroom or curriculum music and an optional module of academic music, initially referred to as 'special music' until the introduction of the BEd in 1974 when it became known as academic music. The BA in humanities and university linkage initially with University College Dublin and subsequently with Dublin City University brought a new dimension to the academic life of St Patrick's College, including the Music Department.

While many of the students attending St Patrick's College emerged from a broadly similar social and educational context, their musical experience and identity varied widely from the almost negligible to the highly sophisticated and focused. Many of those students with a strong sense of musical identity had already been engaged with Irish traditional or classical music while others had been members of brass or wind bands or, in more recent times, musical theatre or popular music. All brought their own particular musical identities and gifts to the department, which warmly welcomed and embraced the rich variety that such diversity afforded. Prior to the dissolution of the college in 2016, students could undertake studies in music or music education at both undergraduate and postgraduate levels including BA, BEd, MA, MEd, and PhD.

Students are the essence and centrality of any university college and the music department in St Patrick's College always held this principle and philosophy at the heart of its mission. A sense of delight and pride in the achievements of past students in the arenas of teaching, performance, composition, musicology, and music administration was shared by staff and students alike. Many of these achievements have been referred to in earlier chapters of this publication. In this chapter, six graduates offer their individual perspectives on their studies in the music department and the impact these studies have had on their subsequent careers. The period covers a thirty-four year time span from 1979 to 2013, during which many new programmes and other innovations were introduced to the College.

The six perspectives which follow are written by students who graduated from a variety of programmes, BA, BEd, and PhD over that period. Miriam O'Sullivan and Denise Morgan are active as teachers at primary and secondary school levels respectively while Gavan Ring and Conall Ó Breacháin are internationally recognised as performers of opera (Ring) and rock/pop (Ó Breacháin). Paul Gilgunn is a musicologist, composer and performer, while Colman Pearce continues his distinguished career as conductor, pianist and composer. Collectively, their perspectives present a portrait of the aims, ambitions and achievements of the music department of St Patrick's College in the thirty or more years prior to its incorporation into DCU.

Miriam O'Sullivan (BEd, 1979-1982)

In conversation with other graduates of St Patrick's College, the common theme that often arises is the musical experiences we were fortunate to share on that very convivial campus in the late 1970s and early 1980s. The range of musical encounters was diverse and interesting. During the lunch break for example, the canteen might play host to such performers as Freddie White or Luka Bloom. How lucky we were to be exposed to performers who were the best of their genre without even having to leave the building! Such experiences informed us in a surreptitious way, teaching us skills for life, like listening intently, participating wholeheartedly and maybe most importantly of all, sharing and appreciating music in a communal setting as a core activity, an integral aspect of our formation as teachers.

Then there were the great performance opportunities provided by the College's performing groups. These ranged from large scale musical productions such as *The Pirates of Penzance*, expertly directed by Colum Ó Cléirigh to the sumptuous choral presentations of motets and madrigals by Seán Mac Liam's madrigal group in the hallowed setting of the college chapel. Lunchtime performances in the music room gave individual students and small groups the chance to demonstrate their flair in full view of an audience of peers. This, I can confess, was no mean feat for a country girl who had never had an audience other than the fawning guests in her family's B&B.

The experience of and participation in live music was a high priority in St Patrick's College. I have a fond memory of my academic music class, all seven of us, being taken to Cork for a night by Colum Ó Cléirigh to see a performance of Stravinsky's *Petrouchka*. To call this experience exotic would be an understatement! I recall with vivid clarity the action and colour on the stage that night, apart from the wonderful music. I was entranced and virtually transported to a folk scene somewhere deep in the heart of Russia.

The detailed study of orchestral music at St Patrick's College brought us to musical horizons far beyond our life experience at this time. We soaked up the richness and complexity of great works, presented to us in the most approachable way by the Head of Department, Seán Hayes, a very erudite gentleman who wore his learning lightly. In my own case, his influence led to numerous nights spent listening astutely to the National Symphony Orchestra and many other wonderful visiting orchestras at the NCH. Such was my enthusiasm for orchestral music that I subsequently studied flute and played an active part in many bands and orchestras in the Dublin area. I am still, to this day, an active chamber musician.

Through the specific study of curriculum music, we engaged with the skills, methodologies and content necessary to deliver a music education to children in primary school. An outstanding memory I have is of seeing the young John Buckley doing a demonstration music lesson with his class of boys from Holy Spirit Boys National School, Ballymun. John was the first person I witnessed using the methodologies of Kodály with a primary school class, and it left a profound impression on me. That single experience provided me with the impetus to explore this methodology further, leading to hundreds of hours of tuition by the best of Irish and Hungarian specialist teachers, John O'Flynn amongst them. Since I started teaching in 1982, this methodology has been an integral part of my daily classroom routine. I know that exposure has propelled many of my own pupils in a variety of musical directions.

The formal study of Irish music was done under the tutelage of Caitlín Uí Éigeartaigh. My own impression of Caitlín was that she was the living embodiment of the *aisling* with her long blonde hair, piercing blue eyes and fine bone structure. I couldn't have imagined anyone more appropriate to deliver the subject. She provided an in-depth study of the history and structure of Irish music, with particular reference to cataloguing tunes, and becoming familiar with the great collections of Bunting and others. This is a well of information to which I refer and return on a regular basis, still updating my knowledge of the genre using the tools I was given in those intense lectures many years ago.

The collective musical experiences of my life in St Patrick's College nourished my hunger for musical skill and knowledge in a way that was to have a marked influence on the direction both of my private and professional lives. I realised at an early stage that music was the universal language which would bring me into contact with many like-minded, and often colourful people. The seed that was sown in that music department led me in many musical directions, as much for the social opportunities as the musical ones. Let me tell you about some of them!

My involvement in a chamber choir called Eblana, directed by John O'Flynn brought me great satisfaction through learning a repertoire of polyphonic European and Irish chamber choral works. The pleasure that can be derived from making music collectively with human voices is uniquely satisfying and even therapeutic, as choral sound has the power to convey such meaning. Eblana was a great vocal laboratory, focused on exploring and developing choral repertoire and technique, and bringing an accomplished standard of performance to many discerning audiences.

Playing what I'd call a 'social' instrument was always an aspiration of mine. By 'social', I really mean easy to carry so that I could always be ready to play solo or blend in with other instruments. So, shortly after leaving St Patrick's College, I bought myself a concert flute. 'Why the flute?' you might ask. Well, for a start I liked the sound of it and felt assured, having heard James Galway, that I could aspire to the same standard! Given its portable size, the flute generated ample opportunities to become involved in a wide range of musical communities. It opened doors to brass and wind bands, orchestras, chamber music groups, music courses at home and abroad, a performer's diploma, in short, a lifetime of social engagement, and even on some rare occasions, payment!

On the professional front, a solid foundation in music education gave me the appetite to engage children with music. This led me to become involved with school choirs, recorder groups, tin whistle bands, performances at 'Córfhéile na Scoileanna' and musical collaborations with other schools.

In the late 1990s I was fortunate to be seconded from my teaching position to become music programmer at The Ark, a cultural centre for children, where our youngest participants came to be exposed to high quality experiences in every area of the arts. This was a whole new world of endeavour. It called upon my skills as an educator as well as my particular knowledge of, and involvement in music, to devise and commission music experiences for children from 4-13 years old. It also regularly necessitated the design and delivery of professional development workshops for primary teachers who brought their classes along to the events. There is no doubt in my mind that the solid foundation in music and music education I received in my undergraduate years in St Patrick's College equipped me with the skills to face this challenge with confidence.

An opportunity to deliver professional development in the 1999 Music Curriculum to primary teaching colleagues was another wonderfully enriching experience. It came by way of a Department of Education secondment to the Primary Curriculum Support Programme (PCSP). I became a full-time member of a national team of thirty teachers whose role was to design and deliver a two-day training programme in the music curriculum for all primary teachers. A tall order indeed! Fortunately, the years spent honing my skills as a primary music educator in my classroom fuelled me with the passion I needed to convince other teachers not just of the need for a music education, but of the right of each child to experience it in the primary classroom. This commitment to promoting music as a core element of curriculum was something that took root in my undergraduate training in St Patrick's College.

In conclusion, I am very grateful indeed for the music education I received in St Patrick's College. It was an institution which delivered a quality education in music. In my own case, it shaped me, not just as a teacher of music but as a vibrant, happy human being, living life to the full every day through music, and like the pied piper, leading the children on behind me!

Gavan Ring (BEd, 2005-2008)

At fifteen years of age, I resolved to become a primary school teacher. Given my mother's life-long involvement in education I was intimately familiar with the teaching profession from a very young age – one could say that I wanted to enter into the family business, so to speak! Music, of course, was always the driving force in my life; I was an avid organist and had a promising singing voice. I had attended secondary school at St Finian's College Mullingar as a member of the Schola Cantorum music scholarship programme so I was equally keen to ensure my continued development as a musician alongside my studies in education. St Patrick's College Drumcondra, centrally located in Dublin where my singing teacher, Mary Brennan, was based and boasting one of the best music departments in the country, was the obvious choice for me.

Although I never pursued a career in the primary school after I graduated, the skill set I developed in the field of education at St Patrick's College has proven invaluable to me over the years. In particular, the processes that govern the practice of reflective pedagogy have become central to my continuing artistic and professional development. So much of my craft as an operatic artist involves constant engagement with pedagogues such as singing teachers, repertoire coaches, language coaches, dance instructors, conductors and directors and whenever my schedule allows, I also mentor young opera singers and present lectures, lecture recitals and master classes. I firmly believe that a deep understanding of pedagogical concepts is a necessary, vital and symbiotic component to the artistic endeavour as it demands comprehensive practice reflection.

The musical education I received at St Patrick's College was nothing short of remarkable. Comprising a staff of highly prolific Irish composers, accomplished conductors and seminal musicologists, the music department was always a hive of stimulating vibrancy and dynamism. The formal academic courses were inspirational; to this day, Rhona Clarke's first year module on early music and Seán Mac Liam's third year module on verismo opera remain etched in my memory as acmes of an almost three-decade long musical education that has taken me all the way to doctorate level. Dr Marion Doherty, who was head of the music department during my time at St Patrick's College, was also profoundly influential in that, recognizing my abilities in particular as a singer, she created multiple, full-scale, solo performance opportunities for me such as Mozart's *Requiem in D minor*, Handel's *Messiah*,

Haydn's *Creation* and Gilbert & Sullivan's *Trial by Jury*. She also accompanied me on piano in a full, solo lunchtime recital in my third year (these were normally reserved for visiting professional performers) and provided me with my first, thrilling, foray into conducting where I was given the reins as maestro of the college orchestra for works by Beethoven and Mozart. It must be said, however, that Dr Doherty was able to fashion a great deal of these performance platforms as, during my time at St Patrick's College, the music department found itself with an embarrassment of riches in terms of student performers – current West End star Brian Gilligan, all Ireland champion sean-nós singer Cian Kerins, sopranos Christine Smyth and Chloe Kenny along with virtuoso cellist Ruth O'Leary are but some of a plethora of my class contemporaries who wouldn't have been out of place in any of the major performance conservatoires in the world. In fact, Brian, Cian and I famously formed a vocal trio called 'The Three Baritones' (even though Brian was and has always been a tenor!) and we sang for several important college functions including representing the College at Áras an Uachtaráin for then President Mary McAleese.

I remember that in my second year I was beginning to sense that perhaps primary school teaching was not the career path I was going to pursue and thus talk of changing institutions for a music performance-related degree programme entered the ether. I agonized for months about this, discussing at length the possibilities with members of the music department at St Patrick's College (who, I might add, were incredibly magnanimous and supportive throughout), my singing teacher and my family. In the end, I decided to complete my studies at St Patrick's College and then, instead of entering the teaching profession, I opted to pursue postgraduate studies in music performance at the Royal Irish Academy of Music – a decision that I feel has since been wholly vindicated. In retrospect, I am immensely relieved that I stayed the course (if one will pardon the pun!) at St Patrick's College. I am tremendously proud of my status as an alumnus of such an illustrious institution and the exceptionally well-rounded and multi-faceted education I received there has stood to me as an unrivalled corner stone in my progression not only as an operatic performer but also crucially, as a musicologist and pedagogue.

Colman Pearce (PhD, 2003-2009)

As September 2003 loomed (the month and year I was due to officially retire from my orchestral conducting position at RTÉ), I began to get excited at the prospect of having more time with which to compose. In a very busy career as a conductor, my creative output had been quite limited by lack of 'composing oases' - those zones of quietude which I needed to stimulate the imagination, and work with my musical ideas. With the possibility of producing new compositions, it occurred to me that these works might be used to obtain a PhD. But where? I didn't want to attend classes, and that ruled out most universities both here and in the United States, my two preferred locations.

One day, having finished a project with the RTÉ National Symphony Orchestra, recording music by John Buckley, John and I had a celebratory drink, as one does! I mentioned my compositional aspirations to him, and the possible link to achieving a Doctorate. John asked whether I really wanted to work for a PhD, in that he was just about to recommend me for an honorary doctorate to DCU. I told him that I would much prefer to achieve the degree by research, and John said that he thought St Patrick's College, in conjunction with DCU, could confer a PhD for composition. This was a new possibility for his college, created by the fact that John, a recipient of a PhD in composition, had recently been appointed to a staff position. Heretofore, there had never been a full-time lecturer in St Patrick's College with John Buckley's qualifications. John assured me that he would investigate the specific situation, and inform me of his findings.

Yes, it would be possible! St Patrick's College had not had the facility before, but now that Dr Buckley was on the staff with his PhD for composition, the College was enabled to provide what I needed. I duly registered as the first student of the College to pursue this particular course. I was shortly joined by Kevin O'Connell, already well established as a composer, and desirous to achieve a similar PhD.

I was pleased to be enrolled in St Patrick's College. I knew John Buckley very well, and he laughingly pointed out that years ago I had been his mentor and now he was my supervisor! My other overseer was Seán Mac Liam, whom I had not previously met, and he proved to be both charming and rigorous in his shaping of my academic style for my thesis. Seán said that he thought that I might be eligible for a partial scholarship, and he delivered on this, which helped to defray some of my expenses in the first two years. My course was to be for a minimum of four years, and as I was about to sign on, John rather hesitantly said he had a question for me. Did I have a primary degree? - he had assumed that I did, but he awaited my answer with - bated breath?! Yes, I had; a BMus awarded in 1960 by UCD – John was delighted!

The Head of the Music Department in St Patrick's College was Marion Doherty, whom I knew and whose work as a harpsichordist and choral director I much admired. Also on the staff was (and still is) the amiable and talented Patricia Flynn, who revealed to me that I was eligible to use a large rather secluded room available for doctoral students alone. This was to be a haven for me for both composing music and my thesis. I created a college 'first' by once working throughout the night in this room in 2008 – a practice not condoned by the College (I didn't know!), and subsequently officially banned. The Security Guard on duty that night was dealing with an unprecedented situation, and he was too kind to ask me to finish my work!

For my thesis I chose the very broad-spectrummed subject of 'Creativity' as manifested in humankind since our time began. I touched upon crafts, science, imagination, human ingenuity and inventiveness in general, and gradually honed in on the core of my topic, the Arts, with special emphasis and treatment of music.

Typically, a thesis such as this involved a lot of research - I suppose most theses do! I spent many hours in the excellent Cregan Library in St Patricks College, where I was a book-reader and not a computer-reader! The most difficult part of working to achieve my PhD was reading books by musicologists; I found most of them overly clinical, and simultaneously turgid in style. The sound created by composers, the expressive qualities conveyed by music, the satisfying structures in good compositions ('architecture in sound'), were somehow diminished, by footling and inconsequential musical minutiae in many of the books I ploughed through. And, of course, in common with many to whom I spoke, I developed a love/hate relationship with footnotes, including 'mine own' - however, they were obviously a *sine qua non* of academic scholarship!

Seán Mac Liam and John Buckley kept my 'feet to the coals' in shaping my thesis, and very gradually I scaled this Mount Parnassus. My submitted compositions were: *Day Dream, Night Dance* for solo guitar, *Toccata Festiva* for solo piano, *Six Yeats Songs*, a song-cycle, *What's in a Name?* for trumpet and piano, and two orchestral pieces - *Concerto for Two Mandolins*, and a cantata *Like as the Waves* for three solo singers, SATB chorus and large orchestra. These were reviewed by John Buckley, and he made many helpful suggestions which I incorporated.

In 2008 I was almost 'there' but didn't quite get everything finished in time for the deadline. The following year, despite a three-month concert tour of the United States with the Dublin Philharmonic Orchestra, I completed my requirements. My examiners were Rhona Clarke, composer and lecturer in St Patrick's College and Eibhlis Farrell, composer and distinguished academician, as external examiner. 'Sitting in' was John O'Flynn, newly appointed Head of Music in St Patrick's College, succeeding Marion Doherty. I was awarded a PhD in Research, and was duly conferred in November that year (2009) – at 71, perhaps the oldest in the annals of the College to have so achieved! But I'll leave that research (and footnoting!) to others! I enjoyed my time spent in the cloistered ambiance of this historic college, and am grateful to my mentors there. BEIR bua!

Conall Ó Breacháin (BEd, 1999-2002)

John Duignan and I met in St Patrick's College, Drumcondra. The campus was a relatively short stroll from my family home in Clontarf. John is from the lake-side village of Knockvicar in Co. Roscommon. Despite sporadic childhood dalliances with formal musical training, neither John nor I had had much legitimate experience of musical composition and performance before entering the College. Our friendship and musical collaboration, which at this point has lasted almost twenty years, was initially sparked by conversations in the College's social hub – the 'small canteen' - as we shared our favourite albums and argued over the virtues of our favourite bands. These initial conversations would be the bedrock from which We Cut Corners would eventually emerge.

We Cut Corners therefore began in St Patrick College. Back then, we went by the rather more pragmatic and resolutely less imaginative moniker of 'Conall and John', but St Patrick's College was where John and I first forged our friendship, first shared our musical tastes and tipples and first collaborated as songwriters and musicians. Between 1999 and 2002, when we both completed our undergraduate degrees in education, I have strong memories of the refracted sunlight bouncing off sepia-tinged corridors, the hustle of students scampering to lecture theatres, the bustle of the canteen and common rooms as the population scrambled for sustenance during short break periods. St Patrick's College was a unique place. It was heavily coloured with the rich history of the past, the vibrant buzz of the present and the hum of possibility that waited in the future. We Cut Corners and the music that we have written and recorded owe St Patrick's College a great debt of gratitude. It initially fostered our enthusiasm and has continued to support our growth and development.

Culture is tacit, difficult to recognize in the moment, particularly as a typically self-conscious teenager. The sanctuary of hindsight of course, facilitates elucidation. There was a compassion, a kindness and a personal feel to the college. It was a community; small enough to feel you belonged, just big enough to allow you to stretch your proverbial wings. As with any such colony or collective, it had its moments and some may argue it was all too colloquial and potentially stifling in its tight-knit nature. For education however, trust, relationships, collaboration and belonging are paramount and in this regard, St Patrick's College enacted the virtues that it espoused. The staff knew the students, the students knew the staff and the students knew each other.

This was a place where vocations were crystallized and career paths forged – everyone taking their first tentative steps in life's long journey - oriented towards a similar goal (education) but often presented along that river with myriad tangents and tributaries. The unique blend of personalities and skillsets drawn to education ensured that not only teachers, but artists, writers, playwrights, musicians and journalists all emerged from the gates of the college.

I *look* back on my time in St Patrick's College and I *hear* music. Pianos were a standard feature in many of the lecture halls and tutorial rooms. Music could be heard spilling from any corner of the college. Our music classes were (thankfully) a compulsory facet of our teacher-training (as it was known at the time). Our music elective (taken in our final year) was a source of true inspiration. Classes in classical music appreciation, musical literacy with an emphasis on tonic-solfa, song-singing and composition, brought to life through dynamic, interactive, collaborative workshops meant we were not just being inspired as music educators but as musicians, as songwriters, as composers and as arrangers of music. Choral recitals, annual song contests, talent shows and lunchtime concerts all intertwined in a symphony of personnel and personality. For those seriously musically inclined, it was a fertile breeding ground. For those with a casual interest in music, it offered scope to explore and experience.

The music rooms were situated in a small but vibrant tributary off the main thoroughfare of the College. All varieties of timbres and textures, from pianos to flutes to clarinets to bassoons, to guitars, to voices and to percussion, could be heard emanating from this cosy enclave. John and I were drawn to the piano rooms and their sympathetic acoustics from the first days we spent together. Hours were whittled in the evenings with two acoustic guitars making our first tentative, often clumsy steps into the field of song writing. There, we discovered the enveloping warmth of harmony-singing. We experimented with our first chord progressions (borrowing heavily from our heroes at the time - Radiohead, Jeff Buckley, Paul Simon, David Bowie) and poured out our earliest melodies. Our love of music was cemented in the halls and hollows, the corridors and common rooms. An annual song-contest provided the impetus for our first musical collaboration, a college play for our first compositional score. John and I have, since then, written and recorded four studio albums (*Today I Realised I Could Go Home Backwards*, 2011, *Think Nothing*, 2014, *The Cadences of Others*, 2016, and *Imposters*, 2018) and a live album (*Strings*, 2015). In 2010, we were signed to the London-based Delphi music company, an ethically-orientated independent record label which has released all of our music to date. Three of our albums have been nominated for the RTÉ choice music award. We have toured in Spain, Germany, Russia and the UK and have played festivals in New York, Groningen, Brighton and Berlin.

The origin of each composition and performance can be traced back to the College. And the influence of the College doesn't end in the embryonic, gestational period we spent there in the first few years of the 21st century. Our second album, *Think Nothing*, released in 2014, featured a significant collaboration with our former music lecturer (and the man behind the inspirational music elective), John Buckley, whose intricate string arrangements add a richness and depth to the music for which we will be forever grateful. Our third record, *The Cadences of Others*, released in 2016, was recorded in the College Chapel, where we turned the church aisles into a live room, and the sacristy into the engineer's control booth. These subsequent collaborations speak to the generosity and nurturing spirit that characterized the College and to the strong ties we have with St Patrick's College.

It's easy to over-sentimentalize your college experience. From Chopin to cheap cider, from Bruner to Buckfast, these were formative, horizon-broadening, heady days. The memory and influence of those days will remain with us for the rest of our lives. As I gaze back on my time spent in St Patrick College, Drumcondra, I can't help but feel that it was a special time indeed.

Paul Gilgunn (BA, 2007-2010)
I attended St Patrick's College as an undergraduate studying music as part of my BA degree from 2007-2010. Initially, Dr Marion Doherty noted my enthusiasm for music and encouraged me in my studies of the subject at the College – despite my somewhat limited practical knowledge of musical notation. Although I had previously undertaken some formal training in guitar styles, music theory, and vocal performance, my earlier musical experiences were characterized by a desire to explore and experiment with the forms, instruments, and techniques of popular music as an electric guitarist and composer/songwriter through performances and recordings. What I learned subsequently at the College – about composition, musicology, performance, and pedagogy – altered my musical trajectory and shaped my subsequent career in music.

Contemporary music was of particular interest, and my studies included tuition from composers Dr John Buckley and Dr Rhona Clarke. John taught instrumental and vocal composition in an insightful and practical way, and these gave a solid grounding in these areas. He generously provided a recording of his orchestral work *Taller Than Roman Spears* (1976-1977), and this was very interesting to me as it featured elements of fully-scored modernist composition and notational forms used in experimental music. Rhona's teaching covered musicology, and practical approaches to composition (including musical techniques and orchestration) that drew upon her work as a composer. I looked forward to these weekly assignments, which led me to develop a working knowledge of aesthetics and techniques in classical music. John O'Flynn's instruction in popular music studies were formative for me at the time also, and I found I had a natural affinity for this area of study. I subsequently began to combine idiomatic elements of music while attending the College; for example, orchestration of music by Radiohead and Thelonious Monk or short graphic and notated works that amalgamated aesthetics and practices from an art music tradition with harmonic, modal, and rhythmic elements from popular music.

These initial studies of formal composition and contemporary popular music served me well and would influence the course of my later work in music. As a composer, my current compositions move across avant-garde classical and underground popular music drawing upon forms, instruments, and techniques from electronica, folk, post-minimalism and rock. This work frequently combines notated and non-notated scores in ensemble performances led by myself as composer-performer, and these works often involve cross-disciplinary activities with literature, video, video games, and visual art. Recent installations and performances of my music include *Okamajigerí* (2015), *I.S. Complex* (2015), *DDÁDADORHELYO* (2016), and I am currently preparing new works for electronics, guitar, synthesiser, and voice, including a studio recording titled *Here We Are Now* (2018). I have also been able to work with leading avant-garde luminaries including Rhys Chatham, Tony Conrad, and Jennifer Walshe. As well as initiating an interest in contemporary musical composition, I also became very interested in contemporary musicology during my undergraduate studies.

In my present work as an educator and researcher, I locate the synthesis of my interests in contemporary musicology to the study of Rhys Chatham's *A Crimson Grail* (Revised Version) (2009), which I undertook for my undergraduate thesis. The music department was supportive – especially, John O'Flynn and my supervisor Rhona Clarke – and this enabled me to explore a distinct new work for electric guitar orchestra from an important artistic figure in the history of twentieth and twenty-first century music. I found it a formative study on a practical and theoretical level, and was proud when it was adjudged to be the best undergraduate musicology dissertation in Ireland that year (2010) by the Council of Heads of Music in Higher Education. This writing led directly to the research I undertook for my doctoral thesis: 'Distillation and Synthesis: Aesthetics and Practice in Rhys Chatham's Music for Electric Guitar' for which I received a PhD in Music from Goldsmiths, University of London in 2017. This reading was situated within major music traditions of the later twentieth century and at the forefront of a nexus of postmodern radical pluralism, operating across the borderline of the avant-garde and the popular. I used a range of research methods: aesthetics, cultural theory, interviews, musical analysis, music theory, and my own experience of performing several of the works.

Indeed, my undergraduate studies at St Patrick's College led to my development as a performer and educator. I furthered my performance practice with studies of guitar (classical and electric) to deepen my understanding of the instrument and extended my repertoire beyond popular music to encompass jazz (Thelonious Monk) and Western art music (Bach and Brouwer). As well as being involved in ensemble and solo performances, I was a member of the college choir too, which included concerts at the Cork International Choral Festival and the Hungarian Embassy, Dublin. The pedagogical approach evident on the music curriculum at St Patrick's College aligned with my own desire to teach music and allowed me to do so. I was also awarded a scholarship to the Kodály Summer School held by St Patrick's College in 2009, which included tuition in solfège, choral conducting, music teaching methods, and choir. Subsequently, I have taught music in a professional capacity for several years, both privately and at institutions in Ireland – musicianship, musical analysis, music theory, performance, popular music, sight-singing and ear-training – including providing lectures, seminars, and tutorials to students at The British and Irish Modern Music Institute Dublin BIMM, (Europe's largest and leading contemporary music college) since 2015. I am also a committee member of the Music Generation South Dublin partnership, working with local funding partners, arts advocates, and music educators to provide access to music education for all young people in that area. The pedagogical focus in my studies at St. Patrick's College – particularly, in relation to music education – inspired much of this subsequent work as an educator, and emphasized the benefits of an informed, open, and welcoming learning environment.

In my time at St Patrick's College, there was a focus upon art music – its composition, performance, and musicological study – as well as very useful tuition in ethnomusicology, popular music, traditional Irish music, and instrumental performance. I used the knowledge and skills that I gained to augment my earlier training and develop as a composer-performer, and become an active and engaged educator as well.

Denise Morgan (BA, 2010-2013)

I began my journey as a BA Music and Irish student in St Patrick's College Drumcondra in August 2010. I had always loved music throughout my time as a secondary school student in Loreto Secondary School Balbriggan. I was a member of the senior choir and was music captain throughout my final year there. I was also musical director of the Mornington Gospel Choir at the time. This involved preparing for rehearsals every Wednesday evening and leading the choir at parish masses, local concerts and events. There was simply no denying that music was the definite option for me at third level.

Our first lecture in St Patrick's College took place in B118, the music room, a place I came to love visiting throughout my time in college where we were greeted by music lecturers John O'Flynn and John Buckley. We were told we would have to do an exam and I remember saying to myself 'Mam was right, college is harder, an exam on the first day!' but I wasn't going to tell her that of course! Thankfully, everyone passed the exam and our musical journey in St Patrick's College began.

As the weeks went on in B118, I started to make great friendships with staff and students alike, friendships I just knew would last a lifetime. I joined the choir, led by John O'Flynn and thoroughly enjoyed every minute of it. We were given opportunities to sing at events both inside and outside the college. The music was always challenging with many parts and was different to pieces that I had sung before. The choir was led by a committee and throughout my time in the college I served both as secretary and chairperson of this committee, experience which has been extremely helpful in my teaching career. I took great pleasure in organizing the annual trip to Cork for the choral festival every year, an unforgettable experience for any music student.

The highlight of most college lunchtimes for me was the weekly concert that was held in the music room, B118. John Buckley led a strong committee that left no stone unturned, ensuring that music students and indeed all students and staff of the College were given the opportunity to experience live music as part of their daily life in the College. I was delighted to be given the opportunity to join the Lunchtime Concerts Committee in second year. Participation by the students was always encouraged and I can fondly remember performing 'The Greatest Day' with my fellow students in first year like it was yesterday.

When I look back on my time in St Patrick's College as a music student, I have nothing but fond memories of the place. The support I received from the department staff was incredible and when times got difficult, there was always a listening ear and a friendly face to get you through. They took an interest in our daily lives outside of the College and always encouraged us in all of our endeavours as young adults at the time. I remember when I ran for Education Officer as part of the St Patrick's College Students' Union, the staff were so encouraging and supported me in whatever way they could along the way when I was elected. They were as proud of us on graduation day as our parents were and we were sad to be saying farewell. A problem shared was always a problem halved especially over a cup of tea in the college canteen.

Not every element of the degree was easy and I remember thinking when John O'Flynn mentioned 'Ethnomusicology' for the first time 'I'm in the wrong room here', but as the weeks went by all became clear eventually. Orchestration and composition were never my strong point as music lecturer Rhona Clarke will tell you but I gave it my best shot and having The Fidelio Trio play my composition live as part of the module in B118 was really an unforgettable experience, despite what my composition may have sounded like.

The Fidelio Trio were artists in residence for a period of the time I spent in St Patrick's College. We were honoured as students to experience their wonderful music as part of our lectures, at college performances and at lunchtime concerts. As a student, I was in awe of their musical abilities and their work ethic and I look back now thinking how lucky I was to have been witness to it all as a young music student. Following on from my graduation in 2013, I received a place on the Professional Diploma in Education Course in Trinity College and began the process of making my dream of becoming a music and Irish teacher a reality. I graduated in 2014 and began teaching in a school in Navan where I found myself as head of the music department. I started my own choir and traditional group and encouraged all things musical as part of daily life in the school including lunchtime performances. I always wanted my students to feel the support that I felt from the lecturers as a student of St Patrick's College and I hope that they did.

We entered the Navan Choral Festival and were placed, something which I and my students were very proud of.

I am now back in Dublin, teaching in St Mary's Secondary School Baldoyle and enjoying every minute of it. I am also the transition year coordinator. Reflecting back on my time in St Patrick's College I know that it was there that I learned many of the skills required within the teaching profession. I am also the Irish and Cultural Officer of Meath GAA and as part of my position I host the County Scór Competitions, competitions that promote all that is good about our beautiful language and rich musical culture throughout the country. I also sit on the National Scór Committee in Croke Park, an opportunity presented to me last year by the president of the GAA that I couldn't refuse.

There was something unique about St Patrick's College, Drumcondra as a third level institution. It had a family atmosphere, a sense of belonging where every student from every corner of the world was welcome. It was home while you were enrolled there and I certainly made memories and friendships that I will cherish for a lifetime of years to come.

Figure 11: Main entrance to St Patrick's College. Photograph by Paul Murphy

Afterword: St Patrick's College Music Department and its place in Irish musical life

Niall Doyle

'Nostalgia isn't what it used to be' is a Peter de Vries quotation I've always liked enormously. At this remove, nostalgia is the warm emotion that first rushes in whenever I think of the three highly formative years I spent as a student in St Patrick's College from 1978 to 1981. As I suspect it will for numerous former students, reading many of the chapters in this book has stimulated pleasurable reminiscence of great experiences, people and friendships. It has enhanced my appreciation of my own time there and the many seminal experiences it provided at such an important time in the life of any young person.

This was perhaps predictable. Less predictable was that it has given me a new understanding of the history of the College in general and of the contribution of the music department in particular. Learning so much I did not know about music in St Patrick's College has brought, through different, well-chosen lenses, a new understanding of the energetic musical idealism, activism and leadership there. It is clear that over generations this created the highly positive culture and powerful sense of mission that I experienced in the College and which are to be seen in the many developments since that time.

Using the nostalgic side of the ledger as a starting point, I'd like to briefly add some personal reminiscence of my time there, and of the strong sense of mission about the teaching of music I experienced in the music department - evident through many of the contributions to this book. Following that, I'd like to offer some reflections on the contributions of music in St Patrick's College to the wider professional musical life in Ireland. Finally, as an extension of that, I'd like to offer some reflection (and perhaps provocation) on the recent history of the national music education 'grand project' and on the future of what I might describe as St Patrick's College 'musical mission' now that we are in what might be termed as the post-St Patrick's era, following its absorption into DCU.

Another graduate perspective

I consider myself very lucky to have attended the College when I did. Apart from all the wonderful experiences that going to college, living away from home in the big city and living-in on campus would always have to offer a student, St Patrick's College was small enough and centred enough to provide a particularly strong and supportive sense of community and collegiality. At the same time, it had sufficient scale and student-body energy to foster a wonderfully rich and diverse set of college experiences and opportunities. This was true both in terms of the education provided and a very dynamic extra-curricular student life. I made great friends there, had great conversation and debate on all manner of topics long into many residence common-room nights, and generally had great fun. For a music-mad student the stimulation offered by academic music study, music teaching experience, and more informal performance activity was very positive and formative. The graduate perspectives in Chapter Eleven of this publication tell individual stories evocatively, and mine here is another in similar vein.

While I had had a truly great and inspiring musician-teacher who conducted my school band, I was largely informally trained through playing music in brass bands and an accidental membership of the Irish Youth Orchestra. I was one of those students referred to in Chapter Three for whom St Patrick's College offered a very suitable alternative to university. The BEd in the College offered me an opportunity to pursue teaching as a profession, which I thought I'd like (and did). It also enabled me to study music formally for the first time, without undertaking a music degree, which I assumed would be unattainable for someone with no formal study of the subject in school. Being an academic music student in St Patrick's College Music Department under the avuncular eye of Seán Hayes and his younger colleagues Colum Ó Cléirigh, Seán Mac Liam and Caitlín Uí Éigeartaigh gave me the satisfaction and confidence of feeling I was at last properly learning how music actually worked, and that I was capable of doing so. Singing as a sort of fractured bass-baritone in Seán Mac Liam's madrigal group/chamber choir, and later establishing and conducting my own church choir were great developmental opportunities, as were performing in and attending student recitals, and hearing occasional professional performances in College (I still have a surprisingly vivid pictorial and aural memory of the Vienna Haydn Piano Trio concert in 1978 referred to Chapter Two).

Having access to Dublin's musical life just down the road from the College was simply fantastic. Attending regular free RTÉ Symphony Orchestra concerts in the St Francis Xavier Hall on Upper Sherrard Street, hearing John Beckett's series of Bach cantata, playing with friends from the Irish Youth Orchestra in Concord Brass Band and the Dublin Training Orchestra, and starting our own brass quintet were all exciting and immersive opportunities. When I began to get paid gigs as a freelance tuba player with the RTÉ orchestras while still in college (I didn't have a lot of competition!), I really felt I was getting somewhere as a 'proper' musician, and that perhaps it was a possible profession. In parallel with academic study, concert-going and performing activity, a hugely formative experience was encountering lecturers in St Patrick's

College who had a genuine, passionate idealism for the importance of teaching in general, and the teaching of music in particular. They were infectiously inspiring people with a real sense of mission and the possibility of transforming Irish life through teaching. There is no doubt that many of us as students were equally inspired.

An utterly revelatory experience I remember vividly was one in which a young teacher from a school in Ballymun brought a full fourth class of boys to the music department recital room and taught a demonstration lesson based on the Kodály approach (as Miriam O'Sullivan also recalls in Chapter Eleven). All the children were asked to compose and write down a short melody in basic staff notation, bring it to someone in the audience, show it to them and sing it for them. When a ten-year-old came to me and did just that (completely naturally and flawlessly) I was just blown away, as I was in general by seeing such great, high quality class teaching. Seeing living proof that deep musical understanding, facility and literacy are perfectly possible to achieve in the 'normal' school population was absolutely inspiring. Being equipped to do the same in our own teaching careers was something many of us in St Patrick's College Music Department were able to test in practice in the classroom too. To me, all of this made the idealism of creating a musically literate and creative population through primary education not just abstract wishful thinking, but a completely feasible proposition.

I had the great pleasure getting to know that inspiring young teacher (John Buckley) in many path-crossings later in musical life. Reflecting on all of this in writing this piece, there is something particularly appropriate about John's 're-arrival' as a leading figure in the music department of St Patrick's College in 2001. It is very clear from many of the chapters in this book that the culture of energetic and practical idealism I experienced lived on very strongly right up to the present, and John Buckley's re-emergence in the middle of that stream at that point seemed particularly positive and appropriate.

Reading of the development, leadership and activism of the music department in the preceding book chapters it is clear that under successive leadership it always had that powerful sense of belief and mission at its core: that it could inspire, form and equip teachers to create a universally musical population through our schools, where acquiring a full musical understanding and experience would not just be a matter of chance or family background. I was aware of and strongly influenced by this in my own time at the College. It has been fascinating to read of its origins, strength and clear continuity through several generations before and since. This sense of transformative mission is at the heart of all great education and educators and it seems clear from the insights provided in the different chapters in this book that it has been a constant cultural core of St Patrick's Music Department - something I will return to below.

St Patrick's College and professional music life

A strong thread that emerges from the different chapters in this book is that the College, at various times and in different ways throughout its history, both reflected and contributed to wider professional music-making and the development of musical life in Ireland. John Buckley's comprehensive chapter on music performance at the College illustrates one strong strand of this. Since the 1960s St Patrick's College has had an impressive history as a venue for external professional performing groups. Its most dramatic peak was during the 1960s and early 1970s when it was an important venue for the RTÉSO. Those concerts were high points of engagement of national-level music making with the student body, and began an important drawing-in of audiences from outside the College's high institutional walls. This engagement was sustained in later years through a wide range of amateur music and musical theatre groups using the fine auditorium at the College as a performing space.

Chamber music in the College has had a constant presence since that time, and the catalogue of solo musicians and chamber groups who performed there as detailed in Chapter Two is a long and impressive one. This produced a sustained strand of some very high-quality performances for students at the College. The combination of these concerts with regular recitals by students was an important formative influence, integrating student activity with the professional, and creating a sense of the student-musician community as an aspect of the wider professional music scene in Ireland.

The formative value of undertaking amateur performance to high standards in a professional music context extended beyond the smaller academic music student community to large-scale choirs and the presentation of musicals – a feature of the College's musical life that has been gratifying to see so well captured in this book. These performances provided highly memorable, enjoyable and developmental experiences for large numbers of students over many years. The deep value of such musical encounters for students' personal and professional lives is perhaps difficult to measure or appreciate fully, but it is illuminating to see a strong sense of that personal impact emerge in the graduate perspectives, as well as having the extent of the activity documented more formally in other chapters. It has been particularly interesting to read about the presence and development of Irish traditional music at the College (less a concern of mine in my own College days) and the manner and extent to which this reflected the movement towards a greater 'mainstreaming' of traditional music in wider Irish musical and cultural life.

It is clear too, and fascinating to read as a developmental overview, that while traditional and popular music activities were always present among the student population (and Irish traditional music was always a valued strand of formal music study), from Marion Doherty's era there was a very clear broadening and deepening of practical engagement by the music department with these genres. It can also be observed that this wider practical engagement with non-classical music was paralleled by changes in the academic music component of the BEd and BA over those years. This was both responsive to and reflective of shifts and developments in public engagement and discourse about music in wider society.

Looking at more recent years, Chapter Ten on the Fidelio Trio residency, as well as references to it elsewhere, can also be read as the emergence of a theory-into-practice initiative by the music department. It seems clear that there was a strong integrative-holistic impulse behind this project, animated by a goal of blending professional music making with active composition, performance study and music education. This residency provided a unique source of deep engagement and enrichment for students and outside communities. In many ways it is a case study which captures much of the music philosophy and spirit of the music department over the many decades of its existence.

A feature to emerge from this book's multiple-lens overview is that over its long history, St Patrick's College in many ways can be seen as a highly active national music environment in microcosm – with every aspect of music, from composition to performance to audience-membership, formal academic study and music teaching (of course) woven strongly through the formal and informal life of the College. John O'Flynn's chapter on engagement and research details many contributions to wider music education organizations and movements by St Patrick's College music staff over many years. These range from the highly influential Kodály Society engagement (evolving from the era of Colum Ó Cléirigh), to more recent engagement with the SMEI, SMI, CHMHE, and governance involvement in a number of influential music organizations such as the MAI, Music Network, IMRO and the CMC.

For most of its institutional life, St Patrick's College, like other colleges of education, has had a singular vocational purpose. Given that, it is an interesting aspect that the formative process in the College was one which also produced significant numbers of people who went on to careers in other professions, including public life, business and the arts. One of the dimensions of this book is that it also illustrates a thread of graduates and staff from St Patrick's College whose major professional lives and contributions have been in music, and it would be an omission not to highlight this here. I am conscious that in illustratively naming individuals I am certainly omitting many more who are also worthy of mention. John Buckley and Rhona Clarke are two notable figures from the College who have made a significant contribution to Irish composition and have professional reputations built on substantial bodies of fine work. A string of professional performers has continuously emerged from St Patrick's College also – well documented throughout Chapter Two. As well as being reminded of luminaries like Kathleen Tynan and Victor Merriman, I was interested to find that singers Gavan Ring and Brian Gilligan are St Patrick's College graduates – all, and many others like them, making their mark and contribution in wider musical life. The recent postgraduate programmes in the music department since the formal association with DCU in 1993 have also seen other significant musical figures such as conductor Colman Pearce and composer Kevin O'Connell undertaking PhD studies there. In the sphere of academic music the contribution of St Patrick's College staff and students to musicology and music education studies of various kinds has also developed over this period.

Musical career inclinations and wanderings have also meant that the occasional St Patrick's College graduate has appeared in other areas of the profession such as music management. I have to offer myself as some chequered evidence on that score, and one of the unexpected pleasures of reading Chapter Five by Teresa O'Donnell was discovering that Fachtna Ó hAnnracháin - a fine man I was fortunate to meet in his later life and one of my predecessors as Director of Music in RTÉ - was also an alumnus of the College. Of the various music professionals of my acquaintance who spent time as students in the College, it seems that we all had something of a musical worldview in common as a result. Our engagement with education and teaching was something that gave us a particular sense of the importance of good music teaching for the development of every individual, and also for the health of music in the country – one where the vast majority of individuals did not and still do not have an opportunity to fully develop that immensely rewarding and fulfilling dimension of themselves. The sense of mission by which I was deeply influenced in my time in the College has been a guiding force of my professional life since and it continues to be transmitted though the work of many other of the College's music graduates working in various areas of musical life.

This strand of contribution to and influence on national music and cultural life is a facet that has been and continues to be of value. The most important contribution of the music department in St Patrick's however has been the extent to which it has shaped and contributed to the development of primary music education, and to the preparation of College graduates to teach music in schools.

Recent and future history: where now for St Patrick's College's primary music mission?

This brings me to some thoughts on the recent past, present and future of that core mission so evident throughout this book. Reading through the different chapters has stimulated interesting reflections and perspectives on that mission. One of the most striking moments was reading the reference in Daithí Ó Corráin's historic overview to a stark official report of Irish primary school music education in 1900 by Peter Goodman that 'only one quarter of the 12,000 teachers were registered as competent to teach the music curriculum music at that time'. Writing almost 120 years ago, Goodman focused on an issue which despite many changes and developments has remained relevant to primary music education development ever since.

The development of primary music education in Ireland since Goodman's time has followed a twin-track approach to which the College has been a major contributor and leader. The first of these has been the development of a curriculum of quality that did justice to the individual student's musical potential and the right to have that potential fulfilled while remaining true to the unique nature of the art form itself. The second is the critical partner of this - developing teacher education to enable the competent implementation of the music curriculum. It has been instructive to discover in a number of the book's chapters a sense of constant drive, effort and work of real and lasting value in both of these areas. In broader educational contexts, there were some major landmarks in this process. These included two major curriculum developments leading to new music syllabuses, in 1971 and in 1999 respectively. Also significant were two major shifts in teacher formation with the introduction of the three-year BEd in 1974 and the four-year BEd in 2012 (these are comprehensively documented in Chapter Three). There is a salutary story arc across these and it is worth exploring here before considering where that driving music-education mission of St Patrick's College might be taken in the future.

The 'new' curriculum of 1971 was still new when I started as a student in St Patrick's College, and for music it really represented a very large leap forward. Influenced by Kodály music education principles, the curriculum was very well developed and designed, and was a strong basis for a transformation of the musical experience of children in Irish schools, of their future musical lives and development, and by extension of the musical life of the country. It was admirably ambitious, idealistic and uncompromising in terms of setting out to deliver a best-practice music education in Irish schools. As with any such curriculum, it required the teacher to have a solid grasp and internalized understanding of the fundamentals of music - a sort of basic music 'system-comprehension'. The introduction of the three-year BEd in

1974 was the primary instrument by which new teachers were to be developed and equipped to teach the new curriculum, (along with in-service development for the existing teaching body). Those musically literate students taking academic music as part of their BEd degree were always likely to be most easily formed into successful teachers of the new music curriculum. These students constituted a small minority however, and the core principle underpinning the primary school system was that the generalist classroom teacher would teach every subject. As a result, much rested on the capacity of curriculum music courses to form confident and competent music teachers among the general student body (along with effective supplementary professional development for the existing teacher body).

Referring to the above, Daithí Ó Corráin's fine opening historic survey contains insightful commentary worth highlighting here again. He illustrates how general progress and the underlying issue of teacher efficacy in teaching music progressed from the introduction of the new curriculum. Given the subject requirements of teachers of the new music curriculum, the 1976 INTO survey's statement that only 50% of teachers were dissatisfied with their ability to teach the new curriculum seems a remarkably low figure at this remove. Other perspectives in subsequent years painted a bleaker picture. The 1985 Arts Council report *Deaf Ears?* by Donald Herron stated bluntly that a majority of Irish children left school 'musically illiterate, with little or no vocal or aural training, and with a repertoire of songs that is usually learned by rote'. Writing a decade later in 1995, in *Irish Musical Studies* 3, Frank Heneghan discussed the persistent issue bedevilling attempts to implement the music curriculum when he wrote that most newly trained teachers were ill-equipped to undertake the imaginative teaching of music 'simply because their own acquired skills are necessarily so rudimentary'. Herron and Heneghan (in particular) were writing at times when it might have been expected that the impact of BEd formation and curriculum in-service supports would have begun to produce a significant impact on children emerging from primary school years. Herron and Heneghan's judgements provided a fairly stark and unfortunately accurate evaluation.

A quarter of a century after the great optimism engendered by that new curriculum and the introduction of the BEd, their transformative promise lay largely unfulfilled. The reasons seemed clear. The curriculum was laudable, but the low provision of in-service support and the limited time available for curriculum music studies in the BEd in St Patrick's College and elsewhere could not bridge the large and disabling gap in music 'system understanding' for the vast majority of serving teachers and new-entrant undergraduates. Without this being addressed, the vast majority of teachers could not become capable and confident in implementing the music curriculum. Almost a century after Peter Goodman's observation of the low level of music teaching competence in Irish national schools, there seemed to be clear evidence that, despite the curriculum advances and higher standards of music education in the system as a whole, this fundamental problem had not changed. Furthermore, the gap had arguably widened between the ambition of the primary music curriculum and the capacity of primary teachers to implement it.

The introduction of the 1999 music curriculum was the next major step in attempting to address this persistent core problem. Undoubtedly the 1999 curriculum introduced progressive developments, most fundamentally in placing the virtuous triangle of composing, performing and listening/responding at its heart - the basis of an integrated experience and understanding of music. It also made strenuous efforts to address the reality of the music skills gap in the teaching profession. My impression at the time was that this was a pragmatic trade-off, an attempt at an 'art-of-the possible' curriculum, one in which the significant objective of enabling delivery of the curriculum by classroom teachers with significant musical skill and knowledge gaps became a substantial shaping influence on the curriculum itself. It is arguable that in some ways, the envisioned music education experience was partly compromised to enable easier, average-classroom-teacher delivery.

Some 1999 curriculum changes were an honest, realistic attempt to bridge the curriculum-teaching skills gap in the interests of broadly delivering on a perhaps less ambitious, but nonetheless substantive and well-grounded curriculum. Music education idealism was still evident, if arguably in more pragmatic form, and in this it still adhered to the principle that 'music is for every child and for every teacher' (as discussed by Yvonne Higgins in Chapter Seven). The question now, some twenty years later, is whether this has succeeded or is succeeding. I am conscious that I am short of hard empirical evidence for the assertion. However, my own impression is that it has not worked and is not working, that what progress has been made is limited relative to the scale of the problem and that a child receiving a solid basic music education in primary school in Ireland is still very much the exception rather than the rule.

More than anything else, this impression is a result of watching my own children, nieces and nephews and children of friends come through primary school post-1999. For most pupils, music education in primary school was not significantly better than my own typically threadbare one in the mid-1960s and early 1970s. It seems that the educational ambition of the 1999 curriculum has also not been met, and that sadly the teaching of music in primary school remains quite variable. It appears to be the case that the most children can hope for is to be fortunate enough to have perhaps one or two teachers in their primary school years who have sufficient competence and confidence to deliver the music curriculum well for those years. A great many children may never have even that. In this context, major changes planned to the BEd in 2012 offered a glimmer of hope. With the addition of an extra year to make it a four-year degree, there was some possibility to increase the quantity and intensity of training in delivery of curriculum music in a way that might have increased the music teaching capacity of BEd graduates.

While I have been somewhat out of touch with these matters myself in recent years, I found it particularly surprising and disappointing to read in Chapter Three that the BEd changes were ones which actually reduced the time given to curriculum music studies – with obvious consequences. This seems like an extraordinary reversal, as was the simultaneous removal of academic study of arts subjects to degree level within the BEd. This meant that the small annual cohort of BEd students, which previously had a high-level academic music training in college and therefore most likely to make an impact on music development in their schools, was also capped off. The disappointment and frustration that this represented for those leading primary school music education in the College is evident. With the recent absorption of St Patrick's College into DCU and the dilution of focus on its core mission it must have represented something of a watershed moment of reversal and uncertainty for those most centrally involved.

All of this is understandable and may seem to be a somewhat downbeat coda for Irish primary music education at the end of the independent era of St Patrick's College. However, there are perhaps also reasons to be more optimistic as we stand at a crossroads, not just for the new context in which responsibility for music education now lies with the DCU Institute of Education, but also for wider Irish primary music education policy. It now seems clear that in relatively recent history, respectively from 1971 and 1999, the two major attempts to realize the reasonable goal of a high-quality basic music education for every primary schoolchild have failed. In both cases the cause has been the same – an inability to equip the general teaching population, either in their BEd studies or through in-service professional development, with a sufficient level of music understanding, skills and confidence to teach the music curriculum well. There has long been a question as to whether it would ever be practically and politically possible, with so many competing and loud-voiced demands, to secure commitments to deliver the higher levels of in-degree and in-service music training and support necessary to succeed where the two major curricular reforms so far have not. The changes to the BEd in 2012 would seem to indicate that at the highest policy-making levels, whether consciously or tacitly, there has been a backing away from further attempts to follow this approach. This represents a significant choice at policy level to withdraw support from raising music teaching abilities in the general teaching profession to the required standard. If this is the case (and given the salutary experience of the two big moves to realize change on this model, it is easy to see how this evolved) then it points to a clear new direction for the next phase: a move toward national delivery of the music curriculum by specialist primary teachers with the necessary skill levels to deliver it. This would be a break with the ideal in previous curricula of 'music being for every child and for every teacher' and its alignment with the central Irish primary education organizing model of all-subjects delivery by the single classroom teacher. It is not that these two things are undesirable or unattainable – they are the ideal. However, Irish primary music education policy, over two major attempts, has now proven incapable, unable or unwilling to invest or prioritize on supporting the delivery of this model.

The diminution of the role of music and music education in the four-year BEd introduced in 2012 creates a major roadblock (if not a cul-de-sac) for the longstanding principle that music is for every teacher which underlay both the 1971 and 1999 curricula. Now may be the time for the national music education mission to change its longstanding direction of travel and advocacy. The advent of the specialist primary music teacher for primary schools may now be the only feasible way to break this vicious circle, that is, the low levels of general musical understanding in the typical BEd intake - reflective of the general population - with the resulting large difficulties in equipping BEd graduates with sufficient understanding and mastery to teach a good music curriculum.

If specialist music teachers could be accommodated within the primary education system, perhaps after another generation the typical BEd entrant intake would have a considerably higher level of music system understanding. This in turn would enable the possibility of a musically competent general teaching population and a return to Kodály-based ideals as a more easily attainable goal. I don't underestimate the enormous challenges facing attempts to have a policy focus, commitment and investment in specialist curriculum music teaching brought about at national level. It may be more productive however to pursue this approach in advocacy for change, than to continue in a vein where two great attempts have not succeeded, and where a diminution of that approach in national policy is already evident if not yet explicitly stated.

Perhaps here is where the St Patrick's College music mission can continue to be a leading force in the DCU era. Over the years, the

College music department has developed a cohort of experienced BEd graduates who are well positioned to be in the vanguard of a specialized primary music-teaching force within the general teaching population. College graduates and music staff continue to be amongst the thought-leaders in Irish music education, and that tradition is part of the valuable DNA it has carried into the DCU faculties of humanities and education. It is now undoubtedly a time for change, contribution and leadership in deciding what direction the future history of Irish primary music education will take. One of the themes evident in many of the chapters in this book is that of a powerful sense of continuity of the mission that drove music in St Patrick's College over generations being absolutely intact through the association with and merging into DCU. Coming at the end of that epoch, this book describes and in many ways also typifies the continuing vigour of that sustained contribution and determined, idealistic spirit very well.

No doubt this sense of mission has many challenges to face in the new situation, but equally it has perhaps a greater range of opportunities and a larger canvas on which to influence and shape policy and practice. I would be hopeful that the sense of dynamic drive and mission for music education in Ireland will run just as powerfully in the DCU faculties of humanities and education as it did consistently in the independent St Patrick's College from the time of Peter Goodman to the very recent past. Based on the evidence of what has gone before and a powerful sense of continuity evident throughout this book, there is every reason to be confident that the future history of primary music education in Ireland (and with it the fundamental health of music in the country) will be continue to be shaped and influenced for good by that enduring spirit.

Appendix A: List of full-time music lecturers in St Patrick's College 1883-2016*

Compiled by John Buckley

Peter Goodman (1883-1892)
Theodore Logier (1884-1944)
Joseph Seymour (1892-1910)
Samuel Myerscough (1910-1913)
Louis O'Brien (1912-1921)
Clyde Twelvetrees (1912-1913)
James McKenna: Vocal Music (1915-1918)
John Redmond (1918-1949) Education:
          (1920-1949) Supervisor of Schools
Seán Hayes (1949-1985)
Colum Ó Cleirigh (1971-1998)
Kathleen Hegarty (1972-1977) Part-time (1977-1985)
Seán Mac Liam (1977-2012)
Marion Doherty (1985-2008)
Patricia Flynn (1998-2016)
Breda O'Shea (1998-1999)
John Buckley (2001-2016)
Mary O'Flynn (2008)
John O'Flynn (2008-2016)
Rhona Clarke (2012-2016) Part-time (1999-2012)

Teaching Fellows
Yvonne Higgins (2000-2001)
Eimear Ní Mhaolmhuaidh (2003)
Marie-Louise Bowe (2014-2015)
Orla Flanagan (2015-2016)

Research Fellows
Ailbhe Kenny (2006-2008)
Thomas Johnston (2013-2016)
Áine Mangaoang (2015-2016)

*Part-time lecturers in either academic music or curriculum music are listed in Chapter Three. See also Chapter Five for references to part-time lecturers in traditional music.

Appendix B: Programmes of Lunchtime Concerts Given by Guest Performers November 2003 - March 2016

Compiled by John Buckley

2003

19 November 2003	Fergal Warren (piano)
Debussy	*Estampes*
Barber	*Piano Sonata*
3 December 2003	John Feeley (guitar)
Albeniz	*Suite Espanola*
John Feeley	*Arrangements of Irish Melodies*
John Buckley	*Guitar Sonata No. 1* (3rd Movement)

2004

11 February 2004	Aran Mac Giolla Bhríde (pipes), Simon Mac Giolla Bhríde (flute), Ciara Nic Ghiolla Bhríde (fiddle), Roisín Chambers (fiddle and songs) *Programme of Irish Traditional music*
18 February 2004	Geraldine Meade (soprano), Fergal Warren (piano)
Scarlatti	*O Cessate di Piagarmi*
Thomas Ford	*Fair, Sweet, Cruel*
Handel	*O Sleep, Why Dost Thou Leave Me*
Purcell	*Hark! The Echoing Air*
Fauré	*Les Berceaux*
Schubert	*Die Forelle*
Montsalvatge	*Canción de Cuna Para Dormir a un Negrito*
Strauss	*Mein Herr Marquis (Laughing Song)*
Havelock Nelson	*The Black Cat*
Flanders and Swann	*A Word on my Ear*
25 February 2004	Currafin String Quartet
Beethoven	*String Quartet, Op. 18, No. 5*
21 April 2004	Cliona Warren (bassoon), Vourneen Ryan (flute), Mary McCague (piano)

274   *Appendix B: Programmes of Lunchtime Concerts*

Handel	*Sonata in A minor*
Villa-Lobos	*Bachianas Brasileiras No. 6*
Morricone	*Gabriel's Oboe*
Rimsky-Korsakov	*Flight of the Bumble Bee* (for bassoon and piano)
5 May 2004	Niamh Williams (piano), Séan Williams (violin)
Elgar	*Salut d'Amour, Op. 12*
Nolck	*Hungarian Dance, Op. 196, No. 5*
Shostakovich	*Romance* (from *The Gadfly*)
12 May 2004	Fergal Warren (piano), David Noone (poetry reading)
Ravel	*Ondine*
Schubert	*Sonata in B flat, D960* (Movements I and II)
David Noone	*Poetry reading*
Gershwin	*Three Preludes for Piano*
10 November 2004	Anthony Byrne (piano)
Mozart	*Piano Sonata in C, K330*
Ireland	*The Island Spell*
Granados	*Allegro de Concierto, Op. 46*
17 November 2004	Liam Kennedy (mandolin) - with 2nd year music students *Programme of Irish traditional music*
1 December 2004	Geraldine O'Doherty (harp)
Croft	*Sarabande and Ground*
Spohr	*Fantasie in C minor*
Britten	*Interlude* (from *'A Ceremony of Carols'* Op. 28)
John Buckley	*Two Lullabies for Deirdre*

2005

2 February 2005	Martin O'Leary (piano)
Janáček	*In The Mists*
Martin O'Leary	*Geantraí*
9 February 2005	Antonin Prihod (violin and viola), Petra Lexova (violin), Marion Doherty (piano)

Appendix B: Programmes of Lunchtime Concerts 275

Corelli	*Sonata da Camera in C major*
Bach	*Double Concerto in D minor* (2nd movement)
Dvořák	*Humoreske in G*
de Falla	*Two Spanish Folksongs: Nana & Canción*
Glinka	*Elegy: Do Not Tempt Me*
Khachaturian	*Sabre Dance*
6 April 2005	Alec O'Leary (guitar), Michael O'Toole (guitar)
Granados	*Spanish Dance No. 5, Spanish Dance No. 2*
Pierre Petite	*Toccata*
Piazzolla	*Tango No. 1, Tango No. 2*
De Falla	*La Vida Breve*
13 April 2005	Edward Holly (piano)
Rachmaninov	*Three Preludes*
Jezek	*Toccata*
Liszt	*St Francis De Paul Walking on the Waters*
20 April 2005	Julie Maisel (flute), Colman Pearce (piano)
Katherine Hoover	*Kokopeli* for solo flute
Charles DeLaney	*'. . . and the strange unknown flowers . . .'* for solo flute
John Rutter	*Suite Antique* for flute and piano
16 November 2005	William Dowdall (flute)
Bach	*Partita in A minor*
Mozart/Mercadente	*Variations on 'La ci Darem'*
Debussy	*Syrinx*
Takemitsu	*Itinerant*
John Buckley	*Two Fantasias for Alto Flute*
7 December 2005	Colm 'Stride' O'Brien (piano) *Ragtime, Stride Piano and Musicals*

2006

25 January 2006	Aoife Nic Athlaoich (cello), Rhodri Clarke (piano)
Beethoven:	*Sieben variationen über das duett 'Bei Männern, welche liebe fühlen' aus der Oper 'Die Zauberflöte'*

Britten	*1st Suite for Solo Cello Op. 72* (3 final movements)
Piazolla	*Le Grand Tango*

1 February 2006	Anthony Byrne (piano)
	Music by Chopin

8 February 2006	Aileen Cahill (piano)
Schumann	*Papillons, Op. 2*
Debussy	*La terrasse des audiences du clair de lune* (*Préludes, Book II*)
	Des pas sur la niege (*Préludes, Book I*)
	Feux d'Artfice (*Préludes, Book II*)
Schumann	*Intermezzo* from '*Faschingschwank aus Wien*'

26 April 2006	Virginia Kerr (soprano), Colman Pearce (piano)
Stanford	*There's a Bower of Roses* (from *The Veiled Prophet*)
arr. Hughes	*I Have a Bonnet*
Lambert	*She is Far From the Land*
arr. Hughes	*The Leprechaun*
Colman Pearce	*Six Yeats Songs* (World Premiere)

15 November 2006	Barbara Murray (piano)
Bernstein	*Touches* (*Chorale, Eight Variations and Coda*)
Haydn	*Sonata in C, Hob. XVI/50*
Gershwin	*Preludes 2 and 3* (from *Three Preludes for Piano*)

6 December 2006	Benjamin Dwyer (guitar)	
De Falla	*Homenaje a Debussy*	
	Miller's Dance	
Villa Lobos	*Prelude No. 1*	
John Buckley	*Guitar Sonata No. 1* (*Movements 2 and 3*)	
Benjamin Dwyer	*Song for Her*	
	Three Études	
	Étude No. 1	*Relentless*
	Étude No. 6	*African Print*
	Étude No. 9	*Why not? Mr. Buckley*

2007

21 January 2007	Aisling Ennis (harp), Aisling Connolly (guest harpist)
Croft	*Sarabande and Ground*
Buckley	*endless the white clouds...*
Traditional arr. Connolly	*Goltraí* (peformed by Aisling Connolly)
Fauré	*Impromptu*
21 February 2007	Kevin Carberry (flute), Marion Doherty (piano)
Fauré	*Morceau de Concours*
C.P.E. Bach	*Solo Sonata in A minor* (1st Movement)
Griffes	*Poem*
John Buckley	*Fantasia No. 1 for Alto Flute*
Briccialdi	*Carnival of Venice*
18 April 2007	The Fidelio Trio
Martin O'Leary	*Bluescape* (World Premiere)
Ravel	*Piano Trio*
25 April 2007	Dublin City String School (director Niamh Kelly)
	Programme of string music for school orchestra
2 May 2007	Jenny Dowdall (cello), David Leigh (piano)
Beethoven	*Sonata in G minor, Op. 5, No. 2*
Piazolla	*Le Grande Tango*
14 November 2007	Vivienne Hassell (soprano), Marion Doherty (piano)
Strauss	*Meinem Kinde, Op. 37, No. 3*
Schubert	*Im Frühling*
Handel	*But Who May Abide* (from *Messiah*)
Duparc	*Au pays où se fait la guerre*
Schumann	*Mondnacht* (from *Liederkreis, Op. 39*)
Puccini	*Quando M'en Vo'* (from *La Bohème*)
28 November 2007	Róisin Ní Bhríain (flute), Debbie Armstrong (piano)
Wagner arr. Liszt	*Liebestod* (from *Tristan and Isolde*)
Brahms arr. Roderick Seed	*Sonata in E flat* for flute and piano

Karg-Elert	*Sonata Appassionata in F sharp minor, Op. 140* for solo flute

2008

23 January 2008	Gavan Ring (baritone), Marion Doherty (piano)
Mozart	*Hai! Già Vinta la Causa!* (from *Le Nozze di Figaro*)
Duparc	*L'invitation au voyage*
Schubert	*Erlkönig*
Vaughan Williams	*Silent Noon*
Mendelssohn	*It is Enough!* (from *Elijah*)
Lerner & Lowe	*If Ever I Would Leave You* (from *Camelot*)
Thomas Moore	*Believe Me, If All Those Endearing Young Charms*
Gounod	*Avant de quitter ces lieux* (from *Faust*)
9 April 2008	Martin Johnson (cello), Colman Pearce (piano)
Haydn	*Divertimento in D* (transcribed by Piatigorsky)
Schumann	*Three Fantasy Pieces, Op. 73*
Fauré	*Après un rêve, Op. 7*
Rachmaninov	*Andante* (from *Cello Sonata, Op. 19*)
Popper	*Hungarian Rhapsody, Op. 68*
16 April 2008	Colm 'Stride' O' Brien (piano) *Ragtime and Stride Piano Extravaganza* Scott Joplin, Gershwin, Fats Waller
12 November 2008	William Dowdall (flutes)
John Buckley	*Two Fantasias for Alto Flute*
Rhona Clarke	*Four Songs*
John Buckley	*Winter Echoes* *Sea Echoes*
CPE Bach	*Solo Sonata in A minor*
26 November 2008	Anna Fliegerová (violin), Marion Doherty (piano)
Leclair	*Sonata in G major for two violins* (with Michael Romanovský)
von Biber	*Ciacona*
John Buckley	*A Few Notes for Jim*
Martinů	*Arabesques*

2009

11 February 2009	David MacKenzie (violin), Josh Johnson (piano), Andrew Csibi (double bass) *Cool Jazz & Hot Rhythms*
22 April 2009	Colma Brioscu (piano)
Esposito	*My Irish Sketch Book Op. 71.*
Debussy	*Reflets dans l'eau*
Liszt	*Consolation No. 3 in D flat*
Esposito	*Impromptu in A flat, Op. 62*
21 October 2009	Willicher Emmaus Kantorei, (conductor: Klaus - Peter Pfeifer)
Pachelbel	*Singet dem Herrn*
Hammerschmidt	*Schaffe in Mir Gott, ein Reines Herz (Psalm 51)*
Haydn	*Aus dem Dankliede zu Gott*
Bob Chilcott	*So liebt Gott die Welt*
Elgar	*Ave Verum Corpus*
Bruckner	*Locus Iste*
Marco Frisina	*Alto e Glorioso Dio*
Purcell	*To the Hills and the Vales*
Dowland	*Come Again*
Friedrich Silcher	*Ich Weiß Nicht, Was Soll es Bedeuten*
Iván Eröd	*Viva la Musica*
Arr. Stanford	*Quick! We Have but a Second*
11 November 2009	John Feeley (guitar)
J. S. Bach (arr. Feeley)	*Prelude & Gigue* (from *Cello Suite No. 1 in D*)
John Buckley	*Lullaby No. 1 for Deirdre*
Albéniz (arr. Feeley)	*Rumores de la Caleta*
Albéniz (arr. Feeley)	*Suite Espanola*
Trad. (arr. Feeley)	*Bí a Íosa im Chroíse* (*Christ be in my Heart*)
Carolan (arr. Feeley)	*Mrs Bermingham's Air & Jig*
Carolan (arr. Feeley)	*Planxty*
25 November 2009	Róisín Ní Bhríain (flute), Rhoda Dullea (piano)
Schumann	*Three Romances for Flute and Piano Op. 94*
John Buckley	*Three Pieces for Solo Flute*
Poulenc	*Sonata for Flute and Piano*

2010

3 February 2010	Clíodhna Ní Aodáin (cello), Marion Doherty (piano and harpsichord)
Vivaldi	Sonata No. 6 in B flat major
Rameau	Premier Livre de Pièce de Clavecin Prelude –Sarabande I and II - Menuet
Debussy	Romance
Fauré	Après un rêve
John Buckley	Dialogue for solo cello (World Premiere)
Saint-Saëns	The Swan (from Carnival of the Animals)
10 February 2010	Julie Feeney (composer – performer), Cormac de Barra (harp)
Julie Feeney	Programme of original material
21 April 2010	Anthony Byrne (piano)
Chopin	Polonaise in A, Op. 40, No. 1
Chopin	Scherzo No. 3 in C sharp minor, Op. 39
Chopin	2 Waltzes, Op. 64
Chopin	3 Waltzes, Op. 70
Chopin	Polonaise in A flat, Op. 53
28 April 2010	Imelda Drumm (mezzo-soprano), St Patrick's College Choir, (conductor - John O'Flynn), Colman Pearce (piano)
Schumann	Frauenliebe und Leben
Gounod	Que fais-tu, blanche tourterelle (from Romeo and Juliet)
John Buckley	Haiku Seasons
Rutter	A Prayer of St Patrick
Kern	All the Things You Are
Di Marco	Up the Ladder to the Roof
13 October 2010	Duluth Vocal Jazz Ensemble, (conductor: Tina Thielen-Gaffey)
Michael Jackson	Medley Tribute
A musical history tour	Voca People Medley
arr. Marsh	Uninvited
arr. Marsh	Sing a Song of Songs
arr. Ray	Star Spangled Banner
arr. Makarof	Butterfly

Sting, arr. Idea of North — *Straight to my Heart*
Lennon and McCartney, arr. Fox — *In My Life*
Gershwin, arr. Fawcett — *Summertime*

10 November 2010	Cormac Ó hÁodáin (horn), Kathrine Barnecutt (viola), Marion Doherty (piano)
John Buckley	*Sirato* for solo viola
John Buckley	*Sonata for Solo Horn*
Linda Buckley	*Do You Remember the Planets?* for viola and tape
Aloys Fleischmann	*Cornucopia* for horn and piano
24 November 2010	William Dowdall (flutes)
John Buckley	*Constellations* for multiple flutes (bass flute, alto flute, C flute, piccolo and 13 pre-recorded flutes)
Rhona Clarke	*Elegy* for alto flute solo
Stephen Matthews	*Te Ao Marāma* (alto flute, C flute, electronics)
Benjamin Dwyer	*Crow* for amplified sliding flute and tape

2011

23 February 2011	Elina Hakanen (violin), Aileen Cahill (piano)
Franck	*Violin Sonata* (1st Movement)
Schnittke	*Violin Sonata No. 1*
Gluck	*Mélodie*
2 November 2011	Thomas Johnston (uilleann pipes, low whistle), Lindsay Moynagh (Irish harp)
	Programme of Irish traditional music
16 November 2011	Pavlos Kannelakis (guitar)
de Falla	*Homenaje a Debussy*
Bach	*Lute Suite No. 1 BWV 996 (Prelude, Presto, and Sarabande)*
Albeniz	*Granada*
Mamangakis	*Suite for Solo Guitar New Excursion (Var. IV and Romance)*
John Buckley	*Guitar Sonata No. 2* (3rd and 4th movements)

30 November 2011	William Dowdall (flute), Andreja Malir (concert harp)
Martin Lodge	*Pan Dreaming* for solo flute (World Premiere)
Brian Boydell	*A Pack of Fancies for a Travelling Harper*
Martin Lodge	*Feadóg mhór oíche spéirghealaí* for solo flute (World Premiere)
John Buckley	*les oiseaux rêvent dans les arbres* for solo flute (World Premiere)
arr. John Buckley	*Irish Melodies* for flute and harp - *Eleanor Plunkett, Two Jigs*

2012

8 February 2012	Martin Johnson (cello), Colman Pearce (piano)
Dvořák (arr. Furse)	*Gypsy Songs, Op. 55, No. 1 - 2*
Delius	*Sonata for Cello and Piano*
Dvořák (arr. Furse)	*Gypsy Songs, Op. 55, No. 3 - 5*
Bruch	*Kol Nidrei, Op. 47*
Dvořák (arr. Furse)	*Gypsy Songs, Op. 55, No. 6 - 7*

15 February 2012	Anthony Byrne (piano)
Debussy	*Reflets dans l'eau*
John Buckley	*And Wake the Purple Year*
Debussy	*Children's Corner*
Lecuona	*Malaguena*
Gottschalk	*Souvenirs d'Andalouise*

14 March 2012	Apáczai Csere János Choir, Hungary, (conductor: Tamás Váray)
Gregorian	*Sanctus, Sanctus*
Kodály	*Stabat Mater*
Handel	*Győzelmet vettél* (Victory Chorus from *Judas Maccabaeus*)
Kodály	*Ének Szent István királyhoz* (Song of St Stephen the King)
Irish folksong	*Ír népi ének ....Az úton....* (....On the road....)
Erkel Ferenc	*Szózat* (Voive)
Kodály	*Esti Dal* (Evening Song)
Liszt	*O Salutaris Hostia*
Liszt	*Ave Maria*
Sapszon Ferenc	*Hala Dal* (Song of Thanksgiving)
James E. Moore	*An Irish Blessing*
Henry Smith	*Ride the Chariot*

Appendix B: Programmes of Lunchtime Concerts 283

25 April 2012	The Kildare International School of Musical Excellence for Young Musicians (director: Bernadette Hayden) *Programme of chamber, vocal, and junior orchestra music*
17 October 2012	Mary Dullea (piano)
Bach arr. Hess	*Jesu Joy of Man's Desiring*
Schumann	*Arabeske Op. 18*
Cage	*In a Landscape*
Rachmaninoff	*Prelude in G major, Op. 32, No. 5*
	Prelude in G minor, Op. 23, No. 5
Jonathan Nangle	*grow quiet gradually*
Albeniz	*Triana*
7 November 2012	Flute Éire Ensemble (director: Julie Maisel)
Kathy Farmer	*Flourishes*
Christopher Caliendo	*Siempre Domingo*
Bernstein	
arr. Mel Orriss	*Overture to Candide*
Arr. Elliot del Borgo	*Irish Suite* (adapted by Daniel Dunne)
John Buckley	*Fantasia and Variations on Irish Melodies*
21 November 2012	Conor Linehan (piano) *Programme of Jazz improvisations*
12 December 2012	The Fidelio Trio See Appendix E

2013

30 January 2013	Aoife Nic Athlaoich (cello), Martin Joyce (piano)
John Buckley	*Dialogue* for solo cello
Beethoven	*Cello Sonata No. 2, Op. 5, No. 2*
13 February 2013	The Fidelio Trio See Appendix E
10 April 2013	The Fidelio Trio See Appendix E

17 April 2013	William Dowdall (flutes),
	Izumi Kimura (piano)
Houston Dunleavy	*Traces* for solo flute with glissando headjoint
John Buckley	*Piano Prelude No. 1*
	(*The Cloths of Heaven*) for piano
Houston Dunleavy	*Lux Perpetua* for solo bass flute
Rhona Clarke	*Four Songs* for solo flute
Benjamin Dwyer	*Four Japanese Pieces* for flutes and piano
16 October 2013	Robin Michael (cello), Mary Dullea (piano)
	See Appendix E
6 November 2013	Elizabeth Hilliard (soprano),
	David Bremner (piano)
Rhona Clarke	*The End of Day*, five songs for soprano and piano.
Seóirse Bodley	*Rondo for Éamonn*,
	Love-Song
David Bremner	*Knot*
Siobhán Cleary	*Caoineadh Airt Uí Laoghaire*
Peter Moran	*Vowels*
20 November 2013	Fionnuala Moynihan (piano)
Haydn	*Sonata in A major: Hob XVI:5*
Haydn	*Sonata in C major: Hob XVI:3*
Haydn	*Sonata in Ab major: Hob XVI:43*
Chopin	*Étude Op. 25, No.7*
Chopin	*Berceuse Op. 57*
4 December 2013	The Fidelio Trio
	See Appendix E

2014

12 February 2014	Síle Denvir (harp & vocals),
	Thomas Johnston (uilleann pipes & whistles),
	Kieran Munnelly (flute & vocals),
	Eoin Ó Beaglaoich (concertina),
	Programme of Irish traditional music

Appendix B: Programmes of Lunchtime Concerts

19 February 2014	We Cut Corners (Conall Ó Breacháin, John Duignan) with String Quartet
We Cut Corners	*Songs from recent albums*
5 March 2014	The Fidelio Trio
	See Appendix E
7 May 2014	The Fidelio Trio
	See Appendix E
1 October 2014	The Fidelio Trio
	See Appendix E
8 October 2014	Aylish Kerrigan (mezzo-soprano), Diao Ke (tenor), Dearbhla Collins (piano)
Luigi Denza	*Occhi di fata*
arr. John Buckley	*The Bard of Armagh, Kitty of Coleraine* (from *Four Irish Folk Songs*)
Schubert	*Der Wanderer an den Mond*
Schumann	*Mit Myrten und Rosen*
Weill	*Seeräuber Jenny*
Weill	*Das Lied von der Harten Nuss*
Zhang Rui	*Poem for a Dead Lover*
Lu Zaiyi	*Yearning*
15 October 2014	Svetlana Rudenko (piano)
Bach	*Partita No. 1 in B flat Major, BWV 825*
John Buckley	*The Silver Apples of the Moon*
	The Golden Apples of the Sun
Scriabin	*5 Preludes Op. 74*
Rachmaninov	*Preludes Op. 32, No. 8 in A minor, No. 12 in G sharp minor*
19 November 2014	Cora Venus Lunny (violin)
	Selections from Cora's Venus Lunny's programme included music by: Sebastian Adams, Richard Gill, Jennifer Walshe, Andrew Hamilton Daniel Barkley, Kian Geiselbrechtinger
10 December 2014	The Fidelio Trio
	See Appendix E

2015

21 January 2015	The Fidelio Trio See Appendix E

4 February 2015	Muireann Mulrooney (soprano), Dearbhla Collins (piano)
Mozart	*Voi Che Sapete* (from *Le Nozze di Figaro*)
Mozart	*Se il Padre Perdei* (from *Idomeneo*)
Poulenc	*Les gars qui vont à la fête*
Strauss	*Allerseelen*
Barber	*Sure on This Shining Night*
arr. Herbert Hughes	*Marry Me Now* (traditional)
Puccini	*O Mio Babbino Caro* (from *Gianni Schicchi*)
Massenet	*Il est doux, il est bon* (from *Herodiade*)
Bernstein	*I Feel Pretty* (from *West Side Story*)
arr. John Buckley	*Down by the Salley Gardens* (traditional)

18 February 2015	Líadan: Síle Denvir (harp), Deirdre Chawke (piano accordion), Valerie Casey (fiddle), Catherine Clohessy (flute) *A programme of Irish traditional music*

15 April 2015	The Fidelio Trio See Appendix E

14 October 2015	Rhona Clarke (piano)
Chopin	*Nocturne in D flat, Op. 27, No 2*
Chopin	*Nocturne in C minor, Op. 48, No. 1*
Chopin	*Nocturne in E minor, Op. 72, No. 1*
Chopin	*Prelude in D flat, Op. 28, No. 15*
Chopin	*Ballade No. 3 in A flat, Op. 47*

21 October 2015	Conor Linehan (piano)
Linehan	Piano Improvisations

28 October 2015	Imelda Drumm (mezzo-soprano), Dearbhla Collins (piano)
Gluck	*O Del Mio Dolce Ardor*
Brahms	*Die Mainacht*
Brahms	*Von Ewiger Liebe*
Debussy	*Noël des enfants*
Fauré	*Les berceaux*

Elgar	*Where Corals Lie*
Harty	*Sea Wrack*
Kern	*Can't Help Lovin' Dat Man of Mine*
Massenet	*Va laisse couler mes larmes* – (from *Werther*)
Bizet	*Seguidilla* (from *Carmen*)
18 November 2015	Thomas Johnston (uilleann pipes and whistles),
	Niamh Dunne (fiddle and vocals),
	Hajime Takahasi (guitar),
	Sile Denvir (harp and vocals)
	A programme of Irish traditional music

2016

10 February 2016	Sanja Romic (oboe),
	Fionnuala Moynihan (piano)
Vincent Kennedy	*Meditation on the Book of Kells*
John Buckley	*The Silver Apples of the Moon, The Golden Apples of the Sun* for piano
Nimrod Borenstein	*Duo Concertant*
Dejan Despic	*Ethno Sonata*
Mendelssohn	*Song Without Words* (*Andante in E flat major*)
17 February 2016	Martin O'Leary (piano)
Seóirse Bodley	*In Quiet Celebration...*
James Wilson	*5 Preludes, Op. 87*
John Buckley	*3 Lullabies for Deirdre*
Kevin O'Connell	*Berceuse*
John McLachlan	*December (Winter Music)*
Peter Moran	*Transcript 4*
9 March 2016	John O'Flynn (baritone),
	Colman Pearce (piano)
Mozart	*An Chloë*
	Das Lied der Trennung
	Dans un bois solitaire
Berlioz	*Villanelle*
Fauré	*Après un rêve*
	Lydia
Massenet	*Nuit d'Espagne*
Tchaikovsky	*Don Juan's Serenade*

Debussy	*Beau Soir*
	Mandoline
Joan Trimble	*Inis Fál*
	The County Mayo

Appendix C: Participation by choirs of St Patrick's College at the Cork International Choral Festival, 1972-2015

Compiled by John O'Flynn

* denotes set competition piece

Year	Competition	Choir and Conductor	Piece 1	Piece 2/3
1972	Competition for Irish Choirs	Cantóirí Choláiste Phádraig, Colum Ó Cléirigh	'An Cóisire' * arr. R. Ó Frighill	'Orchard' from *Six Chansons* * P. Hindemith 'Ecce Quomodo Moritur Justus' J. Hand
1973	Competition for Irish Choirs	Cantóirí Choláiste Phádraig Colum Ó Cléirigh	'Éirigí Suas' * arr. Pilib Ó Laoghaire	'Come Away Death' * R. Vaughan Williams 'Factus Est Repente' Gregor Aichinger
1974	Competition for Irish Choirs	Cantóirí Choláiste Phádraig Colum Ó Cléirigh	'I Love My Love' * G. Holst	'Ballad of Green Boom' * B. Britten 'Christus Factus Est' F. Anerio
1976	Competition for Irish Choirs	Cantóirí Choláiste Phádraig Colum Ó Cléirigh	'Jesu, Dulcis, Memoria' * T.L da Vittoria	'Yarmouth Fair'* P. Warlock, arr. C. A. Gibbs 'Bí Meidhreach a Bhanba!' arr. P. Ó Ceallaigh
1987	Competition for Youth Choirs of Mixed Voices	Cantóirí Choláiste Phádraig Colum Ó Cléirigh	'Esti Dal' Z. Kodály	'Cór na Síog' arr. É. Ó Gallchobhair

Appendix C: Participation at the Cork International Choral Festival

Year	Competition	Choir	Piece	Composer
1988	International Competition for Youth Choirs	Cantóirí Choláiste Phádraig Colum Ó Cléirigh	'An Raibh Tú ag an gCarraig' arr. T.C. Kelly	'Jubilate Deo' W.A. Mozart
1988	Open National Competition for Mixed Choirs	Cantóirí Choláiste Phádraig Colum Ó Cléirigh	'Túrót Eszik a Cigány' Z. Kodály	'Jesu Dulcis' T.L. de Victoria 'An Cóisire' arr. R. Ó Frighill
1988	National Competition for Chamber Choirs	Cantóirí Choláiste Phádraig Colum Ó Cléirigh	'All Lust und Freud' H.L. Hassler	'Esti Dal' Z. Kodály
1989	Open National Competition for Mixed Voices	Cantóirí Choláiste Phádraig Colum Ó Cléirigh	'Gagliarda' H.L. Hassler	'Exsultate Justi' G.P. da Palestrina 'Cuimhní Cré' C. Ó Cléirigh
1989	National Competition for Youth Choirs (1st Place)	Cantóirí Choláiste Phádraig Colum Ó Cléirigh	'Il Est Bel et Bon' P. Passereau	'The Bluebird' C.V. Stanford
1989	National Competition for Youth Choirs	Cantóirí Choláiste Phádraig Colum Ó Cléirigh	'Hark All Ye Lovely Saints' T. Weelkes	'Ballad of Green Boom' from *Five Flower Songs* B. Britten
1990	Open National Competition for Mixed-Voice Choirs	Cantóirí Choláiste Phádraig Colum Ó Cléirigh	'Gagliarda' H.L. Hassler	'Jubilate Deo' O. di Lassus

Appendix C: Participation at the Cork International Choral Festival

1990	National Competition for Youth Choirs (Mixed-Voice)	Cantóirí Choláiste Phádraig Colum Ó Cléirigh	'Túrót Eszik a Cigány' Z. Kodály	'Ave Vera Virginitas' J. des Prez
1990	National Competition for Youth Choirs (Equal-Voice)	Cantóirí Óga Choláiste Phádraig Colum Ó Cléirigh	'Ave Maria' Z. Kodály	'Cill Chais' arr. A. Fleischmann
1991	National Competition for Youth Choirs (Mixed-Voice)	Cantóirí Choláiste Phádraig Darragh McGonigle	'Jesu, Dulcis Memoria' T.L. de Victoria	'Gagliarda' H.L. Hassler
1991	National Competition for Youth Choirs (Equal-Voice)	Cantóirí Óga Choláiste Phádraig Darragh McGonigle	'Esti Dal' Z. Kodály	'Onomatopée' G. Nuyts
1992	National Competition for Mixed-Voice Choirs	St Patrick's Music Society, Colum Ó Cléirigh	'Il Est Bel et Bon' P. Passereau	'An Raibh Tú ag an gCarraig' arr. T.C. Kelly
1992	National Competition for Equal-Choirs (Confined)	Cantóirí Óga Choláiste Phádraig Colum Ó Cléirigh	'Villő' from *Boborvidéki Bőjti Szokás* Z. Kodály	'Cill Chais' arr. A. Fleischmann

Appendix C: Participation at the Cork International Choral Festival

Year	Competition	Choir	Piece	Additional Piece
2008	National Competition for Youth Choirs	Cantairí Choláiste Phádraig Ruth O'Leary	'Thugamar Féin an Samhradh Linn' R. Clarke	'Tea for Two' V. Youmans, arr. C. Balandras
2008	National Comp. Church Music	Cantairí Choláiste Phádraig Ruth O'Leary	'Gloria' from *Missa de Angelis* Anon.	'Lift Thine Eyes' from *Elijah* F. Mendelssohn
2008	National Competition for Light, Jazz and Popular Music	Cantairí Choláiste Phádraig Ruth O'Leary	'Can't Help Lovin' That Man' J. Kern, arr. N. Hare	'Big Spender' C. Coleman, arr. N. Hare
2009	National Competition for Light, Jazz and Popular Music	St Patrick's Choral Society John O'Flynn	'Shenandoah' arr. L. Spevacek	'Lean on Me' B. Withers, arr. P. Schmutte
2010	National Competition for Light, Jazz and Popular Music	St Patrick's College Choir John O'Flynn	'All the Things You Are' J. Kern, arr. G. Arch	'Up the Ladder to the Roof' F. Wilson & V. DiMirco arr. M. Brymer
2011	National Competition for Light, Jazz and Popular Music	St Patrick's College Choir Rhona Clarke	'You'll Never Walk Alone' R. Rogers & O. Hammerstein	'Money, money, money' B. Anderson & B. Ulvaeus
2012	National Competition for Youth Choirs (1st Place)	St Patrick's College Choir John O'Flynn	'Hark All Ye Lovely Saints' T. Weelkes	'Calmes des Nuits' C. Saint-Saëns

Appendix C: Participation at the Cork International Choral Festival

2012	National Competition for Light, Jazz and Popular Music	St Patrick's College Choir, John O'Flynn	'Moon Glow' W. Hudson, I. Mills & E. Delange, arr. G. Arch	'Libertango' A. Piazzolo, arr. O. Escalada
2012	National Competition for Church Music	St Patrick's College Choir, John O'Flynn	'Dixit Maria' H.L. Hassler	'Pater Noster' A. De Klerk
2013	National Competition for Youth Choirs (2nd Place)	St Patrick's College Choir, John O'Flynn	'Fire, Fire!' T. Morley	'The Bluebird' C.V. Stanford
2014	National Competition for Youth Choirs (2nd Place)	St Patrick's College Choir, John O'Flynn	'If Ye Love Me' D.A. White	*Three Hungarian Folk Songs* M. Seiber
2015	National Competition for Youth Choirs (2nd Place)	St Patrick's College Choir, John O'Flynn	'Sure on This Shining Night' S. Barber	'Tambur' L. Bardos

Appendix D: Music and Music Education Dissertations and Theses, 2000-2016

Compiled by John O'Flynn

2000

Siobhán Keane, 'A "write an opera" project in a school for children with physical and learning disabilities', MEd

Assumpta Kerins, 'Beginning classroom music: an investigation into musical experience and achievement during the first six months of formal schooling', MEd

Caitríona Ní Threasaigh, 'Attitudes of generalist primary school teachers towards music teaching: implications for inservice education', MEd

2002

Deirdre Cullen, 'Enculturation, music education and instrumental learning in the traditional Irish music experience: a case study of one Gaelscoil', MEd

Eimear Ní Mhaolmhuaidh, 'Researching the need for music lesson materials in Gaelscoileanna and their design, trial and assessment', MEd

Una O'Kelly, 'Listening and responding to music in the revised primary music curriculum (1999): a case study in music development', MEd

Anne Purcell, 'Big boys don't sing: a comparative study of the attitudes of 4th and 6th class boys towards singing', MEd

2004

Yvonne Higgins-Murphy, 'The composing process in classroom music: an investigation into its theory and practice', MEd

Daniel Walsh, 'The design and evaluation of prototype software for teaching and learning chord progression in music', MA (research)

2005

Patrice Bowe, 'Performance recital accompanied by the research essay "An analysis of Frank Corcoran's *Trauerfelder* (1995)"', MA

Eileen Brogan, 'The solo piano music of Philip Martin: an assessment of his teaching and concert repertoire', MA

Eimear Carroll, 'The sacred choral commissions of the Cork annual seminar on contemporary choral music - tradition in modernity', MA

Aisling Connolly, 'The contribution of Dr. Joseph Groocock to music education in Ireland (1935-1997)', MA

Orla Coughlan, 'Portfolio of original compositions with analytical commentary', MA

Nicola Corbet, 'Performance recital accompanied by the research essay "The solo harp music of Brian Boydell"', MA

Clara Donohue, 'An analysis of selected solo piano music by contemporary female Irish composers', MA

Noreen Gavin, 'Innovation and influences in the music of Mícheál Ó Súilleabháin', MA

Amanda Geary, 'Computer aided teaching and learning: a study of the use of music technology in melodic composition', MA

Richard Gill, 'The influence of Ligeti's compositional techniques on my compositions', MA

Regina Killoran, 'Performance recital accompanied by the research essay "Jewishness in the cello music of Ernest Bloch and Max Bruch"', MA

Emer Moloney, 'Harmony and dramatic impact in Puccini's operatic style', MA

2006

Loreto Desmond, 'Music leadership: the in-school management of music in primary schools', MEd

Ailbhe Kenny, 'Symbolising sound: an investigation into musical understandings revealed through visual representations of music at primary level', MEd

Helen Lawless, 'Musical perception among five and six year old children', MEd

Lisa Maloney, 'Different genres of music: investigating the responses of children', MEd

Evelyn O'Donoghue, 'Listening and responding to music in middle standards of the primary school: an experiment in resource-based teaching and learning', MEd

Sandie Purcell, 'Portfolio of original compositions with research essay: influences and organising principles in selected chamber music of Dr. Gráinne Mulvey and their influence on my own compositions', MA (research)

Laura Wickham, 'An exploration of child-centred teaching of piano for six/seven year-old children', MEd

2007

Cathal Clinch, 'Stanford's *Magnificat* and *Nunc dimittis in E flat*: a performing edition', MA

Lisa Dowling, 'The Suzuki method: an assessment of its educational and musical vitality', MA

Leslie Eager, 'Ways of engaging young people with contemporary Irish music', MA (research)

Éadaoin Kelly, 'Text setting in the madrigals of John Wilbye', MA

Denise Kerrigan, 'A stylistic chronology of selected sacred works by Thomas Tallis', MA

Maria Kirrane, 'Verismo and motivic development in Puccini's *Tosca*', MA

Laura Meally, 'Portfolio of original compositions with research essay: a technical and aesthetic assessment of Messiaen's *Quatuor pour la fin du temps*', MA

Róisín Nic Athlaoich, 'Bach's Solo Cello Suite No. 1: The Performance and Interpretive Value of Schenkerian Analysis', MA

Kevin O'Connell, 'Portfolio of original compositions with analytical commentary', PhD

Seamus O'Connor, 'Emotion in film-music: the evocation of fear in horror films', MA (research)

Raymond Ryan, 'Liszt's transcriptions of Schubert's songs: a comparative analysis of three selected works', MA

Maria Westvall, 'Webs of musical significance: a study of student-teachers' musical socialisation in Ireland and Sweden', PhD

Niamh Williams, 'John Rutter's *Requiem*: the origins of and influences on his musical style', MA

2008

Eoin Mulvany, 'Portfolio of original compositions with research essay', MA (research)

2009

Colma Brioscú, 'Performance recital accompanied by the research essay 'Irish and Victorian idiom in Michele Esposito's *My Irish sketch book*', MA

Maura Flynn, 'An Analysis of Britten's *Turn of the Screw*', MA

Caitríona Keenan, 'Rachmaninoff's *Morceaux de Fantasie* and the Emergence of a Personal Voice', MA

Vincent Kennedy, 'Portfolio of original compositions with analytical commentary', MA

Anne-Marie O'Regan, 'The songs of children's composer Dorothy Parke 1904-1990', MA

Colman Pearce, 'Portfolio of original compositions with analytical commentary', PhD

Dianne Steen, 'The therapeutic and enhancing effects of music and their application in the classroom', MEd

2011

Clare Donegan, 'Music as a Way of Being: The Role of Music in the Unique Intercultural Context of the European School', MA (research)

Matthew Quinn, 'An investigation of post-primary teachers' experiences of and opinions on performance education within the Senior Cycle of the Music curriculum', MEd

Martina Sexton, 'Exploring the potential benefits of an informal music programme for the development of pupils in the Senior Cycle of a primary school of designated educational disadvantage', MEd

Claire Shortall, 'Singing with my friends: an exploration of the nature of the choral experience for the members of a boys' primary school choir in inner city Dublin', MEd

Maeve Trimble, 'The wider benefits of music education in the primary school', MEd

Sarah Ward, 'Music and free-play: a case study of four and five year old children', MEd

2012

Sinead Gaskin-O'Connell, '"Scherzando": how primary teachers can be supported to engage in composing, particularly in the early years', MEd

Teresa O'Donnell, 'The Music Association of Ireland: A Cultural and Social History', PhD

2013

Emma Grufferty-Slevin, 'Peace Proms: An investigation into the contribution a music education project can make in promoting values of citizenship, peace, tolerance and unity in children', MEd

Yvonne Slevin, 'A music based language skills intervention for children with specific speech and language disorder', MEd

2014

Mairéad Berrill, 'Towards the inclusion of group music-making in Irish second-level classrooms', PhD

2015

John Bonner, 'The Arklow Silver Band: an analytical study of the performance practices and repertoire of a successful brass band on the east coast of Ireland (1968-2015)', MA

Anna Bourke, 'Performance Recital accompanied by the research essay "Russianness in the Solo Piano Works of Sergei Rachmaninov"', MA

Rachael Byrne, 'Musical Shades of Grey: An Exploration of Crossover Between Classical and Popular Music', MA

Joanne Doherty, 'An Analysis of Selected Postminimalist Piano Works in Light of their Minimalist Roots', MA

Amy Fahy, 'Composing in the Community: An Examination of Three Music Commissions with Music Generation', MA

Deirdre O'Hare, 'Performance Recital accompanied by the research essay "Violin techniques and interpretation - Developments from the Baroque era to the 21st century, and their effects on the performer"', MA

Karl Reardon, 'A Neglected Symphonist: Individuality and Eclecticism in Selected Symphonies of C.P.E. Bach', MA

Patrick Reddy, 'Exploring Music and Identity in Grime: Towards an Analytic Model', MA

2016

Michelle Finnerty, 'Interpreting the musical cultures of children in Ireland: an ethnography exploring children's perspectives and voices in middle childhood experiences of music in Cork', PhD*

* Joint registration with UCC

Appendix E: List of Events During The Fidelio Trio Residency and Festivals, 2012-2016

Compiled by John O'Flynn

CONCERTS AND FESTIVALS, September 2012 – July 2015
(*All concerts in St Patrick's College, unless otherwise indicated*)

Year One (2012-2013)

21 September 2012	Culture Night, Room D115, Darragh Morgan (violin), Mary Dullea (piano)
Pärt	*Spiegel im Spiegel*
Enescu	*Andantino Malinconico*
Franck	*Violin Sonata in A*
17 October 2012	Lunchtime Concert, B118 (Music Room), Mary Dullea (piano)
Bach arr. Hess	*Jesu Joy of Man's Desiring*
Schumann	*Arabeske Op. 18*
Cage	*In a Landscape*
Rachmaninoff	*Prelude in G Major Op. 32, No. 5; Prelude in G Minor Op. 23, No. 5*
Jonathan Nangle	*grow quiet gradually*
Albéniz	*Triana*
6 December 2012	B118 at 6.30pm, Darragh Morgan (violin), Mary Dullea (piano)
Cage	*Nocturne for Violin & Piano*
John Buckley	*A Few Notes for Jim* for solo violin
Rhona Clarke	*Tread Softly*
Schumann	*Sonata in A Minor Op. 105* for violin & piano
12 December 2012	Lunchtime Concert, B118, The Fidelio Trio
Stephen Gardner	*The Mayfly*
Schoenberg arr. Eduard Steuermann	*Verklärte Nacht*
11 February 2013	Evening Concert, Auditorium, Robin Michael (cello), Mary Dullea (Piano)

Schubert	*Sonata in A minor* ('Arpeggione')
Debussy	*Cello Sonata*
Brahms	*Cello Sonata No. 2*

13 February 2013	Lunchtime Concert, B118, The Fidelio Trio
Piers Hellawell	*Etruscan Games*
Gabriel Fauré	*Piano Trio in D Minor Op. 120*

6 March 2013	Evening Concert, Mahony Hall The Helix, The Fidelio Trio
Schumann	*Piano Trio No. 3 in G Minor Op. 110*
Fergus Johnston	*Piano Trio* (world premiere, Fidelio Trio commission funded by the Arts Council/An Chomhairle Ealaíon)
Arensky	*Piano Trio No. 1 in D Minor Op. 32*

10 April 2013	Lunchtime Concert, B118, The Fidelio Trio
Linda Buckley	*Galura*
Maurice Ravel	*Piano Trio*

3 July 2013	Evening Concert, Auditorium, The Fidelio Trio
Beethoven	*Piano Trio in E flat Major Op. 1, No. 1*
Ed Bennett	*Slow Down*
Schumann	*Piano Trio No. 1 in D Minor Op. 63*

Year Two (2013-2014)

20 September 2013	Culture Night, B103, The Fidelio Trio
Chick Corea	*Addendu*
John Harbison	*Piano Trio No. 2*
Darius Brubeck	*Tugela Rai*
Micheál Ó Súilleabháin	*Fidelio Unsung*

16 October 2013	Lunchtime Concert, B118, Robin Michael (cello), Mary Dullea (piano)
Janáček	*Podhádka (Fairytale)*
Dvořák	*Silent Waldesruhe (Silent Woods)*
Brahms	*Sonata No. 1 in E minor Op. 38*

1-3 November 2013: 1st Fidelio Trio Winter Chamber Music Festival at Belvedere House

The Fidelio Trio with Robert Plane (clarinet), and Patricia Rozario (soprano)

1 November 2013	Opening Evening Concert: Poulenc Celebration
Poulenc	*Cello Sonata*
Poulenc	*Clarinet Sonata*
Poulenc	*Fiançailles pour rire*
Stravinsky	*The Soldier's Tale*
2 November 2013	Lunchtime Concert
Messiaen	*Quatuor pour la fin du temps* (*Quartet for the End of Time*)
2 November 2013	Early Evening: Schumann and Brahms
Schumann	*Fantasiestücke for clarinet and piano*
Brahms	*Scherzo from FAE Sonata*
Schumann	*Selected songs*
Schumann	*Adagio & Allegro for cello and piano*
Brahms	*Clarinet Trio Op. 114*
3 November 2013	Afternoon Closing Concert
Schubert	*Notturno in E flat major*
Britten	*Third Suite for Solo Cello*
John Buckley	*Piano Trio* (world premiere, Fidelio Trio commission funded by the Arts Council/An Chomhairle Ealaíon)
Shostakovich	*Seven Romances on Verses by Alexander Blok Op. 127*

4 December 2013	Lunchtime Concert, B118, The Fidelio Trio
Raymond Deane	*Marche Oubliée*
Beethoven	*Piano Trio Op. 70 No. 1* ('Ghost')
5 February 2014	Evening Concert, Mahony Hall The Helix, The Fidelio Trio
Mendelssohn	*Piano Trio No. 1 in D minor Op. 49*
Graham Fitkin	*Lens*
Erich Korngold	*Piano Trio Op. 1* (Concert followed by CD launch of *From Vienna, Volume 1* (Naxos))

5 March 2014	Lunchtime Concert, B118, The Fidelio Trio
Donnacha Dennehy	*Bulb*
Schumann	*Piano Trio No. 2 in F major Op. 80*

7 May 2014	Lunchtime Concert, B118, The Fidelio Trio
Agustín Fernandez	*Trio*
Harrison Birtwistle	*Piano Trio*

10 May 2014	3rd Women and Music in Ireland Conference, Lunchtime Concert, B118, The Fidelio Trio
Nicola LeFanu	*Piano Trio*
Rhona Clarke	*Piano Trio No. 2*
Sally Beamish	*The Seafarer* (with John Buckley, narrator)

9 Jul 2014	Evening Concert, Auditorium, The Fidelio Trio
Arturo Fuentes	*MIMIK* (world premiere)
Ronan Guilfoyle	*A Little Blues*
Saint Saëns	*Piano Trio No. 2 in E minor Op. 92*

Year Three (2014–2015)

1 October 2014	Lunchtime Concert, B118, The Fidelio Trio
Mozart	*Piano Trio in B flat major K502*
Michael Nyman	*Time Will Pronounce*

5–7 December 2014: 2nd Fidelio Trio Winter Chamber Music Festival at Belvedere House

The Fidelio Trio with Nicholas Daniel (oboe) and Meghan Cassidy (viola). Premieres of new works by Gerald Barry and Seóirse Bodley

5 December 2014	Opening Concert
Gerald Barry	*Fanfare for solo oboe* (world premiere)
Schubert	*String Trio in B flat major D471*
Mozart	*Oboe Quartet in F major K370*
Barry	*New work for violin and piano* (world premiere)
Mozart	*Piano Quartet No. 1 in G minor K478*

6 December 2014	Lunchtime Concert
Schumann	*Three Duos for Oboe and Piano*, arr. Howard Ferguson
Schumann	*Piano Quartet in E flat major Op. 47*
6 December 2014	Evening Concert
Arvo Pärt	*Fratres* for violin and piano
Sofia Gubaidulina	*Chaconne* for solo piano
Alfred Schnittke	*Stille Musik* for violin and cello
Shostakovich	*Sonata for Cello and Piano in D minor Op. 40*
7 December 2014	Afternoon Closing Concert
Haydn	*Piano Trio in G major Hob.V:25* ('Gypsy')
Seóirse Bodley	*Piano Trio* (world premiere, Fidelio Trio commission funded by the Arts Council/An Chomhairle Ealaíon)
Dvořák	*Piano Trio in E minor Op. 90* ('Dumky')

10 December 2014	Lunchtime Concert, B118, The Fidelio Trio
Mendelssohn	*Variations Concertantes Op. 17* for cello and piano
Suk	*Ballade & Serenade* for cello and piano
John Adams	*Road Movies* for piano and violin
21 January 2015	Lunchtime Concert, B118, The Fidelio Trio
B. Schlepper-Connolly	*Ekstase II* (Irish premiere)
Mark Bowden	*Airs No Oceans Keep* (Irish premiere)
Percy Grainger	*Colonial Song*
25 February 2015	Judith Weir Evening Concert, Auditorium, The Fidelio Trio
Fauré	*Piano Trio Op. 120*
John Buckley	*Piano Trio*
Judith Weir	*Piano Trio Two* (Irish premiere)
Schoenberg (arr. Steuermann)	*Verklärte Nacht*
15 April 2015	Lunchtime Concert, B118, The Fidelio Trio
Dorothy Ker	*Onaia* (world premiere)
Mozart	*Piano Trio in E major K542*

8 July 2015   Evening Concert, Auditorium, The Fidelio Trio
Martin O'Leary   *Bluescape*
Liszt, arr. Saint-Saëns   *Orphée* ('Poeme Symphonique')
Chausson   *Piano Trio in G minor Op. 3*

THE FIDELIO TRIO WINTER CHAMBER MUSIC FESTIVALS, 2015 and 2016

4-6 December 2015: 3rd Fidelio Trio Winter Chamber Music Festival at Belvedere House

The Fidelio Trio with Carol McGonnell (clarinet), William Dowdall (flute), Richard Watkins (French horn)

4 December 2015   Opening Evening Concert
Ravel   *Piano Trio*
Bartok   *Contrasts*
Debussy, arr. Sally Beamish   *La Mer* (Irish premiere)

5 December 2015   Lunchtime Concert
Telemann   *Sonata for Flute and Violin, TWV 40:111*
Handel-Halvorsen   *Passacaglia*
John Buckley   *les oiseaux rêvent dans les arbes* for solo flute
Villa-Lobos   *The Jet Whistle*
Poulenc   *Flute Sonata*

5 December 2015   Evening Concert
Beethoven   *Piano Trio in D major Op. 70 No. 1* ('Ghost')
Beethoven   *Sonata in A major for Cello and Piano Op. 69*
Beethoven   *Trio for Clarinet, Cello and Piano in B flat major Op. 11*

6 December 2015   Afternoon Closing Concert
Dukas   *Villanelle* for French horn and piano
Satie arr. John White   *New Set of Pieces for Piano Trio*
Benjamin Dwyer   *Nocturnal after Benjamin Britten* (Irish premiere)
Brahms   *Horn Trio in E flat major Op. 40.*

2-4 December 2016: 4th Fidelio Trio Winter Chamber Music Festival at Belvedere House

The Fidelio Trio with Matthew Jones (viola), Chi-chi Nwanoku (double bass), Joan Rodgers (soprano)

2 December 2016	Opening Evening Concert: 'Music from the Czech Lands +'
Sam Perkin	*"FREAKSHOW"* (Irish premiere)
Martinů	*Duo for Violin and Cello No. 2*
Janáček	*Violin Sonata*
Smetana	*Piano Trio in G minor Op. 15*
3 December 2016	'Schubertiade' Lunchtime Concert
Schubert	*Arpeggione Sonata for Viola and Piano D821*
Schubert	*Trio in B flat Sonatensatz D28*
3 December 2016	'Schubertiade' Evening Concert
Schubert	*Auf dem Strom D943*
Sebastian Adams	*2013.8*
Schubert	Selected *Lieder*
Schubert	*Trout Quintet D667*
4 December 2016	Afternoon Closing Concert ('A Different Game')
Rhona Clarke	*A Different Game* (world premiere)
Ina Boyle	Selected songs
Ann Cleare	*93 million miles away* (world premiere, GlasDrum commission funded by the Arts Council/An Chomhairle Ealaíon)
Clara Schumann	*Piano Trio in G minor Op. 17*

Appendix E: List of Fidelio Trio Events, 2012-2016

WORKSHOPS, SEMINARS AND COMMUNITY ACTIVITIES, October 2012 – July 2015

Year One (2012-2013)

Saturday 20 October 2012
Seminar on String Teaching and Learning
Seminar leaders Darragh Morgan and Robin Michael, B118 St Patrick's College (in association with DIT Conservatory of Music & Drama): workshop day with a focus on string learning in conservatory and community settings, concluding with a performance of Ravel's *Sonata for Violin and Cello*.

Saturday 8 December 2012
Composition Forum at St Patrick's College, supported by the Contemporary Music Centre: Selected submissions by established and emerging international composers performed by the Fidelio Trio and discussed in open workshop format.

Sunday 9 December 2012
Rehearsal and Performance of John Cage's *MusiCircus*, St Patrick's College: Marking the Cage centenary, a rehearsal and performance involving the Fidelio Trio working alongside amateur and professional musicians and other artists and groups.

Tuesday 11 December 2012:
Annual Carol Service, The Chapel, St Patrick's College: Darragh Morgan (violin) and Mary Dullea (piano) performed "Sé fáth mo bhuadhartha', arr. Havelock Nelson for Darragh Morgan and 'Down by the Salley Gardens', arr. Benjamin Britten, transcribed by D. Morgan.

Thursday 13 December 2012
Secondary School Performances/Workshops by the Fidelio Trio at St Patrick's College.

Friday 14 December 2012
Primary School Performances/Workshops by the Fidelio Trio at St Patrick's College.

Friday 8 March 2013
Intervarsity Composition Forum at St Patrick's College in association with CHMHE (the Council of Heads of Music in Higher Education): Workshop led by the Fidelio Trio focusing on selected submissions to

the Undergraduate Composition Forum, open to all third level undergraduates in Ireland.

Monday 8–Tuesday 9 April 2013
Performances/Workshops at the Ark by the Fidelio Trio in association with the Ark Cultural Centre for Children; on Tuesday evening a short recital for teachers by the trio was preceded by a talk by John O'Flynn on musicians and artists working in schools and in higher education institutions.

Wednesday 10 April 2013
Annual John McGahern Evening hosted by the English Department of St Patrick's College. The Fidelio Trio made a guest performance alongside Claire Keegan, creative writing fellow in the English Department and Nuala Ní Dhomhnaill, writer-in-residence at the College's Roinn na Gaeilge [Irish department].

Monday 1– Friday 5 July 2013
Performances/Workshops during in-service music courses on St Patrick's College Campus: a) Primary teachers attending music in-service courses engaged with the Fidelio Trio in performances directed towards the performing, listening and composing strands of the primary school curriculum; b) Chamber Music at Kodály Summer School, St Patrick's College in association with the Kodály Society of Ireland (KSI). The Fidelio Trio worked closely with faculty and students on the chamber music components of this established music summer school.

Year Two (2013-2014)

Friday 20 September 2013
Chamber Music in Schools Workshop at St Patrick's College: Interactive workshop led by The Fidelio Trio for tutors and other interested professionals, featuring St Ultan's Senior Primary School Orchestra and their teachers.

Tuesday 5 November 2013
Lecture Performance for MA in Music St Patrick's College: Darragh Morgan (violin) and Mary Dullea (piano) performed short excerpts of twentieth-century as part of the 'Music and Modernity' module.

Thursday 5 December 2013
Composition Forum, St Patrick's College: All-day workshop with readings of new works for piano trio from the residency's second international call for scores.

Monday 3 February 2014
Composer Focus – Joe Cutler, St Patrick's College: Joe Cutler, Head of Composition at Birmingham Conservatoire presented a seminar in which he explored pieces he wrote for the Fidelio Trio, with live performances by the trio.

Thursday 6 February 2014
Lecture Performance for MA in Music at St Patrick's College: Exploratory talk and performance of Graham Fitkin's Piano Trio *Lens* with the Fidelio Trio.

Monday 3–Tuesday 4 March 2014
Performances/workshops for Children at The Ark: The Fidelio Trio, St Patrick's College and The Ark: two workshops for children; additional concert for teachers with pre-concert talk by John Buckley on the subject of classical music in the primary school.

Thursday 6 March 2014
Performances/workshops with Secondary School Groups, St Patrick's College Interactive discussion and performances by the Fidelio Trio.

Friday 7 March 2014
Intervarsity Composition Forum at St Patrick's College in association with CHMHE (The Council of Heads of Music in Higher Education): Selected works from a call for scores from undergraduate composers nationwide received in-depth readings by The Fidelio Trio. Featuring the student composers Stephanie Hasler O'Mahony (WIT), Sebastian Adams (RIAM), Chloe PoYee Wong (Maynooth), Elliot Murphy (TCD), Kevin Free (DIT) and Rachael Ann McArney (SPD).

Friday 9 May 2014
Performances/workshops with Primary and Secondary School Groups, St Patrick's College: Interactive discussion and performances by the Fidelio Trio for over 100 students from local schools.

Friday 9 May 2014
Symposium on Engagement between the Higher Education & Arts Sectors, Croke Park Conference Centre: Invited presentation by Darragh Morgan (The Fidelio Trio) and John O'Flynn

(St Patrick's College) 'The Fidelio Trio Residency at the Music Department, St Patrick's College'. The symposium was opened by Jimmy Deenihan TD, Minister for Arts, Heritage and the Gaeltacht. Later that day the Trio performed Robert Schumann's *Piano Trio No. 2 in F* to a representative audience of national arts organisations and higher education stakeholders in Ireland.

Saturday 10 May 2014
3rd Women and Music in Ireland Conference, St Patrick's College. A lunchtime performance by the Fidelio Trio featured female composers.

Monday 7 – Friday 10 July 2014
Chamber Music at Kodály Summer School: St Patrick's College In association with the Kodály Society of Ireland (KSI); workshops with Louth Music Partnership Strings.

Year Three (2014-2015)

Friday 5 – Sunday 7 December 2014
European Chamber Music Teachers Association Autumn Gathering: The first gathering in Ireland of the European Chamber Music Teachers Association (ECMTA) hosted by St Patrick's College Music Department in association with The Fidelio Trio and coinciding with the Trio's second Winter Chamber Music Festival. In addition to concerts, a range of guest speakers - including Raymond Deane, Miriam Roycroft, Ferenc Szucs, John O'Flynn, Christopher Marwood, Sharon Rollston and John O Kane - provided insights into chamber music instruction and activities in Ireland. The meeting also featured the ECMTA Members' Forum, master classes and thematic work groups.

Monday 8 December 2014
Performances/lectures at Mater Dei Institute of Education in association with MDI Music Department.

Tuesday 9 December 2014
Fidelio Trio Primary School Visits/Workshops: The Fidelio Trio presented workshops in primary school classes in North Dublin following liaison between the Trio, local schools and BEd students on school placement.

Tuesday 9 December 2014
Annual Carol Service, The Chapel, St Patrick's College: The Fidelio Trio performed *Piano Trio in D Minor, 2nd Movement* (Gabriel Fauré) and *Wiegenlied* (Johannes Brahms) with St Patrick's Alumni Choir.

Sunday 22 February 2015
International Composition Forum, St Patrick's College: All day workshop with readings of new works for piano trio from an international call for scores, convened by Rhona Clarke. Featuring Composers Anthony Green (US), Peter Moran (IRL) and Daniel Barkley (NIRL).

Wednesday 25 February 2015:
Composer Focus: Judith Weir Master of the Queen's Music
Judith Weir visited St Patrick's College for a performance by The Fidelio Trio of her *Piano Trio Two*; a pre-concert interview between Judith Weir and John Buckley focused on Weir's extensive output as a composer and on her role as Master of the Queen's Music.

Thursday 26 February 2015
Performances/workshops by The Fidelio Trio with Secondary School Groups, St Patrick's College: Interactive discussion and performances for eighty-five students from Larkin Community College, St Aidan's CBS, Dominican College, and Pobalscoil Rosmini.

Saturday 11 April 2015
Intervarsity Composition Forum at St Patrick's College in association with CHMHE (Council of Heads of Music in Higher Education) Selected works from a call for scores from undergraduate composers nationwide received a day long in-depth reading by The Fidelio Trio.

Tuesday 14 April 2015
Fidelio Trio Schools' Performances: 'Music and Myth' at the Ark Cultural Centre for Children, in association with Dublin City Council's MusicTown festival: The Fidelio Trio gave two performances with question and answer sessions for primary school children. The myth-themed programme featured works by Bartók, Ravel and Beethoven.

Wednesday 15 April 2015
Composer Focus: Dorothy Ker, St Patrick's College: Following the world premiere of *Onaia*, New Zealand composer Dorothy Ker unraveled her new work in a discussion and demonstration with The Fidelio Trio.

Monday 6 – Friday 10 July 2015
Chamber Music at Kodály Summer School, St Patrick's College in association with the Kodály Society of Ireland (KSI). Coaching undertaken by the Fidelio Trio prior to the final concert.

Index

References to illustrations are in **bold**.

2RN 1, 27, 136. *See also* Raidió Éireann; RTÉ
98FM 211

'ABC Sharp' 185
academic music 67, 70, 76, 87, 88, 92, 117, 243, 244
accordion 49, 116, 121
'Active Music Making: The Kodály Approach' 153, 166-170
Acton, Charles 114, 161
Adam 28, 137
    'The Comrade's Song of Hope' 28, 137
African drumming 182, 236
Afro-Celt Sound System 119
'Afternoons in the Atrium' 147
Airs & Graces 165
Alive-O 119
All Hallows Campus 5, 123
All Hallows Seminary 139
Amhrán Náisiúnta / 'Amhrán na bhFiann' 137, 139
Amica Voce choir 146
An Chomhairle Ealaíon *see* Arts Council
An Cumann Gaelach 121, 135
An Curaclam Nua (1971) 60, 128
Andor, Éva 167, **168**
An Foras Feasa 191
An Páistín Fionn 137
An Poc ar Buile 113
An Roinn Oideachas *see* Department of Education
An Seomra Chaidrimh 123
An tOireachtas 120, 121
ANAM 2018 123
Annie Get Your Gun 54
Aosdána 94, 98, 190
    Saoí of 98
    Toscaireacht of 190
Apáczai Csere János Choir 53
Áras an Uachtaráin 248
Arensky 230
Ark Cultural Centre for Children, The 223, 236, 246

Armagh Piper's Club 118
Around the Fire 112
Arts Council, The 4, 19, 86, 94, 97, 185, 194, 210, 223, 224, 225, 226, 229, 233, 234, 239, 266
Arts-education interface 223, 224-226
Arts-in-education 185-187, 195
Arts in Education Charter (2013) 224-226
arts programming 4
Association for the Advancement of Music in Education 189
Association of Irish Composers 190
Aspiro choir 197
aural training 16, 19, 69, 80, 128, 129, 136, 154, 160, 173, 255. *See also* listening and responding to music
Aurehl, Bo 163, 165

B118 Music Room 46, 48, 181, 195, 229, 230, 255, 256
BA degree 1, 2, 48, 60, 61, 66, 68, 71, 73-74, 76, 77, 80-81, 86, 88-90, 95, 105, 117-120, 143, 146, 147, 148, 188, 237, 238, 239, 243, 255, 263
Bach, J. S. 41, 66, 88, 145, 254, 260
    Christmas Oratorio 41
BAJH programme 80, 81
Baker, Davina 65, 145, 146
Balfour, Arthur 10
Balladmakers, The 112
Bangor Choral Festival 143
Bantock
    'Swing Low Sweet Chariot' 139
Barnecutt, Kathrine 71
Barnes
    'All Through the Night' 138
Barry, Gerald 98
    Fanfare for solo oboe 98
Base, The 187

Index

Bartók, Béla 50, 95, 153-154, 164, 165
   Out of Doors 162
   Romanian Dances 50
Bates, Enda 96
Beamish, Sally 100
   arrangement of Debussy's *La Mer* for piano trio 100
Bean, Fr Louis 8
Beatles, The 207
Beckett, John 260
BEd degree 2, 20-21, 30, 48, 60-61, 63-73, 76-81, 86-88, 92, 93, 95, 96, 105, 115, 117-119, 140, 143, 146, 147, 157, 162, 171, 182, 186, 188, 193, 201, 233-238, 243, 244, 247, 250, 259, 263, 265, 266, 268-270
Beethoven 31, 34, 36, 42, 66, 230, 239, 248
   Egmont Overture 42
   Piano Concerto No. 3 42
   Piano Concerto No. 4 42
   Romance in G 50
   Symphony No. 1 144
   Symphony No. 2 34
   Symphony No. 3 'Eroica' 36
   Symphony No. 5 42
   Symphony No. 8 31
   Violin Concerto 36
Beirt Eile 113
Belfast Harp Festival (1792) 119
Belvedere House 9, 10, 39, 98, 205, 217, 223, 231, **232**
Bennett, Fr James 15
Beo go Deo 119
Berg
   Violin Concerto 36, 37
Bergin, Grace 167
Berlioz 54, 145
Bernstein
   Chichester Psalms 143
Berrill, Mairéad 71, 187, 193
Best, Paula 162
BIMM *see* British and Irish Modern Music Institute
Black, Mary 119
Blackpool Sentinel, The 211
Bloom, Luka 44, 244
Blunnie, Róisín 167, 170, 172, 200, 238

Board of Commissioners of National Education in Ireland *see* Commissioners for National Education
Board of Public Works 10
Bodley, Lorraine Byrne 71, 192
Bodley, Seóirse 37, 98, 111, 116
   Dancing in Daylight 98
   September Preludes for flute and piano 38
Boland, Majella 81
Bolger, David 55
Bologna declaration (1999) 78
Bombay Bicycle Club 48
   'Shuffle' 48
Bonner, John 237
Born, Georgina 201, 205
Borodin
   Polovtsian Dances 42
Bothy Band 119
Bourke, Anna 145
Boydell, Barra 163, 164
Boyle, Ina 100
Bowden, Mark
   Airs No Oceans Keep 100
Bowe, Marie-Louise 51, 71
Bowie, David 252
Bradby, Barbara 197
Bradshaw, Albert 161, 163, 167, 170
Brahms 28, 35, 50, 230, 239
   Academic Festival Overture 35
   'Cradle Song' 28, 230
   Piano Trio No.3 in C minor 239
   Violin Sonata No. 1 50
Breathnach, An tAthair Pádraig 105, 109, 110
   Ár gCeól Féinig 110
   Ceól ár Sínsear 110, 111
   Fuínn na Smól 109
   Sídh-Cheól 110
   Songs of the Gael 110
   Traditional Irish Airs 110
Breen, Dan 15
'Breffni Parade' 43
Brennan, Helen 235-236
Brennan, Louise 49
Brennan, Mary 247
Brennan, Michelle 49
Bridge, Frank
   'Peter Piper' 28

'Bridge Over Troubled Waters' 48
British and Irish Modern Music
    Institute 255
Britten, Benjamin 143
    Ceremony of Carols 143, 144
Brogan, Eileen 71
Brouwer 254
Browne, John 182
Brunnock, Moylan 54
Buchbinder, Rudolph 39
Buckley, Jeff 252
Buckley, John 55, 70, 71, 76, 78,
    81, 94, 98, **99**, 100, 121,
    122, 142, 145, 146, 157, 161,
    163, 181, 185, 186, 188, 189,
    190, 191, 194, 201, 224, 229,
    230, 236, 239, 245, 249,
    250, 252, 253, 255, 256,
    261, 264
    A Few Notes for Jim 50
    And Wake the Purple Year 100
    Dialogue 100
    Fantasia and Variations for
        flute ensemble 100
    *Les oiseaux rêvent dans les
        arbres* 100
    Piano Trio 98, 99
    Sea Echoes 100
    Taller Than Roman Spears
        253
    Winter Echoes 100
    Words Upon the Window Pane
        189
Buckley, Linda 53
Bunting, Edward 117, 245
Burke, Pat 47
busking *see* street musicians
Butler, Eoin 186
Byrne, Aisling Drury 42, 164
Byrne, Anthony 51
Byrne, Jennifer 73
Byrne, Lynda 42
Byrne, Martin 217
Byrne, Fr Peter 10, 11, 14, 15
Byrne, Rachael 167, 235

Cabaret 113
Cage, John 89, 147, 238
    MusiCircus 147, 238
Cahill, Aileen 51
'caint na ndaoine' 109
Caminiti, Giuseppe

Concerto for Cello 36
Caminiti, Vincenzo 36
Cant, Anne 40, 41
Cantairí Óga Átha Cliath 162
Cantóirí Avondale, 143
Cantóirí Choláiste Phádraig [St
    Patrick's College Singers]
    44, 45, 140-142
Carissimi
    Jephte 46
Carney, Leonora 164
Carolan *see* O'Carolan, Turlough
Carolan, John 15
Carolan, Nicholas 111, 118
Carpendale, Harry 163
Carysfort Training College *see* Our
    Lady of Mercy College,
    Carysfort
Cas Amhrán 116
Cascelli, Antonio 192
Casey, Karen 119
Cassidy, Eva 48
Castiglioni, Niccoló
    Tropi 38
Castleknock College 8
Catholic University of Ireland 22,
    65 *see also* National
    University of Ireland
Cavan Association 43
CCÉ *see* Comhaltas Ceoltóirí
    Éireann
Cecilian movement in Ireland 1,
    131, 132, 149
Céili House 55, 122
Ceiliúradh Choir 172
cello 36, 42, 47, 50, 91, 92, 100,
    165, 224
Celtic Congress 112
Celtic Connections festival 123
Celtic studies 118
Ceol Tíre 115
Ceolta Éireann 114
Ceoltóirí Chualann 113
Chalaftri, Vicky 50
Chanticleer choir 169
Charles University, Prague 50
Chieftains, The 44
CHMHE *see* Council of Heads of
    Music in Higher Education
Chopin 39, 51, 252
    Ballade No. 3 54

choral conducting 71, 128, 142, 144, 161, 162, 169, 183, 254
choral music in Ireland 3, 28, 172
chorale 87-88
Christian Brothers 10
Christmas carols
   'Angels We Have Heard on High' 32-33
   'Oíche Shéimh' 33
   'See Amid the Winter's Snow' 33
Chung, Kyung-Wha 36, **37**
Church of Ireland 10
Church of Ireland College of Education (*formerly* Training College) 9, 22, 148, 153, 166
Clancy, Pádraig 123
Clandillon, Seamas 28
Chatham, Rhys
   A Crimson Grail 254
clarinet 26, 91
Clarke, Rhona 51, 53-54, 70, 76, **79**, 81, 94, 98, 142, 147, 190, 191, 200, 201, 228, 238, 247, 250, 253, 254, 256, 264
   Piano Trio No. 2 98
Cleare, Ann 53
Cleary, Andrea 102, 192, 217
Clinch, Cathal 143
Club Chonradh na Gaeilge 123
Club na Múinteoirí 138
Clyne, Fr Simon (Sam) 21, 159
CMC *see* Contemporary Music Centre, The
Coghill, Rhoda 100
Cohen, Sara 192, 212, 219
CoisCéim Dance Theatre 55, 226
Coláiste Chonnachta 111
Coláiste Móibhí 18
Coleman, Ciara 167, 170
College of Music, Dublin *see* DIT Conservatory of Music and Drama
Collins, Dearbhla 51, 68
Comhaltas Ceoltóirí Éireann 105, 121, 122, 170
Comhaltas Pléaracha 121
ComhaltasLive 55, 122, 123

Commissioners of National Education 7, 9, 12-15, 108, 129
Common Ground 187
composition commissions 18, 35, 41, 86, 94, 96-102
composition studies 3, 4, 60, 73, 75-77, 80, 85-102, 170, 177, 179, 184, 193, 201, 237, 238, 244, 248, 249-256, 263-264
composition workshops 71, 85, 91-92
concertina **48**, 49, 116, 117, 121, 122
Concorde 100
Concorde Brass Band 260
Conrad, Tony 254
Conradh na Gaeilge *see* Gaelic League
Contemporary Music Centre, The 86, 96, 101, 179, 191, 223, 263
continuing professional development (CPD) 167
Conway, Saoirse 123
Coolahan, John 63
Cooling-Nolan, Deirdre 41
Cooper, Cáit Lanigan 159, 162
Cooper, Gemma 121
Cór Cois Laoi 141
Cór Fhéile na Scoileanna Baile Átha Cliath 178, 246
Corcoran, Frank 38, 116
   Chamber Sonata 38
Corcoran, Rachel 239
Cork International Choral Festival 4, 41, 45, 139, 140, 145-147, 157, 163, 165, 171, 174, 178, 254, 255
Cork School of Music 163
Cox, Gareth 178
Council of Heads of Music in Higher Education 91, 92, 179, 190, 191, 223, 238, 254, 263
Cranitch, Matt 105, 118
Creamer, Seán 138, 159, 162, 165, 181
Cregan, Fr Donal 15, 18, 20, 29, 30, 31, 32, 34, 97, 140
Cregan Library 105, 109, 111, 213, 218, 250

Crémer, Seán *see* Creamer, Seán
Croke Park 27
Croke Park Conference Centre 227
Crowley, Deirdre 45
Cuirm Cheoil agus Drámuíocht na Macléinn 27, 138
Cuisle an Cheoil 116
Cullen, Fr Edmund J. 16
Cullen, Cardinal Paul 8, 16, 22, 65
Cuore choir 172
cultural activism 106-109, 112
cultural nationalism 106, 131
Culture Night 213, 229, 230
Culwick Choral Society 41, 172
Culwick, James 41
Cumann Cheol Tíre Éireann 115
Cumann Gaelach *see* An Cumann Gaelach 121
curriculum music 2, 59, 61, 69, 70-71, 76, 79, 81, 85, 87, 92, 115, 187, 196, 226, 233, 244, 245
Curtis, Louise **79**
Curwen method 59, 128, 129, 131
Cutler, Joe 53, 98

DAHG *see* Department of Arts, Heritage and the Gaeltacht
Daly, Síle 91
Dancing in Daylight: Contemporary Piano Trios from Ireland 98
Dandelion Market 210
Daniel, Nicholas 98
Darcy, David 183
Dave Fanning Show 211
Davies, Peter Maxwell
  Eight Songs for a Mad King 38
Davis, Ben 148
DCU *see* Dublin City University
DCU Lumen Chorale 172
DCU Music Society 148
DCU Music Society Choir 148, 172
DCU Orchestra 51
de Baróid, Máire 121
de Bromhead, Jerome
  Hy Brasil 41
de Buitléar, Róisín 102, 217, 218
de Burca, Aingeala 71
De La Salle College 8, 14
de Noraidh, Liam 111

de Regge, Earnán 111
'Cumha Eoghan Ruaidh Uí Néill' 138
Deane, Raymond 53
Debussy 39, 48, 54, 66
  La Mer 100
Decca label 36
Dee, Alan
  Adam and Eve 40
Deegan, Paul 143
Deenihan, Jimmy 224
Delius 165
Delphian label 98
DeNora, Tia 206
Denvir, Síle 53, 55, 120, 121, 218
Department of Arts, Heritage and the Gaeltacht 224, 225, 227
Department of Education and Science *see* Department of Education and Skills
Department of Education and Skills 15, 16, 17, 18, 20, 21, 62, 63, 64, 65, 110, 116, 128, 160, 167, 184, 191, 192, 224, 225, 246
Department of Posts and Telegraphs 27
DES *see* Department of Education and Science/Department of Education and Skills
Desmond, Loretta 71
Devally, Liam 105, 113
  Songs of the Emerald Isle 113
Devane, Andrew 18, 205
Dexter, John 41
'Didn't my Lord Deliver Daniel' 145
'Dindirrindin' 148
DIT Conservatory of Music and Drama 91, 163, 192, 196, 200, 237
Doherty, Marion 46-47, 49-50, 68, 70, 76, 86, 91, 118, 142, 143, **144**, 149, 165, 166, 182, 183, 186, 190, 247, 248, 250, 253, 263
Dolan, Ruth 123
Donatoni, Franco
  Etwas Ruhiger im Ausdruck 38
  Puppenspiel No. 1 37
Donegal Democrat 28

Donizetti,
    'Hark the Solemn Music' 28
Donlon, Eileen 41
Donoghue, Celia 163
Doolan, Grace 123
DOP *see* Dublin Orchestra Players
Douglas, Gordon 71
Dowdall, Jenny 53
Dowdall, William 53, 100
Dowland, John 145
Downes, Niamh 123
Doyle, Niall 4
Doyle, Susan 91
Drumcondra Education Centre 181
Drumcondra Music Education
    Conference, The 196, 200
Drumcondra Teachers' Centre *see*
    Drumcondra Education
    Centre
Drumm, Imelda 52, 65, 68, 146
Drury, Martin 229
DSO *see* Dublin Symphony
    Orchestra
Dublin Castle 224
Dublin City University 1, 2, 7, 21-22, 25, 30, 72, 74, 86, 87, 98, 101, 120, 122, 123, 128, 131, 148, 189, 192, 196, 223, 231, 232, 240, 243, 244, 249, 259, 264, 268, 269, 270
    Institute of Education 5, 171, 268
Dublin Corporation 133, 210
    Public School Competition 133
'Dublin Differently' 209
Dublin Diocesan Commission on
    Liturgical Music 189
Dublin Festival of Twentieth-
    Century Music 36, 190
Dublin Grand Opera Society 112
Dublin Inquirer 211
Dublin Municipal College of Music 68
Dublin Music Map 4, 205, 215, **216**, 217, 219
Dublin Orchestral Players 43
Dublin Philharmonic Orchestra 250
Dublin Symphony Orchestra 42
Dublin Tourism 210
Dublin Training Orchestra 260

Duffy, Áine 123
Duignan, John 51, 250
Dullea, Mary 223, 229, 230, 238
Duluth Vocal Jazz Ensemble 53
Dundalk Institute of Technology 91, 117, 191
Dunne, Frank 41
Dunne, Veronica 32, 163
Duruflé 142, 145
Dvořák
    Cello Concerto 42
Dwyer, Benjamin 51, 53, 100
    Nocture after Benjamin Britten 100
Dyer, Elizabeth 71

ear training *see* aural training
Early Childhood Ireland 185
Eblana Chamber Choir 245
'Ecce Sacerdos Magnus' 25
ECTMA *see* European Chamber
    Music Teachers' Association
ECTS *see* European Credit
    Transfer and
    Accumulations System
Educational Company of Ireland 111
Educational Research Centre 18
EHEA *see* European Higher
    Education Area
Éigse an Cheoil 116
Elliott, David 199
Enchiriadis choir 142, 143
Enchiriadis Treis choir 142, 166
engagement and research 177-202
English school system 11
Ennis, Aisling 51
Enniscorthy Choral Society 172
Enya 210
Erasmus students 49-50, 146, 147
Erdei, Ida 163
Erdei, Péter 156, 157, 171, 174
Escribano, Maria 76
Espeland, Magne 192
ethnography 77, 193, 196, 211, 219
ethnomusicology 60, 65, 73, 74, 76, 80, 119, 153, 160, 254, 256, 264
European Chamber Music
    Teachers' Association 200, 223, 231

European Credit Transfer and
    Accumulation System 78,
    119
European Higher Education Area
    78
Evening Herald 26, 32, 40, 42
extemporization 97

Fáilte Ireland 3, 179, 196, 205,
    208, 209, 210, 215
Fanshawe, David 41
    African Sanctus 41
Farhat, Hormoz 163
Farrell, Eibhlis 250
Farrell, Margaret O'Sullivan 168,
    169
Faulkner, Pádraig 17, 20
Fauré, 46, 54, 143, 230
    Piano Trio in D Minor 230
    Requiem 46, 143
Feeley, John 51
Feeney, Julie 71
Feis Ceoil 113
Ferguson, Christine 174
Ferguson, Evonne 217
Fernandez, Augustin 53
Ferriter, Diarmuid 135
fiddle 117, 118, 121, 122, 123
Fidelio Trio, The 4, 53, 86, 92, 97-
    102, 147, 168, 169, 178, 188,
    191, 199, 200, 217, 223-241,
    232, 233, 256, 262
Finer, Sara 71
Finnegan, Ruth 219
Finnerty, Michelle 187, 193
Finzi, Gerald 201
Fire I' the Flint, The 97
Fitkin, Graham 53
Fitzgerald, Mark 192
Fitzpatrick, John 163
Fox, Charlotte Milligan 111
Flanagan, Orla 71, 144, 167, 171,
    172
Fleadh Cheoil na hÉireann 120,
    122
Fleischmann, Aloys 68, 127, 140,
    141, 157, 159, 161
Fleming, Brian 183
Fleming, Cathal 181
Fliegerová, Anna 50, 51
Flood, Patrick 123
Florestan Trio 98

flute 38, 49, 91, 94, 100, 118, 121,
    181, 245, 246, 252
Flute Éire 100
Flynn, Fr James 15
Flynn, Rev John E. 25
Flynn, Maura 71
Flynn, Patricia 47, 70, 71, 74, 76,
    79, 81, 91, 93, 98, 101, 102,
    120, 182, 183, 185, 188, 189,
    190, 191, 192, 193, 194, 195,
    196, 197, 200, 201, 217,
    228, 231, 239, 249
Fogarty, Willie 122
Folk Music Socity of Ireland 115
Forde manuscripts 115
Fox, Gerard 181
Franck
    Symphony in D minor 43
Freeman's Journal 2, 25, 133
Frith, Simon 206
Froebel College of Education 171
Frobel Department of Primary and
    Early Childhood Education
    226
Fuaim (the Association for the
    Promotion of Primary-Level
    Music Education) 182, 191,
    196
Fuentes, Arturo 98
    MIMIK 98
funded research 194-196

GAA *see* Gaelic Athletic
    Association
Gabór, Lilla 167
Galway, James 246
Gael Linn 112-114, 121
Gaelic Athletic Association 112
Gaelic culture 63
Gaelic League 14, 109, 111, 112
Gaelic Revival 1, 131
Gaelic sports 105
Gaeltachtaí 17, 18
Gaiety Theatre 27, 31, 136
Gaffney, Lauryn 54
    Big Shot 54
Galligan, Geraldine 46
Gardner, Stephen 53
Gaskin-O'Connell, Sinéad 93
Gathering, The 199
Gearty, John 71
Geary, Amanda 96

Gershwin 48
Gibson, John 42
Gilbert and Sullivan 44, 45, 47,
    248
  The Mikado 44
  The Pirates of Penzance 44,
    45, 244
  Trial by Jury 47, 248
Gilgunn, Paul 4, 167, 244, 253-255
  DDÁDADORHELYO 254
  Here We Are Now 254
  I.S. Complex 254
  Okamajigerí 254
Gillen, Gerard 77, 162
Gilligan, Brian 47, 49, 248, 264
GlasDrum 101-102, 179, 192, 205,
    217-220, 231, 232
Glinka 42
Glover, Sarah 129
Goethe Institute Choir 159, 162
Golden Triangle Chorus 162
Goodman, Peter 13, 25, 28, 59, 65,
    105, 107, 109, 128-133, 149,
    177, 265, 267
Gorman, Martina 121
Gounod 26, 28
  Faust 28
  Messe des Orphéonistes 26
Grace, Mary 123
Graceland 207
Graduate Diploma in Education
    70, 71, 192
Graham, Len 162
Grant, Evelyn 71
Grease 54
Gregorian chant 26
Gregory, Lady Augusta 138
  Éirí na Gealaighe [The Rising
    of the Moon] 138
Griffith, Dave 209
Grimson, Brian 40
guitar 41, 47, 49, 50, 51, 93, 250,
    252, 253, 254

Hackett, Marian 186
Hamel, Peter Michael 97
Handel 28, 43, 138
  Concerto in B flat for harp 43
  'Hallelujah Chorus' 28
  Messiah 247
Hanrahan, Kieran 122
Hansard, Glen 210

Hardebeck, Carl 110, 111, 139
  'Och, Och, Éireagh Leigeas Ó'
    139
harmonium 14, 26, 68, 133, **134**
harmony & counterpoint 3, 60,
    65-67, 80-89, 95
harp 43, **48**, 51, 53, 108, 109, 116,
    118, 121, 122, 123, 143, 165,
    207, 218, 238
harpsichord 100, 143, 162, 165,
    249
Hassler, J.
  'Cantate Domino' 138
Hayden, Berna 71
Haydn 31, 39, 45, 55, 143
  Creation 45, 141, 247
  Missa in Tempore Belli 143
  Symphony No. 103 (Drumroll)
    31
Hayes, Michael 16
Hayes, Seán 33, 35, **66**, 67, 70, 86,
    94, 97, 113, 115, 116, 135,
    137-140, 145, 149, 159, 178,
    188, 189, 244, 260
  'Seán Ó Duibhir an Ghleanna'
    138
  'Tórramh an Bharaille' 139
Healy, Darragh 121
Heaney, Joe 119
Heffernan, Honor 163
Hegarty, Kathleen *see* Uí
    Éageartaigh, Caitlín
Hegarty, Patricia 163, 172, 174
Hegarty, Susan 147
Helix, The 49, 98, 146, 148, 223,
    230, 240
Hellawell, Piers 53
Hello, Dolly! 40
Heneghan, Aisling 165
Heneghan, Frank 19, 196, 266
Herron, Anne Marie 234
Herron, Donald 266
Hertfordshire County Youth
    Orchestra 42
Hesmondhalgh, David 206
Heverin, Emma 237
Higgins, Anna-Marie 71
Higgins, Yvonne 71, 93, 143, 163,
    171, 172, 174, 185, 196, 200
Higher Education Authority 78
Hildrick, Maria 216
Hilliard, Elizabeth 52

Index

Hoddinott, Alun 94
Holstead, Rachel
   Ardee Dances 197
Holy Spirit Boys National School 245
Holy Spirit Girls National School 186, 187
Hopefield Secondary School, Antrim 43
Horncastle, F.W. 108
Horton, Julian 192
Horsley, Erika 91
Hot Press 53, 210
Hothouse Flowers 102, 218
Houlahan, Micheál 171
Hugh Lane Gallery 163, 164
Hughes, Anthony 159, 161
Hullah, John 11, 13
humanities 3, 7, 21, 59, 60, 62, 63, 72, 85, 128, 148, 179, 188, 227, 270
Hungarian Embassy 43, 147, 254
Hungarian-Irish Music Festival 146
'Hush my Babe' 145
Hyde, Douglas 14, 106
   'The Necessity for De-Anglicising Ireland' (1892) 106
hymnody 133
Hynes, Ellen 121

IFUT *see* Irish Federation of University Teachers
improvisation 51, 85, 86, 90, 97
IMRO *see* Irish Music Rights Organization
in-service training 3, 16, 21, 93, 128, 130, 136, 179, 180-183, 236
Institute for Research in Irish Historical and Cultural Traditions *see* An Foras Feasa
Intermediate Certificate examination 183
International Celtic Congress 115
International Kodály Society 190
International Society for Music Education 191
INTO *see* Irish National Teachers' Organisation

IRA *see* Irish Republican Army
Ireland Funds 192
Ireland is Singing 112
Irish America Society 112
Irish-Austrian Society 38, 39, 40, 43
Irish Baroque Orchestra 197
Irish Civil War 15
Irish Composers Project 191
Irish dance music 66
Irish Echo 53
Irish Federation of University Teachers 190
Irish Festival Singers 113
Irish Folk Music Society 189
Irish Free State 16, 110, 128
Irish-German Society 112
Irish identity 76, 95, 105
Irish Independent 31, 38, 39, 138
Irish Journal of Education, The 18
Irish Kodály Society 153, 165, 166, 167
Irish language 14, 15, 16, 27, 63-64, 105, 107, 109-112, 114, 120, 121, 134-138, 140, 142, 257
Irish Minstrel, The **108**
Irish Music Education 195
Irish Music Rights Organization 190, 263
Irish Musical Studies 266
Irish National Teachers' Organisation 19, 140, 180, 182, 266
Irish Press 31, 32
Irish Republic 128
Irish Republican Army 15
'Irish Rock 'n' Roll Museum Experience' 209
Irish School Weekly 111
Irish Times, The 117, 211
Irish Tourism *see* Fáilte Ireland
Irish traditional music 1, 2, 16, 46, 49-55, 60, 64, 65, 67, 73, 74, 76, 80, 105-124, 160, 162, 196, 201, 207, 215, 245, 255, 263
   'Farrell O'Gara' 123
   'Janine's Fancy' 123
   'The Frost is All Over' 122
   'The Young Fair Maidens' 122

Irish Traditional Music Archive 118
Irish traditional music society *see* Tradsoc
Irish traditional songs 1, 16, 27, 28, 63, 64, 107, 109, 120
 'Ag an mBoithrín Buí' 137
 'Aillíliú na Gamhna' 109
 'An Abhainn Laoi' 109
 'An Caipillín Bán' 113
 'An Draighneán Donn' 116
 'An Dreoilín' 109, 111
 'An Londubh 'gus an Chéirseach' 137
 'An Maidrín Rua' 111, 137
 'An Poc ar Buile' 116
 'An Raibh Tú ar an gCarraig?' 116
 'An Spailpín Fánach' 109
 'Bíonn Cuimhne Fuar Agam' 137
 'Bó na Leath-Adhairce' 137
 'Cailín na Gruaige Doinne' 137
 'Caoine na hAoine' 116
 'Carraig Donn' 137, 138
 'Cill Chais' 109
 'Cumha Eoghan Ruaidh Uí Néill' 138
 'Dún do Shúile' 114
 'Eamonn an Chnuic' 28, 109
 'Im' Aonar Seal' 116
 'Killarney's Lakes and Dells' 28
 'Mar Mheath Uaim' 111
 'Ó Cé h-é seo?' 137
 'O Donnell Abu' 28
 'Ó Suilleabháin ag Fágáil na Sléibhte' 137
 'Och, Och, Éireagh Leigeas Ó' 139
 'Óró 'sé do Bheatha 'bhaile' 111
 'Peigín Leitir Móir' 116
 'Róisín Dubh' 111
 'Seán Ó Duibhir an Ghleanna' 116, 138
 'Seothín Seothó' 111
 'Slán le Máigh' 28, 109
 'Úna Bhán' 116
 'The Croppy Boy' 113
 'The Language of Éire' 109
 'The West's Awake' 113
 'Thugamar Féin an Samhradh Linn' 113
 'Tórramh an Bharaille' 139
 'Túirne Mháire' 111
Irish Volunteers 14
Irish World Academy of Music and Dance 118, 200
Irish Youth Orchestra 260
Ittzés, Mihály 161, 163
Ives, Charles 95

Jaffrey, Marc 194
Janáček 239
Jári, Ferencs 146, 147, 166
Jári, Melinda 147, 166
Jerome Hynes Young Composers Competition 94
John Barker Totally Irish 211
Johns, Jasper 89
Johnson, Martin 53, 91
Johnston, Fergus 97, 98
 Piano Trio 97
Johnston, Thomas 53, 71, 81, 120, 121, 187, 195, 200, 201
Jones, Jaime 192
Journal of Music, The 211
Joy, Muireann 172
Joyce, P. W. 108
Junior Certificate Music Syllabus 183, 184, 185

Kamenkivo, Valentina 165
Kannelakis, Pavlos 51
Kavanagh, Lillian 163
Keane, Siobhán 93, 170, 196
Kearns, Cian 49
Keegan, Claire 230
Keegan, Niall 118
Kelly, Cyril 33
Kelly, Declan 143
Kelly, Denise 143, 162, 165
Kelly, Éadaoin 71
Kelly, Frank 162
Kennedy, Vincent 191
Kenny, Ailbhe 71, 93, 183, 194, 195, 197
Kenny, Aisling 71, 81
Kenny, Chloe 248
Keogh, Daire 123, 229
Keogh, Doris 181
Ker, Dorothy 53, 99
 Onaia 99
Kerins, Assumpta 71, 196
Kerins, Caoimhe 122

Index 325

Kerins, Cian 248
Kerr, Virginia 51-52
Kerrigan, Aylish 52
Kerrigan, Denise 71
keyboard harmony 68, 80
Kíla 119
King, Clare 50
Kings of Leon 49
   'Use Somebody' 49
King's Place, London 100
King's scholarship 14
Kirk, Barbara 121
Kirrane, Maria 71
Kiss, Katalin 161, 163
Knerova, Dasha 50
Knowing the Score 194, 196, 197
Kocsár, Balázs 163
Kocsár, Ildikó Herboly 161, 163, 167
Kocsár, Miklós 165
Kodály Choral Library 161
Kodály Institute, Kecskemét 153-175
Kodály method 71, 116, 129, 140, 142, 153-175, 245, 261, 265, 269
Kodály Society of Ireland 146, 166, 167, 183, 190, 236, 263
Kodály Summer Schools 43, 146, 157, **164**, 165, 166, 167, 181, 183, 236, 254
Kodály, Zoltán 3, 30, 31, 95, 129, 142, 145, 148, 153-157, 164, 165, 174
   'Ave Maria' 165
   'Cohors Generosa' 148
   Dances of Galanta 31
   'Esti Dal' 165
   Missa Brevis 165
   'Ode to Music' 157
   Sonata for Solo Cello 164
   'Túrót Eszik a Cigány' 165
Kokas, Klára 169
Kortvési, Kata 167, 169
Kovacs, Brigetta 167
Kozlova, Barboro 50
Krucká, Markéta 50, 146
Kulezic-Wilson, Danijela 192

Laetare choir 172
Laighléis, Ciarán 27
Land War 9

Lane, Aideen 40
Larchet, John F. 111
Lawless, Helen 71
Leahy, Niamh 123
Leaving Certificate 17, 18, 183, 184
LeFanu, Nicola 100, 101, 200
   Piano Trio 100
Léhar
   The Merry Widow 44, 45
Lexova, Petra 91
Líadan 53, 119, 121
LibFocus 211
Lillis, David 31
Linehan, Conor 51, 55
listening and responding to music 19, 20, 69, 71, 85, 93, 140, 160, 170, 181, 184, 185, 209, 228, 240, 244, 245, 267
Liszt Academy of Music, Budapest 30, 156
Liszt, Franz 43, 164, 165
Little Museum of Dublin 209
Little Shop of Horrors see Menken, Alan
Lloyd Webber, Andrew 48
Loans for Non-Vested Schools and Training Colleges (Ireland) Act 10
Logier, Theodore 132, 133
London Symphony Orchestra 36
Lott, Pixie 49
Louth Music Partnership Strings 237
Lunny, Cora Venus 51
Lutosławski
   Symphony No. 2 37
Lynch, Charles 162
Lynch, Fionán 15
Lynch, Sheryl 81
Lyric FM 145, 163, 185, 223
   Choirs for Christmas 145

MA degree 3, 74, 75, 76, 94, 95, 179, 192, 193, 229, 237, 244
Mac Cába, Éanna 161
Mac Daid, J.
   'Cailín na Gruaige Doinne' 137
Mac Gearra, Criostóir 138
Mac Liam, Seán 45, 46, 47, 67, 68, 70, 74, **75**, 76, 95, 96, 140, 142, 145, 149, 181, 183, 184,

185, 188, 193, 197, 245, 247, 249, 250, 260
'In Tenebris' 140
'The Self Unseen' 140
The Sources of Continental Music in Britain c.1450 – c.1650 46
macalla/echo **101**, 102, 217
macaronic songs 118, 119
MacGoris (*also* McGoris), Mary 31, 39
MacGrianna, Seosamh 137
An Páistín Fionn 137
MacManus, Francis 27
MacNeill, Eoin 14, 16, 109
Madrigal '75 choir 45
MAI *see* Music Association of Ireland
Major and Minor 185
Maher, Carrie 71, 196
Maher, John 238
Maisel, Julie 53, 100
Malahide Singers and Orchestra 41
Malir, Andreja 144
Malirsh, Victor 34
Mamma Mia! 54
Mangaoang, Áine 192, 200, 201, 205, 213, 214, 217, 231
Mannion, Máire 170
'Mapping Popular Music in Dublin' 3, 196, 200, 205-220
Marenzio, Luca 142
Marín, Oscar 50
Marino Institute (*formerly* College) of Education 70, 118, 147, 171, 226
Marlborough Street Training College 8, 10
Martin, Nicole 123
Mary Immaculate College, Limerick 8, 20, 171, 178, 195, 197, 200, 225, 226
Massenet 54
Massey, Victoria 168, 169
Master of the Queen's Music 98, **99**
Mater Dei Institute of Education 4, 22, 147, 148, 200, 223, 238, 240
Maynooth synod 8, 9
Maynooth University 117, 191, 192

Mayo International Choral Festival 147
McAleese, Mary 248
McAuliffe, Mary Ryng 182
McBride, Seán 209
McCabe, Edward 9, 10
McCague, Donal 121
McCague, Mary 91
McCann, Gabrielle 77
McCarthy, Marie 63, 105, 109, 134, 135, 178, 192, 199
McCarthy, N. St. John 162
McEniry, Caitríona 71
McEvoy, Clare 71, 145, 168, 170, 171
McEvoy, Eleanor 162
McGahern, John 230
McGahon, Colette 168, 169
McGann, Judith 146
McGonigle, Darragh 142, 144
McGowan, Alfred (Alf) 138
McKay, Brian 143, 144, 166, 171
McLaughlin, Lorraine 49
McLoughlin, Irma 217
McManus, Ruth 147
McNally, Aonghus 47
McNally, R. 28
McNamara, Brian 165
McSwiney, Veronica 31, 32
Meade, Geraldine 49
MEd degree 61, 74, 75, 93, 95, 179, 192, 193, 196, 244
MEND *see* Music Education National Debate
Mendelssohn 42, 145
Violin Concerto 42
Menken, Alan
The Little Shop of Horrors 40-41
Merrigan, Joan 165
Merriman, Victor 45, 264
Messiaen
Quatuor pour la fin du temps [Quartet for the end of time] 231
Metal Ireland 211
Métier label 98
Michael, Robin 223
Millar, John 81
Millersville University 171
Milne, John 41
minimalism 94, 253

Molière
Le Medecin malgré lui 137
Molloy, Niamh **48**, 123
Molloy, Richard 238
Monk, Thelonious 253, 254
'Moon River' 145
Moore, Christy 44, 119
   The Box Set 44
   'Nuke Power' 44
Moore, Thomas 108, 119
   'Dear Harp of my Country' 109
   'My Gentle Harp' 109
   'Oft in the Stilly Night' 137
   'Oh, Breathe not his Name' 28
   'Rich and Rare' 109
   'Sweet Inisfallen' 109
   'The Young May Moon' 113
Moran, Peter 170, 195
Morgan, Darragh 223, 227, 229, 230, 238
Morgan, Denise 4, 244, 255-257
Morley, Thomas
   'Now is the month of maying' 138
Morning Airs 113
Mornington Gospel Choir 255
Mornington Singers 165, 172
Morrison, George 111
Moynihan, Fionnuala 51, 68, 201
Mozart 31, 32, 36, 39, 54, 247
   Divertimento No. 17 in D, 32
   Exultate Jubilate 32
   Il Seraglio 31, 40
   'Laudate Dominum' 146, fn65
   Overture to *The Marriage of Figaro* 36
   Piano Concerto No. 20 31, 32
   Requiem in D minor 247
   Violin Concerto No. 5 31
Mullen, Marian 144
Mulligan, Meabh 123
Mulrooney, Muireann 51
Mulvany, Eoin 94, 191
   PX2 94
Municipal School of Music, Cork 161
Municipal School of Music, Dublin 138
Munnelly, Kieran 121
Murphy, Michael 200
Murphy, Paul 44, 47, 141
Murphy, Regina 71, 93, 163, 166, 170, 174, 185, 200
Murphy, Róisín 217
Murray, Barbara 51
music
   Afghan 97
   African 41, 182
   African-American 138
   avant-garde 37, 254
   Baroque 49, 67, 87
   chamber music 4, 49, 86, 94, 229
   choral 1-3, 34, 44, 69, 76, 86, 111, 127-149, 201
   classical 2, 30, 46, 49, 50, 51, 60, 64, 95, 142, 155, 251
   Classical period 67, 87
   contemporary 31, 42, 51, 73, 76, 85-102, 114, 119, 120, 253, 254, 255
   dance 31, 42, 43, 49, 50, 55, 66, 115, 118, 119
   East Asian 181
   electro-acoustic 86, 96
   electronic 92, 95, 207
   European 41, 66
   experimental 86, 89, 94-95
   film 60, 76, 201, 237, 239
   folk 50, 115, 129, 145, 147, 160
   folksong 53, 95
   gospel 145
   Indian classical 97
   instrumental 2, 12, 64, 68, 69, 76, 85, 111, 147, 255
   Irish art music 80
   Irish opera 73, 189
   jazz 2, 51, 53, 73, 121, 163, 201, 207, 254
   mash-up 51
   musicals 2, 44, 49, 145
   nineteenth-century 67, 201, 237
   opera 2, 34, 40, 49, 189, 244, 247
   orchestral 2, 86, 94, 244, 245
   popular 2, 49, 50, 53, 60, 65, 73, 76, 118, 119, 147, 197, 201, 208, 215, 244, 253, 254, 255
   Renaissance period 138, 142
   Romantic period 87
   ragtime 51

328   Index

rock 50, 51, 244
romantic 46
sacred 53, 147
sean nós 49, 114, 118, 119, 120, 248
South Asian 181
traditional *see* Irish traditional music
twentieth-century 49, 67, 169, 201, 237
twenty-first century 254
western art music 60, 64, 80, 107, 253, 254, 255
world 71
music analysis 65, 67, 72-74, 77, 160, 193, 238, 254
Music and Modernity (module) 76, 94, 238
Music and National Identity (module) 76, 95
Music Association of Ireland 36, 179, 190, 193, 263
music criticism 72, 73, 74, 76
music education 4, 59, 60, 73, 74, 110, 148, 177, 179, 195, 196-201, 255, 267-269. *See also* curriculum music, music pedagogy
Music Education Gathering **198**, 199, 200, 231
Music Education National Debate 196, 197, 199
Music Educators' Orchestra 195, 198
Music for the Hour 113
Music Generation 120, 179, 192, 195, 196, 197, 223, 254, 255
music history 65-67, 72, 73, 75, 77, 119, 193, 245, 254
Music Network 190, 192, 263
music pedagogy 61, 62, 131, 153, 155, 158, 160, 165, 167, 173, 193, 227, 247, 248, 253, 255
music technology 60, 71, 73, 76, 80, 95-96, 170, 184, 193
music theory 60, 64, 80, 85, 130, 131, 160, 253
music tourism 207, 211
musical techniques 65, 72-74, 76-77, 80, 86, 88, 253
musicology 4, 60, 75, 76, 77, 80, 119, 120, 138, 177, 179, 201, 229, 237, 239, 244, 248, 250, 253, 254, 256, 264
'My Johnny's a Soldier' 145
Myerscough, Samuel Spencer 132
Myler, Thomas 40

Na Casadaigh 115
Nangle, Jonathan 53
National Board of Education 8-13, 15-16, 107, 128. *See also* Department of Education
National Children's Choir 138
National Concert Hall 33, 49, 94, 163, 164, 181, 245
  'Rising Star' series 94
National Council for Curriculum and Assessment 3, 85, 183, 185
  Primary Curriculum Support 130, 246
National Institutes of Higher Education 21
National Programme Conference 16
National Programme of Primary Instruction (1922) 59
National schools
  curriculum 7, 11, 69, 85, 92, 93, 107, 128, 129, 130, 139, 153, 158, 170, 172-174, 178, 179, 180, 182-186, 201, 228, 235, 247, 265-269
  denominational system 7-8
National Symphony Orchestra *See* RTÉ National Symphony Orchestra
National Teacher (NT) Diploma 3, 62, 66, 69, 86-87, 94, 115, 182
National University of Ireland 2, 20, 30, 65, 66, 67, 72, 74, 94, 115
nationalism 63, 64, 107, 131, 134
Navan Choral Festival 257
NCCA *see* National Council for Curriculum and Assessment
NCH *see* National Concert Hall
NDRC Digital Exchange 213
Nemes, László 167, 170
Neved, Yavor 50
New Dublin Voices 172
Ní Aodáin, Clíodhna 53, 100

Index

Ní Argáin, Aoife 122, 238
Ní Bhaoill, Máire 120
Ní Bhraonáin, Evonne 115
Ní Bhrían, Róisín 53
Ní Cheallaigh, Moya 47
Ní Chiardh, Eithne *see* Vallely, Eithne
Ní Chiosáin, Bairbre 114
Ní Choilm, Máire 120
   Nuair a théid sé fán chroí 120
Ní Chonaráin, Siobhán 170
Ní Chondúin, Mairéad 170
Ní Dhomhnaill, Nuala 230
Ní Mhaicín, Éadaoin **48**, 122, 123
Ní Mhaolmhuaidh, Eimear 71
Ní Mheara, Bebhinn 163
Ní Raghallaigh, Áine 109
Ní Shé, Bríd 61, 64, 70, 171, 172
Ní Shúilleabháin, Niamh 50
Nic Aodha, Orla 102, 192, 217
Nic Athlaoich, Aoife 53
Nic Athlaoich, Róisín 71, 144
Nic Eoin, Máirín 177
Nicolai
   The Merry Wives of Windsor 40
Notes for Teachers 64
NSO *see* RTÉ National Symphony Orchestra
Nugent, Mary 118, 119, 167, 170, 171, 174, 196
NUI *see* National University of Ireland
NUI Maynooth 91
Nyman, Michael 239
   Poczatek 240
   Yellow Beach 240
NYU Steinhardt 170

Ó Beaglaoich, Eoin 121
O'Breacháin, Conall 4, 51, 244, 250-253
O'Briain, Anne 91
Ó Briain, Stan 111
   Amhrán na mBeach Fián 111
   Ceol na Scol 111
   Clasceadal na Scol 111
   Cór na Scol 111
   Déanamís Ceol 111
O'Brien, Aideen 143
O'Brien, Colm 'Stride' 51
O'Brien, Louis 14, 133
O'Brien, Mary Amond 71
O'Brien, Vincent 111, 133
O'Byrne, Dympna 174
O'Carolan, Turlough 115, 116
O'Carroll, John 140
Ó Ceallaigh, Sam 123
Ó Ceallaigh, Tadgh 112
Ó Cléirigh, Colum 44-45, 67, 70-71, 140-142, 145, 149, 156, 157, **158**, 159, 160, 162, 163, 165, 166, 167, 171, 172, 174, 175, 178, 181, 185, 189, 190, 244, 261, 263
O'Connell, Kevin 94, 191, 192, 193, 249, 264
O'Connell, Lorraine 170, 171
O'Connell Music Society 40
O'Connor, Gerry 197
O'Connor, Jennifer Madsen 81, 100, 200
O'Connor, Maura 187
O'Connor, Sinéad 210
O'Doherty, Geraldine 51
Ó Donnchadha, Gary 191
Ó Donnchadha, Tadhg (Tórna) 14, 137
   'Bíonn Cuimhne Fuar Agam' 137
O'Donnell, Mary Louise 118, 119
O'Donnell, Teresa 71, **75**, 119, 193
O'Donovan, Ite 162, 164
O'Driscoll, Peter 161, 186
Ó Dubhghaill, Brian 159, 162
O'Flanagan, Rachel 217
O'Flynn, John 45, 51, 53, 55, 74, 75, 76. 78, 81, 95, 102, 144, 149, 163, 166, 167, **168**, 171, 172, 187, 188, 189, 190, 191, 192, 196, 197, 200, 205, 213, 214, 216, 217, 227, 231, 236, 239, 245, 250, 253, 254, 255, 256
O'Flynn, Liam 189
O'Flynn, Mary 71, 143, 144, 162, 163, 186
Ó Gadhra, Pádraig 139
Ó Gallchobhair, Éamonn 111
O'Gorman, Aisling 236
O'Grady, Geraldine 31, 32
O'Grady, Moya 43, 165
O'Halpin, Barry 200, 235

Ó hAnnracháin, Fachtna 111, 113-114, 264
Ó hAodáin, Cormac 53
Ó hAodha, Seán see Hayes, Seán
O'Hara, Mary 119
Ó hEidhin, Mícheál 116
Ó Laoghaire, An tAthair Peadar 109
   Séadna 109
   Mo Sgéal Féin 109
Ó Laoghaire, Pilib 141
O'Leary, Jane 100
O'Leary, Martin 51, 53
O'Leary, Michael 165
O'Leary, Ruth 142, 144, 248
Ó Lionard, Iarla 119
Ó Loinsigh, Fionán
   An Doctúir Bréige 137
Ó Maonlaí, Liam **101**, 102, 217
Ó Moráin, Donal 114
Örebro University 193
Ó Riada, Seán 111, 113, 119, 141
   Mise Éire 111
   Ó Riada sa Gaiety 113
O'Rourke, Mary 72
O'Rourke, Pádraig 41
Ó Sé, Seán 105, 113
O'Shea, Breda see Ní Shé, Bríd
O'Shea, Caitríona 186
Ó Síocháin, Seán 105, 112
Oslizlok, Danusia 168
Ó Súilleabháin, Eoghan 138
Ó Súilleabháin, Mícheál 118, 161, 199
O'Sullivan, Chris 53
O'Sullivan, Miriam 4, 174, 244-247, 261
O'Sullivan, Paul 123
O'Sullivan, Terry 44
O'Toole, Peter 102, 217
oboe 91, 98
Oifig an tSoláthair 114
Oklahoma! 40
Oravecz, György 43
orchestration 73, 77, 80, 88-9, 237, 238, 253, 256
Our Lady of Mercy College, Carysfort 8, 20, 21
Our Lady of Mercy Training College, Baggot St 9
Oxford University 201

Pad, Zoltán 167
Page, Nick
   Nursery Rhyme Cantata 197
Palestrina Choir, The 162
Pan-Celtic Festival 120
Park Singers, The 162, 165
Passereu, Pierre
   'Il est bel et bon' 142
Patterson, Annie 28, 110, 111, 137
   'Ó Suilleabháin ag Fágáil na Sléibhte' 137
Paul McIntyre Trio 201
Paul, Tibor 29, 30, 31, 32, 33, 34, 35, 36, 96, 139
payment by results 128
Pearce, Colman 4, 37, 53, 54, 91, 94, 144, 191, 193, 244, 248-250, 264
   Concerto for Two Mandolins 250
   Day Dream 250
   Like as the Waves 250
   Night Dance 250
   Six Yeats Songs 53, 250
   Toccata Festiva 250
   What's in a Name? 250
Pearse, Patrick
   The Singer and the King 55
Pearson, William 37
performance studies 25-55, 60, 67-68, 73-77, 80, 86, 93, 160, 179, 184, 193, 201, 229, 237, 243, 244, 247, 248, 253, 255, 256, 259, 263
Pergolesi
   Magnificat 46
Perosi, Dom Lorenzo 26
   'Benedictus' 26
   'Credo' 26
   The Raising of Lazarus 26
   The Resurrection of Christ 26
   The Transfiguration 26
Pestalozzi, Johann Heinrich 155
Petit, Fr James 8
Petrie, George 108, 117
PhD degree 3, 74, 86, 94, 96, 179, 187, 193, 196, 198, 243, 243, 248, 249, 250, 254, 263
philosophy 61
Phoenix Hall 31
piano 4, 26, 31-32, 38-43, 46-47, 51, 54, 87, 88, 90, 92, 94,

97, 98, 99, 100, 110, 123,
162, 165, 169, 186, 201, 223,
227, 229, 230, 238, 239,
240, 244, 248, 250, 251,
252, 260
Piggott manuscripts 115
plainchant 133
Plane, Robert 231
Planxty 119
Platthy, Sarolta 167
Pogues, The 119
Poires, Anna 7
'Popular Music in Ireland' 197
Possible Selves in Music 195, 196
Postgraduate Diploma in
 Education 93, 233
Potter, A. J. 18, 35, 94, 96-97, 225
 Lúireach Phádraig [St Patrick's
 Breastplate] 35, 96-97, 139
Power, Eoin 143
Power, Karen 198
 *Always Considering Kitchen
 Sinks* 198
Powis Commission (1870) 12
Pragrová, Anna 50, 146
premiere performances 38, 41, 53,
 94, 96-102
preparatory colleges 16, 17, 18
Presley, Elvis 207
Previn, André 36
Prey Trio, The 91
Prihoda, Antonin 91
primary schools *see* National
 schools
Professional Masters in Education
 93
Programme for Research in Third
 Level Institutions 194
Prokofiev, Sergei 55, 165
 *Peter and the Wolf / The Wolf
 and Peter* 55
Provisional government 15, 16
PRTLI *see* Programme for
 Research in Third Level
 Institutions
psychology of music 77, 80
Puccini
 Il Tabarro [The Cloak] 40
Pulcinella Ensemble 37
Purcell, Anne 71, 185
Purcell, Edward C.,
 'Passing By' 137

Purcell, Sandie 94, 193

Quality and Qualifications Ireland
 62
Queen's scholarship 10, 14
Queen's University Belfast 91, 192
Quinn, Bernadette 208
Quinn, Ruairí 224
quodlibet 51

Raidió Éireann 17, 27, 29, 30, 31,
 96, 97, 111, 114
Raidió Éireann Singers 29
Raidió Éireann Symphony
 Orchestra *see* RTÉ
 National Symphony
 Orchestra
Raidió Teilifís Éireann *see* RTÉ
Radiohead 252, 253
Rao, Doreen 169
Ravel
 Piano Trio 239
RÉ *see* Raidió Éireann
RÉ Light Orchestra *see* RTÉ Light
 Orchestra
Réamonn, Seán (*see also*
 Redmond, John J.)
 'Ag an mBoithrín Buí' 137
 'Péarla an Bhrollaigh Bán' 137
 'Sean-fheara-Chonnacht' 137
Redmond, John J. (Gus) 17, 27,
 28, 136, 137, 138, 145, 149
RÉSO *see* RTÉ National
 Symphony Orchestra
Respighi
 The Fountains of Rome 31
Revised Primary School Music
 Curriculum (1999) 60, 70,
 228, 243, 247, 267
Revised Programme of Instruction
 (1900) 12, 59
Revised Programme of Instruction
 for Music in National
 Schools (1939) 59-60, 136
Rhattigan, Hannah 123
'Rhythm of Life, The' 145
Right Note, The 185
Ring, Gavan 4, 47, 49, 144, 201,
 244, 247-248, 264
'Road to the Isles' 137
Robinson, Ken 89
Robinson, Lennox 137

The Whiteheaded Boy 137
Roche, Simon 216
'Rock 'n' Stroll: Dublin's Music Trail' 209, 210, 217
Roinn na Gaeilge 55, 120, 121, 218
Romic, Sanja 53
Rosen, Albert 36
Rosen, Hans Waldemar 29
Rossini
   Overture to *The Barber of Seville* 34
   Signor Bruschino 38
Rossmayer, Richard 38
Rowesome, Leo 114
Royal Birmingham Conservatoire 98
Royal Irish Academy of Music 68, 91, 94, 139, 171, 192, 200, 248
Rozsnyai, Zoltán 165
RTÉ 1, 35, 38, 40, 113, 122, 141, 186, 223, 224, 248, 252, 260, 264
RTÉ 2FM 211
RTÉ Concert Orchestra 42
RTÉ Light Orchestra 44, 113, 114.
   See also RTÉ Concert Orchestra
RTÉ National Symphony Orchestra 18, 30, 31, 32, 33, 34, 35, 36, 42, 44, 114, 139, 164, 165, 224, 225, 245, 249, 272, 245, 249, 260, 262
RTÉ Symphony Orchestra *see* RTÉ National Symphony Orchestra
RTÉ Young Musician of the Year 162
Rudenko, Svetlana 51
Russell, Fr John 15
Ruthmann, Alex 170
Rutter, John 145
Ryan, Amy 147, 167, 171, 172
Ryan, Connie 162
Ryan, Archbishop Dermot 141, 160
Ryan, Karen 47
   'By all appearances' 47
Ryan, Síle 121

Saint-Saëns 145, 147
   'Calmes des Nuits' 147
Samuelson, Arvin 137

'Road to the Isles' 137
San Diego Fringe Festival 54
Sandford, Irene 41
Saturday Night 112
Scahill, Adrian 192
Schlepper-Connolly, Benedict 53, 100
   Ektase II 100
Schoenberg 88
Schubert 32, 39, 48, 165, 239
   Symphony No. 8 in B minor (unfinished) 32
Schumann 201, 239
Seamus Heaney Lectures 97, 179, 188, 189
Seaver, Deirdre 45, 160, 165
Second Vatican Council 189
Seiber 145
'Send down the Rain' 145
serialism 94
Sexton, Martina 71
Seymour, Joseph 26, 132, 133, 149
   'Laudate' 26
   'Tantum Ergo' 26
   'The Bells of Shandon' 132, 133
Sheedy, Claire 172
Sheekey, Mark 146
'Shenandoah' 145
Sherlock, Bernie 163, 166, 167, 172
Shiel, Conor 91
Shostakovich 55
Sibelius 32, 33, 36
   Finlandia 32, 33
   Violin Concerto 36
sight-reading 16, 68, 129, 130, 136, 173, 255
Simon, Paul 252
'Sinner Man' 145
Sisters of Mercy 8
Slattery, Annette 235
Sliabh Luachra 118, 119
Sliabh na mBan Set Dancers 162
Slógadh 43, 114, 121
Smale, Alan 42
SMEI *see* Society for Music Education in Ireland
Smetana 39, 40, 43
   Blaník 43
   Dvě Vdovy [The Two Widows] 40
SMI *see* Society for Musicology in Ireland

Šmídová, Květa 50
Smith, Adrian 192
Smith, Gillian 100, 162, 165
Smyth, Christine 248
Social Semiotics 219
Society for Music Education in Ireland 179, 191, 197, 199, 200, 223, 231, 263
Society for Musicology in Ireland 179, 191, 200, 263
sociology 61
sociology of music 77
solfège 80, 156, 160, 168, 254
song arrangement 69, 71
song cycles 51
'Songs of a Starry Night' 145
SPARC *see* St Patrick's College Repertory Company
special education courses 20, 30
Spitalfields Festival 98
Spratt, Geoffrey 161
St Francis Xavier Hall 35, 37, 260
St John's Art Centre, Cork 146
St John the Baptist Church, Drumcondra 218, 220
St Joseph's Choral Society 138
St Mary's College, Belfast 8
St Mary's Pro-Cathedral 162, 164, 165
St Patrick's Boys National School 133, 166
St Patrick's Campus (DCU) 5
St Patrick's College
 Academic Council 77, 188
 auditorium 34-5, 38, 39, 40, 44, 96, 102, 139, 144, 162, 163, 165, 189, 218, 230, 262
 alumni 4, 93, 94, 105, 264
 buildings and infrastructure 8-11, **11**, 18, 20, 22, 25, 34
 carol services 34, 46, 55, 140, 145, 230
 concerts 4, 18, 25-55, 80, 97, 99, 100, 114, 115, 120, 121, 161, 162, 165, 168, 169, 181, 201, 208, 210, 215, 218, 223, 224, 229, 230-233, 241, 251, 254, 255, 256, 260, 261
 development and growth 7-22
 drama 27, 54, 112, 137
 early years 25-29

female students 3, 9, 14, 17, 20, 30, 128, 140
 incorporation into DCU 1, 4, 8, 25, 30, 47, 76, 80, 81, 86, 87, 101, 102, 122, 128, 131, 148
 mature students 20, 66
 musical productions 34, 40-41, 44, 54, 140
 postgraduate programmes 21, 60-61, 71-76, 85, 93, 94, 118, 177, 192, 264
 song contests 34, 44, 46, 252
 students' union 44, 54, 105
 undergraduate programmes 21, 61, 63, 70, 72, 85
St Patrick's College Alumni Choir 147, 230
St Patrick's College Choir 2, 17, 18, 27, 28-29, 32, 35, 38, 44, 45-46, 68, 127-149, **146**, **148**, 165, 225, 254. *See also* Cantóirí Choláiste Phádraig *and* DCU Music Society Choir
St Patrick's College Madrigal Choir 46, 140, 244, 260
St Patrick's College Musical Society 42
St Patrick's College Repertory Company 55
St Patrick's Practising Schools 28
St Patrick's Teacher Training College *see* St Patrick's College
St Paul's School, Greenhills 46
St Stephen's Singers 42
St Vincent de Paul Society 135
staff notation 64, 116, 129, 130
Stages of the Rising 55
Stakelum, Mary 70, 171
Stanford, Charles Villiers 142, 145
 'The Bluebird' 142
Stephens, Wendy 170
stick notation 156, 173
Stockholm Youth Choir 163
Stord/Haugesund University 192
Strauss, Johann
 Tales of Old Vienna 38
Strauss, Richard
 Horn Concert No. 1 in E flat major 34

Stravinsky
  Petrouchka 244
street musicians 214
strings, writing for 87
Sugrue, Ciarán 194
Sunday Miscellany 33
Sunday Tribune, The 117
Swain, Mark 123
Swanwick, Keith 192, **199**
Sweeney, Eamon 187
Sweeney, Eric 37, 41, 91
  Canzona 37
Sweet Charity 40
Szabó, Klara 50
Szirányi, Borbála 167

Tacka, Philip 171
Tal, Adi 223
Tanham, Gaye 226, 227
Tartini 165
Tchaikovsky 36, 45, 54
  Nutcracker Suite 45
  Violin Concerto 36
Teaching Council of Ireland 21, 62, 79
Teaching the Unteachable 91
Téarmaí Ceoil 64
Technological University Dublin 171
theory of music *see* music theory
Thompson, Bryden 164
Thompson, Mary Shine 97, 188
  The Fire I' the Flint 97
Three Baritones, The 248
Thumped 211
Timoney, Thérèse 41
tin whistle 49, 53, 93, 118, 120, 121, 246
Toibín, Niall 114
tonic solfa 13, 25, 64, 109, 111, 116, 129, 130, 131, 156, 165, 173, 251
Tórna *see* Ó Donnchadha, Tadgh
Tourdion Chamber Choir 172
Townsend, Declan 161
Tradsoc 54, 55, 120, 122, 123
training colleges 8-10 *see also under individual entries*
Travers, Dr Pauric 21, 147, 166
Treacy, Seán 15
Trevelyan, George 9
Trimble, Joan 54, 100

Trinity College Dublin 37, 46, 96, 117, 163, 171, 197, 256
Tsioulakis, Ioannis 192
Turchi, Peter 217
'Turtle Dove, The' 145
Twomey, Denis 40
Tynan, Kathleen 44, 143, 162, 264

U2 192, 209, 210
U2 Experience, The 209
Ua Braoin, Donnchadh 127, 137
Ua Briain, B.
  'An Londubh 'gus an Chéirseach' 137
  'An Maidrín Rua' 137
  'Bó na Leath-Adhairce' 137
  'Ó Cé h-é seo?' 137
UCC *see* University College Cork
UCC Madrigal Group 45, 140
UCD *see* University College Dublin
Uí Éigeartaigh, Caitlín (Kathleen Hegarty) 67, 70, 115-117, 140, 161, 189, 245
uilleann pipes 53, 114, 118, 121, 161, 189
Un Coeur en Hiver 239
Unbearable Lightness of Being, The 239
Universities Act (1997) 188
University College Cork 110, 139, 141, 157, 159, 160, 192
University College Dublin 20, 66, 67, 72, 118, 122, 159, 161, 163, 192, 243, 249
University of Iowa 143, 144
University of Limerick 118, 119, 197, 200
University of Liverpool 192
University of London 192, 254
University of Michigan 192
University of Sheffield 229
University of Western Hungary 146
University of York 100, 200
Upbeat 185

Vallely, Brian 118
Vallely, Eithne 118
  Sing a Song and Play It 118
Vallely, Fintan 105, 117, 118
  Timber: The Concert-Flute Tutor 117

Index

The Companion to Irish Traditional Music 117
Velická, Helena 50
Verdi 30, 43
    operas 30
    overture to *Nabucco* 43
Victoria (Vittoria), 138, 142
    'Domine Non Sum Dignus' 138
Victory, Gerard 35, 97
Vienna Boys Choir 38, **39**
Vienna Haydn Trio 39, 260
Vincentian Order 3, 8, 21, 142, 159, 230
viola 91, 143
violin 31, 36, 38, 41, 42, 47, 50, 51, 91, 92
visiting composers 96-102
Viva Voce chamber choir 143, 147, 172
Vivaldi 46, 142, 143
    Gloria 46, 142, 143
    Magnificat 142
vocal music & training 2, 12, 14, 16, 19, 64, 69, 77, 81, 85, 119, 121, 127-149, 154, 247, 253
Vogler Quartet 55, 228
Voice Squad, The 119
Volans, Kevin 91

Wagner 42
    Siegfried Idyll 42
Wallace, Stephen 168
Wallfish, Elizabeth 197
Walsh, Daniel 96, 166, 167, 170, 193, 236-237
Walsh, Fr Patrick A. *See* Breathnach, An tAthair Pádraig
Walsh, Archbishop William J. 10, 11, 25, 26
Walshe, Jennifer 254
Walton 42
War of Independence 15
Warren, Fergal 49, 50, 51
Waterford Institute of Technology 91
Watkins, Kathleen 113
We Cut Corners 51, **52**, 251
    Imposters 252
    Strings 252
    The Cadences of Others 252

Think Nothing 252
Today I Realised I Could Go Home Backwards 252
Weelkes
    'Hark All Ye Lovely Saints' 147
Weir, Judith 53, 98, **99**
    Piano Trio Two 98
Werner, Gregor Joseph 50
    Trio Sonata No. 3 50
Westval, Maria 71, 193
Wexford Festival Opera 94
Whelan, Hannah 123
White, Freddie 244
White, Harry 105, 192, 199
'Whiteheaded Boy, The' 137
Wickham, Laura 71
Wicklow Opera Group 40
Wilhelm, G.L.B. 12
Wilhelm-Hullah method 12
Wilkinson, Colm 40
Williams, Niamh 46, 71, 185
Willicher Emmaus Kantorei 53
Wilson, James 94
Winter Chamber Music Festival 4, 98, 100, 102, 223, 224, 230, 231, **232**, **233**
Witt, Franz Xaver 26
Wiz, The 54
Wizard of Oz, The 54
Wolf-Ferrari
    Susanna's Secret 40
women
    marriage bar 17
Women and Music in Ireland Conference 100, 200
Woodward, Sheila 199, 231
woodwind 88
Woodworth, Anne 41
World War II 112
Wylde, Donagh 171, 172

Yeats, Caitríona 43
Yeats, William Butler
    Words Upon the Window Pane 189

Zezere Arts Festival 171

www.ingramcontent.com/pod-product-compliance
Lightning Source LLC
Chambersburg PA
CBHW050835230426
43667CB00012B/2013